Intelligent Data Security Solutions for e-Health Applications

Intelligent Data Centric Systems

Series Editor

Fatos Xhafa

Intelligent Data Security Solutions for e-Health Applications

Edited by

Amit Kumar Singh

Department of Computer Science and Engineering,
NIT Patna, Patna, Bihar, India

Mohamed Elhoseny

Faculty of Computers and information Sciences,
Mansoura University, Dakahlia, Egypt

ACADEMIC PRESS

An imprint of Elsevier

ELSEVIER

Academic Press is an imprint of Elsevier
125 London Wall, London EC2Y 5AS, United Kingdom
525 B Street, Suite 1650, San Diego, CA 92101, United States
50 Hampshire Street, 5th Floor, Cambridge, MA 02139, United States
The Boulevard, Langford Lane, Kidlington, Oxford OX5 1GB, United Kingdom

Library of Congress Cataloging-in-Publication Data
A catalog record for this book is available from the Library of Congress

British Library Cataloguing-in-Publication Data
A catalogue record for this book is available from the British Library

ISBN: 978-0-12-819511-6

For information on all Academic Press publications
visit our website at https://www.elsevier.com/books-and-journals

Publisher: Mara Conner
Editorial Project Manager: Gabriela Capille
Production Project Manager: Paul Prasad Chandramohan
Cover designer: Victoria Pearson

Typeset by SPi Global, India

Working together
to grow libraries in
developing countries

www.elsevier.com • www.bookaid.org

Contents

CHAPTER 3   An OpenSim guided tour in machine learning for e-health applications.. 57

Mukul Verma, Muskan Dawar, Prashant Singh Rana, Neeru Jindal, and Harpreet Singh

CHAPTER 4   Advances and challenges in fMRI and DTI techniques 77

Ranjeet Ranjan Jha, Gaurav Jaswal, Aditya Nigam, and Arnav Bhavsar

CHAPTER 5 **Homomorphic transform-based dual image watermarking using IWT-SVD for secure e-healthcare applications 91**

Priyank Khare and Vinay Kumar Srivastava

CHAPTER 6 **An analysis of security access control on healthcare records in the cloud 113**

P. Chinnasamy, P. Deepalakshmi, and K. Shankar

Contributors

Hiba Abdel-Nabi
Department of Computer Engineering, Princess Sumaya University for Technology Amman, Amman, Jordan

Abhinav Adarsh
Department of ECE, Motilal Nehru National Institute of Technology Allahabad, Prayagraj, India

Ali Al-Haj
Department of Computer Engineering, Princess Sumaya University for Technology Amman, Amman, Jordan

K.V. Arya
Information and Communication Technology, ABV-Indian Institute of Information Technology and Management Gwalior, Gwalior, India

Gaurav Bhatnagar
Indian Institute of Technology Jodhpur, Karwar, India

Arnav Bhavsar
Indian Institute of Technology Mandi, Mandi, India

P. Chinnasamy
Department of Information Technology, Sri Shakthi Institute of Engineering and Technology, Coimbatore, Tamil Nadu, India

Muskan Dawar
Computer Science and Engineering department, Thapar Institute of Engineering & Technology, Patiala, Punjab, India

P. Deepalakshmi
Department of Computer Science and Engineering, Kalasalingam Academy of Research and Education, Srivilliputtur, Tamil Nadu, India

Rajasi Gore
Computer Science and Engineering Department, Motilal Nehru National Institute of Technology Allahabad, Prayagraj, India

Ritu Gothwal
Computer Science and Engineering Department, Thapar Institute of Engineering and Technology (TIET), Patiala, India

Wahidah Hashim
Institute of Informatics and Computing Energy, Universiti Tenaga Nasional, Kajang, Malaysia

M. Ilayaraja
School of Computing, Kalasalingam Academy of Research and Education, Krishnankoil, Tamil Nadu, India

Gaurav Jaswal
National Agri-Food Biotechnology Institute, Mohali, Punjab, India

C. Jeyamala
Department of Information Technology, Thiagarajar College of Engineering, Madurai, India

Ranjeet Ranjan Jha
Indian Institute of Technology Mandi, Mandi, India

Neeru Jindal
Electronics and Communication Engineering Department, Thapar Institute of Engineering
& Technology, Patiala, Punjab, India

Priyank Khare
Department of Electronics & Communication Engineering, MNNIT Allahabad, Prayagraj,
Uttar Pradesh, India

Manju Khurana
Computer Science and Engineering Department, Thapar Institute of Engineering and Technology
(TIET), Patiala, India

Basant Kumar
Department of ECE, Motilal Nehru National Institute of Technology Allahabad, Prayagraj, India

Shailesh Kumar
Department of ECE, Motilal Nehru National Institute of Technology Allahabad, Prayagraj, India

Andino Maseleno
Institute of Informatics and Computing Energy, Universiti Tenaga Nasional, Kajang, Malaysia

Ashish Nanda
Faculty of Engineering and Information Technology, University of Technology Sydney, Sydney,
NSW, Australia

Aditya Nigam
Indian Institute of Technology Mandi, Mandi, India

Shashwat Pathak
Department of ECE, Motilal Nehru National Institute of Technology Allahabad, Prayagraj, India

Eswaran Perumal
Department of Computer Applications, Alagappa University, Karaikudi, India

Prashant Singh Rana
Computer Science and Engineering Department, Thapar Institute of Engineering & Technology,
Patiala, Punjab, India

J. Jennifer Ranjani
Department of Computer Science & Information Systems, Birla Institute of Technology
and Science, Pilani, India

Amiya Kumar Sahu
Department of Computer Science and Engineering, International Institute of Information
Technology Bhubaneswar, Bhubaneswar, India

Sima Sahu
St. Martin's Engineering College, Secunderabad, India

K. Shankar
Department of Computer Applications, Alagappa University, Karaikudi, Tamil Nadu, India

Suraj Sharma
Department of Computer Science and Engineering, International Institute of Information Technology Bhubaneswar, Bhubaneswar, India

Shivendra Shivani
Computer Science and Engineering Department, Thapar Institute of Engineering and Technology (TIET), Patiala, India

Amit Kumar Singh
Department of Computer Science and Engineering, NIT Patna, Patna, Bihar, India

Ghanshyam Singh
Department of Electrical and Electronics Engineering Science, Auckland Park Kingsway Campus, University of Johannesburg, Johannesburg, South Africa

Harpreet Singh
Computer Science and Engineering Department, Thapar Institute of Engineering & Technology, Patiala, Punjab, India

Harsh Vikram Singh
Department of Electronics, Kamla Nehru Institute of Technology (KNIT), Sultanpur, Uttar Pradesh, India

Satendra Pal Singh
Indian Institute of Technology Jodhpur, Karwar, India

Rohini Srivastava
Department of ECE, Motilal Nehru National Institute of Technology Allahabad, Prayagraj, India

Vinay Kumar Srivastava
Department of Electronics & Communication Engineering, MNNIT Allahabad, Prayagraj, Uttar Pradesh, India

Prabhat Thakur
Department of Electrical and Electronics Engineering Science, Auckland Park Kingsway Campus, University of Johannesburg, Johannesburg, South Africa

Rohit Thanki
C. U. Shah University, Wadhwan, Gujarat, India

Shailendra Tiwari
Computer Science and Engineering Department, Thapar Institute of Engineering and Technology (TIET), Patiala, India

Mukul Verma
Computer Science and Engineering department, Thapar Institute of Engineering & Technology, Patiala, Punjab, India

Preface

In recent times, implementing e-health solutions has become a trend among various research teams at a national/international level. It primarily focuses on employing the latest information and communication technologies to cater to the requirements of people associated with the health industry: healthcare professionals, patients, and policy makers. E-health applications such as telemedicine, teleradiology, teleophthalmology, and telediagnosis are very promising and have great potential. They can play a very important role in service provision by improving access, equity, and quality through connecting healthcare facilities and healthcare professionals, and diminishing geographical and physical barriers. However, the transmission and access technologies of medical information raise critical issues that urgently need to be addressed, especially those related to security. Furthermore, medical identity theft is a growing and dangerous crime. Stolen personal information can have negative financial impacts, but stolen medical information cuts to the very core of personal privacy. Medical-related identity theft is an escalating threat that already costs billions of dollars each year, and altered medical information can put a person's health at risk through misdiagnosis, delayed treatment, or incorrect prescriptions. Yet the use of hand-held devices to store, access, and transmit medical information is outpacing the privacy and security protections on those devices. Therefore the authenticity of information and related medical images is of prime concern, as they form the basis of inference for diagnostic purposes. Potential researchers are using a number of imperceptible marks to ensure tamper proofing, cost effectiveness, and guaranteed originality of medical records. However, robustness, security, and efficient image archiving and retrieval of medical data/information against attacks are interesting and challenging areas for researchers in the field of e-health applications.

Outline of the book and chapter synopsis

To address the foregoing challenges, this book presents recent trends in terms of security, processing, and applications at the global level. In the chapters, we provide potential thoughts and methodologies that help senior undergraduate and graduate students, researchers, programmers, and industry professionals create new knowledge for the future to develop efficient techniques/frameworks for healthcare applications.

The book contains 16 thought-provoking chapters.

Chapter 1 provides a novel approach to the security of medical images based on zero watermarking incorporating perceptual hashing. For this purpose, robust invariant features are extracted based on scale invariant feature transform (SIFT) and discrete cosine transform (DCT), respectively. Local features are determined by the descriptor of the most stable SIFT key points, whereas for global features the preprocessed medical image is transformed into the DCT domain followed by singular value decomposition. A digital signature for medical images is constructed using a binary watermark and the hash value, which is useful in the authentication of medical images. The hash value is generated by combining global and key local features. The simulation results show that the proposed scheme has good robustness against various signal processing attacks as well as geometric attacks. This technique is useful in the authentication and integrity verification of medical images during transmission across channels and storage in databases. The approach plays a vital role in other image processing applications like identification and classification of digital images.

Chapter 2 describes a novel separable and blind joint encryption/watermarking algorithm that provides security for transmitted medical images. The frequency domain algorithm combines cryptography, as a preprotection mechanism, and digital watermarking, as a postprotection mechanism, to provide the required security requirements. The algorithm is based on a special type of watermarking called reversible data hiding that guarantees the exact recovery of the original image after the embedded data have been extracted. Extensive experiments using four different medical modalities, and four different sizes of the same modality, have been conducted to evaluate the performance of the proposed algorithm.

Chapter 3 presents a quick summary of critical application areas of OpenSim in e-healthcare and how it is related to neuromusculoskeletal systems. A detailed investigation of the existing literature is presented, which covers 3D virtual learning environments, OpenSim projects, technical requirements, repurposing for different medical specialties, joint kinematics, joint kinetics, muscle forces, muscle activations, etc. Furthermore, the limitations, challenges, and opportunities for conducting a biomechanical simulation are also highlighted. Details of kinematics models, human musculoskeletal system control, and dynamics are also presented. The chapter concludes by considering open research issues and future trends.

Chapter 4 presents an extensive review of magnetic resonance imaging (MRI) nuts and bolts, including quantitative methods used to assess brain structure integrity. MRI methods for assessing network connectivity of the brain using diffusion tensor imaging and functional MRI are discussed in conjunction with the joint analysis of both. Next, traditional and deep learning-based classifiers are discussed in detail, which can be used for the classification of several mental diseases.

Chapter 5 provides an efficient dual image watermarking technique that uses the fusion of homomorphic transforms, integer wavelet transforms, singular value decomposition (SVD), and Arnold transform for e-healthcare applications. The simulation results clearly illustrate the remarkable robustness and perceptual invisibility of the proposed scheme when subjected to various nongeometric and geometric attacks. Moreover, the results highlight the improvement in robustness of the proposed technique over other recently reported schemes.

Different access controls in electronic health record (EHR) security advertisement approval processes are introduced in Chapter 6. Furthermore, the chapter presents an extensive review of different access control requirements, types, and their security analysis alongside basic usage in medical applications. The plausibility of setting up a security administration model is shown by proposing an e-healthcare system for a secure e-healthcare condition as a safe personal health record system. Finally, access control instruments for healthcare application with proper security analysis and execution assessment subsequent to contrasting and different access control mechanisms are introduced.

Chapter 7 presents the potential frameworks that exploit the cognitive-inspired internet of medical things to resolve the issue of spectrum scarcity in wireless body area networks (WBANs). The potential frameworks with their pros and cons as well as major research challenges with probable solutions are discussed. Because security and interference with human body organs are of prime concern due to direct human body involvement, security concerns and interference management techniques are illustrated.

Chapter 8 presents blockchain technology and a support vector machine-based security model for e-healthcare systems. The model is verified in terms of throughput, energy, and security-level measures, and shows its usefulness for healthcare applications.

Chapter 9 explores various machine learning-based algorithms to ensure the security of EHRs in e-healthcare applications. The chapter confirms that machine learning can revolutionize the healthcare industry by enhancing healthcare services for future generations.

Chapter 10 introduces a new watermarking scheme using a bioinspired algorithm for the security of medical images. In this chapter, the intelligent watermarking scheme based on a genetic algorithm is discussed with its different features. Also, an image watermarking scheme using hybridization of DCT–SVD and a genetic algorithm (GA) is developed and analyzed for the security of medical images. Here, GA is used for the optimization of scaling factors based on the nature of medical images and watermark logos. Comparative analysis also shows that the performance of the proposed scheme is better (in terms of robustness) than many existing state-of-the-art techniques.

Chapter 11 introduces in detail the need for security in WBANs, attacks on WBANs while collecting and transmitting data, and surveys on existing data security advancements. It can be seen from the chapter that many algorithms have been proposed, but there is still a need for new and efficient algorithms that are 100% safe from any attacks.

Chapter 12 presents Internet of Things (IoT)-enabled intelligent diagnostic solutions for e-healthcare. The focus of this chapter is on providing an IoT-enabled cloud-based diagnostic solution framework for various diseases, namely cataracts, cardiovascular diseases, the risk of falling, and diabetes-related diseases.

Chapter 13 discusses the current state-of-the-art security challenges, importance of ubiquitous utilization of IoT, and machine learning in the e-health system. It also investigates the gaps and trends in this area to provide valuable visions for industrial environments and researchers.

Chapter 14 presents a despeckling method to remove speckle noise from ultrasound images. Along with the statistical approach with benefits such as wavelet transform, another procedure called Gaussianization is introduced for correctly modeling ultrasound images and estimating unknown parameters. The obtained numerical results show that the threshold value is estimated accurately and the noise removed effectively.

Chapter 15 presents a comprehensive study of various smart e-healthcare scenarios that utilize advancements in the field of wearable medical sensors and efficient body area networks (BANs). Various challenging issues and comparisons of various competing communication technologies for BANs along with upcoming network protocols for e-health applications are also discussed in detail.

Finally, Chapter 16 discusses a secure, lightweight authentication protocol between a healthcare wearable device and its user. The scheme uses the cryptographic hash function and X-OR functionalities only. It is tested by the well-known formal security verification tool AVISPA to show its robustness against various attacks related to authentications. The secure establishment of a shared secret key is also shown by the well-known BAN authentication logic. Furthermore, the computational cost of the scheme is calculated and compared with other work to prove its efficiency.

To conclude, we would like to sincerely thank all the authors for submitting their high-quality chapters to this book, and the large number of reviewers who have provided helpful comments and suggestions to the authors to improve their chapters.

We especially thank the *Intelligent Data-Centric Systems: Sensor Collected Intelligence* Series Editor Prof. Fatos Xhafa for his continuous support and excellent guidance.

We would also like to thank Gabriela Capille, Editorial Project Manager, Elsevier S&T Books, for her helpful guidance and encouragement during the creation of this book.

We are sincerely thankful to all authors, editors, and publishers whose works have been cited directly or indirectly in this book.

The editors believe that this book will be helpful to senior undergraduate and graduate students, researchers, industry professionals, and providers working in areas that demand state-of-the-art solutions for healthcare applications.

Special Acknowledgments

The first author gratefully acknowledges the authorities of the National Institute of Technology Patna, India, for their kind support.

The second author gratefully acknowledges the authorities of Mansoura University, Egypt, for their kind support.

Amit Kumar Singh
Mohamed Elhoseny

Perceptual hashing-based novel security framework for medical images

1

Satendra Pal Singh and Gaurav Bhatnagar
Indian Institute of Technology Jodhpur, Karwar, India

1 Introduction

In recent years, advanced developments in information and communication technology have changed the medical environment through medical information management systems at hospitals where medical thin films have replaced hard copies of medical images [1]. Medical information systems have enabled applications such as telemedicine for medical images where healthcare professionals exchange electronic patient records (EPRs) over the internet worldwide. An EPR contains information regarding the patient's health, such as laboratory tests, historic pathology, radiology, physical examinations, etc. [2, 3]. An EPR that includes images, diagnostic reports, etc. can be transmitted over communication channels using the Internet. However, this transmission may not be secure unless robust encryption is used. This type of transmission poses a significant threat, as it contains essential patient medical information. Specifically, the routing strategy for many routers makes the data vulnerable to obstruction and may result in the tempering/modification of medical data during transmission over the Internet. The distortion or tempering of the medical data may lead to the wrong diagnosis. Due to the rapid development of telediagnosis, security of the medical image becomes an important issue [4, 5]. For this purpose, many solutions such as watermarking, hashing, and encryption have been proposed in the literature. Among these, watermarking provides multilabel support in the security of digital data. Digital watermarking consists of two main components: (1) watermark embedding and (2) watermark extraction. In the embedding process, a watermark considered as a weak signal is imperceptibility embedded into the host image, whereas in the extraction the process watermark is extracted from the watermarked image. The embedding of a watermark distorts and alters the host image and as a result, fidelity of the image is slightly changed. However, this fidelity change mainly depends upon the applications. In some applications, limited fidelity loss is allowable as long as host and watermarked images remain perceptually similar. On the other hand, medical imaging applications are sensitive to embedding distortion and have stringent constraints to prohibit permanent loss of image fidelity in watermarking. For example, the artifacts in the patient's medical image may cause misdiagnosis and corresponding treatment may lead to life-threatening consequences [6]. Therefore several zero-watermarking systems have been developed to secure the digital data without disturbing the

Intelligent Data Security Solutions for e-Health Applications. https://doi.org/10.1016/B978-0-12-819511-6.00001-7

1

fidelity of the image [7]. A more appropriate multipurpose solution can be achieved by combining zero watermarking and perceptual hashing.

In general, there are two types of hashing technique [8–11]. The first are cryptographic hashing techniques, which are useful for nonchanging multimedia data such as passwords or files. These types of technique are very sensitive to the input data; if a single bit of data is changed, then the corresponding hash value will be completely changed and as a result, data are considered to be nonauthentic. Classic hash functions such as MD-5 or SHA-1 [12] are not suitable for the authentication of multimedia data. On the other hand, content-based hashing techniques are applicable to common signal processing operations such as image scaling, enhancement, cropping, and JPEG compression. These operations alter the pixel values but do not change the perceptual content of the image. An image hash is a small binary string that can be obtained from the appropriate image hash function. It extracts the intrinsic feature of the image and generates the hash value. Robustness and security are two main aspects of a hash function. Robustness implies that the hash value of the perceptually similar image must be approximately the same. In contrast, security of the hash function can be obtained by generating the hash value based on a secret key. The use of secret keys plays a vital role in security as the hash value cannot be easily counterfeited or obtained unbeknown to the correct secret keys.

Generally, hashing techniques can be categorized, based on the feature extraction process, into two groups, namely (1) global feature and (2) local feature techniques. The global feature usually represents the structural layout of the image holistically, including texture features, invariant moments, shape descriptors, gray-level features, and frequency characteristics, whereas the local feature quantifies the comprehensive local variations in the small patches. In the literature, scale invariant feature transform (SIFT) is the most widely used technique for local feature extraction. It essentially determines the key points in the image, which can be described based on scale, orientation, and position of the considered points. These feature points have excellent robustness to rotation, scale, and brightness changes. Clearly, global and local features have their own merits and demerits; however, it is obligatory to integrate them smartly in pursuit of improved robustness and security.

A number of image-hashing approaches [13–17] have been designed and proposed in the existing literature. However, to achieve the desired level of robustness and security for a universally optimal scheme remains a challenging task. In [13], Monga et al. proposed a two-stage framework for perceptual image hashing using feature points, where an end-stopped wavelet transform is employed for feature detection. Then, an iterative process is followed to obtain the final hash value. A similar approach has been discussed in [14]. Swaminathan et al. [15] developed an image-hashing technique-based Fourier-Mellin transform and controlled randomization process. This method is rotation invariant and provides better robustness against geometric distortions. Khelifi et al. [16] computed an image hash based on virtual watermark detection using Weibull distribution, but the method is unable to detect the small change in area of the content. Lv et al. [17] proposed a hashing method on the basis of SIFT features and a Harris corner detector. In this approach, key points are obtained using the SIFT detector, from which the most stable points are then retained using the Harris corner detector. Tang et al. [18] presented an image-hashing technique based on tensor decomposition. This method shows limited robustness against geometric operations, especially for large degree rotations. An image-hashing approach based on a combination of local and global features was developed by Ouyang et al. [19]. These features are obtained by a SIFT detector and Zernike moments, respectively. This method is resilient to geometric operations but less sensitive to content manipulation.

In the literature, numerous zero-watermarking approaches [20–27] have been proposed over the last few years. In [20], the authors represented a zero-watermarking system based on higher-order cumulants. The technique showed good robustness to general image processing attacks but struggled against image rotation attacks. In [21], the authors presented a watermarking scheme using singular value decomposition (SVD) and shearlet transform. In this work, an essential property, namely image directional features and matrix norm, is used in the construction of the zero watermark. In [22], the authors presented a watermarking scheme using multiresolution wavelet transform and piecewise logistic chaotic. In [23], the authors proposed a watermarking framework where adaptive Harris corner detection and lifting wavelet transform were combined to generate a feature map to construct the zero watermark. In [27], the author reported a watermarking scheme using discrete wavelet transform and principal component analysis (PCA). PCA is employed on the approximation wavelet component to generate a feature map to construct a zero watermark of desired size, and the resultant image is registered into a database for the protection of the intellectual property right.

In this chapter, a novel approach for the security of a medical image has been proposed based on zero-watermarking incorporating perceptual hashing. For this purpose, robust invariant features are extracted based on SIFT and discrete cosine transform (DCT), respectively. The local features are determined by the descriptor of the most stable SIFT key points, whereas for global features, the preprocessed medical image is transformed into the DCT domain followed by SVD. The intermediate hashing sequence is quantized using the Hessian matrix. A binary watermark is first encrypted using an Arnold cat map, then the encrypted watermark, along with the final hash sequence of the respective medical image, constructs a digital signature, which can be used for authentication purposes at the later stage.

2 Mathematical preliminaries

In this section, a brief overview of the methodologies that underpin the rest of the chapter is illustrated. These methodologies include SIFT, SVD, nonlinear chaotic map, and DCT.

2.1 SIFT features

SIFT is a widely used feature detection technique proposed by Lowe [28]. It extracts robust feature points, which are invariant to image rotation, scaling, limited affine distortion, change in illumination, and projective transformation. The main steps used in feature extraction using the SIFT algorithm are summarized as follows:

1. *Scale-space extrema detection*: The feature points are detected using a SIFT detector by searching local maxima using difference of Gaussian (DoG) at different scales of the considered image. Let $f(x, y)$ be the input image, then the corresponding scale space can be defined as:

$$L(x,y,\sigma) = G(x,y,\sigma) * f(x,y) \tag{1}$$

where $*$ is the convolution operator, $G(x,y,\sigma) = (1/2\pi\sigma^2)e^{-(x^2+y^2)/2\sigma^2}$ is the variable-scale Gaussian function, and σ denotes the scale. For stable feature points, the DoG is computed by the difference of two nearby scales, separated by a multiplicative factor k as:

$$\begin{aligned} D(x,y,\sigma) &= (G(x,y,k\sigma) - G(x,y,\sigma)) * f(x,y) \\ &= L(x,y,k\sigma) - L(x,y,\sigma) \end{aligned} \tag{2}$$

The process is illustrated using a Gaussian pyramid as shown in Fig. 1. To determine the local maxima and minima of $D(x, y, \sigma)$, each sample point is compared to all its neighbors. For example, the middle point in Fig. 2 is compared with its eight neighbors at the same scale and nine neighbors at upper and lower adjacent scales, respectively. The estimated extreme values are the candidate feature points. If it is a local extremum, then the point is considered to be the potential key point.

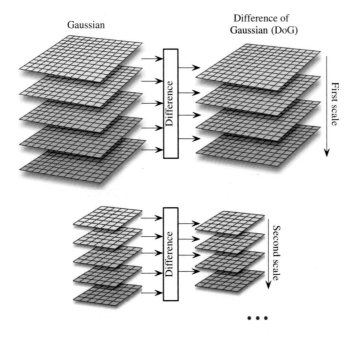

FIG. 1

Creation of a scale-space pyramid for scale invariant feature transform features.

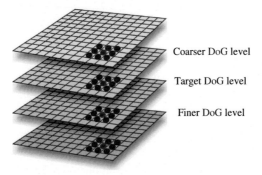

FIG. 2

Comparison of extreme value points obtained from scale invariant feature transform.

2. *Keypoint localization*: The final key points are purely dependent on the stability of potential key points. The more accurate key point locations are determined using Taylor series expansion of scale space. If the intensity at this extremum is lower than some threshold then the key point is removed as the structure has low contrast. Also, the edge effect will be removed to increase the stability and enhance the antinoise capability.

3. *Orientation assignment*: Sampling is performed around the neighbor of the key point location and the orientation histogram is used to count the gradient direction of neighboring pixels. The subsequent modifications in the image transformed to the orientation, scale, and position provides invariance to the transformation.

4. *Keypoint descriptor*: A neighbor is taken around the key point, then a local coordinate is created with the main direction of key point at 0 degrees to ensure rotation invariance. An illustration is shown in Fig. 3.

2.2 Nonlinear chaotic map

In chaotic systems, nonlinear chaotic maps play an important role in engineering, biology, and economics due to their versatile properties such as ergodicity, mixing property, and sensitivity to initial conditions. A simple example of a chaotic phenomenon is a logistic map [29], which describes the population growth model over time evaluation and can be defined as:

$$x_{n+1} = \mu x_n (1 - x_n) \tag{3}$$

where $x \in [0, 1], 0 \le \mu \le 4$, and $n = 0, 1, 2, \dots$. This map exhibits chaotic behavior when $3.5699 \le \mu \le 4$. However, it has some drawbacks such as nonuniform behavior in a chaotic region. This issue can be overcome by increasing the nonlinearity and it then is known as a generalized logistic map (GLM). Mathematically, GLM can be defined as:

$$x_{n+1} = \frac{4\mu x_n (1 - x_n)}{1 + 4(\mu^2 - 1)\, x_n (1 - x_n)} \tag{4}$$

where $n = 0, 1, 2, \dots, k$. When $0.6795 \le \mu \le 0.4324$, the map lies in the chaotic state. The same can be verified by Fig. 4, where the Lyapunov exponent of the GLM is illustrated. Clearly, the positive value of the Lyapunov exponent in the whole domain confirms the chaoticity of the map.

Image gradient   Key-point descriptor

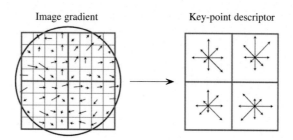

FIG. 3

Generation procedure of SIFT feature descriptor.

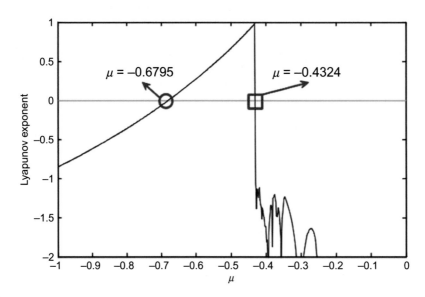

FIG. 4

Lyapunov exponent of the GLM.

2.3 Singular value decomposition

SVD is an optimal matrix decomposition technique, which is useful in many practical applications, including least square problems and multivariate analysis. Recently, SVD has been used in image processing applications such as digital watermarking, image coding, recognition, and multimedia hashing. In contrast, SVD plays an important role in the generation of various hash functions.

Mathematically, the SVD [30] of a matrix A of size $m \times n$ can be expressed as:

$$A = \mathcal{U} * \Sigma * \mathcal{V}^T \tag{5}$$

where $\mathcal{U}$ and $\mathcal{V}$ are orthogonal matrices of size $m \times m$ and $n \times n$, respectively. In addition, matrices $\mathcal{U}$ and $\mathcal{V}$ represent a rotation and reflection in m- and n-dimensional subspace. Also, Σ is a diagonal matrix of size $m \times n$ with rank r, where $r = \min(m,n)$ and leading diagonal elements represent the singular values. In particular, singular values represent brightness of an image and a corresponding singular vector describes the geometric characteristics of the image.

2.4 Discrete cosine transform

The DCT is a well-known transform in mathematics, which essentially transforms a signal from the spatial domain to the frequency domain. It decomposes a signal into a series of cosine harmonic functions. Due to its decorrelation property and better energy compaction, it has been used in many applications such as data compression and pattern recognition. Mathematically, a 2D DCT transform [31] can be defined as:

$$\mathcal{F}^{dct}(u,v) = \mathcal{R}(u)\mathcal{R}(v)\sum_{x=1}^{M}\sum_{y=1}^{N} f(x,y) \cos\left[\frac{u(2m+1)\pi}{2M}\right] \cos\left[\frac{v(2m+1)\pi}{2N}\right] \tag{6}$$

where $u, v = 1, 2, \ldots, M$. The factors $\mathcal{R}(u)$ and $\mathcal{R}(v)$ are given as:

$$\mathcal{R}(u) = \begin{cases} \dfrac{1}{\sqrt{M}}, & u = 0 \\[2mm] \sqrt{\dfrac{1}{M}}, & 1 \le u \le M - 1 \end{cases}$$

$$\mathcal{R}(v) = \begin{cases} \dfrac{1}{\sqrt{N}}, & v = 0 \\[2mm] \sqrt{\dfrac{1}{N}}, & 1 \le v \le N - 1 \end{cases} \qquad (7)$$

3 Proposed technique

The proposed image-hashing technique has three steps: image preprocessing, feature extraction, and hash generation. Using these steps, the hash value can be computed for a given image, which can be further utilized in different applications. Let f represent the input image of size $M \times N$ and H be the corresponding hash value. The length of the hash value entirely depends on the size of the considered image. Therefore input image $f(x, y)$ is resized to $M \times N$ using bilinear interpolation to ensure that each image has a hash value of the same length.

3.1 Perceptual feature extraction

The SIFT technique is applied for key point-based feature extraction as follows:

1. Apply SIFT to the preprocessed input image f. Let $f_p = \{P_i | i = 1, \cdots, \ell\}$ and $\delta_p = \{\delta_i | i = 1, \cdots, \ell\}$ be the key points and corresponding scale factors, respectively.

2. Select n most stable key points f_p^s that represent the object in the image, as follows:
   (a) The key points from the set f_p are arranged in decreasing order according to their scale factors.
   (b) The repeated points P_t with the same scale factor δ_t are removed.
   (c) The top n number of key points $f_p^s = \{P_i | i = 1, \ldots, n\}$ are selected as the candidate key points.

3. Consider the feature descriptors $f_p^{(d)}$ corresponding to key points f_p^s and obtain a new vector using absolute difference of adjacent values as follows:

$$f_p^{(d_i)} = \begin{cases} |d_{i+1} - d_i|, & i \le 127 \\ |d_0 - d_{127}|, & \text{otherwise} \end{cases} \qquad (8)$$

where $d_i, i = 1, \ldots, 127$, denotes the descriptor value.

4. Obtain a binary string as follows:

$$H_s = \begin{cases} 0, & f_p^{(d_i)} \le M \\ 1, & \text{otherwise} \end{cases} \qquad (9)$$

where M is a predefined value that divides the vector into nearly two equal parts.

3.2 Hash generation process

In this section, the core idea used in the design of a robust hashing framework has been discussed. For this purpose, consider a gray-scale image F of size $M \times N$ as the input to the hash function and the resultant hash value is a binary sequence of length ℓ. The main steps of the hash generation process can be summarized as:

1. Apply a normalization process [32] to the image F. Let $F^{(N)}$ denote the normalized image.
2. Partition the normalized image $F^{(N)}$ into nonoverlapping blocks $\{B_j | j = 1, 2, ..., \ell\}$ of size $z \times z$, where $\ell = (M \times N)/z^2$.
3. Generate a random sequence S using a secret key S_{key} and a nonlinear chaotic map:

$$S = \{S_j | j = 1, 2, ..., L \leq \ell\} \quad \text{where } S_j \in \{0, 1\} \tag{10}$$

4. Create an array S_r from S for block selection as follows:

$$S_r = \lfloor (S * 2^{12}) \rfloor \bmod \ell \tag{11}$$

5. Select the random blocks from S_r as follows:

$$B_s = \{B_j | j = 1, 2, ..., S_s \text{ and } s = 1, 2, ..., L\} \tag{12}$$

6. Apply DCT transformation to the block B_s:

$$B_s^{(f)} = DCT\{B_s\} \tag{13}$$

7. Perform SVD on the transformed coefficients $B_s^{(F)}$:

$$B_s^{(f)} = U_s^{(f)} S_s^{(f)} V_s^T(f) \tag{14}$$

8. Obtain a vector h using left and right singular vectors corresponding to the highest singular value as $h = [U_h^{(f)}, V_h^{(f)}]$.
9. Construct a 2D array H by stacking the elements of h and applying the SVD to it:

$$H = U^{(H)} S^{(H)} V^{H(T)} \tag{15}$$

10. Create a Hessian matrix Q using $U^{(H)}$ and V^H at each position (x, y) as follows:

$$Q_m(x, y) = \begin{bmatrix} q_{11}^m & q_{12}^m \\ q_{21}^m & q_{22}^m \end{bmatrix} \tag{16}$$

where $m \in \{U^{(H)}, v^{(H)}\}$ and coefficients $q_{11}^m, q_{12}^m, q_{21}^m, q_{22}^m$ are defined as:

$$q_{11}^m = m(x+1, y) + m(x-1, y) + m(x, y) \tag{17}$$

$$q_{12}^m = q_{21}^m = m(x+1, y) + m(x, y-1) + m(x, y) \tag{18}$$

$$q_{22}^m = \frac{1}{4}[m(x+1, y+1) - m(x+1, y-1) - m(x-1, y+1) + m(x-1, y-1)] \tag{19}$$

11. Obtain a binary matrix as follows:

$$F_m(x, y) = \begin{cases} 1, & |Q_{U^{(H)}}| \leq |Q_{V^{(H)}}| \\ 0, & \text{otherwise} \end{cases} \tag{20}$$

12. Stack the elements of matrix (F_m) into a vector H_f.
13. Obtain a vector H_c using concatenation of H_s and H_f.
14. The vector H_c is randomly permuted to generate the final hash vector H_f^m.

3.3 Watermark construction

1. Obtain a hash vector H_f^m to the input medical image f as described in Section 3.2.
2. Encrypt the binary watermark w using an Arnold map [33] to generate encrypted watermark $\overline{W}$.
3. Produce a zero watermark using an XOR operation between the H_f^m and $\overline{w}$:

$$w_z = XOR(H_f^m, \overline{w}) \tag{21}$$

4. Finally, a zero watermark and all the secret keys signed by the owner using the digital signature technique [34] are registered to the database. Mathematically:

$$D_s^z = Sig_{opk}(w_z, U_{Key}) \tag{22}$$

where Sig_{opk} denotes a digital signature function based on the owner's private key U_{Key}.

3.4 Watermark verification

The verification process can be summarized as follows:

1. First, validate the digital signature D_s^z using the private key U_{Key} to confirm the security. After successful verification, the authentication process may proceed further, otherwise the process will be terminated.
2. Obtain a hash vector H_f^m to the input medical image f as described in Section 3.2.
3. Obtain an encrypted watermark using an XOR operation between the H_f^m and D_s^z:

$$\overline{w} = XOR(H_f^m, D_s^z) \tag{23}$$

4. Obtain the original watermark using the inverse encryption process and check the authenticity of the watermark.

4 Experimental results and discussion

The effectiveness of the proposed technique is examined using the Matlab platform on a system with an i5 processor and 4 GB of RAM. For this purpose, the standard gray-scale medical images, namely head, brain, ultrasound, and X-ray images of size 256×256, are considered as the experimental images as shown in Fig. 5. A perceptual hash sequence is first generated by extracting the invariant features from the medical image. For this purpose, the local salient features are obtained using the SIFT technique, whereas global features are obtained from the DCT domain. A binary watermark is then considered and coupled with the obtained hash sequence to construct the zero watermarks for the experimental images. These zero watermarks are finally used for the authentication of medical images whenever required.

The robustness of the proposed technique is evaluated using a series of image processing attacks such as average and median filtering, Gaussian blur, additive Gaussian noise, salt and pepper noise, speckle noise, resizing, cropping, rotation, scaling, histogram equalization, contrast and brightness

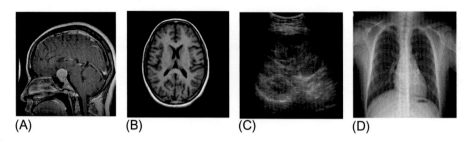

FIG. 5

Experimental images: (A) head, (B) brain, (C) ultrasound, and (D) X-ray.

adjustment, JPEG compression, and row and column deletion. For authentication purposes, a zero watermark is extracted from the possible attacked medical image using the secret key and then compared with the registered watermark. To identify the zero watermark, normalized correlation coefficients (NCCs) are estimated between the original and extracted zero watermarks. The NCCs can be determined as follows:

$$\rho(\mathcal{W}_1, \mathcal{W}_2) = \frac{\sum_{i,j}(\mathcal{W}_1 - \mu_{\mathcal{W}_2})(\mathcal{W}_2 - \mu_{\mathcal{W}_2})}{\sqrt{\sum_{i,j}(\mathcal{W}_1 - \mu_{\mathcal{W}_2})^2}\sqrt{\sum_{ij}(\mathcal{W}_1 - \mu_{\mathcal{W}_2})^2}} \tag{24}$$

where $\mathcal{W}_1$ and $\mathcal{W}_2$ are the original and extracted zero watermarks with respective mean values of $\mu_{\mathcal{W}_1}$ and $\mu_{\mathcal{W}_2}$. The values of ρ lie between the range from $[-1, 1]$. If the value of ρ is 1, then it indicates perfect correlation, whereas if the value of ρ is 0, then it shows no correlation between the watermarks. In addition, performance of the proposed scheme is also analyzed by estimating the bit error rate (BER) for the extracted watermark. Mathematically, BER can be determined as follows:

$$BER = \frac{E_B}{m \times n} \times 100\% \tag{25}$$

where $m \times n$ is the total number of bits in the watermark, whereas E_B denotes the number of error bits in the extracted watermark. The smaller value of BER describes better similarity between the watermarks. Moreover, the robustness of the proposed scheme, in view of hashing sequences, is exploited using normalized hamming distance (NHD). Mathematically, the NHD can be computed as follows:

$$NHD = d(\mathcal{H}_1, \mathcal{H}_2) = \frac{\sum_{j=1}^{N}|(\mathcal{H}_1(j) - \mathcal{H}_2(j))|}{N} \tag{26}$$

where $\mathcal{H}_1(j)$ and $\mathcal{H}_2(j)$ represent the jth element of the hash $\mathcal{H}_1$ and $\mathcal{H}_2$, respectively. The estimated NHD can be divided into two sets: $I_1 = [0, \lambda]$ and $I_2 = [\lambda, b]$, where $b > \lambda$ and $\lambda > 0$ are prefixed threshold values. If NHD belongs to set I_1, the image pairs are considered as perceptually similar, whereas if NHD belongs to set I_2, then it indicates that image pairs are not identical or the image is maliciously modified.

For performance analysis of the proposed technique, additive Gaussian noise (20%) is applied to the medical image as shown in Fig. 6A. Then, zero watermark is extracted from the attacked medical image and compared with the original one in terms of normalized correlation (NC) and BER. Moreover, noise

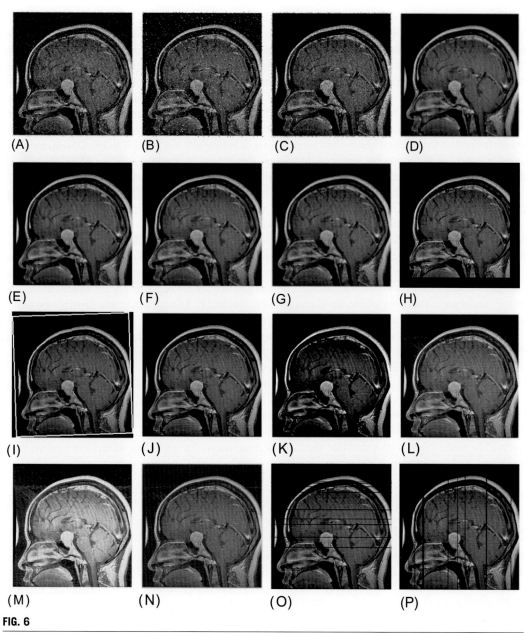

FIG. 6

(A) Gaussian noise addition (20%), (B) salt and pepper noise (20%), (C) speckle noise (20%), (D) Gaussian blur (13 × 13), (E) average filter (3 × 3), (F) median filter (3 × 3), (G) resizing (256 → 128 → 256), (H) cropping (10% area), (I) rotation (5 degrees), (J) image scaling (scale factor = 1.5), (K) contrast adjustment (decreased by 40%), (L) brightness adjustment (increased by 40%), (M) histogram equalization, (N) JPEG compression (20%), (O) row deletion (10R), (P) column deletion (10C).

addition operation is extended to salt and pepper (20%) and speckle noise (20%) addition as shown in Fig. 6B and C, respectively. These operations are also applied to the experimental images and the extracted watermark is compared with the original watermark. The obtained results indicate that the proposed technique has good performance against additive noise operations. Image blurring is another common image processing attack and therefore Gaussian blurring is applied to the medical images with filter size 13×13. The blurred medical image (shown in Fig. 6D) is used for the generation of a watermark and then NC and BER are determined between the watermarks. Image filtering is another common operation in image processing. For this purpose, average and median filtering operations are performed on the medical images and filtered images are depicted in Fig. 6E and F. Operations such as enlargement or reduction are performed to fit the image into the desired size. To do so, the size of medical images is reduced to 128×128 (Fig. 6G) and then increased to its original size.

The effectiveness of the proposed scheme is also investigated against geometric attacks. For this purpose, the image cropping operation is applied to the medical images. In this process, an area of medical image is cropped, which leads to information loss. The resultant cropped image with 90% remaining area is shown in Fig. 6H. For rotation, the image is rotated by 5 degrees in a counterclockwise direction as shown in Fig. 6I. Image scaling is another frequently used operation in real life. The size of the medical images is scaled with a scale factor of 1.5 and is depicted in Fig. 6J. In general, to change the lightness or darkness of an image, contrast and brightness adjustments are widely used. The images undergoing these operations are depicted in Fig. 6K and L. To adjust the tonal distribution of the image histogram, equalization is a widely used tool and is also considered. The resultant image after histogram equalization is depicted in Fig. 6M. Image compression is a frequently used application in day-to-day life. A lossy encoding process is used for storage and transmission of the digital data to reduce the memory requirement. Hence, efficiency of the proposed technique is also tested against JPEG compression (20%) and the estimated result is depicted in Fig. 6N. Finally, results for row and column deletion operation, wherein 10 rows and columns are deleted randomly, are shown in Fig. 6O and P. The zero watermark is generated after these attacks and is compared with the registered zero watermark in terms of NC, BER, and NHD. The obtained results are shown in Tables 1–3, respectively. The tables clearly illustrate that the proposed technique has excellent robustness against both geometric and general image processing attacks.

5 Robustness analysis

The robustness of the proposed technique is measured using NHD against different standard operations. In the first experiment, Gaussian noise is added to medical images with different variances 0.02, 0.04, 0.06, 0.08, 0.10, and 0.12, respectively. The perceptual hash is generated for the noisy and original medical images and the corresponding NHD is estimated as shown in Fig. 7A. The experiments are also explored for other noisy operations. Salt and pepper noise and speckle noise are applied to the medical images with different noise densities 0.02, 0.04, 0.06, 0.08, 0.10, and 0.12, respectively, and the obtained results are depicted in Fig. 7B and C. The robustness of the proposed technique is also verified against Gaussian blurring. The estimated NHDs for blurred images with different filter sizes from 3×3 to 13×13 are shown in Fig. 7D. The minimum NHD is 0.01 for the ultrasound image and the maximum NHD is 0.19 for the X-ray image.

Table 1 Estimated correlation coefficients in watermark extraction after attacks.

Operations	Normalized correlation			
	Head	Brain	Ultrasound	X-ray
Gaussian noise addition (20%)	0.8044	0.7024	0.7314	0.6651
Salt and pepper noise (20%)	0.9110	0.7441	0.7058	0.6481
Speckle noise (20%)	0.8650	0.8601	0.8243	0.6055
Gaussian blur (13 × 13)	0.9481	0.8912	0.8017	0.6772
Average filter (3 × 3)	0.9793	0.9328	0.9681	0.5512
Median filter (3 × 3)	0.8545	0.5875	0.7216	0.6512
Resizing (256 → 128 → 256)	0.8784	0.7746	0.8656	0.8496
Cropping (10%)	0.8939	0.7883	0.7024	0.6474
Rotation (5 degrees)	0.6651	0.6896	0.6761	0.6139
Scaling (scale factor = 1.5)	0.8578	0.7184	0.9200	0.7193
Histogram equalization	0.6175	0.5308	0.6163	0.5274
Contrast adjustment (40%)	0.8925	0.9104	0.9456	0.7006
Brightness adjustment (40%)	0.9208	0.7409	0.8369	0.7249
JPEG compression (20%)	0.8786	0.7956	0.8209	0.7274
Row deletion (10 rows)	0.7569	0.7000	0.7536	0.7361
Column deletion (10 columns)	0.7122	0.7956	0.7209	0.7474

Table 2 Estimated bit error rate in watermark extraction after attacks.

Operations	Bit error rate			
	Head	Brain	Ultrasound	X-ray
Gaussian noise addition (20%)	0.0944	0.1488	0.1344	0.1876
Salt and pepper noise (20%)	0.0416	0.1280	0.1472	0.1904
Speckle noise (20%)	0.0624	0.0704	0.0880	0.1876
Gaussian blur (13 × 13)	0.0976	0.0544	0.0992	0.1616
Average filter (3 × 3)	0.0128	0.0336	0.0160	0.1920
Median filter (3 × 3)	0.0672	0.2064	0.1392	0.1744
Resizing (256 → 128 → 256)	0.0608	0.1326	0.0672	0.0771
Cropping (10%)	0.0496	0.1337	0.1488	0.1840
Rotation (5 degrees)	0.1648	0.1552	0.1884	0.1776
Scaling (scale factor = 1.5)	0.0656	0.1276	0.0572	0.1408
Histogram equalization	0.1744	0.2184	0.196	0.2224
Contrast adjustment (40%)	0.0496	0.0448	0.0272	0.1504
Brightness adjustment (40%)	0.0368	0.1296	0.0816	0.1376
JPEG compression (20%)	0.0576	0.1024	0.0896	0.1260
Row deletion (10 rows)	0.1216	0.0683	0.1148	0.0701
Column deletion (10 columns)	0.0805	0.0350	0.1331	0.0946

Table 3 Estimated normalized hamming distance after attacks.

Operations	Normalized hamming distance			
	Head	**Brain**	**Ultrasound**	**X-ray**
Gaussian noise addition (20%)	0.0896	0.1413	0.1474	0.1804
Salt and pepper noise (20%)	0.0395	0.1231	0.1550	0.1931
Speckle noise (20%)	0.0592	0.0668	0.0835	0.2021
Gaussian blur (13 × 13)	0.0227	0.0516	0.0942	0.1534
Average filter (3 × 3)	0.0531	0.0319	0.0151	0.1899
Median filter (3 × 3)	0.0638	0.1656	0.0486	0.1656
Resizing (256 → 128 → 256)	0.0577	0.1621	0.0638	0.0668
Cropping (10%)	0.0471	0.1735	0.1882	0.1978
Rotation (5 degrees)	0.1793	0.1565	0.1686	0.1961
Scaling (scale factor = 1.5)	0.0623	0.1184	0.1899	0.1686
Histogram equalization	0.2082	0.1848	0.1920	0.1835
Contrast adjustment (40%)	0.0471	0.0668	0.0835	0.0805
Brightness adjustment (40%)	0.0349	0.1337	0.1322	0.1398
JPEG compression (20%)	0.0576	0.0972	0.1443	0.1872
Row deletion (10 rows)	0.1216	0.0683	0.1148	0.0701
Column deletion (10 columns)	0.0805	0.0350	0.1331	0.0946

The robustness of the proposed technique is tested against filtering operations. The perceptual hashes are generated for the average- and median-filtered image with different filter sizes 3, 5, 7, and 9, and the respective NHDs are depicted in Fig. 8A and B. In addition, experiments are further extended to various other operations like contrast and brightness change. The contrast of medical images is decreased from 5% to 30% with five step sizes and the brightness of images is also increased in the similar ratio. The results are shown in Fig. 8C and D. The robustness of technique is also investigated against geometric operation. The size of the image is decreased using the scale factor from 0.9 to 0.5 and is increased by 1.1 to 1.5. The NHD between the hash pairs of the scaled and original images is depicted in Fig. 9. Finally, JPEG compression is employed on the medical images with 10% to 50% compression and the NHD is computed between the hash pairs of original and compressed versions. The resultant NHD of JPEG compression is shown in Fig. 10. From the robustness analysis of the foregoing experimental results, it can be observed that the proposed technique achieves good robustness against underlying attacks.

6 Key sensitivity analysis

A good watermarking technique should be sensitive to its secret key. The experimental images shown in Fig. 5 are used to measure the sensitivity analysis of the proposed technique. For this purpose, wrong secret keys are used to generate the watermarks for the medical images. Then, correlation is evaluated between the original and other watermarks, generated from the original and wrong secret keys,

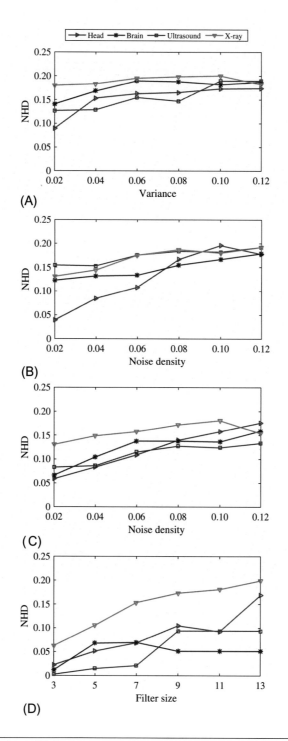

FIG. 7

Robustness against operations: (A) Gaussian noise addition, (B) salt and pepper noise, (C) speckle noise, and (D) Gaussian blur.

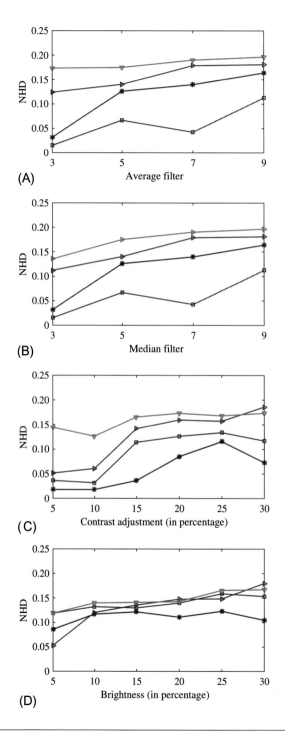

FIG. 8

Robustness against operations: (A) average filter, (B) median filter, (C) contrast adjustment, and (D) brightness adjustment.

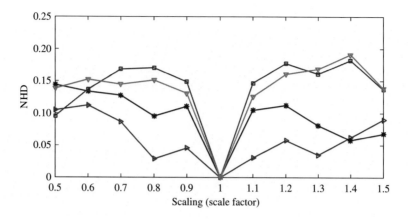

FIG. 9

Robustness against image scaling with different scale factors.

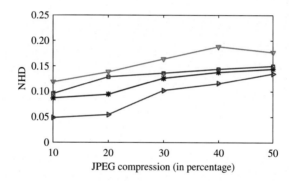

FIG. 10

Robustness against JPEG compression with different compression ratios.

respectively. The estimated results show that correlation coefficients are small in comparison to the attacked medical images. Due to limited space, the key sensitivity of the "Brain" image is presented. First, a secret key is used in the generation of a watermark for the "Brain" image, after which 100 different keys other than the original one are used to generate a watermark for the same medical image while keeping all other parameters unchanged. The correlation between the watermark corresponding to true and 100 secret keys is measured and shown in Fig. 11.

7 Computational time complexity

Computational time complexity is another important aspect that defines the feasibility of the approach. Time complexity refers to the time required for constructing the zero watermark and the execution time is measured in terms of CPU cycles. Remarkably, optimal implementation of a particular algorithm

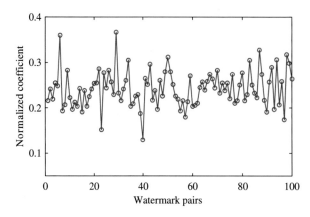

FIG. 11

Key sensitivity for the watermark.

Table 4 Computational time complexities of the proposed technique.				
Process	**Time (in s) for the image**			
	Head	**Brain**	**Ultrasound**	**X-ray**
Watermark 1	1.8869	1.8329	1.8214	1.7446
Watermark 2	1.9438	1.8659	1.801	1.7746
Watermark 3	1.8972	1.8384	1.8053	1.7697
Watermark 4	1.9018	2.0904	1.8883	1.7658

may have lower time complexity than a less optimal one for a given hardware platform despite the fact that the two implementations produce identical results. The execution time is measured using the Matlab platform on a system with an Intel core i5-2.27 GHz processor with 4 GB of RAM. The code is executed 10 times for each experimental image by considering the four different watermarks having the same size as the original one, and the average times for the experimental images are shown in Table 4.

8 Conclusion

In this chapter, a robust framework was presented for security of the medical images using perceptual hashing by extracting the invariant features based on SIFT and DCT transform. A digital signature for medical images is constructed using a binary watermark and the hash value, which is useful in the authentication of the medical images. The hash value is generated by combining the global and key local features. The simulation results show that the proposed scheme has good robustness against various signal processing attacks as well as geometric attacks. This technique is useful in the authentication and integrity verification of the medical images during transmission across channels and storage in the database. The approach plays a vital role in other image processing applications like identification and classification of digital images.

References

[1] M. Elhoseny, G. Ramírez-González, O.M. Abu-Elnasr, S.A. Shawkat, N. Arunkumar, A. Farouk, Secure medical data transmission model for IoT-based healthcare systems, IEEE Access 6 (2018) 20596–20608.

[2] S. Kaihara, Realisation of the computerised patient record; relevance and unsolved problems, Int. J. Med. Inform. 49 (1) (1998) 1–8.

[3] C.K. Tan, J.C. Ng, X. Xu, C.L. Poh, Y.L. Guan, K. Sheah, Security protection of DICOM medical images using dual-layer reversible watermarking with tamper detection capability, J. Digit. Imaging 24 (3) (2011) 528–540.

[4] X. Kong, R. Feng, Watermarking medical signals for telemedicine, IEEE Trans. Inf. Technol. Biomed. 5 (3) (2001) 195–201.

[5] F. Cao, H.K. Huang, X.Q. Zhou, Medical image security in a HIPAA mandated PACS environment, Comput. Med. Imaging Graph. 27 (3) (2003) 185–196.

[6] X. Guo, T.G. Zhuang, Lossless watermarking for verifying the integrity of medical images with tamper localization, J. Digit. Imaging 22 (6) (2009) 620–628.

[7] C.P. Wang, X.Y. Wang, Z.Q. Xia, C. Zhang, X.J. Chen, Geometrically resilient color image zero-watermarking algorithm based on quaternion exponent moments, J. Vis. Commun. Image Represent. 41 (2016) 247–259.

[8] F. Tao, W. Qian, Image hash authentication algorithm for orthogonal moments of fractional order chaotic scrambling coupling hyper-complex number, Measurement 134 (2019) 866–873.

[9] J. Guan, Y. Li, J. Sun, X. Wang, H. Zhao, J. Zhang, Z. Liu, S. Qi, Graph-based supervised discrete image hashing, J. Vis. Commun. Image Represent. 58 (2019) 675–687.

[10] B. Topcu, H. Erdogan, Fixed-length asymmetric binary hashing for fingerprint verification through GMM-SVM based representations, Pattern Recognit. 88 (2019) 409–420.

[11] M. Sapkota, X. Shi, F. Xing, L. Yang, Deep convolutional hashing for low-dimensional binary embedding of histopathological images, IEEE J. Biomed. Health Inform. 23 (2019) 805–816.

[12] S. Singh, G. Bhatnagar, A robust image hashing based on discrete wavelet transform, in: International Conference on Signal and Image Processing Applications (ICSIPA), 2017, pp. 440–444.

[13] V. Monga, B.L. Evans, Perceptual image hashing via feature points: performance evaluation and tradeoffs, IEEE Trans. Image Process. 15 (11) (2006) 3452–3465.

[14] V. Monga, B. Evans, Robust perceptual image hashing using feature points, in: IEEE International Conference on Image Processing, vol. 1, 2004, pp. 677–680.

[15] A. Swaminathan, Y. Mao, M. Wu, Robust and secure image hashing, IEEE Trans. Inf. Forensics Secur. 1 (2) (2006) 215–230.

[16] F. Khelifi, J. Jiang, Perceptual image hashing based on virtual watermark detection, IEEE Trans. Image Process. 19 (4) (2009) 981–994.

[17] X. Lv, Z.J. Wang, Perceptual image hashing based on shape contexts and local feature points, IEEE Trans. Inf. Forensics Secur. 7 (3) (2012) 1081–1093.

[18] Z. Tang, L. Chen, X. Zhang, S. Zhang, Robust image hashing with tensor decomposition, IEEE Transactions on Knowledge and Data Engineering 31 (3) (2019) 549–560.

[19] J. Ouyang, Y. Liu, H. Shu, Robust hashing for image authentication using SIFT feature and quaternion Zernike moments, Multimed. Tools Appl. 76 (2) (2017) 2609–2626.

[20] Q. Wen, T.F. Sun, S.X. Wang, Concept and application of zero-watermark, Acta Electron. Sin. 31 (2) (2003) 214–216.

[21] J. Zhao, X.W. Zhang, S. Fan, W. Zhang, A strong robust zero-watermarking scheme based on shearlets' high ability for capturing directional features, Math. Probl. Eng. 1 (2016) 1–12.

[22] J.K. Kou, L.X. Wei, Zero-watermarking algorithm based on piecewise logistic chaotic map, Commun. Eng. Des. Mag. 34 (2) (2013) 464–468.

[23] F. Li, T. Gao, Q. Yang, A novel zero-watermark copyright authentication scheme based on lifting wavelet and Harris corner detection, Wuhan Univ. J. Nat. Sci. 5 (2010) 408–414.

[24] C. Wang, X. Wang, Z. Xia, C. Zhang, Ternary radial harmonic Fourier moments based robust stereo image zero-watermarking algorithm, Inform. Sci. 470 (2019) 109–120.

[25] T.-Y. Fan, H.-C. Chao, B.-C. Chieu, Lossless medical image watermarking method based on significant difference of cellular automata transform coefficient, Signal Process. Image Commun. 70 (2019) 174–183.

[26] H. Zheng, C. Wang, J. Wang, S. Xiang, A new reversible watermarking scheme using the content-adaptive block size for prediction, Signal Process. 164 (2019) 74–83.

[27] X. Leng, J. Xiao, Y. Wang, A robust image zero-watermarking algorithm based on DWT and PCA, in: Communications and Information Processing, 2012, pp. 484–492.

[28] D.G. Lowe, Distinctive image features from scale-invariant keypoints, Int. J. Comput. Vis. 60 (2) (2004) 91–110.

[29] M.A. Afarizadeh, S. Behnia, Hierarchy of chaotic maps with an invariant measure and their coupling, Physica D 159 (1–2) (2001) 1–21.

[30] H. Andrews, C. Patterson, Singular value decompositions and digital image processing, IEEE Trans. Acoust. Speech Signal Process. 24 (1) (1976) 26–53.

[31] N. Ahmed, T. Natarajan, K.R. Rao, Discrete cosine transform, IEEE Trans. Comput. 100 (1) (1974) 90–93.

[32] S.P. Singh, G. Bhatnagar, A robust watermarking scheme based on image normalization, in: IEEE 14th International Colloquium on Signal Processing & Its Applications (CSPA), 2018, pp. 140–144.

[33] L.S.B. Gao, Color image encryption based on gyrator transform and Arnold transform, Opt. Laser Technol. 48 (2016) 530–538.

[34] T.H. Chen, G. Horng, W.B. Lee, A publicly verifiable copyright-proving scheme resistant to malicious attacks, IEEE Trans. Ind. Electron. 52 (1) (2005) 327–334.

Frequency domain based data hiding for encrypted medical images

2

Hiba Abdel-Nabi and Ali Al-Haj

Department of Computer Engineering, Princess Sumaya University for Technology Amman, Amman, Jordan

1 Introduction

The evolution in computer and communications technologies has been advancing rapidly in recent years. Such advances have facilitated the exchange and transmission of information via vulnerable insecure public networks. On the other hand, and despite all of these appealing advantages, the security of the transmitted information can be violated easily and consequently may lead to the illegal disclosure of private information. Therefore providing security services such as confidentiality, authenticity, integrity, protection, and safe transmission of transmitted information has become a vital and an essential task.

This chapter focuses on providing security for transmitted medical images because of their important and crucial role in telehealth medical applications. The intra- and interhospital exchange of medical images and the ease of making digital copies, editing, and distributing these images via unsecured public networks have brought about the essentiality of securing transmitted medical images [1,2]. Indeed, medical images are sensitive to any manipulation that may threaten the lives of patients, and at the same time disrupt the credibility of medical institutions.

In recent years it has become a fact that any powerful scheme developed for securing transmitted medical images must be based on two techniques: cryptography to achieve confidentiality and digital watermarking to achieve authenticity and integrity. Encryption plays the role of a preprotection tool since it becomes ineffective when the image is decrypted, and consequently its integrity and authenticity become hard to validate. These are the benefits of watermarking, which acts as an a posteriori control tool allowing the image content to be still available for interpretation while the remainder is protected. Accordingly, any security scheme that combines cryptography and digital watermarking will efficiently secure medical images while being encrypted or decrypted.

As a consequence, because of the sensitive nature of medical images they cannot tolerate any distortion that may lead to privacy violation or severe complications due to misdiagnosis. Therefore reversible data hiding (RDH) techniques that operate on encrypted images need to be developed to provide the required security. RDH offers exact and perfect recovery of the original image after the embedded data have been extracted. This reversibility is considered an attractive and valuable feature from which medical images can benefit to attain security while being transmitted. In RDH schemes the embedded data are made fragile so that any tampering or modification of the watermarked image results in an authentication error. Moreover, because of the security vulnerabilities discussed earlier, medical images are often transmitted and stored in encrypted form to protect their contents, and thus there is always a need to provide security for encrypted medical images.

Most existing RDH schemes operate on plain images. These schemes exploit the redundancy inherently available in plain images to provide the required reversibility. Extending these RDH schemes to operate on encrypted images is not straightforward. This is because encryption algorithms, which are used to encrypt the plain image, minimize the existing redundancy in the image, thus preventing the RDH algorithm from making use of the redundancy it needs to operate normally.

In this chapter, an effective joint watermarking encryption algorithm is developed and evaluated. The proposed algorithm uses dual watermark embedding in the frequency and encrypted domains. The algorithm embeds dual watermarks: the encrypted domain watermark and the frequency domain watermark. The two watermarks are embedded in different frequency sub-bands to avoid any mutual interference and to allow for direct and independent access to each watermark. Partial encryption is used to encrypt one of the sub-bands by means of a permutation-based encryption algorithm.

The proposed algorithm benefits from the advantages offered by the frequency domain. One major benefit is the high embedding capacity the frequency domain offers. Another benefit is the high imperceptibility that the watermarked image exhibits because it operates on the coefficient level, not the pixel level. That is, by virtue of embedding in the coefficients of the frequency transforms, any distortion caused by the watermarking process is distributed irregularly over the entire image, making illegal detection of the watermark more difficult. Moreover, the proposed algorithm is separable, which allows for the watermark extraction to be independent from the decryption of the watermarked image. A direct result of separability is that the authenticity and integrity of the medical image can be verified while preserving the privacy of the original content of that image. This can be achieved by virtue of the multiple keys used by the algorithm to control access to the medical images at different stages.

The remainder of the chapter is organized as follows. In Section 2 a brief overview of a number of related works in RDH schemes for encrypted images is given. Section 3 describes the two functions responsible for providing reversibility to the proposed algorithm. A detailed description of the proposed algorithm is given in Section 4. Section 5 gives an in-depth analysis of the experiments conducted to prove the effectiveness of the proposed algorithm. In addition, Section 5 presents performance evaluation results and compares these results with a number of recent state-of-the-art studies. Finally, in Section 6, concluding remarks and future work directions are outlined.

2 Literature survey

This section gives a short survey of a selected set of published RDH algorithms. The algorithms are classified either in terms of the data hiding domain, whether it is a spatial domain or a frequency domain, or in terms of the format of the original cover image, whether it is a plain image or an encrypted image. RDH is an active research area driven by the need for effective and reliable data hiding schemes for all type of images, with emphasis on medical images.

A separable joint data hiding algorithm that manipulates the encrypted images is proposed in [3]. The algorithm jointly embeds two watermarks in both the spatial and encrypted domains using the idea of partial encryption to avoid any interference between the two watermarks. The algorithm randomly selects the majority of pixels of the cover image and embeds the watermark using histogram shifting (HS). These watermarked pixels are then encrypted using a standard substitution encryption such as

Advanced Encryption Standard (AES). The remaining unselected pixels are left unencrypted and used at a later stage to embed another watermark. This scenario has been adopted to achieve separability and to create multiple levels of security of the cover image in which authenticity and integrity can be verified in both the spatial and encrypted domains.

Zhang [4] proposed a joint encryption and watermarking scheme by encrypting the entire cover image by stream encryption. The encrypted image was then segmented into nonoverlapping blocks in which secret bits were embedded. This was done by toggling the three least significant bits (LSBs) of half the pixels in that block. At the receiver side, and for every decrypted block, fluctuation of its pixel values is used to extract the embedded bit and recover the original image. The main advantage of this proposed algorithm is low computational complexity. A major disadvantage is that some errors may occur in the extraction phase because the smoothness of each block does not utilize all the pixels. Hong et al. [5] enhanced the performance of Zhang's algorithm by proposing a better correlation between adjacent blocks using a different estimation formula. The formula is based on a side-match scheme that lowers the error rate by generating the absolute vertical and horizontal differences of the pixels of the blocks followed by taking their summation. However, this is a nonseparable scheme since data extraction is done after decrypting the encrypted watermarked image.

The separable scheme proposed by [6] creates a sparse space to hide any side information by compressing the LSBs of the encrypted cover image. Data extraction and image recovery depend on the spatial correlation in the original image. In [7], a room is vacated for embedding before the encryption process. The idea behind this algorithm is that a space on the cover image is preserved for data hiding before encryption takes place. The algorithm divides the image into two parts, A and B, according to a first-order smoothness function and rearranges A in front of B. Then, the LSBs of A are embedded into B with a standard RDH algorithm and a required watermark is embedded in their place. The image is then encrypted using a stream cipher and delivered to a service provider for data embedding.

Instead of using the encrypted images to embed the secret data, the scheme proposed in [8] estimates some of the image pixels before the encryption takes place to embed the data in the resulting estimation errors. Two types of encryption are adopted in this scheme: the standard AES to encrypt the pixels that will not be estimated by the scheme, and a special encryption technique to encrypt the estimating errors.

A framework that divides the image pixels into blocks of a certain size is proposed in [9]. It employs a new encryption strategy to encrypt each block using a key stream generated from the encryption key that differs for each block. Each generated block is then randomly permutated, which maintains the neighboring pixels' correlation in the encrypted domain. In [10], a joint RDH and encryption algorithm is introduced for securing medical images. To achieve separability, the algorithm embeds two different watermarks simultaneously: one watermark in the spatial domain and one watermark in the encrypted domain to attain high embedding capacity. The algorithm utilizes different types of encryption methods such as substitution based and transposition based to guarantee complete image encryption. It randomly divides the image pixels into two halves or groups that are used separately to embed the two watermarks using HS. One watermark is embedded before encryption and the other watermark is embedded after encryption.

In [11] another separable scheme is proposed that utilizes the bitplanes concept. It merges the plain watermarked image with its encrypted watermarked counterpart image to form a single image with double the number of bitplanes of the original image. Therefore the algorithm can be thought of as double sided regarding the encryption coverage: partial encryption of the single generated image and full encryption when the two images are separated and processed at the receiver side. The hiding keys are generated by feeding the side information required by the RDH algorithm through a key generator.

An adaptive block-level prediction-error expansion-based scheme is proposed in [12]. The scheme can be used to embed the data in the plain and encrypted images. The image is divided into 2×2 blocks that are used to embed the secret data into each block by expanding the prediction-error produced using a new proposed predictor called the best linear predictor (BLP). A joint scheme that operates in the frequency domain and is based on integer wavelet transform (IWT) and Arnold map permutation is proposed in [13]. Perfect restoration of the original cover image is achieved through IWT. After encrypting the middle- and high-frequency sub-bands of the wavelet coefficients using Arnold permutation encryption, the data are embedded using the HS method.

A novel RDH scheme for encrypted images that adopts many techniques such as IWT, HS, and orthogonal decomposition is proposed by Xiong et al. in [14]. Perfect reversibility is achieved by embedding the secret data in the independent subvector of the orthogonal coefficients. In [15], another scheme that operates in both the frequency and encrypted domains is proposed. A permutation encryption is used to encrypt the cover image. The IWT is then used to decompose the encrypted image into four sub-bands. The scheme losslessly compresses the location map of the most significant bitplanes of the high-frequency coefficients of the encrypted image. It then concatenates it as part of the embedded payload. After that, the scheme uses these high-frequency coefficients to embed the secret data by bits replacement.

3 Theoretical background

The proposed algorithm is an RDH algorithm. To achieve the desired reversibility, the algorithm makes use of an RDH algorithm known as HS and a frequency domain transform known as IWT. Both HS and IWT are key functions in furnishing the reversibility of the proposed algorithm. In this section, brief descriptions of HS and IWT are given.

3.1 Histogram shifting RDH method

An efficient RDH algorithm that modifies the histogram of the cover image is proposed by Ni et al. [16]. The algorithm generates the histogram of an image, then a pair or more of **peak** points that have the maximum number of pixels and **zero** (minimum) points are found. A gap or a space for data hiding is generated by shifting the histogram between the peak point and the zero point toward the latter. In other words, if the peak and zero points are denoted by P and Z, respectively, and assuming that $P < Z$ without loss of generality, then the histogram that is bounded by the $P+1, Z-1$, is shifted to the right by 1 causing the point P to disappear and a gap to be generated in the histogram. Now, while scanning the cover image, if a pixel with value P is found, 1 bit of the watermark will be embedded by modifying this value. If the additional bit is 1, then it is incremented by 1, otherwise, no modification is done.

This scheme is known for the very little distortion it introduces in the watermarked image, in addition to its low computational complexity. However, this scheme has some disadvantages. The payload size is limited by the frequency of peak point in the histogram that may be insufficient. Also, this scheme is not blind, i.e., it requires the availability of the side information represented by the peak and zero points that were used in the embedding phase, along with the watermarked image. It is worthwhile noting that multiple pairs of peak and zero points can be used to increase the embedding capacity of the cover image. A utilization of peak point and zero point is found in Fig. 1A where the peak and zero points are defined, while the shifted histogram before embedding the data is shown in Fig. 1B. The figure shows that the original histogram is shifted from peak point toward the zero point to generate the required gap to embed the data. Fig. 1C represents the watermarked histogram with the disappeared peak point due to data embedding.

One major drawback of the traditional HS method is its nonblindness. That is, the side information of this method, such as the peak point and zero point, must be transmitted alongside the watermarked image. The proposed algorithm overcomes this limitation by using an LSB substitution scheme, which embeds this side information in the LSBs of selected pixels in the boundary regions of the image. This approach achieves the required blindness and thus eliminates the difficulty of transmitting the

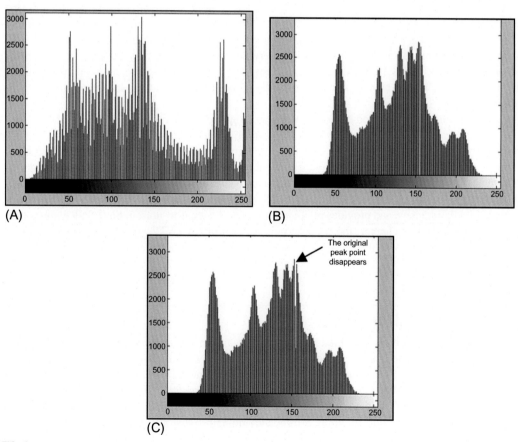

FIG. 1

(A) Histogram of original image. (B) Shifted histogram. (C) Histogram of watermarked image.

auxiliary data required by the HS method separately. Therefore an LSB substitution scheme is adopted with the original HS method to guarantee blind extraction.

3.2 Integer wavelet transform with lifting scheme

The multiresolution representation offered by operating in the frequency domain is useful in analyzing the information content of an image. It presents the image at different resolution levels, thus providing a time frequency representation of the image without changing its information content. Converting an image into the frequency domain is done by reversible mathematical transforms that map the pixel values onto a set of coefficients.

A popular family of frequency domain transforms is the wavelet transform family. The traditional wavelet transforms, such as the discrete wavelet transform (DWT), are based on floating point operations. This leads to loss of information because of the truncation or rounding off errors caused by representing the transforms' coefficients in floating points. Therefore DWT is not suitable for reversible watermarking schemes since the exact recovery of the original cover image may not be guaranteed and the watermark extraction will fail. To overcome this limitation, and since every detail in the medical image is important, an invertible integer-to-integer wavelet transform based on a lifting scheme is proposed in [18,19]. This transform preserves all the information by mapping the integers of the original image pixels to an integer coefficient and thus achieving the required reversibility. The lifting scheme is used since it significantly reduces the computation time and speeds up the computation process.

A lossless data hiding method based on IWT was proposed by Xuan et al. [17]. The authors found more bias between 1s and 0s starting from the second bitplane to the higher bitplanes of the IWT coefficients. The data are hidden in one or more bitplanes of the middle- and high-frequency coefficients of the IWT. The original bitplanes are compressed losslessly by arithmetic coding and then concatenated with payload. As a preprocessing step to prevent grayscale overflowing during data embedding, histogram modification or integer modulo addition is applied. However, this method is computationally intensive and provides relatively lower peak signal-to-noise ratio (PSNR) values than the other RDHs. In this chapter, the proposed algorithm utilizes IWT2, which performs 2D lifting wavelet decomposition with respect to the orthogonal wavelet Cohen-Daubechies-Feauveau lifting scheme.

4 The proposed algorithm

This proposed algorithm is implemented in the frequency and encrypted domains. It provides high embedding capacity because it embeds two watermarks: one in each domain. The encrypted domain and the frequency domain watermarks are embedded in different sub-bands to avoid any interference or interaction between them and to give access to them separately. Unlike the spatial domain RDH schemes, which are based on pixel-level modification of the original image, reversible methods operating in the frequency domain apply a frequency domain transform, such as wavelet transform, on the original image. The frequency domain transform performs some sort of coefficient-level modification, followed by inverse transformation to obtain the watermarked image. This kind of embedding in the coefficients distributes the distortion caused by the embedding process irregularly over the image, making the detection of the watermark more difficult. Watermark embedding and extraction procedures will be described in detail in this section.

4.1 Watermark embedding procedure

The embedding procedure consists of four phases: the image preprocessing phase to prevent overflow and/or underflow, the image segmentation phase to generate the required sub-bands, the frequency domain watermark generation phase, and the overall data embedding phase.

4.1.1 Phase 1—Image preprocessing

When a watermark is embedded into a certain frequency transform's coefficients, it is always possible that the embedding process will cause an overflow or an underflow for some image pixels after applying the inverse IWT. An overflow means that the grayscale values of some pixels in the transformed image may exceed the upper bound (255) or the lower bound (0) for an 8-bit grayscale image. To prevent the overflow and underflow from happening, and to ensure the algorithm's reversibility, image preprocessing in the spatial domain is done before applying frequency transformation and prior to watermark embedding. A histogram modification that narrows the histogram from both extremes toward the center is applied on the original image as a required preprocessing step. However, the side information that contains information about that narrowing must be embedded into the image as part of the total payload, which is used later in the postprocessing phase to recover the cover image.

The preprocessing modification used in this algorithm will map the lowest 16 grayscale values to a grayscale value of 15, while the highest 16 grayscale values are mapped to the grayscale value of 240, as done in [17]. This will narrow down the histogram of the image to the range [15,240] instead of the normal range of [0,255]. Fig. 2A and B provides an example of the normal histogram of an image and the corresponding narrowed histogram, respectively.

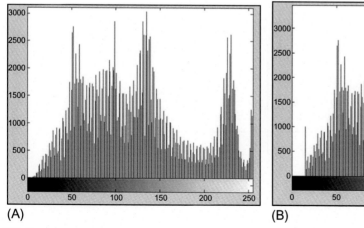

(A)   (B)

FIG. 2

The range of pixel values of the original image is narrowed at the two extremes to avoid overflow or underflow. (A) Normal histogram. (B) Narrowed histogram.

4.1.2 Phase 2—Image segmentation

Applying a one-level IWT2 on the input image produces four frequency sub-bands denoted as the lower sub-band (LL), the middle sub-bands (LH, HL), and the higher sub-band (HH). One other notation that is commonly used to represent the sub-bands is as follows: the approximation sub-band (CA) and the details sub-bands (CH, CV, CD). Fig. 3 shows the sub-band structure of a one-level wavelet decomposition of an image. Each sub-band represents a different degree of resolution of the original image. The size of each sub-band is equal to one-fourth the original image size. This decomposition offers flexibility in choosing the most appropriate position of the embedded data, based on the specific requirements of data hiding applications.

The low-frequency sub-band indicates the miniature of the image that represents the most important part of the image. On the other hand, the high- and middle-frequency sub-bands indicate pixel differences in different directions, which represents variations of the image. Therefore to enhance the quality of the decrypted image, the frequency domain watermark is usually embedded in the middle sub-bands. Any data embedding in the low-frequency sub-band results in a change that affects the visual quality of the image. Consequently, the low-frequency sub-band will not be used in frequency domain watermark embedding. Similarly, the high-frequency sub-band will be used for data embedding because it can be easily destroyed by compression or scaling operations. As a result, the middle frequency sub-bands are the best choice for embedding as long as the embedding rate is sufficient. If the embedding rate is insufficient, then the higher sub-band can be used since reversible data hiding produces a fragile watermark.

Within the same sub-band, each coefficient consists of multiple bitplanes. In the lower bitplanes, the distribution of 1s and 0s is random with equal probability. Thus it will result in a low compression rate when compressed losslessly using arithmetic coding. However, the bias between the 0s and 1s starts to increase as we move to higher bitplanes. Therefore the higher the bitplane, the more bias occurs, and as a result a good compression ratio is provided. On the other hand, any change in the higher bitplanes affects the coefficients further, and thus produces distortion to the image.

LL ≡ CA lower / approximation sub-band	**HL ≡ CH** middle / horizontal details sub-band
LH≡ CV middle / vertical details sub-band	**HH≡ CD** higher / diagonal details sub-band

FIG. 3

One-level IWT2.

In summary, for frequency domain embedding, the optimal selection that preserves the image quality and makes the watermarked sub-bands perceptually the same as the original sub-bands is the middle and/or the higher sub-bands with one or more middle bitplanes of the coefficients in these sub-bands. On the other hand, the lower sub-band is the best choice of sub-band to be encrypted and then used for embedding the encrypted domain watermark. This is because the lower sub-band contains most of the details and approximation of the original image. Therefore encrypting this sub-band will provide an encrypted image; however, this encryption is considered partial encryption since the middle and higher sub-bands remain unencrypted.

4.1.3 Phase 3—Frequency domain payload generation phase

As stated in the image segmentation subsection, frequency domain embedding is done in the middle bitplanes. To be specific, embedding is done in the fourth bitplane of the wavelet coefficient in the middle and/or higher sub-bands. To ensure exact image restoration, the selected bitplane must be compressed losslessly using the arithmetic encoding technique, and then this compressed bit stream must be embedded in the image as part of the payload. The total frequency domain payload that is embedded in place of the chosen bitplane is given as:

$$frequency\ domain\ payload = (freq\ wm) \cup (side\_info1) \cup (compressed\ bitplane)$$
$$\cup (watermark\ height) \cup (watermark\ width) \tag{1}$$

where *freqwm* represents the frequency domain watermark, *side_info1* represents the information used to prevent overflow and underflow, *compressed bitplane* represents the losslessly compressed original bitplane that is needed for exact image recovery, and *watermark height* and *watermark width* represent the height and width of the frequency domain watermark.

4.1.4 Phase 4—Data embedding phase

A detailed description of the embedding procedure of the proposed algorithm is given in this subsection. A block diagram of the procedure is shown in Fig. 4, a detailed flowchart of the embedding steps is shown in Fig. 5, and an embedding example is shown in Fig. 6.

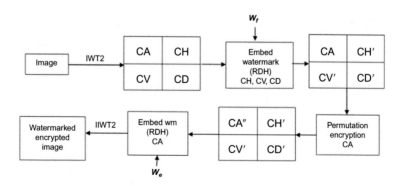

FIG. 4

Block diagram of the data embedding phase in the proposed algorithm.

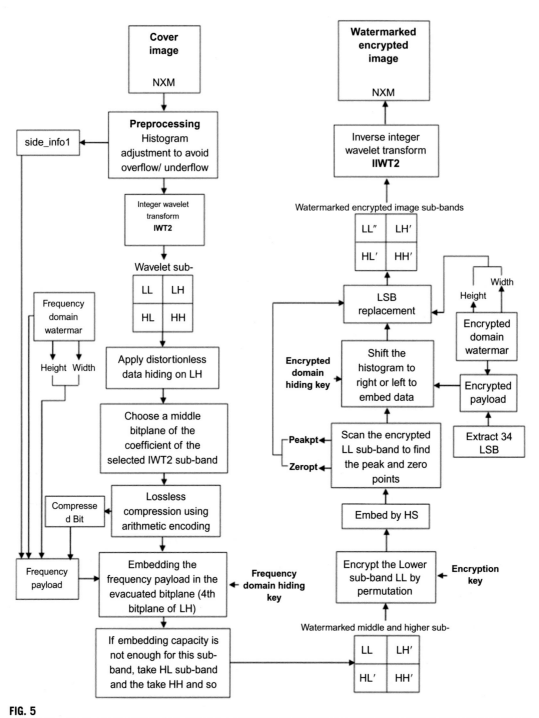

FIG. 5

Flowchart of embedding procedure.

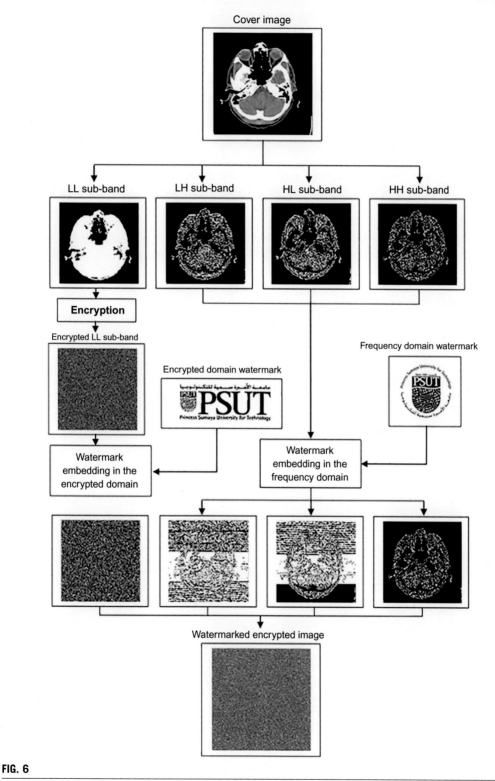

FIG. 6

Example of data embedding by the proposed algorithm.

Inputs: Cover image I with size $M \times N$ (where M, N are the height and width of the cover image), encrypted domain watermark W_e, frequency domain payload W_f.

Output: Watermarked encrypted image I''.

Step 1: Decompose the cover image by applying the IWT2 transform. This operation will produce four multiresolution sub-bands: lower, middle, and higher sub-bands. The four sub-bands CA, CH, CV, CD are shown in Fig. 4.

Step 2: Embed the frequency domain payload in the middle and higher sub-bands using the distortionless data hiding method. Note that the three sub-bands are used for embedding the frequency domain payload to increase the hiding capacity. The resultant image is called the frequency domain watermarked image.

Step 3: Encrypt the lower sub-band CA by pixel permutation using a predefined key. Note that the lower sub-band contains the approximation of the image, thus encrypting this sub-band will convert the image into meaningless data.

Step 4: Embed the encrypted domain watermark in the encrypted lower sub-band CA using the HS method.

Step 5: Apply the inverse IWT2 transform on the modified sub-bands to get the final watermarked encrypted image.

4.2 Watermark extraction procedure

The watermark extraction procedure is the direct reversal of the watermark embedding procedure. The watermarked encrypted image is decomposed using the same wavelet transform used in the embedding process, which means that the higher three sub-bands are processed to extract the frequency domain watermark. To extract the encrypted domain watermark, inverse HS is applied to the lower encrypted sub-band. A restored image can be obtained by decrypting the lower sub-band. The operational steps of the watermark extraction procedure are illustrated in Fig. 7 and described hereafter. A detailed flowchart of the watermark extraction steps is shown in Fig. 8 and an extraction example is shown in Fig. 9.

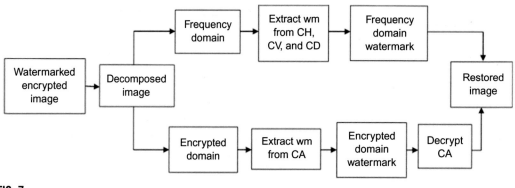

FIG. 7

Block diagram of data extraction procedure of the proposed algorithm.

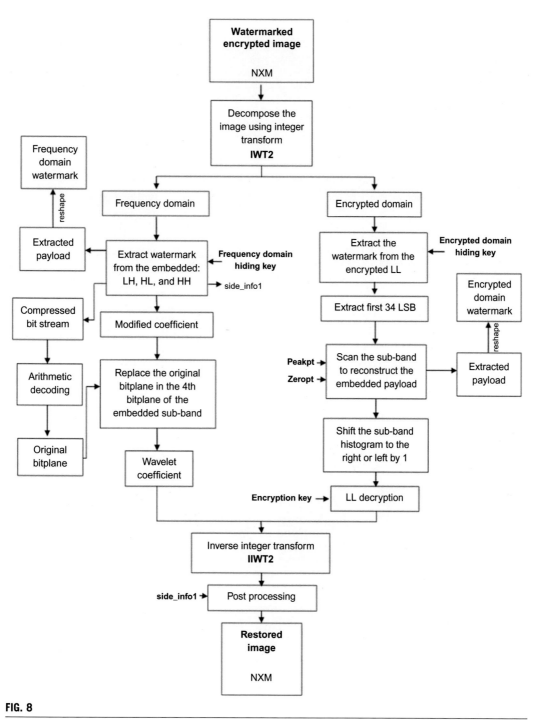

FIG. 8

Flowchart of extraction procedure of the proposed algorithm.

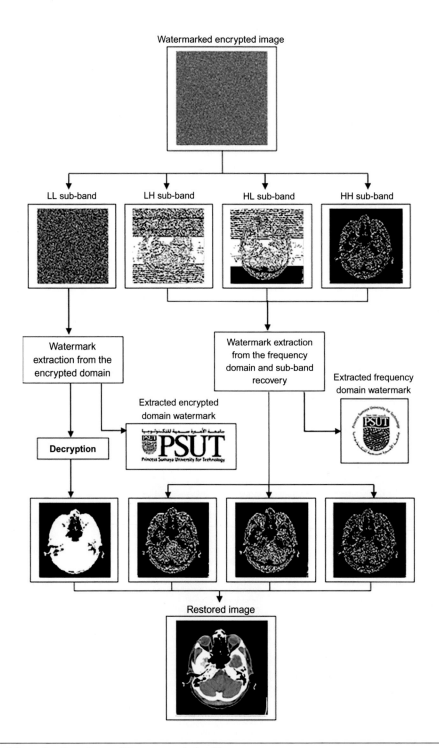

FIG. 9

Example of the extraction phase of the proposed algorithm.

Input: Watermarked encrypted image I''.
Outputs: Cover image I, encrypted domain watermark W_e, frequency domain watermark W_f.
Step 1: Apply IWT2 to the watermarked encrypted image to get the four sub-bands.
Step 2: Extract the frequency domain watermark from the middle and higher sub-bands CH, CV, and CD.
Step 3: Decode the compressed extracted bitplane and place it in its original location.
Step 4: Extract the encrypted domain watermark from the CA sub-band using HS.
Step 5: Apply the inverse IWT2 on the decrypted CA sub-band.
Step 6: Restore the changes that have been done to the image pixels at the beginning of the data embedding phase to prevent any possible overflow or underflow. A new mapping is done according to the side_info1 extracted from the frequency domain payload and the shifted pixels are returned to their positions, i.e., widening the modified histogram.

5 Performance evaluation

This section presents the performance evaluation results obtained for frequency domain watermarking, encrypted domain watermarking, and for the two domains together—the combined domain. First, the test images and the list of metrics used to evaluate the effectiveness of the algorithm are described. Second, the performance results for each domain are presented. Finally, the results of the available pure embedding capacity, the encrypted image entropy value, and the image quality measured with respect to the capacity are included.

5.1 Test images

The performance of the proposed algorithm has been evaluated using two sets of test images. The set is a collection of 8-bit grayscale medical images of different modalities, including computed tomography (CT), magnetic resonance imaging (MRI), ultrasound, and X-ray images. These images have a resolution of 2048×2048, and they are shown in Fig. 10. The second set of images consists of four CT images with sizes 256×256, 512×512, 1024×1024, and 2048×2048, as shown in Fig. 11. The CT images are used to evaluate the performance of the algorithm for images having the same modality. The 512×512 CT image, shown in Fig. 12A, has been taken as an example to demonstrate the performance of the proposed algorithm and to visualize the simulation results. Fig. 12B shows the corresponding encrypted watermarked image. The frequency domain watermark with size 275×268 is shown in Fig. 13A, while the encrypted domain watermark with size 305×98 is shown in Fig. 13B.

5.2 Performance evaluation metrics

The performance of the proposed algorithm has been evaluated with respect to the following three metrics: embedding capacity, visual quality, and entropy. A brief description of each metric is given hereafter.

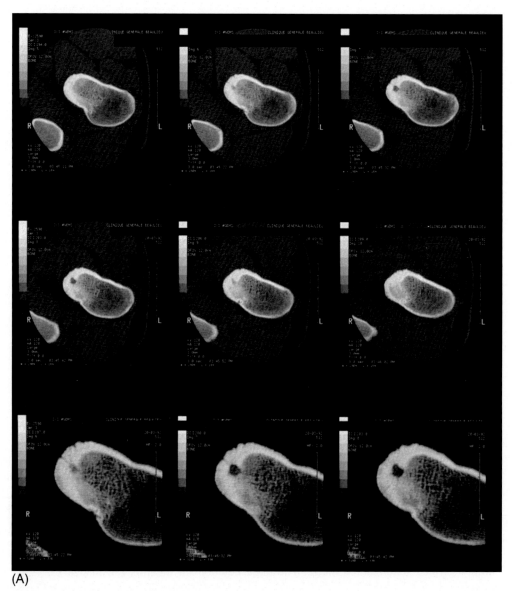

(A)

FIG. 10

General medical images. (A) Computed tomography image.

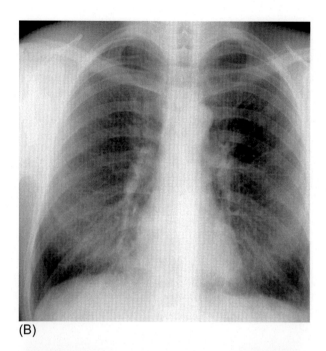

(B)

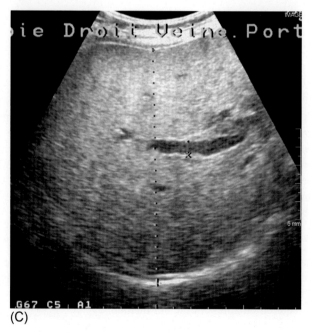

(C)

FIG. 10, CONT'D

(B) X-ray image. (C) Ultrasound image.

(Continued)

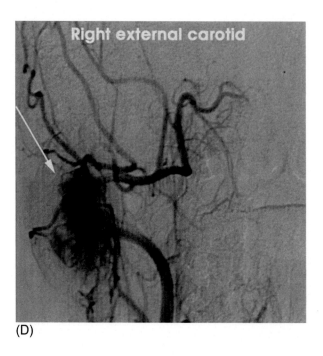

(D)

FIG.1O, CONT'D

(D) Magnetic resonance imaging image.

5.3 Embedding capacity

When computing the total embedding capacity of RDH schemes the side information must be taken into consideration. Two sets of side information are required: the first set of side information is essential to extract the embedded watermark, and the second set of side information is used to allow for exact image recovery at the receiver's side. Such information includes the original LSBs that were evacuated to embed the first type of side information.

The maximum number of pure embeddable pixels after excluding the bits that are used to embed the side information can be calculated as follows:

$$Maximum\ number\ of\ embeddable\ pixels = number\ of\ pixels\ of\ the\ peak\ value - |sideinfo| \tag{2}$$

where the side information represents the bit length of the original LSB that is concatenated with the embedded payload and represents the watermark width, the watermark length, the peak point, and the zero point. Although this method decreases the embedding capacity, calculated using Eq. (3), it nevertheless provides the required blindness of the HS method:

$$Maximum\ Embedding\ Capacity\ (bpp) = \frac{\#\ of\ pixels\ with\ peak\ point}{image\ length\ \times\ image\ width} \tag{3}$$

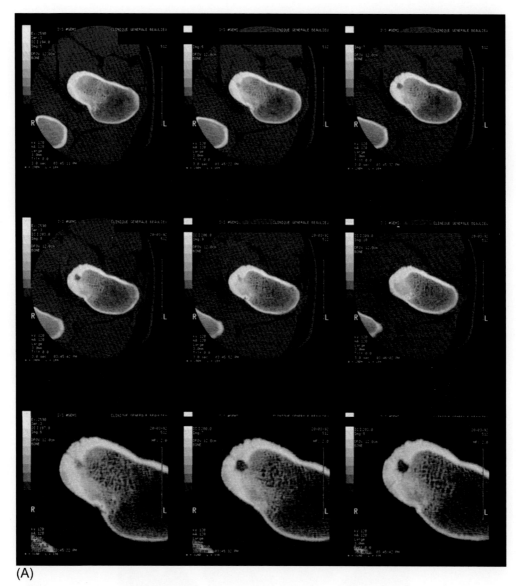

(A)

FIG. 11

Computed tomography medical images with different sizes. (A) 2048 × 2048.

(Continued)

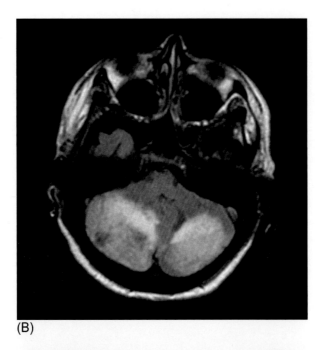

(B)

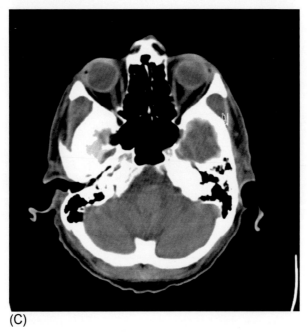

(C)

FIG.11, CONT'D

(B) 1024 × 1024. (C) 512 × 512.

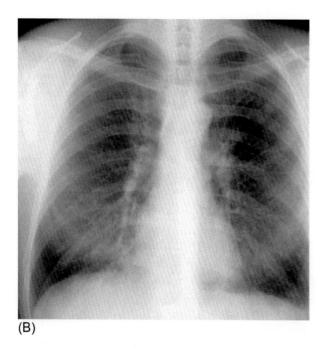

(B)

FIG.11, CONT'D

(D) 256 × 256.

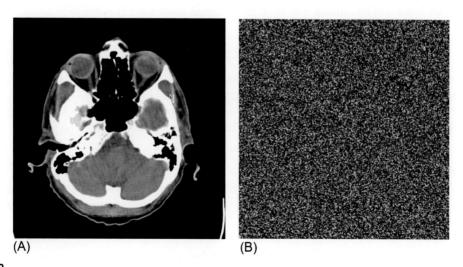

(A)   (B)

FIG. 12

(A) Computed tomography (CT) medical image. (B) Encrypted watermarked CT image.

(A)   (B)

FIG. 13

The dual embedded watermarks. (A) Frequency domain watermark. (B) Encrypted domain watermark.

5.4 Image visual quality

The PSNR is used to measure the fidelity or the quality degradation between the original cover image and the corresponding watermarked image, and the degree of distortion the proposed algorithm applies on the image. The PSNR is calculated in dB as:

$$PSNR\,(dB) = 10\log_{10}\frac{(255)^2}{MSE} \tag{4}$$

where the mean square error (MSE) value represents the cumulative squared error between the original and the restored images. In case of full reversibility, MSE will be zero and its corresponding restored image PSNR value will be infinite. The MSE is calculated using Eq. (5) as follows:

$$MSE = \frac{\sum_{m=1}^{M}\sum_{n=1}^{N}[I(m,n)-I'(m,n)]^2}{M\times N} \tag{5}$$

The PSNR will be calculated in each domain. In the frequency domain the PSNR will be calculated between the frequency domain sub-bands of the image and the corresponding watermarked sub-bands, whereas in the encrypted domain the PSNR will be calculated between the encrypted domain sub-band of the image and the corresponding watermarked encrypted sub-band after encryption.

5.4.1 Entropy

This metric indicates the level of randomness, and thus security, of the encrypted image. More randomness in an encrypted image means a higher entropy value and therefore a more secure scheme. The entropy is calculated using Eq. (6):

$$entropy = -\sum_{k=0}^{M-1}P_k\log_2 p_k \tag{6}$$

where M represents the number of gray levels and is equal to 8 in the used test images, and p_k is the probability associated with gray level K.

5.5 **Performance of the proposed algorithm in the frequency domain**

The effectiveness of the proposed joint algorithm in the frequency domain is measured with respect to two items: the maximum available embedding capacity each sub-band can offer and the amount of distortion introduced to each sub-band measured by the PSNR. The results obtained using the first set of test images are illustrated in Fig. 14 where the maximum embedding capacities for different modalities are compared.

The embedding capacities listed in Table 1 correspond to the number of embeddable bits after removing the bits used for embedding the compressed bitplane. In addition, a PSNR value of INF indicates that the corresponding sub-band is not used for data embedding because the embedding capacity provided by the previous sub-band is sufficient to embed the required data. In general, the high-frequency sub-band is compressed losslessly with a better compression rate than the compressed

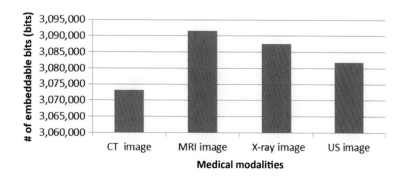

FIG. 14

Total embedding capacity for different medical modalities in the frequency domain.

Table 1　Capacity and PSNR results in the frequency domain, using a watermark of 300 × 300.				
	CT image	**MRI image**	**X-ray image**	**US image**
Original LH, HL, HH sub-bands size (bits)	1,048,576	1,048,576	1,048,576	1,048,576
Compressed LH sub-band size (bits)	24,495	20,274	21,149	20,479
LH sub-band PSNR (dB)	40.8868	41.7378	41.5285	41.1890
Embedding capacity of LH sub-band (bits)	1,024,081	1,028,302	1,027,427	1,028,097
Compressed HL sub-band size (bits)	31,223	17,050	20,142	26,357
HL sub-band PSNR (dB)	INF	INF	INF	INF
Embedding capacity of HL sub-band (bits)	1,017,353	1,031,526	1,028,434	1,022,219
Compressed HH sub-band size (bits)	16,921	16,921	16,921	17,070
HH sub-band PSNR (dB)	INF	INF	INF	INF
Embedding capacity of HH sub-band (bits)	1,031,655	1,031,655	1,031,655	1,031,506
Total capacity (bits)	3,073,089	3,091,483	3,087,561	3,081,822
CT, *computed tomography;* MRI, *magnetic resonance imaging;* PSNR, *peak signal-to-noise ratio;* US, *ultrasound.*				

middle-frequency sub-bands can achieve. The MRI modality has the best results in terms of high compression rate compared with the other modalities. Consequently, it offers the highest embedding capacity in the frequency domain. Generally speaking, the four modalities achieved almost close embedding capacities, represented by the number of available embeddable bits after excluding the bits that are used to store the compressed bitplanes.

In addition, the four modalities introduced an almost equal amount of visual quality degradation when the same watermark is embedded in each of them. This can be seen clearly by the close PSNR values of the middle frequency sub-band, as shown in Fig. 15.

The results of the experiments using the second set of CT images with varying sizes are listed in Table 2 and illustrated in Fig. 16. As seen in Table 2, the worst results in terms of the different sub-band bitplane compression rate belong to the CT 256 image and thus the achieved embedding capacity that is needed to embed the payload and the other side information is small compared with the images with

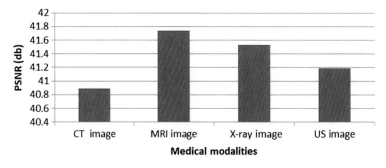

FIG. 15

Peak signal-to-noise ratio values for different medical modalities for the LH sub-band.

Table 2 Results of different medical image sizes in the frequency domain with a watermark size of 300 × 300.

	CT 256	CT 512	CT 1024	CT 2048
Original LH, HL, HH sub-band size (bits)	16,384	65,536	262,144	1,048,576
Compressed LH sub-band size (bits)	9350	8950	4326	24,495
LH sub-band PSNR (dB)	33.3118	31.8428	35.8441	40.8868
Embedding capacity of LH sub-band (bits)	7034	56,586	257,818	1,024,081
Compressed HL sub-band size (bits)	9095	9905	4360	31,223
HL sub-band PSNR (dB)	33.3587	32.63109	INF	INF
Embedding capacity of HL sub-band (bits)	7289	55,631	257,784	1,017,353
Compressed HH sub-band size (bits)	10,627	6262	4237	16,921
HH sub-band PSNR (dB)	32.1506	INF	INF	INF
Embedding capacity of HH sub-band (bits)	5757	59,274	257,907	1,031,655
Total capacity (bits)	20,080	171,491	773,509	3,073,089

CT, *computed tomography*; PSNR, *peak signal-to-noise ratio*.

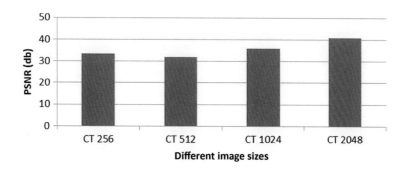

FIG. 16

Peak signal-to-noise ratio values obtained for different computed tomography image sizes for the LH sub-band.

Table 3 Performance results of different medical modalities in the encrypted domain.				
	CT image	**MRI image**	**X-ray image**	**US image**
PSNR (dB)	56.8534	63.9370	66.2340	54.9120
Total embedded bits	305 × 98 (29,890)	305 × 98 (29,890)	305 × 98 (29,890)	305 × 98 (29,890)
Max bpp	0.4646	0.0670	0.0327	0.1756
Entropy	4.5069	6.4861	7.0929	6.6179
Bpp, *bits per pixel;* CT, *computed tomography;* MRI, *magnetic resonance imaging;* PSNR, *peak signal-to-noise ratio;* US, *ultrasound.*				

other sizes within the same modality, as can be seen by using all three sub-bands to embed a small watermark. On the other hand, the best compression rate is achieved by the CT 1024 image and the best PSNR value is achieved for the CT 2048 image.

5.6 Performance of the proposed algorithm in the encrypted domain

The effectiveness of the proposed algorithm in the encrypted domain is measured by the maximum available embedding capacity the encrypted sub-band can offer, and the degree of degradation of the watermarked encrypted sub-band with respect to the encrypted sub-band. In addition, the entropy value of the encrypted sub-band is investigated. The results are summarized in Table 3 and illustrated in Figs. 17–19.

The X-ray images achieved the best results is terms of the visual quality (imperceptibility) between the encrypted and watermarked encrypted sub-band. In terms of the embedding capacity, the CT image achieved the highest capacity followed by the ultrasound image. As for entropy, the X-ray image exhibited the best entropy but the least embedding capacity, while the CT image exhibited the worst entropy value of the encrypted sub-band.

The results of the second set of test images are listed in Table 4 and illustrated in Figs. 20–22. In general, the CT images have poor encrypted sub-band entropy values, as can be seen in Table 4. The worst embedding capacity was achieved by the CT 256 image, while the best capacity was achieved by the CT 512 image.

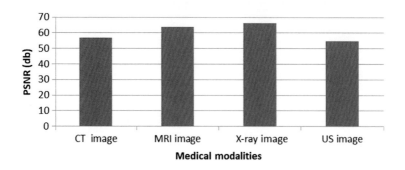

FIG. 17

Peak signal-to-noise ratio values for different modalities for the encrypted LL sub-band.

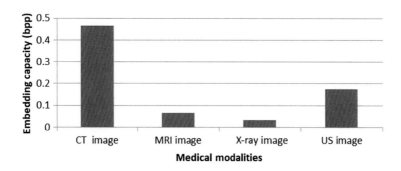

FIG. 18

Embedding capacity for different modalities in the encrypted LL sub-band.

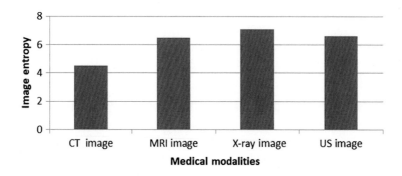

FIG. 19

Entropy of the encrypted LL sub-band for different medical modalities.

Table 4 Performance results of different image sizes in the encrypted domain.				
	CT 256	**CT 512**	**CT 1024**	**CT 2048**
PSNR (dB)	64.4515	55.38174	56.8683	56.8534
Total embedded bits	45 × 13 (598)	305 × 98 (29,890)	(305 × 98) 29,890	305 × 98 (29,890)
Max bpp	0.0076	0.5776	0.3915	0.4747
Entropy value	6.8698	4.2400	5.2043	4.5069
Bpp, *bits per pixel;* CT, *computed tomography;* PSNR, *peak signal-to-noise ratio.*				

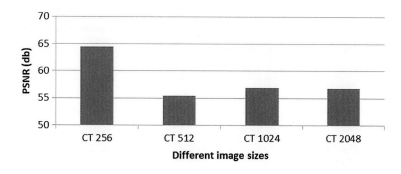

FIG. 20

Peak signal-to-noise ratio values for different computed tomography image sizes for the encrypted LL sub-band.

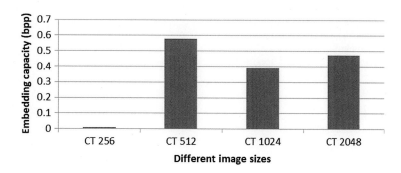

FIG. 21

Embedding capacity for different computed tomography image sizes for the encrypted LL sub-band.

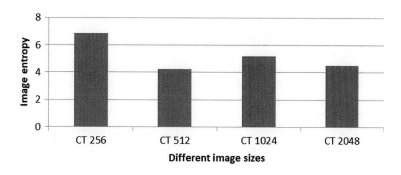

FIG. 22

Entropy for different computed tomography image sizes for the encrypted LL sub-band.

5.7 Combined performance of the frequency and encrypted domains

The performance results of the proposed algorithm in the frequency and encrypted domains are presented in this section. A summary of the results is given in Tables 5 and 6, followed by detailed analysis of the pure embedding capacity, encrypted image entropy, and visual quality.

Table 5 Performance results of the combined image for different medical modalities.

	CT image	MRI image	X-ray image	US image
Total embedded (bits)	3,073,089+497,825 (3,570,914)	3,091,483+70,220 (3,161,703)	3,087,561+34,296 (3,121,857)	3,081,822+184,098 (3,265,920)
Max bpp	0.8514	0.7538	0.7443	0.7786
Entropy value	6.0954	6.6186	7.2652	7.1594

Bpp, *bits per pixel;* CT, *computed tomography;* MRI, *magnetic resonance imaging;* US, *ultrasound.*

Table 6 Performance results of the combined image for different CT image sizes.

	CT 256	CT 512	CT 1024	CT 2048
Total embedded (bits)	20,080+1240 (21,320)	171,491+37,854 (209,345)	773,509+102,640 (876,149)	3,073,089+497,825 (3,570,914)
Max bpp	0.3253	0.7986	0.8355	0.8514
Entropy value	7.3710	7.1689	6.4374	6.0954

Bpp, *bits per pixel;* CT, *computed tomography.*

5.7.1 Pure embedding capacity

The total pure embedding capacity is the sum of the pure capacity each operating domain can offer. The proposed algorithm uses the integer transform-based method to embed data in the frequency domain, and the HS method to embed data in the encrypted domain. A single pair of peak and zero points is used when taking the measurements in the simulation, thus the embedding capacity can be increased rapidly if two or more pairs are used to embed the data.

Fig. 23 shows that the proposed algorithm achieved good results for all types of tested medical modalities. This is because the algorithm operates in the frequency domain. Note that only the fourth bit-plane of the middle- and higher-frequency sub-bands is used for measuring the embedding capacity. Fig. 24 investigates the effectiveness of the proposed algorithm in terms of the maximum available pure embedding capacity of the same modality. The CT 256 image has the poorest performance compared with the other images due to its small size, while the best performance was achieved by the CT 512 image.

Encrypted image entropy: Image entropy is used to measure the randomness of the encrypted image and also as an indicator of the degree of security of the encryption algorithm; the higher the entropy value of the encryption algorithm, the more robust the algorithm against the cryptanalysis attacks. On the other hand, a higher entropy value indicates that the randomness of the image is maximum and thus the data redundancy is small and fewer data can be embedded reversibly in the image. The medical modality that achieved the best entropy value is the X-ray images, as can be seen in Fig. 25, while the CT images achieved the worst results. This result validates the tradeoff relationship between the modality's available embedding capacity and its encrypted image's entropy values. This is

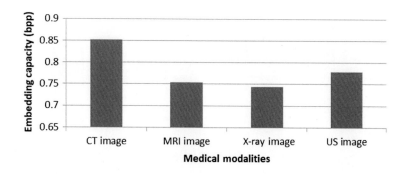

FIG. 23

Combined embedding capacity for different medical modalities.

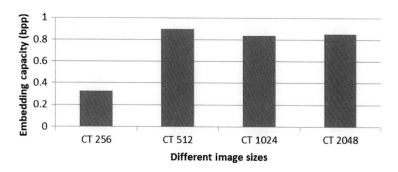

FIG. 24

Combined embedding capacity for different computed tomography image sizes.

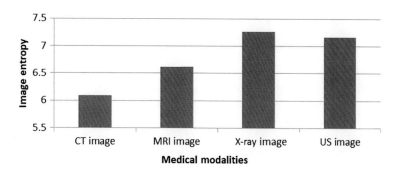

FIG. 25

Combined image entropy values for different medical modalities.

obvious for the CT images, which achieved the best pure embedding capacity, yet were the worst in terms of entropy.

Fig. 26 compares the overall combined image entropy for CT images of different size images. As can be noticed from the figure, the achieved entropy values are small. This is because the CT modality has the lowest entropy value among the other medical modalities. It can be seen that the entropy value

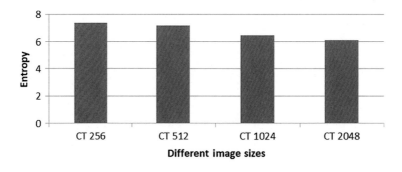

FIG. 26

Combined image entropy values for different computed tomography image sizes.

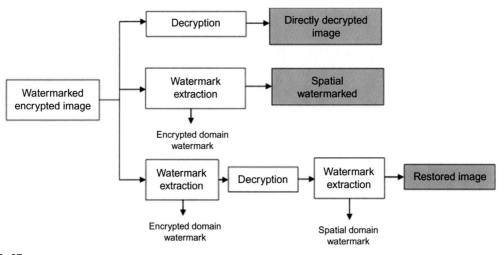

FIG. 27

The three stages at which the peak signal-to-noise ratio values are calculated.

decreases as the image size increases. These results of entropy values within the same modalities provide extra evidence of the existing tradeoff between the offered embeddable capacity and the entropy value of the overall encrypted image.

Image quality versus embedding capacity: There are three types of images the user can produce at the receiving end: a directly decrypted image without any watermark extraction, a decrypted image after the extraction of the encrypted domain watermark, and a perfectly recovered image. The PSNR is used to measure the fidelity or the quality degradation between the original cover image and the corresponding watermarked image, and the degree of distortion proposed.

Multiple PSNR values are used for performance measurements in the conducted experiments; these values are shown in Fig. 27 and described hereafter.

- PSNR between the overall combined image after applying a direct decryption without any watermark extraction in any domain and between the original image.
- PSNR between the decrypted overall combined image, after extracting the encrypted domain watermark and without frequency domain watermark extraction, and between the original image.
- PSNR between the recovered combined image, after extracting the two domain watermarks and applying a decryption, and between the original image.

The PSNR results at different extraction stages, as previously described, are given in Tables 7 and 8 for the two sets of test images. As should be expected, the PSNR values of the directly decrypted images are lower than the PSNR values of the partially decrypted watermarked images for which the encrypted domain watermark is extracted. An infinite PSNR value obtained for the restored image is proof that the image has been completely and exactly restored. In addition to the PSNR values, the two tables show the bits per pixel (bpp) values that represent the actual embedded payload size in each domain.

Table 7 PSNR values at different stages for different medical modalities.

	Directly decrypted watermarked image			Decrypted image with partial watermark		Restored image
	PSNR (dB)	Spatial embedded bpp	Encrypted embedded bpp	PSNR (dB)	Spatial embedded bpp	PSNR (dB)
CT	47.1195	0.0215	0.0071	51.3986	0.0215	∞
MRI	49.4067	0.0215	0.0071	51.1361	0.0215	∞
US	46.9383	0.0215	0.0071	52.2033	0.0215	∞
X-ray	49.3521	0.0215	0.0071	50.7283	0.0215	∞

Bpp, *bits per pixel;* CT, *computed tomography;* MRI, *magnetic resonance imaging;* PSNR, *peak signal-to-noise ratio;* US, *ultrasound.*

Table 8 PSNR values at different stages for different CT image sizes.

	Directly decrypted watermarked image			Decrypted image with partial watermark		Restored image
	PSNR (dB)	Spatial embedded bpp	Encrypted embedded bpp	PSNR (dB)	Spatial embedded bpp	PSNR (dB)
CT 256	38.5727	0.2779	0.0091	39.2130	0.2779	∞
CT 512	37.9943	0.3430	0.1140	41.4422	0.3430	∞
CT 1024	43.1126	0.0858	0.0285	47.6637	0.0858	∞
CT 2048	47.1195	0.0215	0.0071	51.3969	0.0215	∞

Bpp, *bits per pixel;* CT, *computed tomography;* PSNR, *peak signal-to-noise ratio.*

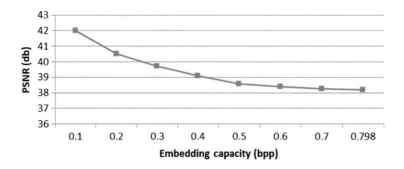

FIG. 28

Peak signal-to-noise ratio versus capacity of the combined CT 512 image.

Fig. 28 shows the PSNR value of the directly decrypted image without any watermark extraction versus varying values of the pure embedding capacity in the combined image. The recorded PSNR values are in the range of 36–40 dB. These values are not sufficiently high for a number of reasons. One reason is that all the frequency sub-bands have been used in the embedding process. Another reason is the preprocessing that was done to prevent the possible overflow and underflow by the histogram narrowing method. One last reason is that the measured PSNR here is for the directly decrypted image without any watermark extraction, which means that its histogram was not yet brought back to its original shape.

5.8 Comparison of the proposed algorithms against state-of-the-art studies

To measure the effectiveness of the proposed algorithm, its performance must be compared with the performance of other recent studies in this field. The comparison will be made despite the fact that the compared algorithms used the standard natural grayscale test images and not medical images.

Separability and image recovery error: To start with, the proposed algorithm is compared with the recent joint encryption watermarking algorithms [3–6,8–15] in terms of both separability and errors generated in the data extraction and image recovery phase. The results are shown in Table 9.

Pure embedding capacity: The choice of the position and the number of bitplanes that will be used to hold the embedded data in the proposed algorithm result in a different available maximum embedding capacity. The higher the position of the bitplane, the higher the offered pure capacity by this bitplane. The reason behind this is that the bias between the 0s and 1s in the eighth bitplane, for example, will be maximal and consequently will result in a high compression rate of the bitplane and thus will lower the size of the side information. However, this comes at the cost of the distortion introduced into the directly decrypted image. Increasing the number of used bitplanes will help increase the embedding capacity as well, for example, using two bitplanes to embed the data in the fourth bitplane will offer almost double pure embedding capacity. Therefore the results of using both choices, the eighth bitplane and the fourth and fifth bitplanes together in the proposed algorithm, is done when comparing with other studies. The comparison is done on the standard test images: Lena, Baboon, Airplane, Barbara, Peppers, and Boat. It can be seen from the results in Table 10 that the proposed joint algorithm obtains higher embedding capacity in general.

Table 9 Comparison in terms of separability and errors of image recovery.

	[3]	[4]	[5]	[6]	[8]	[9]	[10]	[11]	[12]	[13]	[14]	[15]	Proposed algorithm
Separable	Yes	No	No	Yes	Yes	Yes	Yes	Yes	Yes	No	Yes	Yes	Yes
Error in image recovery	No	yes	Yes	Yes	No	No	No	No	No	No	No	No	No

Table 10 Comparison between the proposed algorithm with related works in terms of pure embedding capacity.

Reference	Lena	Baboon	Airplane	Barbara	Peppers	Boat
[4]	0.0039	0.0010	0.0026	0.0009	0.0049	0.0030
[5]	0.0069	0.0013	0.0100	0.0009	0.0067	0.0050
[6]	0.0329	0.0057	0.0200	0.0124	0.0074	0.0124
[8]	0.0400	0.0130	0.0670	0.0360	N/A	N/A
[9]	0.1208	0.0293	0.1697	0.0924	0.0923	0.0717
[10]	0.0109	0.0106	0.0317	0.0091	0.0113	0.0145
[3]	0.0110	0.0105	0.0317	0.0091	0.0113	0.0143
[11]	0.0217	0.0210	0.0612	0.0180	0.0225	0.0286
[12]	0.5000	0.4000	0.5000	0.5000	0.4000	0.5000
[13]	0.7390	0.6406	0.7317	0.6886	0.7365	0.7365
[14]	0.0400	0.0400	0.0400	0.0400	0.0400	0.0400
[15]	0.8101	0.8285	0.7643	0.7363	0.6811	0.7738
Proposed algorithm (eighth bitplane)	0.7406	0.7430	0.7454	0.7518	0.7428	0.7418
Proposed algorithm (fourth and fifth bitplanes)	1.3847	0.7042	1.3465	1.1555	1.3297	1.2181

PSNR versus pure embedding rate. A further validation of the effectiveness of the proposed algorithm is to compare the PSNR versus pure embedding rate behavior of the proposed algorithm with the same behavior of a recently published algorithm [13]. This algorithm has been particularly chosen for comparison because it operates in the frequency domain and thus has similar features to the proposed algorithm. Comparison is done using the Lena and Baboon test images because these two images exhibit different characteristics and structural complexities. The results are shown for the Lena and Baboon images in Figs. 29 and 30, respectively.

As can be seen in Fig. 30, the algorithm in [13] starts with a high PSNR value for small embedding capacities but this value degrades rapidly until it reaches 24 dB when the embedded payload reaches 0.6405 bpp for the Lena image. On the other hand, the PSNR of the proposed algorithm drops at a slower rate until it reaches 35 dB when the embedding capacity was approximately 1.3 bpp. Therefore the proposed algorithm achieves a higher PSNR value than [13] for embedding capacities of 0.55 bpp

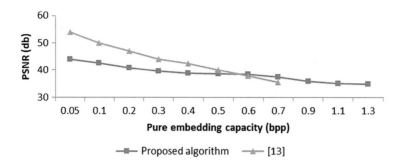

FIG. 29

Peak signal-to-noise ratio versus pure embedding rate of "Lena" of the proposed algorithm with two bitplanes and [13].

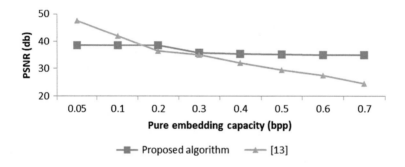

FIG. 30

Peak signal-to-noise ratio versus pure embedding rate of "Baboon" of the proposed algorithm with two bitplanes and [13].

and higher. As a conclusion, the proposed algorithm outperforms [13] in the maximum achievable embedding capacity, while [13] gives better quality of the directly decrypted image given low embedding rates.

Regarding the Baboon curve in Fig. 30, the two algorithms achieved lower PSNR values than those of the Lena image due to the nature of the Baboon image, which contains more texture contents. It can be noticed that the PSNR values of [13] decrease rapidly when the embedding capacity increases, while the PSNR values of the proposed algorithm drop at a slower rate and then remain roughly constant. When the embedding capacity is below 0.1 bpp, [13] gives a higher PSNR value than the proposed algorithm. However, after that the payload of the proposed algorithm outperforms [13] in terms of the PSNR values. That is, the proposed algorithm gives a PSNR value of 35 dB when the payload is approximately 0.6 bpp, while [13] gives a PSNR value of 24 dB for the same embedding capacity. Therefore for the Baboon image, the two algorithms exhibit similar behavior regarding the available embedding capacity, while the proposed algorithm provides a less distorted directly decrypted image at high embedding capacity rates than the algorithm [13].

6 Conclusions and future work

An efficient and separable joint RDH in an encrypted image algorithm was presented in this chapter. The algorithm maintains a tradeoff between the available pure embedding capacity, encrypted image entropy, and the quality of the decrypted watermarked image. The proposed algorithm offers two important advantages. The first is complete blind original image recovery without any errors, and the second is the variety of access control privileges the algorithm offers to legitimate receivers of the watermarked image. These access control privileges are offered in the form of encryption keys and data hiding keys. Therefore the proposed algorithm guarantees the authenticity and integrity of the transmitted medical images in the frequency and encrypted domains. A potential future work can be carried out in a number of directions. One direction is to enhance and improve the proposed algorithm to obtain better results with respect to embedding capacity and visual image quality. Another direction is to increase the embedding capacity by adopting further pairs of peak and zero points to embed the data using HS. One last direction is to replace the HS method with other RDH methods to reach optimal performance results.

References

[1] G. Coatrieux, H. Maitre, B. Sankur, Strict integrity control of biomedical images, in: Security and Watermarking of Multimedia Contents III, August, Vol. 4314, International Society for Optics and Photonics, 2001, pp. 229–240.
[2] L.O.M. Kobayashi, S.S. Furuie, P.S.L.M. Barreto, Providing integrity and authenticity in DICOM images: a novel approach, IEEE Trans. Inf. Technol. Biomed. 13 (4) (2009) 582–589.
[3] H. Abdel-Nabi, A. Al-Haj, Efficient joint encryption and data hiding algorithm for medical images security, in: 2017 8th International Conference on Information and Communication Systems (ICICS), April, IEEE, 2017, pp. 147–152.
[4] X. Zhang, Reversible data hiding in encrypted image, IEEE Signal Process. Lett. 18 (4) (2011) 255–258.
[5] W. Hong, T.S. Chen, H.Y. Wu, An improved reversible data hiding in encrypted images using side match, IEEE Signal Process. Lett. 19 (4) (2012) 199–202.
[6] X. Zhang, Separable reversible data hiding in encrypted image, IEEE Trans. Inf. Forensic Secur. 7 (2) (2011) 826–832.
[7] K. Ma, W. Zhang, X. Zhao, N. Yu, F. Li, Reversible data hiding in encrypted images by reserving room before encryption, IEEE Trans. Inf. Forensic Secur. 8 (3) (2013) 553–562.
[8] W. Zhang, K. Ma, N. Yu, Reversibility improved data hiding in encrypted images, Signal Process. 94 (2014) 118–127.
[9] F. Huang, J. Huang, Y.Q. Shi, New framework for reversible data hiding in encrypted domain, IEEE Trans. Inf. Forensic Secur. 11 (12) (2016) 2777–2789.
[10] H. Abdel-Nabi, A. Al-Haj, Medical imaging security using partial encryption and histogram shifting watermarking, in: 2017 8th International Conference on Information Technology (ICIT), May, IEEE, 2017, pp. 802–807.
[11] A. Al-Haj, H. Abdel-Nabi, Digital image security based on data hiding and cryptography, in: 2017 3rd International Conference on Information Management (ICIM), April, IEEE, 2017, pp. 437–440.
[12] S. Yi, Y. Zhou, Z. Hua, Reversible data hiding in encrypted images using adaptive block-level prediction-error expansion, Signal Process. Image Commun. 64 (2018) 78–88.

[13] S. Zhang, T. Gao, G. Sheng, A joint encryption and reversible data hiding scheme based on integer-DWT and Arnold map permutation, J. Appl. Math. (2014) 2014.

[14] L. Xiong, Z. Xu, Y.Q. Shi, An integer wavelet transform based scheme for reversible data hiding in encrypted images, Multidim. Syst. Sign. Process. 29 (3) (2018) 1191–1202.

[15] G. Ma, J. Wang, Efficient reversible data hiding in encrypted images based on multi-stage integer wavelet transform, Signal Process. Image Commun. 75 (2019) 55–63.

[16] Z. Ni, Y.Q. Shi, N. Ansari, W. Su, Reversible data hiding, in: Proceedings of the 2003 International Symposium on Circuits and Systems, 2003. ISCAS'03, May, Vol. 2, IEEE, 2003, p. II.

[17] G. Xuan, J. Zhu, J. Chen, Y.Q. Shi, Z. Ni, W. Su, Distortionless data hiding based on integer wavelet transform, Electron. Lett. 38 (25) (2002) 1646–1648.

[18] A.R. Calderbank, I. Daubechies, W. Sweldens, B.L. Yeo, Wavelet transforms that map integers to integers, Appl. Comput. Harmon. Anal. 5 (3) (1998) 332–369.

[19] W. Sweldens, The lifting scheme: a construction of second generation wavelets, SIAM J. Math. Anal. 29 (2) (1998) 511–546.

An OpenSim guided tour in machine learning for e-health applications

Mukul Verma[a], Muskan Dawar[a], Prashant Singh Rana[a], Neeru Jindal[b], and Harpreet Singh[a]

Computer Science and Engineering Department, Thapar Institute of Engineering & Technology, Patiala, Punjab, India[a]
Electronics and Communication Engineering Department, Thapar Institute of Engineering & Technology, Patiala, Punjab, India[b]

1 Introduction

Advances in health management research are going in various directions for the treatment of diseases. Predicting how the human control system can benefit from these new advances is a tremendous challenge in biomechanics. So, to bridge the gaps between health management and bioprocedure analysis and simulation, OpenSim was established. OpenSim is freely available software for simulation and modeling. Basically, it came into existence as an expansion of a musculoskeletal package [1–4] and was used to model human muscle movements such as walking [5] and running [6], and predicting surgical outcomes [7]. It provides users with a "virtual world," with powerful kinematical analytical tools to analyze the working of bones, muscles, tendons, and ligaments of the body, etc. OpenSim helps to analyze the capabilities of individuals and can help them handle various issues from completely different perspectives [1]. Since it was presented to the world, people from across the globe have used it for a broad range of applications, such as biomechanics analysis, medical device sketching, medical science, rehabilitation science, neurobiology analysis, engineering science analysis and design, sports science, computer animation, artificial intelligence analysis, biology, and education [1,2]. Fig. 1 shows the graphical user interface (GUI) of OpenSim.

2 State of the art

An OpenSim-based platform allows anyone to simply develop the model and take a look at new machine learning management methods with physiologically musculoskeletal models [2]. OpenSim can be used for any purpose inclusive of nonprofit business applications with Apache License 2.0. Simulations built by the biomechanics community can be analyzed, changed, enhanced, and tested through multiinstitutional collaboration on the base provided by OpenSim. The OpenSim GUI is coded in Java and the core is coded in C++. OpenSim makes it possible to create contact models, muscle models, and many more exciting models.

Models can use these codes by installing the plugins (which are shared by users), and there is no necessity to change or recompile these codes. Users can create their own models and simulations from

Intelligent Data Security Solutions for e-Health Applications. https://doi.org/10.1016/B978-0-12-819511-6.00003-0

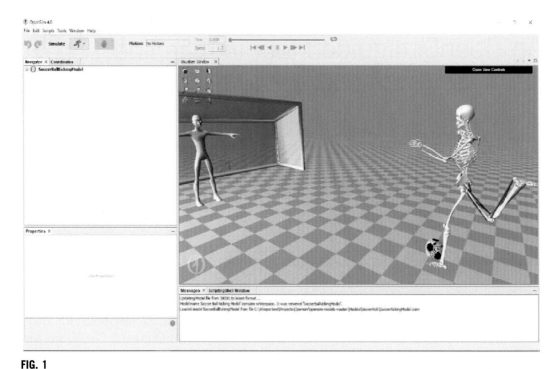

FIG. 1

OpenSim GUI.

the GUI and can also analyze and reference the existing models and simulations. The programs are also freely and anonymously accessible on GitHub, and contributions are readily accepted.

Nowadays, machine learning models use training and testing recommendations to modernize biomechanical data analysis. The potential of several other approaches like deep learning is also used to produce knowledge of human movements. To increase the effectiveness of research in biomechanics, the sharing of data and cross-training are essential. Traditional approaches like inferential statistics are overcome using modern machine learning methods, data mining, and predictive modeling. These approaches provide different advanced solutions compared to traditional ones. Machine learning approaches are trained and interpreted based on well-known reporting standards in comparison with traditional statistical tools. Predictive modeling is used for futuristic accurate predictions by providing an outcome with respect to its output response data with the help of functions. For example, the status of a disease is input and kinematic waveforms are output. In the biomechanics movement field, the use of machine learning techniques is expanding, but evaluation of these studies remains difficult. The use of machine learning approaches is continuously increasing due to large data availability to ensure that valid, as well as reproducible, conclusions are provided. So, good practices in reporting and conducting research that connects biomechanics and machine learning are still needed. Moreover, machine learning methods increase quality and propose further visible standards for future research in this area. The biomechanics and computer science communities have started to work together to model the neural control of movements using reinforcement learning. These joint efforts and advancements will act as a bridge to prepare physiologically accurate biomechanical models [2]. Mostly, reinforcement learning in machine learning is used where environmental actions train the agent and the agent learns to implement a task to increase its output. For example, in OpenSim, an agent of a musculoskeletal model learns to walk by selecting actions of muscle excitations [8]. This method is also used to play the game "Go Well" by training a program; as a result, the program can outperform other humans in gameplay without any input [9]. Future research in this field will enhance the understanding of human neural movements. Hence, it will eventually improve human-machine interfaces. It was discovered that deep reinforcement learning techniques, even with their high processing price, could be strongly utilized as an escalation technique for synthesizing physiological motion in high-dimensional biomechanical systems [10]. Reinforcement learning is a part of machine learning, where an operator learns the optimal policy for performing sequential decision making without complete knowledge of the environment [11,12]. The operator explores the atmosphere by taking action and edit the policy to maximize the reward in RL techniques. General controllers for movement use the latest reinforcement learning techniques. These techniques significantly reduce the need for a user to manually tune the controllers as compared to the formerly discovered gait controllers. As an example, controllers for the locomotion of difficult humanoid models can be trained by reinforcement learning [13,14]. Though these strategies have found solutions that did not have domain-specific data, the ensuing motions were not realistic. One of the key reasons for not using these models is that biologically correct actuators were not used by these models. Its main objectives were [3] to:

- Use reinforcement learning to resolve issues in medical management and to promote the free use of tools in reinforcement learning analysis (the physics simulator, the reinforcement learning environment, and the competition platform that the user can utilize to run the challenges).
- Encourage reinforcement learning analysis in computationally complicated environments, with noisy and highly dimensional action areas, relevant to real-life applications.
- Bridge biomechanics, neurobiology, and computer science communities.

However, the next section discusses the basic musculoskeletal elements and OpenSim capabilities.

2.1 Basic musculoskeletal elements and capabilities of OpenSim

Fig. 2 shows the fundamental components of musculoskeletal simulation in OpenSim. A musculotendon actuator is a significant component of any human musculoskeletal system. These actuators are supposed to be frictionless, massless, extensible strings that attach to and wrap around other structures [15]. Musculotendon models are necessary components of muscle-driven simulations; however, the calculation speed and biological correctness of these models have not been effectively evaluated yet. Muscle-driven simulations depend on computational models of musculotendon dynamics. Generally, parameters like peak isometric muscle force and its corresponding fiber length, muscle's intrinsic extreme shortening velocity, pennation angle, and tendon slack length are specified to customize the generic model for specific muscles. Cross-bridge models and Hill-type models are the two main categories of musculotendon models. Basically, mechanisms for muscle contraction can be explained with the help of cross-bridge models, which also describe the interaction between actin and myosin filaments. It was supposed originally that myosin is attached to actin and makes a cross-bridge among the filaments. After being attached, cross-bridges would cause slipping of the actin filament and the production of force. The

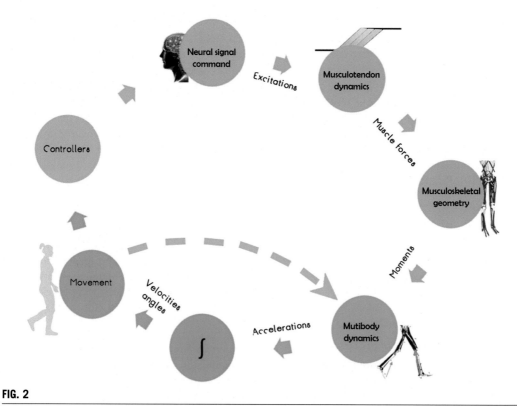

FIG. 2

Simulation of musculoskeletal elements used in OpenSim.

advantages of cross-bridge models are that they are derived from the basic structure of muscles and measure parameters, which are challenging to measure. But due to computational cost, the main focus is on Hill-type models. Hill [16,17] was interested in modeling the external behavior of muscle rather than its underlying physiology. In doing so, a lumped parameter approach was taken, whereby the muscle was modeled as a damped active force generating a contractile element with a parallel elastic element representing its passive elasticity, attached to a series elastic element to represent the tendon. The capacity of muscles to generate force was dependent on length and velocity such that actin and myosin filaments have maximum overlap at an optimal length, producing the greatest capacity to generate force. Force drops as the length deviates from this optimal position in either direction.

The action of movement originates from a complicated coordination/composition of the muscular, sensory, skeletal, and neural systems. Human and animal movements can be analyzed and predicted through the models inculcated in OpenSim. Neural commands to muscles sent as excitations could be calculated from experimental knowledge (e.g., electromyography) or controller models. The force-length and force-velocity values are embodied by OpenSim's Hill-type musculoconnective tissue models, where muscle forces are determined from excitations. OpenSim gives us the freedom to analyze all the different muscle geometries, and also describe muscle orientation parameters and contraction dynamics to be changed by supported tentative knowledge. Users are able to create forward

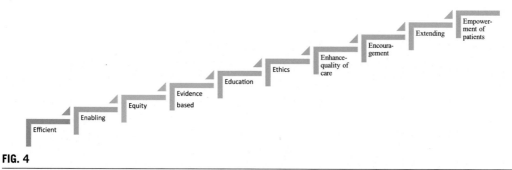

FIG. 4

Ten e's of e-health.

dynamic atmosphere and simultaneously acknowledges that e-health is a combination of both the internet and medicine [30]. Fig. 4 shows the 10 e's within the idea of e-health.

1. Efficiency—This is the assurance given by e-health to enhance efficiency in healthcare, thereby reducing costs. Frequently communication between healthcare and the patient will be the best possible way of decreasing costs [31].
2. Enhancement of quality—Improvement in quality is also one of the issues along with increased efficiency and reduced cost. Quality can be improved by comparing different providers from time to time; noting the suggestions of consumers and many other factors may be included.
3. Evidence based—Efficiency and effectiveness of e-health interventions should not be presumed. It should be evidence based and proven by grueling scientific evaluations. However, in this field much is need to be explored [32].
4. Empowerment of patients and clients—The internet provides the electronic records of patients and knowledge of medicines to consumers. Hence, e-health opens new facilities for patients who are easily accessible.
5. Encouragement for a new relationship: E-health makes and maintains the true partnership between the patient and the health professional, where decisions are taken in a mutual manner. Physicians can continue advanced medical education by online sources and can provide updated preventive information to consumers [33].
6. Enabling the interchange of information and communicating in a consistent way between healthcare institutions.
7. Extending the scope of healthcare beyond its traditional boundaries conceptually as well as geographically. Consumers can easily obtain e-health services online from global suppliers. These facilities can range from very simple advice to complex interventions to pharmaceutical products [34].
8. Ethics—E-health includes new forms of patient-physician interaction such as treatment consent, equity issues, privacy disclosure, etc. These forms avoid threats to ethical issues such as online professional practice.
9. Equity—One of the potentials of e-health is to make healthcare equitable; however, it is also considered that e-health may increase the gap between the "haves" and "have-nots." Some individuals are unable to use computers efficiently or they do not have the skills, money, or

access to networks. Hence, these individuals may be disinterested in adopting the benefits of advances in information technology. The digital world currently runs between young and old, rural and urban populations, rich and poor, male and female, and common and rare diseases. Before diving into the workings of OpenSim we must know the terms that will help us to easily understand the software.

3D virtual learning environments: The learning experiences of students can be enhanced by e-learning media known as the 3D virtual learning environment, which is becoming more popular day by day. This environment allows us to cross the boundaries of the real world and probe the dimensions of a virtual world. No limitations on budgets, natural forces, material strength, or perhaps infrastructural needs and laws are present in this virtual world. The 3D buildings present in the virtual world appear advanced, float in mid-air, or can even be below the deepest ocean because we have the power to control all the laws in this virtual world—even disabling the force of gravity [31]. This will help medical students who wish to achieve an abstract understanding of 3D anatomy, such as bone alignment, ankle, hip, muscle, and complicated movements, from 2D pictures [35,36] because these are in 3D in real life and cannot be properly mapped in 2D. 3D computer graphics (3DCG) are used to give greater visual information to users. By using interactive 3DCG, materials can change the whole mindset of visualizing complex 3D elements and can generate a lot of interest and positivity in medical education; it just has to be integrated into standard education. This interactive 3DCG can prove to be more economical than regular textbooks in medical education and would surely increase the capability of students to grasp complicated anatomical structures [15,37].

Joint kinematics: Training of the relative motion between two successive segments of the body [33,38] is called joint kinematics. If these segments are considered rigid bodies, then relative motion of the links can be defined with the help of six independent scalar quantities for 3D experimental analysis. Three translations and three rotations in human anatomy are described as scalar quantities.

- The data of six autonomous scalar quantities are required to outline the relative motion of the concerned link by 3D experimental analysis (assuming these segments are rigid bodies).
- Sagittal plane: This is also known as the symmetry plane of the human body. It is vertical and passes from the forward to the backward side in the human body.
- Frontal plane (known as longitudinal): This is a vertical plane and is orthogonal to the mesial plane.
- Transverse plane: This is a horizontal plane and is orthogonal to another two alternative planes. Fig. 5 shows three anatomical planes of the human body.

IK: This is the study of motion while not allowing the forces and moments that generate the motion. The aim of IK is to estimate the joint angles of a selected subject from experimental knowledge.

- It helps us to estimate a subject's joint angles through walking by simulating an IK analysis and by collecting walking data experimentally. IK computes a group of joint angles for each time step of recorded motion input and then places the model in a "best matching" configuration based on analyzed results [39].
- This "best matching" configuration is decided by performing a weighted least-squares optimization problem to minimize the marker error. The distance between the model marker and its corresponding experimental marker is called the marker error. Every marker has a corresponding coefficient cost, revealing how powerfully that marker's error term ought to be decreased within the least-squares optimization problem. For every time step, the inverse

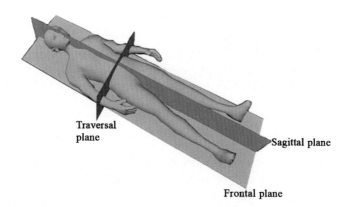

FIG. 5

Anatomical planes of the human body.

mechanic's tool solves for a vector of general coordinates like joint angles that reduce the total weighted marker errors [39]. Fig. 6 shows the typical workflow for generating a muscle-driven simulation after importing experimental data.

The IK tool calculates the set of common angles for each time step and frame of recorded motion. Then, it puts the model in the "best match" configuration of the experimental kinematics. OpenSim solves the weighted least-squares optimization problem and then finds the "best match." The main target is to reduce marker error. The distance between the virtual marker and its corresponding experimental marker is defined as the marker error. The associated weighting value of each marker specifies how effectively the marker's error should be decreased in the case of least-squares problems.

IK tool overview: By changing the joint angles (general coordinates) with time, matching between model markers and experimental markers is performed.

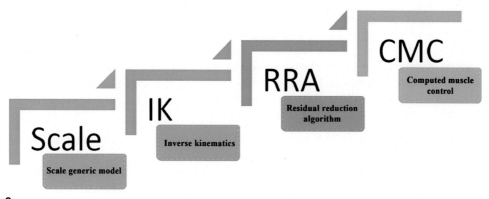

FIG. 6

Typical workflow for generating a muscle-driven simulation after importing experimental data. *CMC*, computed muscle control; *IK*, inverse kinematics; *RRA*, residual reduction algorithm; *Scale,* scale generic model.

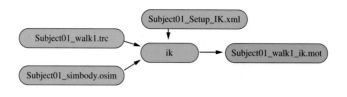

FIG. 7

OpenSim IK tool with inputs and outputs.

Inputs and outputs of the IK tool: The green color shows the experimental data; the red color is used for OpenSim files (.osim); and the blue color shows the settings files. Fig. 7 shows the inputs and outputs of the OpenSim IK tool.

The primary inputs to IK are the following files:

subject01_simbody.osim: By designing a model with the scale tool, a subject-specific OpenSim model is generated, with its adjusted virtual markers.

subject01_walk1.trc: The motion capture system provides experimental marker trajectories along the time of interest.

gait2354_Setup_IK.xml: This file contains all the information for the IK tool as well as marker weightings. These marker weightings are relative and also track the relationship between virtual markers and experimental markers. Less error means a larger weight for a given marker.

subject01_coords.mot: Experimental general coordinate values for joint angles obtained with trials from motion capture devices or other specialized algorithms. We can also specify relative coordinate weights in the tasks file if joint angles are known.

subject01_walk1_ik.mot: This is the output, and a motion file having generalized coordinate trajectories (joint angles as well as translations) is calculated by IK.

Muscle forces: Muscles are modeled as a group of fibers hooked up to connective tissue at pennation angle α. Computational models that represent both skeleton and muscles can actually estimate the muscle forces. In a number of movement tasks to obtain the different muscle forces, musculoskeletal models are used in combination with noninvasive measurements. Dynamic human motion is attained by the initiation of muscles, which then generate force and hence move the joints in an organized manner to finish the determined task requirements. Sometimes, such tasks are essential in addition to the action of the exterior force. The conclusion of this complete procedure mainly depends on the force-generation features of the human muscles, features of the human skeletal system, and the original neuronal system. It is difficult to understand the coupling of this kind of mechanism to observe the applicability of muscle force estimation methods.

- Hill-type muscle model: Muscle is comprised of a contracted component together with a parallel elastic component in series with an elastic connective tissue.
- Modeling muscle force in OpenSim: The muscle may be a complicated actuator and produces an active force up to some peak quantity relying on fiber length and activation.

Human gait dynamics: Analysis of the human gait is a challenging problem in biomechanics due to the involvement of nonlinear human motion equations, foot-ground contact, and muscle dynamics. In spite of a wide number of studies on human gait analysis, it is still challenging to enhance accuracy as well as computational efficiency to predict human gait simulation in evaluative studies. Kinematic features are obtained from a vision-based gait test center and this makes it possible to study the human gait. By using a musculoskeletal simulation platform, the analysis of human gait modeling is possible. This platform provides the degree of human gait stability. Work has already begun to develop a video repository of the human gait (for ordinary and sick individuals) that could broadly be examined to identify walking problems in different humans.

The human gait is a result of complicated coordination between the musculotendinous and fasciculus elements of the human body that work together for legged translation or human body dynamics [40,41]. Osis et al. [42] projected machine learning strategies for the estimation of ground contact events like temporal order for foot strike and toe-off by applying mechanics for each running and walking action. This technique provides promising estimation results and has the possibility to show sturdy temporal order prediction for clinical use. Results show that the model predicted each foot strike and toe-off temporal order between 20 ms of the gold standard and over 95 out of 100 results in running and walking gaits. The machine learning approach continues to produce sturdy predictions for clinical use and should supply a versatile methodology to handle new events and gait varieties. Note that the neural network approach has been conjointly applied to classifying movements [10,40,42–45] or simulating real-time myoelectric control [46,47].

Simulations and analyses of athletic movements using OpenSim applications were provided by Reinbolt et al. [48] where basic outcomes between ground reaction forces, in addition to muscle forces, were shown to minimize the possibility of a patient's injury.

Seth et al. [49] developed a musculoskeletal model of human walking using the OpenSim framework. Postural activities of pathological gait patterns suitable in the biomechanical research community were also simulated. Biomedical researchers also presented another new approach [50] using OpenSim and Matlab/Simulink platforms for dynamic simulation of human movements. This combination of software has developed an innovative area of research to produce treatment solutions for musculoskeletal problems.

4 OpenSim: Musculoskeletal simulation framework

This section presents the basic steps and technical requirements for OpenSim simulations with an example [45,51].

4.1 The OpenSim model

This component creates and shares user-defined models that constitute the dynamics of stiff joints and body parts, which are influenced by different forces to cause motion. This component is an XML file format that contains details related to bodies, joints, constraints, forces, controllers, and components.

4.2 Importing experimental data

The collected experimental data can be analyzed by using this component in the laboratory. The analysis includes the joint angles captured during motion, data related to forces, moments, pressure, electromyography, and marker trajectories. After preparation the data are stored in different files such as marker files, motion files, and store files.

4.3 Scaling

This component allows the scaling up of mass properties and physical dimensions of the general model to create a subject-specific model based on the experimental data, which helps in performing IK and dynamics.

4.4 The inverse problem

In this component, the experimental data are used to perform the inverse dynamics to measure motion kinetics and kinematics. It takes position and force data as input data to calculate the angles, velocities, accelerations, moments, and forces. It further covers IK, static optimization, and inverse dynamics.

4.5 The forward problem

In this component, errors that occur during modeling are reduced by using a residual reduction algorithm followed by CMC, which is used to generate muscle excitations. Furthermore, these muscle excitations are used to drive the model's motion for creating movements. Fig. 8 shows the virtual touch hardware architecture overview.

4.6 Analyzing simulations

This component is used to analyze simulations to answer research queries. The analysis carried out by this component includes body kinematics, point kinematics, muscle analysis, joint reactions, induced acceleration, and force reporter. Technical requirements for simulations are [47]:

CPU: OpenSim does not perform well if it has access to just one computational core; it should have at least a dual-core machine. One idea is to have one core per frequently used region, with two

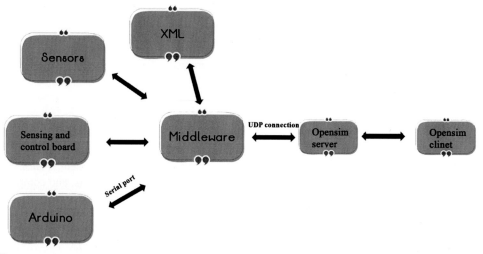

FIG. 8

Virtual touch hardware architecture overview.

more being available. Thus for a four-region simulation, we would require four cores. If those alternative regions were used less often or not used in parallel, one might proceed with a greater core-to-region value.

Memory: 4 GB might be required for a simulator having four such regions. If all the regions are not occupied with avatars simultaneously or wherever there are fewer scripts, the job could be performed with less memory.

Network: Latency along with upload and download bandwidth is necessary. The purpose of upload bandwidth is to provide users with texture data. Thus a poor bandwidth (for example, with 384 kb uploading speed) can result in a poor experience for viewers, probably until the point where they receive all the texture data. The need to upload bandwidth is essential when a user enters a particular region for the first time or after the user cleared his/her asset cache. This implies that the needed bandwidth can differ with the number of textures present in the region.

Database: By default, OpenSim is designed to utilize the SQLite database, which is a plus point since it needs no configuration. MySQL, for instance, is used even for large websites because of its good management of tiny, mediocre, and even huge grids [33].

Simulation example: Inverse dynamics is used to plot different types of forces and moments acting on the body while walking [52–55].

4.7 Methodology

- Import the dataset into OpenSim.
- Generate simulations using the OpenSim workflow.
- Load the files into the inverse dynamics tool and simulate the model.
- Load motion data into the motion folder generated in the result file. Open the results and analyze them.
- Examine forces experienced by the pelvis. Also, examine the change in knee and ankle angle moment with respect to time. Hip flexion and hip rotation can also be observed from the results. Figs. 9–12 detail the simulation results.

5 OpenSim: Plugins, research issues, and future trends
5.1 Plugins

It is a fact that the general set of model elements of OpenSim will not be sufficient with the applications of each user. Therefore we need further classes/categories for performing different functions required by different users. Here, the user-derived categories come into play. These can be defined for a joint, constraint, force, etc. In addition, these custom components/libraries should be accessible from within the OpenSim interface so that users need not define everything again from scratch. So, OpenSim provides a method to load these codes during runtime and provide additional functionality to the OpenSim software; the method uses dynamically linked libraries (DLLs). User's code can be simply compiled as a DLL file by a plugin mechanism provided by OpenSim, which can then be loaded at runtime. A plugin contains a variety of user-defined categories that are stored as a DLL file. Scripts/codes utilizing the tags for a user-defined category would cause OpenSim to form objects of the new category if the plugin was initially loaded in OpenSim. Several currently intrinsic model elements, such as

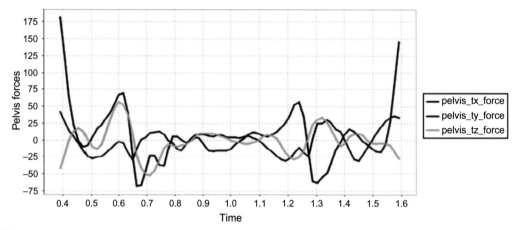

FIG. 9

Simulating and knowing the pelvis forces can help to prevent pelvic fractures. Pelvic fracture often results in massive hemorrhage. Hence, having an approximation of these forces would be of importance.

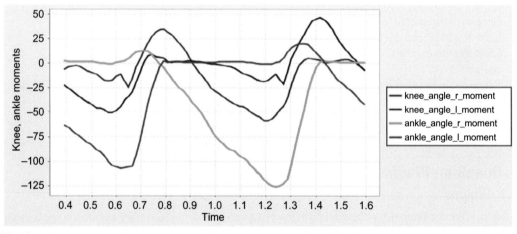

FIG. 10

Knowing knee and ankle angles can help in judging the possibility of suffering a sprain. The knee angles can predict the future possibility of having bow legs or genu valgum.

ligament and ellipsoid joint, were initially added as plugins to satisfy a selected user's requirement. Plugins alter important nonetheless targeted contributions with borderline investment. Plugins alter important nonetheless targeted contributions with borderline investments can jointly function as a straightforward method to share innovations in all fields.

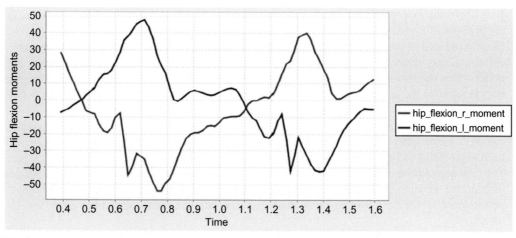

FIG. 11

Flexion can occur around a transverse axis. Flexion is limited by the contact of the thigh with the anterior abdominal wall. Knowing the flexion moments can help to prevent dislocations.

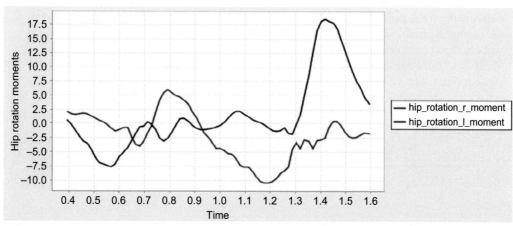

FIG. 12

This plot shows the hip rotation moments experienced by a normal walking person.

5.2 Research issues and future trends

OpenSim is poised to support several endeavors. But there are many problems and trends for the future.

- There should be continuous improvement in the software and online infrastructure to make it even easier for the OpenSim community to share models, algorithms, and data.
- Several teams are working to translate OpenSim to clinical settings, but more work is needed to create user-friendly pipelines and establish OpenSim's utility in treatment planning and evaluation.

- New upcoming fast machine learning-based techniques and data for validation are needed as the applications of musculoskeletal simulation continue to expand.
- Musculoskeletal orientation and joint mechanics are required to grasp how variations such as deformity, age, surgery, or size affect the predictions of a model, and relate to the circumstances under which simulations supporting a general model are applicable to specific subjects. This will help to improve the accuracy of these models.
- It is a serious challenge to demonstrate that simulation will improve treatment outcomes for people with movement disorders. The potential to use subject-specific simulations to grasp the causes of movement deviations and to assess treatment choices is exciting; however, it has not been explored to its full potential.
- The final aim of musculoskeletal modeling and simulation is the prediction of the outcome because of treatment or intervention (surgery, physical coaching, training program, etc.). Computational performance is still the most important challenge especially when models tend to fit biological complexity.
- Muscle-driven simulations produce lots of knowledge. Deploying simulations to discover the principles that control muscle coordination and to attain enhanced clinical outcomes needs tools that can interpret simulations. Developing and diffusing analysis and image tools that give new insights poses a crucial challenge for boosting biomechanical simulation.
- OpenSim is always an open collaboration and peer review for future. A multiinstitutional collaboration constantly tests, analyzes, and improves the OpenSim code. Users are inspired to augment the code, improve models, and produce plugins to support their applications and to share their progress/results with others. As an outcome, simulation-based studies will currently be replicated and tested outside the establishment wherever the simulation was initially designed.
- There is a vision that simulations can augment treatment efficaciousness, cap unsought consequences, and reduce costs. Contributions from the scientific and clinical communities are needed for the refinement of musculoskeletal models and their analyses. Fig. 13 justify that OpenSim can act as a catalyst to push model exchange and inspire modeling innovation, which can be shared by all.

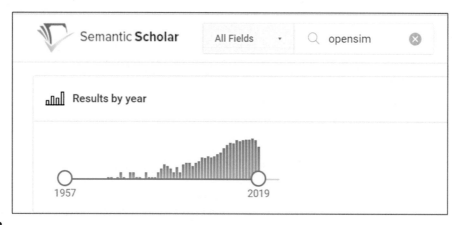

FIG. 13

Increasing publication trends in reputed peer-reviewed journals by semanticscholar.com. The graph ranges from 1957 to July 2019.

References

[1] J.J. Jacobs, G.B.J. Andersson, J.E. Bell, S.L. Weinstein, J.P. Dormans, S.M. Gnatz, N. Lane, J.E. Puzas, E.W. S. Clair, E.H. Yelin, The Burden of Musculoskeletal Diseases in the United States, 1st ed., United States Bone and Joint Decade, Rosemont, 2008.

[2] S.L. Delp, J.P. Loan, A graphics-based software system to develop and analyze models of musculoskeletal structures, Comput. Biol. Med. 25 (1995) 21–34.

[3] S.L. Delp, J.P. Loan, M.G. Hoy, F.E. Zajac, E.L. Topp, J.M. Rosen, An interactive graphics-based model of the lower extremity to study orthopedic surgical procedures, IEEE Trans. Biomed. Eng. 37 (1990) 757–767.

[4] S.L. Delp, F.C. Anderson, A.S. Arnold, P. Loan, A. Habib, C.T. John, E. Guendelman, D. G. Thelen, OpenSim: open-source software to create and analyze dynamic simulations of movement, IEEE Trans. Biomed. Eng. 54 (2007) 1940–1950.

[5] D.G. Thelen, F.C. Anderson, Using computed muscle control to generate forward dynamic simulations of human walking from experimental data, J. Biomech. 39 (2006) 1107–1115.

[6] S.R. Hamner, A. Seth, S.L. Delp, Muscle contributions to propulsion and support during running, J. Biomech. 43 (2010) 2709–2716.

[7] M.D. Fox, J.A. Reinbolt, S. Õunpuu, S.L. Delp, Mechanisms of improved knee flexion after rectus femoris transfer surgery, J. Biomech. 42 (2009) 614–619.

[8] R.S. Sutton, A.G. Barto, Reinforcement Learning I: Introduction; 1998.

[9] D. Silver, J. Schrittwieser, K. Simonyan, I. Antonoglou, A. Huang, A. Guez, T. Hubert, L. Baker, M. Lai, A. Bolton, Y. Chen, T. Lillicrap, F. Hui, L. Sifre, G. van den Driessche, T. Graepel, D. Hassabis, Mastering the game of Go without human knowledge, Nature 550 (2017) 354–359, https://doi.org/10.1038/nature24270.

[10] T.T. Dao, From deep learning to transfer learning for the prediction of skeletal muscle forces, Med. Biol. Eng. Comput. 57 (2019) 1049–1058.

[11] M. Palov, S. Kolesnikov, S.M. Plis, Run, skeleton, run: skeletal model in a physics based simulation, in: AAAI Spring Symposium Series, 2018, pp. 338–343.

[12] S. Escalera, M. Weimer (Eds.), The NIPS '17 Competition: Building Intelligent Systems, Springer, Cham, 2018.

[13] G. Joshi, G. Chowdhary, Cross-domain transfer in reinforcement learning using target apprentice, in: ICRA 2018. Proceedings of 2018 IEEE International Conference on Robotics and Automation, Brisbane, Australia, 21 May 2018, 2018, pp. 7525–7532.

[14] M. Mohammedalamen, W.D. Khamies, B. Rosman, Transfer Learning for Prosthetics Using Imitation Learning, Serial Online. Available from: https://arxiv.org/abs/1901.04772, 2019. (Accessed 28 July 2019).

[15] A. Seth, J.L. Hicks, T.K. Uchida, A. Habib, C.L. Dembia, J.J. Dunne, C.F. Ong, M. S. DeMers, A. Rajagopal, M. Millard, S.R. Hamner, OpenSim: simulating musculoskeletal dynamics and neuromuscular control to study human and animal movement, PLoS Comp. Biol. 14 (2018) 1006223.

[16] H.S. Gasser, A.V. Hill, The dynamics of muscular contraction, Proc. R. Soc. Lond. Ser. B Biol. Sci. 96 (678) (1924) 398–437.

[17] A.V. Hill, The heat of shortening and the dynamic constants of muscle, Proc. R. Soc. Lond. B Biol. Sci. 126 (843) (1938) 136–195.

[18] D.G. Thelen, F.C. Anderson, Using computed muscle control to generate forward dynamic simulations of human walking from experimental data, J. Biomech. 39 (2006) 1107–1115.

[19] D.G. Thelen, F.C. Anderson, S.L. Delp, Generating dynamic simulations of movement using computed muscle control, J. Biomech. 36 (2003) 321–328.

[20] C.T. John, F.C. Anderson, E. Guendelman, A.S. Arnold, S.L. Delp, An algorithm for generating muscle-actuated simulations of long-duration movements, in: Biomedical Computation at Stanford (BCATS) symposium, Stanford University, 21 October 2006, Poster Presentation, 2006.

[21] T.P. Lillicrap, J.J. Hunt, A. Pritzel, N. Heess, T. Erez, Y. Tassa, D. Silver, D. Wierstra, Continuous control with deep reinforcement learning, Serial Online. Available from: https://arxiv.org/abs/1509.02971, 2015. (Accessed 28 July 2019).

[22] J. Schulman, S. Levine, P. Abbeel, M. Jordan, P. Moritz, Trust region policy optimization, in: International Conference on Machine Learning, 6–11 July 2015, Lille, France, 2015, pp. 1889–1897.

[23] http://osim-rl.stanford.edu/docs/home/.

[24] https://github.com/stanfordnmbl/osim-rl/blob/master/docs/_docs/index.md.

[25] https://simtkconfluence.stanford.edu:8443/display/OpenSim/Welcome+to+OpenSimhttp://osim-rl.stanford.edu/docs/home/HOWTO.

[26] C.L. Dembia, A. Silder, T.K. Uchida, J.L. Hicks, S.L. Delp, Simulating ideal assistive devices to reduce the metabolic cost of walking with heavy loads, PLoS One 12 (2017) e0180320.

[27] T.W. Dorn, J.M. Wang, J.L. Hicks, S.L. Delp, Predictive simulation generates human adaptations during loaded and inclined walking, PLoS One 10 (2015) e0121407.

[28] M.S. DeMers, J.L. Hicks, S.L. Delp, Preparatory co-activation of the ankle muscles may prevent ankle inversion injuries, J. Biomech. 52 (2017) 17–23.

[29] C.F. Ong, J.L. Hicks, S.L. Delp, Simulation-based design for wearable robotic systems: an optimization framework for enhancing a standing long jump, IEEE Trans. Biomed. Eng. 63 (2015) 894–903.

[30] A. Seth, R. Matias, A.P. Veloso, S.L. Delp, A biomechanical model of the scapulothoracic joint to accurately capture scapular kinematics during shoulder movements, PLoS One 11 (2016) e0141028.

[31] https://simtk.org/plugins/reports/index.php?type=group&group_id=886&reports=reports.

[32] https://simtk.org/projects/synergy.

[33] https://industryreports24.com/90621/e-health-market-insights-rising-trends-and-global-demand-2019-to-2024/.

[34] G. Eysenbach, What is e-health? J. Med. Internet Res. 3 (2001) e20.

[35] M.S. DeMers, J.L. Hicks, S.L. Delp, Preparatory co-activation of the ankle muscles may prevent ankle inversion injuries, J. Biomech. 52 (2017) 17–23.

[36] R.J.V. Arkel, L. Modenese, A. Phillips, J.R. Jeffers, Hip abduction can prevent posterior edge loading of hip replacements, J. Orthop. Res. 31 (2013) 1172–1179.

[37] https://www.fortlewis.edu/music/Neuromusculo skeletal.aspx.

[38] https://www.sciencedirect.com/topics/materials-science/joint-kinematics.

[39] https://simtk.confluence.stanford.edu:8443/display/OpenSim/Overview+of+the+OpenSim+Workflow.

[40] A. Nandy, P. Chakroborty, A study on human gait dynamics: modelling and simulations on OpenSim platform, Multimed. Tools Appl. 76 (2016) 21365–21400.

[41] F.M.M. Neto, R. Souza, A.S. Gomes (Eds.), Handbook of Research on 3-D Virtual Environments and Hypermedia for Ubiquitous Learning, Information Science Reference, USA, 2016.

[42] S.T. Osis, B.A. Hettinga, R. Ferber, Predicting ground contact events for a continuum of gait types: an application of targeted machine learning using principal component analysis, Gait Posture 46 (2016) 86–90.

[43] M. Atzori, M. Cognolato, H. Müller, Deep learning with convolutional neural networks applied to electromyography data: a resource for the classification of movements for prosthetic hands, Front. Neurorobot. 10 (2016) 1–10.

[44] P. Kutilek, S. Viteckovas, Z. Svoboda, P. Smcka, The use of artificial neural networks to predict the muscle behavior, Cent. Eur. J. Eng. 3 (2013) 410–418.

[45] http://opensimulator.org/wiki/Performance.

[46] P. Soda, S. Mazzoleni, G. Cavallo, E. Guglielmelli, G. Iannello, Human movement onset detection from isometric force and torque measurements: a supervised pattern recognition approach, Artif. Intell. Med. 50 (2010) 55–61.

[47] A. Ameri, E.J. Scheme, E.N. Kamavuako, K.B. Englehart, P.A. Parker, Real-time, simultaneous myoelectric control using force and position-based training paradigms, IEEE Trans. Biomed. Eng. 61 (2013) 279–287.

[48] J.A. Reinbolt, A. Seth, S.L. Delp, Simulation of human movement: applications using OpenSim, Proc. IUTAM 2 (2011) 186–198.

[49] A. Seth, M. Sherman, J.A. Reinbolt, S.L. Delp, OpenSim: a musculoskeletal modeling and simulation framework for in silico investigations and exchange, Proc. IUTAM 2 (2011) 212–232.

[50] M. Mansouri, J.A. Reinbolt, A platform for dynamic simulation and control of movement based on OpenSim and MATLAB, J. Biomech. 45 (2012) 1517–1521.

[51] J. Mateu, M. Lasala, X. Alamán, Developing mixed reality educational applications: the virtual touch toolkit, Sensors 5 (2015) 21760–21784.

[52] F.E. Zajac, R.R. Neptune, S.A. Kautz, Biomechanics and muscle coordination of human walking: Part I: introduction to concepts, power transfer, dynamics and simulations, Gait Posture 16 (2002) 215–232.

[53] https://simtkconfluence.stanford.edu:8443/display/OpenSim/Overview+of+the+OpenSim+Workflow.

[54] https://simtkconfluence.stanford.edu:8443/display/OpenSim33/Tutorial+3+-+Scaling%2C+Inverse +Kinematics%2C+and+Inverse+Dynamics.

[55] https://simtkconfluence.stanford.edu:8443/display/OpenSim/Musculoskeletal+Models.

Further reading

A.F. Huxley, Muscle structure and theories of contraction, Prog. Biophys. Biophys. Chem. 7 (1957) 255–318.

L. Kidzinski, S.P. Mohanty, C. Ong, J.L. Hicks, S.F. Carroll, S. Levine, M. Salathe, S.L. Delp, Learning to Run Challenge: Synthesizing Physiologically Accurate Motion Using Deep Reinforcement Learning; 2018. arXiv: 1804.00198 [cs.AI].

Advances and challenges in fMRI and DTI techniques

Ranjeet Ranjan Jha[a], Gaurav Jaswal[b], Aditya Nigam[a], and Arnav Bhavsar[a]

Indian Institute of Technology Mandi, Mandi, India[a] National Agri-Food Biotechnology Institute, Mohali, Punjab, India[b]

1 Introduction

Neurodegenerative diseases are identified by an ongoing dissipation of neurons associated with the deposition of abnormal proteins, leading to a change of the functional and structural characterization of the human brain. To measure alternation in structural and functional properties, diffusion-weighted imaging (DWI) and functional magnetic resonance imaging (fMRI) (as shown in Fig. 1) have been widely applied simultaneously in these clinical populations. Moreover, these techniques are non-invasive, which helps to examine more in depth the spatial topology and strength of interactions between brain networks without involving cutting or putting instruments inside the brain.

The fMRI technique has been applied to study brain functional activities. In this type of neuroimaging, we measure changes in the brain blood oxygenation-level dependent (BOLD) signal to achieve neural activity in an indirect way. A series of brain images is obtained during an fMRI experiment while the subject is engaged in a set of tasks (task based) or in a resting state.

In the control brain, the main parts of white matter (WM) are myelinated fiber tracts, giving a natural path for water molecules to move along. That is, instead of moving in perpendicular directions, water molecules tend to move along the axon fibers. Based on this basic rule, a matrix of 3×3 has been estimated within the diffusion tensor (DT) model. The estimated matrix is symmetric positive-definite in nature; hence, it has three orthogonal eigenvectors and three corresponding positive eigenvalues. The principal diffusion direction (the direction of the fastest diffusion) is given by the major eigenvector (which has larger eigenvalues). Three positive eigenvalues ($\lambda 1$, $\lambda 2$, $\lambda 3$) of the tensor give the diffusivity in the direction of each eigenvector. Since diffusion tensor imaging (DTI) can detect the diffusion characteristics of each voxel, a natural extension is to evaluate the diffusion connection between adjacent voxels and ultimately induce the complete WM fiber pathways within the entire brain, which is primarily called tractography. These days, the combined study of both fMRI and DTI has been of research interest. It has been observed that the joint study provides extra information about brain anatomy, which further helps when looking into gray matter (GM) functions and WM microstructures for the detection of different brain diseases, such as Alzheimer's, schizophrenia (SZ), epilepsy, etc., at a very early stage. Hence, in this chapter, we explore fMRI, DTI, and the joint analysis of both for various applications. The rest of this chapter is organized as follows: Section 2 discusses

Intelligent Data Security Solutions for e-Health Applications. https://doi.org/10.1016/B978-0-12-819511-6.00004-2

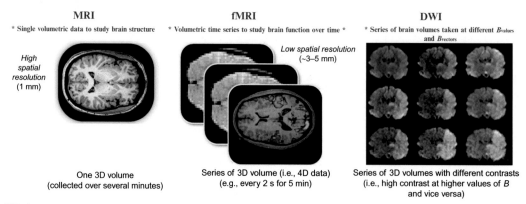

FIG. 1

MRI versus fMRI versus DWI technology.

fMRI analysis and survey, whereas DTI analysis and survey is given in Section 3. Section 4 analyzes fusion analysis of fMRI and DTI, while Section 5 presents classification and prediction methods and scope. Section 6 discusses future directions and challenges. Finally, Section 7 concludes our study with references at the end.

2 fMRI analysis and survey

fMRI utilizes the BOLD signal, which is sensitive to spontaneous neural activity. Especially, functional information of brain networks has been analyzed due to low-frequency oscillations (<0.1 Hz) of the BOLD signal.

In this section, fMRI is discussed, which consists of several stages right from the preprocessing phase until the application phase (as shown in Fig. 2). Here, we have elaborated only the functional connectivity (FC) part, which is crucial in the case of various mental disorders. Moreover, in a later

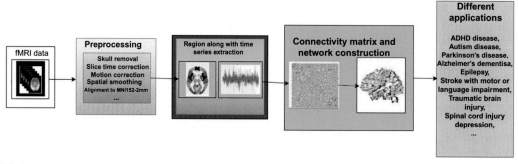

FIG. 2

Flow diagram of fMRI analysis.

section, different classification techniques, namely support vector machine (SVM), artificial neural network, and convolutional neural network, are discussed broadly.

FC calculates the temporal correlation of functional activation in several brain areas and can be defined as mutual information or covariance between time series and pairwise Pearson's correlation coefficients, revealing a particular network.

FC has been acknowledged as a strong biomarker for better knowledge of the pathophysiological procedures of different neurodegenerative illnesses, including frontotemporal dementia, Parkinson's disease (PD), and Alzheimer's disease (AD).

FC represents spatially separated brain region organization and interrelationship. Methods for evaluating and delineating FC play an important role, as the measures used can significantly impact biomarker identification and the precision of classification and prediction of individual subjects.

Normally, FC is assumed to be stationary over the scanning time (usually a few minutes), and a static functional connectivity (SFC) analysis has been applied in most previous fMRI studies. Until recently, interesting research has shown that dynamic brain connectivity can be fruitful in revealing disturbances in disease in the ordinary human brain [1]. Fig. 3 summarizes the essential FC analysis strategies and conceivable network features utilized for prediction/classification problems.

SFC analyses: There are usually three types of approach analyzing SFC from a methodological point of view [2]. The first is a model-driven approach using previous understanding to determine brain region/voxel sets and then restrict the assessment of connectivity to particular regions/voxels. The second method is more data driven and uses clustering or decomposition approaches to map entire brain

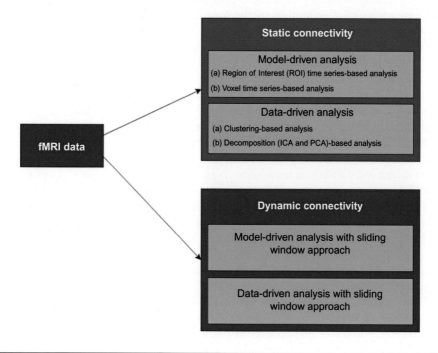

FIG. 3

The essential FC analysis strategies for prediction/classification problem.

functional networks. In such cases, brain voxels allocated to the same element or cluster represent deeply linked regions. The third combines the thinking of the foregoing two processes, first of all extricating coactivated areas using a data-driven approach and then calculating FC between brain areas. We have elaborated a few common approaches in the following.

Model-driven analysis for assessing connectivity among regions or seeds: Brain FC has been widely used in the model-driven strategy. Three primary steps include identifying areas and sizes of regions of interest (ROIs) or voxel areas, calculating representative ROIs or voxel time series, and assessing connectivity (or coupling) between separate ROIs or connectivity between each seed (ROI or voxel) and all other brain voxels. As such, the resulting strengths of FC reflect the connection between the voxels or temporal fluctuation regions selected. ROI-based FC strengths can frequently be taken as features in classification and prediction issues, as the respective connectivity characteristics of a new/testing sample can be calculated directly between the chosen brain areas (or voxels) using the training subjects. While ROIs and voxels are generally determined by subjective experience and previous understanding, the resulting FC can be highly susceptible to empirical choice and display a very distinct pattern for minor ROI modifications. Choosing a reasonable region, including voxels with coherent brain function, is therefore a challenge. Significant research work [3, 4] has tried to delineate a brain parcel by using data from various imaging modalities, but there are still inconsistencies. FC between two representative time series is estimated mostly by computing correlations to evaluate their linear association, but can also be evaluated by mutual information to recognize [5] nonlinear associations. Coherence estimates the linear association in the frequency domain [6] and techniques such as wavelet decomposition [7] can achieve connectivity within a particular frequency.

Data-driven analysis for estimating spatial functional network maps: Data-driven approaches estimating functional networks do not involve the specification of predefined brain areas or voxels as opposed to model-driven techniques. These common approaches include spatial independent component analysis (ICA) [2, 8], principal component analysis (PCA), and clustering techniques [9]. Specifically, ICA is a commonly used strategy that has shown excellent promise in recognizing psychiatric disorder biomarkers such as SZ [10], based on functional networks. Spatial ICA of the fMRI data of an individual subject breaks down the fMRI input matrix (*timepoints × voxels*) into a linear combination of various maximally spatially independent components (ICs), which can be considered as functional brain networks.

Functional network connectivity (FNC) analysis: Analysis of FNC [11] uses an approach combining model-driven and data-driven techniques. Typically, the framework involves two steps. It first conducts various subject group ICA on fMRI subjects, leading to subject-specific functional networks (stated by ICs) and related fluctuations (expressed by time courses (TCs)). The connectivity between any two networks can then be achieved by computing connectivity measurements such as Pearson's correlation between their postprocessed TCs, leading to a connectivity matrix that includes connectivity strengths across all networks. FNC also represents temporal connectivity between distinct brain areas, similar to the ROI-based technique. The distinction between the ROI-based and FNC techniques is that in the FNC analysis, a data-driven technique is applied to fMRI data to produce functionally coactivated brain regions (i.e., regions in one network), whereas in the ROI-based method brain regions are generally chosen through previous expertise (i.e., brain atlas) rather than using in-house fMRI data. Similar to ICA, the number of components in the FNC method must be determined in advance. Typically, FNC methods use a large model order (e.g., 100 or bigger) to provide more comprehensive brain parceling.

Dynamic functional connectivity (DFC) analyses: All of the foregoing analytical methods estimate brain FC by calculating an average full-time sequence (e.g., calculating Pearson's correlation between two ROIs using BOLD signals within 5 or 10 min) and generating a static value to represent the strength of the association. There has been much interest in computing time-resolved connectivity measures and effective applications in defining biomarkers from [12–15] dynamic connectivity over the last few years.

In such analysis, FC of the brain may vary over time (e.g., tens of seconds) rather than be considered static. Such findings tend to expand the information available further, avoiding the powerful hypothesis that brain activity is static over time. While in the latest fMRI literature DFC has emerged as a promising area, some critical remarks on the theory of dynamic connectivity are also available. Laumann et al. [16] proposed that correlations measured by BOLD are comparatively stable over short timescales and may not reflect changes in cognitive content from moment to moment. Although this problem is not yet fully resolved, many fresh studies have shown a connection with dynamic connectivity characteristics between behavior, emotion, and cognition during rest, giving us trust in its prospective usefulness. Since dynamic connectivity has proven to be a helpful method for defining biomarkers, we introduce some typical dynamic connectivity methods and applications.

Sliding time-window-based dynamic connectivity analysis: DFC [17, 18] can be estimated using various techniques. The sliding time-window method [13, 19] is the most commonly used. By evaluating FC in various time windows, current static connectivity strategies can be readily expanded to be time resolved. DFC can then be assessed by evaluating FC between ROIs or voxels in a sliding window that yields various connectivity matrices, performing ICA on fMRI data in various applications to produce dynamic spatial network models, or segmenting network time series (i.e., ICs) into short time series and then computing FNC time-varying patterns. Analysis of dynamic connectivity between brain areas and networks has drawn growing interest. Different methods to further explore the time-varying patterns of connectivity are a continuing job topic. Damaraju et al. [20] computed healthy control and SZ patient dynamic FNC matrices and then clustered the time-varying FNC into different states. It is suggested that states with cortical/subcortical negative connectivity and powerful favorable connectivity between sensory networks demonstrate group similarities between thalamic hyperconnectivity and sensory hypoconnectivity. The sliding time window techniques just described have been used widely and are effective in estimating dynamic connectivity. However, in the absence of norms for setting the window length, there is an obvious limit, although past studies have indicated 30–60 s of window length, which is viable for capturing DFC.

2.1 Application

AD is the most prevalent cause of dementia and has been studied widely using sophisticated MRI methods. The incorporation of resting state (rs)-fMRI in AD image protocols has been particularly advantageous as the difficulty in obtaining the involvement of subjects could affect the outcomes of fMRI related to tasks. Clear proof shows that the default mode network (DMN) FC has declined across the AD continuum, including individuals with full-blown AD dementia and mild cognitive impairment (MCI). Functional rearrangements have shown clinical utility in patients with MCI to predict conversion to AD. The second most prevalent neurodegenerative disorder, PD, is defined by dopamine depletion in the nigro-striatal system leading to progressive functional deficiency.

During clinical progression in patients with PD, widespread functional rearrangements linked to the growth of motor and nonmotor symptoms occur.

PD is the second most common neurodegenerative disease and is characterized by dopamine depletion within the nigrostriatal framework driving to progressive functional disability. Widespread functional improvements related to the development of motor and nonmotor symptoms occur during clinical progression in PD patients. Several rs-fMRI studies have recognized cerebello-thalamo-cortical circuit changes as a main PD hallmark, with the most consistent finding being the decreased activation of the posterior putamen correlating with motor deficiency. Besides, interrupted FC has been connected to the growth of cognitive deficits in PD in the DMN, frontoparietal, salience, and associative visual networks.

3 DTI analysis and survey

DTI has been utilized for measuring the diffusion of water molecules in each voxel. We know that in a cup of water, the diffusion of water molecules in all directions is the same. However, in the case of the brain, diffusion can be isotropic (diffusion is the same in all directions) or anisotropic (diffusion is different in all directions), due to microscopic tissue heterogeneity. In WM, diffusion is anisotropic, since it contains axons that force water molecules to diffuse in a particular direction.

Initially, DWI data are captured, and then DT (3×3) is estimated, which is described by the Gaussian model. The estimated matrix is symmetric positive-definite in nature; hence, it has three orthogonal eigenvectors and three corresponding positive eigenvalues. The principal diffusion direction (the direction of the fastest diffusion) is given by the major eigenvector (which has larger eigenvalues). Diffusivity in the direction of each eigenvector is given by three positive eigenvalues of the tensor ($\lambda 1$, $\lambda 2$, $\lambda 3$).

To better characterize multidirectional fiber design (e.g., fiber crossing) inside single voxels, numerous modern strategies were proposed based on their capabilities to identify numerous dissemination (diffusion) directions, such as diffusion spectrum imaging (DSI) and high angular resolution diffusion imaging (HARDI). HARDI incorporates strategies that procure diffusion data utilizing more than six dissemination directions (such as 32 or higher). These methods generally utilize higher b-values than the standard 1000 for DTI, and/or numerous b-values (multiple shells of information). Another sort of numerous b-value acquisition is DSI.

In this section, DTI is discussed, which consists of several stages right from the preprocessing phase to the application phase (as shown in Fig. 4). Here, we have elaborated mainly the structural connectivity part, which is crucial in the case of various mental disorders. Moreover, in a later section, different classification techniques, namely SVM, artificial neural network, and convolutional neural network, are discussed broadly. Researchers have derived several scalar quantities from DTI data, which mainly partition into two categories, namely diffusion anisotropy and magnitude measures.

Measures of diffusion magnitude: The best and conceivably most valuable scalar is the average of the eigenvalues of the tensor. This average may be alluded to as the mean diffusivity (MD). Note that in clinical imaging, MD maps may be measured utilizing fewer diffusion gradient directions than required for the tensor.

Measures of diffusion anisotropy: Tensor anisotropy measures are proportions of the eigenvalues that are utilized to evaluate the shape of the diffusion. These measures are useful for portraying the

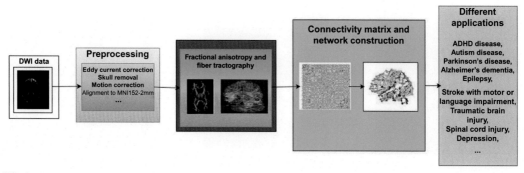

FIG. 4

Flow diagram of DTI analysis.

amount of tissue organization and for finding voxels likely to contain a single WM tract. Fractional anisotropy, or FA, is the foremost broadly utilized anisotropy measure. Its name comes from the fraction of the dissemination that is anisotropic. This can be thought of as the distinction of the tensor ellipsoid shape from that of an idealized sphere. Next, tractography is done by using the afore-mentioned scalar quantities, eigenvectors, and eigenvalues at each voxel. This tract further helps to build the structural connectivity graph. For example, it can be seen in Fig. 5 that initially deterministic tractography has been done for each brain DTI datum. Thereafter, 90 subcortical and cortical brain regions are selected by the automated anatomical labeling (AAL) atlas tool and are coregistered with the DTI tractography image. Next, a symmetric 90 × 90 weighted connectivity matrix is calculated by obtaining the number of connections (WM tracts) between any two regions. Lastly, the graph is built by putting thresholds on the weighted connectivity matrix, where each region is considered as a node.

DTI, in combination with network analysis methods, allows for the in vivo survey of WM tracts and testing of the "disconnectivity hypothesis." The human brain can be considered a small-world arrange-ment as there is a very short separation between neighboring brain regions and the few direct connec-tions to far regions. This small-world network highlights a fast system reaction and empowers the interaction between brain regions in an efficient manner. The connection cost or weight can be given by density measurement, that is, the ratio of the existing connections to the conceivable connections. A high density shows an well-connected network. Moreover, an efficient structural brain connection requires protected axonal wiring and an extensive total wiring volume of the network. Small path lengths and high clustering reflect proficient information exchange over the network with a high capacity to integrate information [21].

Structural network connectivity analysis: Investigation of structural network connectivity in psy-chotic disorders has shown changes in network measures, such as increased characteristic path length and a loss of frontal lobe hub regions. Moreover, studies of the clustering coefficient (CC), a degree of neighborhood cohesiveness showing a stronger neighborhood specialization, appear increased, decreased, and unaltered CC in patients compared to control subjects. Moreover, diminished local efficiency (i.e., how well data circulates over the network) has been found within the (para)-limbic, frontal, and temporal regions, and in the putamen in patients with psychotic disorders compared to control subjects.

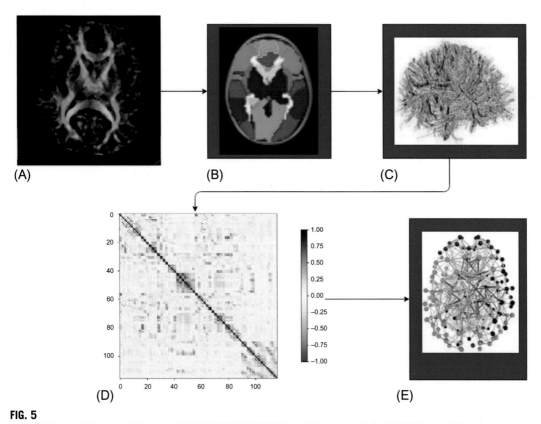

FIG. 5

(A) DTI data are estimated from raw DWI data. (B) 116 Subcortical and cortical brain regions are selected by the AAL atlas tool and coregistered to the DTI data. (C) Brain fiber tracts are estimated. (D) A symmetric 116×116 weighted connectivity matrix is calculated by obtaining the number of connections (WM tracts) between any two regions. (E) The graph is built and visualized by putting thresholds on a weighted connectivity matrix, where each region is considered as a node.

It has been observed that global efficiency (GE) decreases in the case of a mentally disordered patient compared to control subjects [22]. State-of-the-art research also showed reduced GE in patients with psychotic disorders compared to healthy subjects showing less efficient data circulation over the network in common. Hence, network efficiency is capable of providing proof regarding data circulation over the structural network, though clustering shows neighborhood specialization of a node.

For example, initially DTI data is estimated from raw DWI data (as shown in Fig. 5). Thereafter, 116 subcortical and cortical brain regions are selected by the AAL atlas tool and coregistered to the DTI data. Next, brain fiber tracts are estimated using the aforementioned different regions. Then, a symmetric 116×116 weighted connectivity matrix is calculated by obtaining the number of connections (WM tracts) between any two regions. Lastly, the graph is built and visualized by putting thresholds on the weighted connectivity matrix, where each region is considered as a node.

3.1 Application

For SZ, in brain areas there appeared to be critical differences in inconstancy. Changeability diminished in DMNs, such as hippocampus rectus, parahippocampus, temporal lobe (middle temporal pole and inferior temporal gurus), and inferior parietal gyrus, whereas it increased most noticeably in subcortical regions such as the pallidum, thalamus, visual cortex, and putamen. For autism patients, all areas showing noteworthy changes had higher changeability when compared to healthy controls, most essentially within the angular gyrus, rectus, frontal gyrus, superior medial, and medial orbital.

Specifically, the inconstancy of these default network regions was positively associated with the stereotyped, repetitive, and restricted patterns of behavior subscore. For attention deficit hyperactivity disorder (ADHD) patients, the DMN area, including the angular gyrus and posterior cingulate cortex, all appeared to have higher changeability. In contrast, brain areas within the subcortical network, that is, thalamus, appeared to have lower inconstancy in patients with ADHD compared to control subjects. Variability changes in frontal and posterior cingulate regions were related to the severity of ADHD symptoms.

4 Fusion analysis of fMRI and DTI

In this section, the fusion of DTI and fMRI is discussed, which consists of several stages right from the preprocessing phase to the application phase (as shown in Fig. 6). Here, we elaborate only the fusion of the connectivity part, which is crucial in the case of various mental disorders. Moreover, in a later section, different classification techniques, namely SVM, artificial neural network, convolutional neural network, etc., are discussed broadly.

As more and more literature studies have revealed an intimate relationship between WM structures and GM functions, a variety of studies have attempted to combine DTI and fMRI for joint modeling and analysis. Two modalities are integrated with similarly significant positions in the fusion operation, and each facilitates or validates the other. While this integration must be carried out

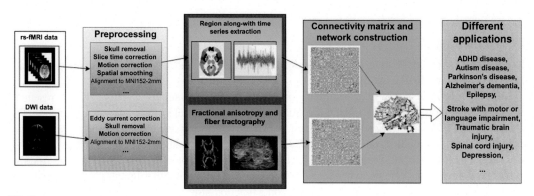

FIG. 6

Fusion of fMRI and DTI along with different preprocessing step.

very closely with regard to the extent and techniques implemented during the combination, these techniques of joint analysis and modeling have demonstrated their supremacy and promise.

When using fMRI and DTI for joint analysis, the outcome of analyzing distinctive modalities will be inferred independently and then combined to perform statistical analysis, such as linear regression, or more complicated models, such as Pearson's correlation coefficient and t-testing. For example, Goble et al. [23] identified clusters (voxels) that show the important age-related difference in functional activation and computed mean FA as well as the respective WM regions' mean percent signal change (PSC). At that point, both Pearson's correlation and the two-sample t-test between mean FA and PSC were conducted. To look at the relationship between structural measure of language lateralization and arcuate fasciculus (AF), Propper et al. [24] calculated the correlation of the laterality indices between DTI measurements and fMRI activations, including AF length and AF volume.

A more sophisticated strategy involves using advanced models to ponder or compare the association between function and structure in a high-order manner, for example, analysis at the network level. To look at the link between the DMN and its fundamental WM microstructure, Teipel et al. [25] implemented two approaches. The primary strategy is a multivariate analysis of variance based on PCA to consider the interactions between FC and MD/FA. DTI and fMRI information were merged in the second approach, and a joint ICA was used from two modalities on the mixed data matrix. Honey et al. [26] adopted a similar strategy to conduct a network-scale joint analysis of structure and function. They parceled the cortex into various subregions [27] that were regarded as nodes on the basis of which the networks of FC and structural connectivity were built. Hypothetical features of the network and dependence between functional and structural networks were explored at that stage.

Joint modeling differs from the aforementioned joint analysis in which fMRI and DTI data are processed separately and then coordinated for statistical analysis together, and joint modeling means that fMRI and DTI data are first formulated, reorganized, and incorporated as a predominant hybrid model compared to using either of these two modalities alone. Bowman et al. [28] developed a novel strategy called anatomically weighted FC to redefine FC by introducing a new metric of distance to characterize FC similarities. Calamante et al. [29] suggested merging fMRI and DTI in a novel manner. The FC and fiber tracking data were combined in this approach to create an entirely new track-weighted FC map. The vital idea is to relate the FC data to the fiber tracts and propagate further to all the voxels that pass through.

4.1 Applications

Here, two types of application namely cognitive neuroscience and clinical neuroscience for joint analysis of DTI and fMRI, are discussed.

Cognitive neuroscience: In a multitude of research, such as aging-related cognition research, integration of DTI and fMRI has played essential roles within the field of cognitive neuroscience. For instance, Ystad et al. [30] efficiently combined rs-fMRI with neuropsychological tests to examine the relationship between modifications in cortical/subcortical fiber tracts and cognitive decreases in aging. ICA's ROIs include subcortical and cortical parts used to extricate the related fiber tracts. The findings encourage a significant correlation between the integrity (FA) of a few fiber bundles and the cognitive measures. Fling et al. [31] examined the motor region's function-structure relationship in young and older adults. The author used structural measures (longitudinal diffusivity, radial diffusivity, mean diffusivity, and fractional anisotropy) and FC of the primary motor cortices (M1) utilizing a motor area template.

The statistical analysis showed that stronger FC between M1 areas is followed by reduced structural connectivity and motor performance in older adults, but not younger ones.

Clinical neuroscience: Commonly, there are at least two reasons for combining fMRI and DTI data with clinical applications. To begin with, the WM structures are significantly deformed or changed for those patients who have lesions such as traumatic damage or tumor. This makes selecting a required ROI from which fiber tractography begins hard and sometimes impossible.

FMRI becomes an additional option to anchor the seed points [32] due to the lack of viable anatomical landmarks. Some clinical studies, including AD/MCI, SZ, autism, mild traumatic brain injury, temporal lobe epilepsy, and posttraumatic stress disorder, have been done using fusion fMRI and DTI modalities.

5 Classification and prediction methods and scope
5.1 Traditional classifiers

In the past few decades, several machine learning-based classifiers have been utilized for the detection of brain disorders. Among different traditional classifiers, SVM [33] is one of the most popular techniques. SVM is a sort of supervised learning classifier, which is based on the concept of finding the optimally separating hyperplane. SVM has several variants with different kernel functions, including the sigmoid kernel, Gaussian RBF kernel, and polynomial kernel, which makes SVM as a nonlinear classifier. As SVM takes features as input, the feature extractor along with several hyperparameters of SVM plays a pivotal role in overall classification/detection accuracy.

Linear discriminant analysis (LDA) could be a generalization of Fisher's linear discriminant and is based on the concept of looking for a linear combination of features that partition two groups. For reducing the overall computational costs and avoiding the overfitting problem, LDA projects data into lower-dimensional space. There exists several other traditional classifiers, namely decision tree, random forest, K-nearest neighbor, etc., which can also be used for performing mental disease classification.

5.2 Deep learning classifiers

In these days, deep learning (DL) has shown favorable results in computer vision and other subdomains. Thus DL strategies have expanded in various areas that have been applied to the classification of brain diseases [34–36]. In contrast to conventional machine learning strategies, DL methods are competent for learning optimal representation straightforwardly from raw data by employing various leveled structures with different levels of complexity. DL strategies consist of several layers with nonlinear functions, which transform input features into high-level abstract features. In other words, in DL, initially, local features have been learned; however, DL can also learn global or abstract features, which further help with classification. There are several DL approaches that can be employed for mental disease classification.

6 Future directions and challenges

This section highlights several challenges in fMRI, DTI, and DL-based approaches for classification. In addition, different future directions are also elucidated for further research.

6.1 Challenges

The fundamental challenges are

- It is worth noting that several measurements for fMRI and DTI data may reflect different connectivities.
- Several preprocessing methods could also affect the resulting structural connectivity and FC strengths, which further affect the overall disease classification result.
- Data can be modified by different DL methods, including encoder-decoder and generative adversarial networks (GANs).

Several critical challenges in DL-based classification are

- During training, it needs a huge amount of computational resources and time due to a large number of parameters in the model.
- Hyperparameter tuning is also a time-consuming process. Initially, we do not know for which values of hyperparameters our model would perform best; hence, we tune parameters again and again.
- Overfitting is also a critical issue in DL methods, which happens when we have fewer data. In the case of DTI and fMRI, normally we have fewer data with a higher feature dimension; hence, this is a candidate for overfitting.
- Interpretability of upshots from the DL method is also challenging in the case of disease classification. In other words, obtaining useful information regarding neurofunctional and neuroanatomical alteration is not easy by utilizing DL-based classifiers.

6.2 Trends and future directions

The different future trends are:

- Structural connectivity and FC can be learned by state-of-the-art DL approaches.
- Structural connectivity and FC can be fused by several powerful conventional neural network-based methods.
- We know that for classification tasks, using DL requires a huge amount of data. However, in the case, disease classification, we do not have that much data. This data scarcity can be solved by performing augmentation on the data.
- Transfer learning can be utilized in a better way to overcome the data scarcity problem.
- A few encoder-decoder-based approaches can be used for solving the overfitting problem in the case of DL-based classifiers.
- A GANs can also be utilized for generating more and more data.

7 Conclusions and important findings

Neuroimaging provides objective information on the structure and function of the brain. Computed tomography and MRI are the fundamental standards in neurological and neuropsychiatric disorders. The foremost common strategy of fMRI takes advantage of the fact that when neurons within the brain become active, the amount of blood flowing through that region is increased. The signal measured in fMRI depends on this alteration in oxygenation and is alluded to as BOLD. However, DTI can detect the diffusion characteristics in each voxel; a natural expansion is to assess the diffusion relationship between adjacent voxels and ultimately collect the entire WM fiber pathways within the brain.

Therefore, efforts were made in this chapter to review MRI nuts and bolts, including quantitative methods used to assess brain structure integrity. MRI methods for assessing network connectivity of the brain using DTI and fMRI were discussed in conjunction with the joint analysis of both. Next, traditional and DL-based classifiers were discussed, which can be used for the classification of several mental diseases.

References

[1] V.D. Calhoun, R. Miller, G. Pearlson, T. Adalı, The chronnectome: time-varying connectivity networks as the next frontier in fMRI data discovery, Neuron 84 (2) (2014) 262–274.

[2] V.D. Calhoun, N de Lacy, Ten key observations on the analysis of resting-state functional MR imaging data using independent component analysis, Neuroimaging Clin. 27 (4) (2017) 561–579.

[3] B. Thirion, G. Varoquaux, E. Dohmatob, J.-B. Poline, Which fMRI clustering gives good brain parcellations? Front. Neurosci. 8 (2014) 167.

[4] M.F. Glasser, T.S. Coalson, E.C. Robinson, C.D. Hacker, J. Harwell, E. Yacoub, K. Ugurbil, J. Andersson, C.F. Beckmann, M. Jenkinson, A multi-modal parcellation of human cerebral cortex, Nature 536 (7615) (2016) 171.

[5] B. Jie, D. Zhang, W. Gao, Q. Wang, C.-Y. Wee, D. Shen, Integration of network topological and connectivity properties for neuroimaging classification, IEEE Trans. Biomed. Eng. 61 (2) (2013) 576–589.

[6] F.T. Sun, L.M. Miller, M. D'Esposito, Measuring interregional functional connectivity using coherence and partial coherence analyses of fMRI data, NeuroImage 21 (2) (2004) 647–658.

[7] F. Skidmore, D. Korenkevych, Y. Liu, G. He, E. Bullmore, P.M. Pardalos, Connectivity brain networks based on wavelet correlation analysis in Parkinson fMRI data, Neurosci. Lett. 499 (1) (2011) 47–51.

[8] Y. Du, Y. Fan, Group information guided ICA for fMRI data analysis, NeuroImage 69 (2013) 157–197.

[9] M. Van Den Heuvel, R. Mandl, H.H. Pol, Normalized cut group clustering of resting-state FMRI data, PLoS ONE 3 (4) (2008) e2001.

[10] A.G. Garrity, G.D. Pearlson, K. McKiernan, D. Lloyd, K.A. Kiehl, V.D. Calhoun, Aberrant "default mode" functional connectivity in schizophrenia, Am. J. Psychiatry 164 (3) (2007) 450–457.

[11] E.A. Allen, E.B. Erhardt, E. Damaraju, W. Gruner, J.M. Segall, R.F. Silva, M. Havlicek, S. Rachakonda, J. Fries, R. Kalyanam, A baseline for the multivariate comparison of resting-state networks, Front. Syst. Neurosci. 5 (2011) 2.

[12] C. Chang, G.H. Glover, Time-frequency dynamics of resting-state brain connectivity measured with fMRI, NeuroImage 50 (1) (2010) 81–98.

[13] Ü. Sakoğlu, G.D. Pearlson, K.A. Kiehl, Y.M. Wang, A.M. Michael, V.D. Calhoun, A method for evaluating dynamic functional network connectivity and task-modulation: application to schizophrenia, Magn. Reson. Mater. Phys. Biol. Med. 23 (5–6) (2010) 351–366.

[14] A. Zalesky, A. Fornito, L. Cocchi, L.L. Gollo, M. Breakspear, Time-resolved resting-state brain networks, Proc. Natl Acad. Sci. USA 111 (28) (2014) 10341–10346.

[15] S. Sadaghiani, J.-B. Poline, A. Kleinschmidt, M. D'Esposito, Ongoing dynamics in large-scale functional connectivity predict perception, Proc. Natl Acad. Sci. USA 112 (27) (2015) 8463–8468.

[16] T.O. Laumann, A.Z. Snyder, A. Mitra, E.M. Gordon, C. Gratton, B. Adeyemo, A.W. Gilmore, S.M. Nelson, J. J. Berg, D.J. Greene, On the stability of BOLD fMRI correlations, Cereb. Cortex 27 (10) (2016) 4719–4732.

[17] X. Chen, H. Zhang, Y. Gao, C.-Y. Wee, G. Li, D. Shen, Alzheimer's Disease Neuroimaging Initiative, High-order resting-state functional connectivity network for MCI classification, Hum. Brain Map. 37 (9) (2016) 3282–3296.

[18] M.G. Preti, T.A.W. Bolton, D. Van De Ville, The dynamic functional connectome: state-of-the-art and perspectives, NeuroImage 160 (2017) 41–54.

[19] R.M. Hutchison, T. Womelsdorf, J.S. Gati, S. Everling, R.S. Menon, Resting-state networks show dynamic functional connectivity in awake humans and anesthetized macaques, Hum. Brain Map. 34 (9) (2013) 2154–2177.

[20] E. Damaraju, E.A. Allen, A. Belger, J.M. Ford, S. McEwen, D.H. Mathalon, B.A. Mueller, G.D. Pearlson, S.G. Potkin, A. Preda, Dynamic functional connectivity analysis reveals transient states of dysconnectivity in schizophrenia, NeuroImage Clin. 5 (2014) 298–308.

[21] S.B. Laughlin, T.J. Sejnowski, Communication in neuronal networks, Science 301 (5641) (2003) 1870–1874.

[22] Q. Wang, T.-P. Su, Y. Zhou, K.-H. Chou, I.-Y. Chen, T. Jiang, C.-P. Lin, Anatomical insights into disrupted small-world networks in schizophrenia, NeuroImage 59 (2) (2012) 1085–1093.

[23] D.J. Goble, J.P. Coxon, A. Van Impe, M. Geurts, W. Van Hecke, S. Sunaert, N. Wenderoth, S. P. Swinnen, The neural basis of central proprioceptive processing in older versus younger adults: an important sensory role for right putamen, Hum. Brain Map. 33 (4) (2012) 895–908.

[24] R.E. Propper, L.J. O'Donnell, S. Whalen, Y. Tie, I.H. Norton, R.O. Suarez, L. Zollei, A. Radmanesh, A. J. Golby, A combined fMRI and DTI examination of functional language lateralization and arcuate fasciculus structure: effects of degree versus direction of hand preference, Brain Cogn. 73 (2) (2010) 85–92.

[25] S.J. Teipel, A.L.W. Bokde, T. Meindl, E. Amaro Jr, J. Soldner, M.F. Reiser, S.C. Herpertz, H.-J. Möller, H. Hampel, White matter microstructure underlying default mode network connectivity in the human brain, NeuroImage 49 (3) (2010) 2021–2032.

[26] C.J. Honey, O. Sporns, L. Cammoun, X. Gigandet, J.-P. Thiran, R. Meuli, P. Hagmann, Predicting human resting-state functional connectivity from structural connectivity, Proc. Natl Acad. Sci. USA 106 (6) (2009) 2035–2040.

[27] B. Fischl, A. Van Der Kouwe, C. Destrieux, E. Halgren, F. Ségonne, D.H. Salat, E. Busa, L. J. Seidman, J. Goldstein, D. Kennedy, Automatically parcellating the human cerebral cortex, Cereb. Cortex 14 (1) (2004) 11–22.

[28] F.D. Bowman, L. Zhang, G. Derado, S. Chen, Determining functional connectivity using fMRI data with diffusion-based anatomical weighting, NeuroImage 62 (3) (2012) 1769–1779.

[29] F. Calamante, R.A.J. Masterton, J.-D. Tournier, R.E. Smith, L. Willats, D. Raffelt, A. Connelly, Track-weighted functional connectivity (TW-FC): a tool for characterizing the structural-functional connections in the brain, NeuroImage 70 (2013) 199–210.

[30] M. Ystad, E. Hodneland, S. Adolfsdottir, J. Haász, A.J. Lundervold, T. Eichele, A. Lundervold, Cortico-striatal connectivity and cognition in normal aging: a combined DTI and resting state fMRI study, NeuroImage 55 (1) (2011) 24–31.

[31] B.W. Fling, Y. Kwak, S.J. Peltier, R.D. Seidler, Differential relationships between transcallosal structural and functional connectivity in young and older adults, Neurobiol. Aging 33 (10) (2012) 2521–2526.

[32] R. Kleiser, P. Staempfli, A. Valavanis, P. Boesiger, S. Kollias, Impact of fMRI-guided advanced DTI fiber tracking techniques on their clinical applications in patients with brain tumors, Neuroradiology 52 (1) (2010) 37.

[33] A. Lord, D. Horn, M. Breakspear, M. Walter, Changes in community structure of resting state functional connectivity in unipolar depression, PLoS ONE 7 (8) (2012) e41282.

[34] S.M. Plis, D.R. Hjelm, R. Salakhutdinov, E.A. Allen, H.J. Bockholt, J.D. Long, H.J. Johnson, J.S. Paulsen, J. A. Turner, V.D. Calhoun, Deep learning for neuroimaging: a validation study, Front. Neurosci. 8 (2014) 229.

[35] T. Iidaka, Resting state functional magnetic resonance imaging and neural network classified autism and control, Cortex 63 (2015) 55–67.

[36] R. Ju, C. Hu, P. Zhou, Q. Li, Early diagnosis of Alzheimer's disease based on resting-state brain networks and deep learning, IEEE/ACM Trans. Comput. Biol. Bioinform. 16 (1) (2019) 244–257.

Homomorphic transform-based dual image watermarking using IWT-SVD for secure e-healthcare applications

Priyank Khare and Vinay Kumar Srivastava

Department of Electronics & Communication Engineering, MNNIT Allahabad, Prayagraj, Uttar Pradesh, India

1 Introduction

Currently, the vast advancement of internet technologies facilitates the transfer of multimedia information such as images and video in a convenient manner. However, these technologies are simultaneously prone to various challenges such as maintaining confidentiality, integrity, and security of multimedia data, especially in medical applications, where significant patient information is being transmitted between different hospitals over digital channels. Therefore there arises a prime requirement for the protection of patient record (PR) data from tampering, which may lead to incorrect diagnosis. Medical image watermarking is the current solution to this problem, which maintains integrity and confidentiality of vital medical information. In the watermarking technique, a watermark image bearing significant information is embedded inside the host image such that vital information remains secure [1–5]. A similar approach is also utilized in medical image watermarking in which multiple watermarks are embedded inside a host medical image, which is further transmitted for several e-healthcare applications.

The main merit of multiple image watermarking is that even if one watermark is tampered with due to unintentional reasons, other watermarks can be efficiently used to deliver vital information. Thus application of multiple watermarking to medical images provides secure transmission of PRs among various e-healthcare agencies providing appropriate healthcare diagnosis in an efficient manner [6–9]. Image watermarking is performed in two domains: spatial and transform domains. The image pixel values are modified for embedding the watermark in the spatial domain [10–12], whereas in the transform domain [13–15] the watermark is embedded by altering the transform coefficients. Out of these two methods, the transform domain approach is extensively preferred as it offers good resilience against attacks. For enhancing the effectiveness of medical image watermarking techniques, several hybrid transform domain techniques are used, such as discrete cosine transform (DCT), discrete wavelet transform (DWT), and single value decomposition (SVD), which remarkably improve robustness and imperceptibility [16–24].

In [25] a dual image watermarking approach using nonsubsampled contourlet transform (NSCT), redundant discrete wavelet transform (RDWT), SVD, and Arnold transform (AT) is reported. A set partitioning in hierarchical tree (SPIHT) algorithm is employed for obtaining the compressed

Intelligent Data Security Solutions for e-Health Applications. https://doi.org/10.1016/B978-0-12-819511-6.00005-4

91

watermarked image. The authors claim that their developed scheme attains high capacity and robustness. Another similar technique is also investigated in [26] where NSCT-RDWT-SVD is again used to embed two image watermarks along with a lightweight encryption technique, which provides extra security to the watermarked image with a lower complexity. This approach is also tested for different wavelet families. Singh [27] suggested an approach that uses lifting wavelet transform (LWT)-DCT. In this method, two watermarks, which comprise a signature and PR, are concurrently embedded inside the colored host image. An encryption technique is also used for both the watermarks, which ensures confidentiality of information. NSCT-RDWT-SVD-based dual image watermarking is investigated in [28] where the host image is subsampled into four images, and out of these the image with maximum entropy is chosen for further transformation. Likewise, both image and encrypted text watermarks are also transformed with NSCT-RDWT-SVD. Encrypting a text watermark with AT increases the security of the scheme. Finally, singular values (SVs) of host image are modified with watermarks SVs to obtain the watermarked image. Another similar technique is developed in [29] where three image watermarks are concealed inside a cover image through fusion of NSCT-DCT-multiresolution SVD transforms. The authors claim that their developed scheme has better robustness against geometrical attacks.

Nonblind image watermarking is established in [30] where patient information is obscured inside a medical cover image using NSCT-DCT-SVD transforms. A fragile watermarking technique is developed in [31] for healthcare purposes, which provides authentication to medical images against tampering. It appears that the developed scheme shows excellent resilience toward malicious tampering attacks. Elhoseny et al. [32] proposed an efficient healthcare system using Rivest-Shamir-Adleman (RSA) and Advanced Encryption Standard (AES) encryption techniques along with DWT. Confidential diagnostic medical data are encrypted with these encryption algorithms and further embedded either in first-level or second-level wavelet coefficients (WCs) of the cover image. Thus this developed scheme provides a secure mechanism for transferring medical data. A secured watermarking technique using chaotic encryption is reported in [33] where an electronic patient record (EPR) is embedded inside a host medical image by using DWT-DCT-SVD. Chaotic encryption is used for encrypting the watermarked image so that the medical watermark image retains its key information.

A multiple watermarking scheme using DWT-SVD is discussed in [34] where image and text watermarks are inserted within the medical image of an eye. Initially, the region of interest (ROI) of an eye image is evaluated, which contains the iris, and over this ROI portion a secure hash algorithm is applied to develop a hash key that is used to strengthen the security of the algorithm. Text and image watermarks are embedded inside the region of noninterest (RONI) portion of the eye image. Singh et al. [35] established a watermarking technique where text and image watermarks are concealed inside the host image. This approach uses a DWT-DCT-SVD combination for embedding, where the image watermark is embedded inside the LL sub-band of the first-level DWT, while the text watermark is embedded in the HH sub-band of the second-level DWT of the host image. An ASCII encryption technique is used for encrypting the text watermark. Thakkar et al. [36] developed a secure watermarking technique where the ROI of the host medical image is evaluated, which is further processed with DWT. Moreover, the LL sub-band of the ROI portion is processed with block SVD operation. Logo image and EPR data are embedded inside these left singular matrices of the host image. Various error correcting codes are used for EPR data, which result in a reduced bit error rate (BER). A semiblind watermarking approach that uses DWT-DCT-SVD is suggested by Srivastava et al. [37], where the middle frequency sub-band is used for watermark embedding. A trigonometric function is utilized for embedding watermark SVs into the cover image. Zear et al. [38] developed a watermarking methodology that is quite helpful in the e-healthcare area. In this process a cover medical image is processed with third-level DWT, then DCT and SVD. The image watermark is processed with AT-DCT-SVD, whereas two text watermarks are used that contain key details regarding the patient, which are encrypted with encoding algorithms such as hamming encoding and arithmetic coding. A watermarked image is attained by embedding three watermarks simultaneously into the host image. Back propagation neural network (BPNN) is employed to make the technique robust against several attacks.

Kannammal et al. [39] suggested watermarking using a nontensor wavelet transform, where a medical watermark image is concealed in the LH sub-band of the host image. Afterward, various encryption techniques such as RSA, AES, and rivest cipher 4 are applied on the watermarked image. Hence, double layer security is provided to the watermarked image. Sharma et al. [40] established secure medical image watermarking for the embedding of multiple watermarks using DWT-DCT. Multiple watermarks use various encryption algorithms for security such as the EPR watermark, which uses message-digest 5, while image watermark uses the RSA algorithm. Hamming codes are also employed on the EPR watermark to obtain a reduced BER. DWT-Schur firefly-optimized multiple watermarking is specified in [41] where various watermarks are embedded inside the RONI of the host medical image. A firefly-optimized algorithm is used to choose the DWT coefficient in which embedding can be performed. Robust image watermarking using DWT is reported in [42] where embedding is performed in significant WCs of LH_2 and LH_3 sub-bands of the host image using the SPIHT algorithm. The noise visibility function is also used to reduce the distortion among WCs for increasing robustness of the technique. So, all the related research and contributions can motivate us to propose a new dual image watermarking algorithm in telemedicine that can protect the integrity of medical data from infringement and help to provide the correct diagnosis for patients with a reduced probability of error.

The layout of the rest of the chapter is as follows. Section 2 emphasizes significant features of the proposed medical image watermarking technique. The basic terminology concerning homomorphic transform (HT), integer wavelet transform (IWT), SVD, and AT is described in Section 3, whereas a proposed watermarking approach is elaborated in Section 4. Analyses of simulation results are illustrated in Section 5, while Section 6 provides a brief conclusion to the chapter.

2 Significant features of the proposed technique

In this work, a novel medical image watermarking technique for e-health applications is proposed, which efficiently uses a combination of HT, IWT, SVD along with AT. In this proposed approach, HT of a host medical image is performed, which results in illumination and reflectance components. A reflectance component is preferred for watermark embedding as this component varies rapidly because of the increase in perceptual invisibility making it difficult to perceive the watermark. Vital attributes of the image are embedded in the watermark of this component, which can resist attacks more efficiently. Furthermore, first-level IWT is applied to the reflectance component, which results in various sub-bands. IWT is preferred over conventional wavelet transform as it offers reduced computational complexity due to direct integer-to-integer mapping.

Two image watermarks are used in the proposed technique where the first image watermark (FIW) is an image, whereas the second image watermark (SIW) is an AT-encrypted PR watermark, which comprises vital patient information. The LL sub-band of the host medical image is used to embed the image watermark, whereas the LH sub-band is chosen for embedding the PR watermark. LL and LH sub-bands are selected for embedding of the watermarks because they ensure robustness and imperceptibility simultaneously. Efficacy of the proposed technique is examined under various attacks with different sets of medical images. Thus salient contributions of the proposed technique are as follows:

- Fusion of various transforms utilized in the proposed technique makes it an effective watermarking algorithm as security, robustness, and imperceptibility are enhanced concurrently.
- The PR watermark is made secure by scrambling it through AT so that only authenticated persons are able to decrypt it. Thus the PR watermark cannot be tampered with or manipulated, which guarantees appropriate health treatment.
- Dual embedding of watermarks inside a host medical image ensures that confidentiality of vital data remains intact. This minimizes the risk of tampering and provides secure transmission of medical information.
- Incorporating SVD into the proposed algorithm increases robustness but possesses the problem of false-positive detection. This problem can be resolved by using a shuffled SVD [43].
- Another merit of the proposed dual image watermarking technique is that it leads to transmission bandwidth reduction.

3 Basic terminologies

A brief description of HT, IWT, SVD and AT is highlighted in this section.

3.1 Homomorphic transform

An image $m(s_1,s_2)$ is assumed to be the product of illumination $i(s_1,s_2)$ and reflectance $r(s_1,s_2)$ components [44–46]:

$$m(s_1, s_2) = i(s_1, s_2)r(s_1, s_2) \tag{1}$$

where (s_1,s_2) in Eq. (1) signifies spatial coordinates of the image.

Two components in Eq. (1) are made separable by applying a logarithm:

$$\ln(m(s_1, s_2)) = \ln(i(s_1, s_2)) + \ln(r(s_1, s_2)) \tag{2}$$

Afterward, frequency domain transformation of Eq. (2) is performed:

$$M(u, v) = M_i(u, v) + M_r(u, v) \tag{3}$$

$M(u,v)$ obtained in Eq. (3) is subjected to a high-pass filter (HPF) $H(u,v)$:

$$F(u, v) = M_i(u, v)H(u, v) + M_r(u, v)H(u, v) \tag{4}$$

The output obtained from the HPF is further processed by inverse frequency transformation and inverse logarithmic operation, which leads to the generation of a reflectance component. The main motive of the proposed approach is to attain robustness and imperceptibility by embedding two watermarks concurrently. Therefore we have selected a reflectance component that possesses important features of the image to achieve better immunity against attacks, whereas its lower energy enhances perceptual invisibility for the human visual system.

3.2 Integer wavelet transform

Sweldens [47] introduced the idea of LWT. The conventional wavelet transform is frequently used in numerous image processing applications such as image watermarking and image compression by assuming input image pixel values to be floating point. It is observed that when integers are available as input the conventional wavelet transform does not produce better results. So, there arises the need for a transform that can conveniently perform integer-to-integer mapping directly. Thus rounding errors are completely eliminated by using IWT [48–50]. Use of IWT provides perfect reconstruction without changing from floating to integer or integer to floating. IWT decomposition primarily comprises three stages: split, predict, and update. In the split stage the original signal is split into odd and even samples, while in the prediction stage new odd samples are estimated from original even samples. In the update stage, an update operator is used, which estimates new even samples with the help of original even samples and the predictor stage output. Various stages of IWT decomposition are depicted in Fig. 1 where $P[.]$ is the predictor operator and $U[.]$ is the update operator. Due to these attributes, IWT is preferred over conventional wavelet transform.

3.3 Singular value decomposition

In image watermarking techniques, SVD is widely used because of its significant merits. In this decomposition a real matrix Q is decomposed into three matrices U, Σ, and V, where U and V are orthogonal matrices denoting left and right singular vectors [51–54]. Σ is a diagonal matrix comprising nonzero SVs arranged in a descending manner. Since SVs are invariant toward slight alterations performed in the image, they offer excellent resilience against geometric attacks:

$$Q = U \Sigma V^T \tag{5}$$

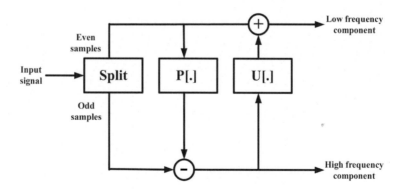

FIG. 1

Schematic of integer wavelet transform decomposition.

3.4 Arnold transform

Medical images that hold important information need to be preserved from unethical tampering that can result in inappropriate diagnosis of the patient. Thus security of these images should be ensured, which can be attained by encrypting these images before transmission over the channel. AT is one of the techniques that can be used for scrambling pixel values of images [55–57]. Due to the scrambling of images, security of the technique is increased because an attacker will not be able to decrypt the correct information. Eq. (6) represents the Arnold transformation of the K-order image:

$$\begin{pmatrix} m_1' \\ m_2' \end{pmatrix} = \begin{pmatrix} 1 & 1 \\ 1 & 2 \end{pmatrix} \begin{pmatrix} m_1 \\ m_2 \end{pmatrix} (\bmod K) \tag{6}$$

Here, $\begin{pmatrix} m_1' \\ m_2' \end{pmatrix}$ represents transformed pixel coordinates of the image from original coordinates $\begin{pmatrix} m_1 \\ m_2 \end{pmatrix}$ after applying AT.

4 Proposed watermarking technique

In this section a proposed watermarking algorithm is elaborated. This proposed watermarking technique constitutes two vital processes: embedding of a watermark and its extraction from an attacked watermarked image. In an embedding algorithm, two image watermarks are concurrently embedded inside the host image. A combination of HT, IWT, SVD along with AT is efficiently used in this proposed technique. To provide confidentiality to a PR watermark, it is scrambled with AT. The selection of a reflectance component ensures that perceptual invisibility and robustness are attained together. A flow diagram for the proposed embedding and extraction algorithms is shown in Fig. 2A and B.

4.1 Embedding process

- Host medical image M is transformed with HT resulting in illumination M_I and reflectance M_R components.
- First-level IWT is applied to the M_R matrix, which yields frequency sub-bands M_{RLL}, M_{RHL}, M_{RLH}, and M_{RHH}.
- SVs of the LL and LH sub-bands are attained by performing SVD:

$$M_{RLL} = U_{RLL} \sum\nolimits_{RLL} V_{RLL}{}^T \tag{7}$$

$$M_{RLH} = U_{RLH} \sum\nolimits_{RLH} V_{RLH}{}^T \tag{8}$$

- First-level IWT of FIW is performed and SVs of the LL sub-band are obtained using SVD as $\sum_{FIW}$:

$$W_{FIW} = U_{FIW} \sum\nolimits_{FIW} V_{FIW}{}^T \tag{9}$$

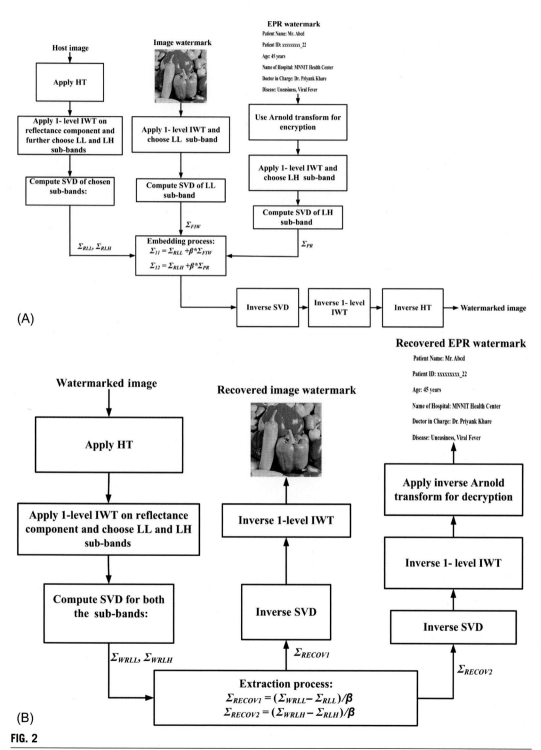

FIG. 2

Flow diagram of the proposed (A) embedding process and (B) extraction process.

- For protecting the integrity of the PR watermark, it is encrypted with AT. Moreover, the first-level IWT of the scrambled PR image watermark is performed and the LH sub-band is selected whose SVs $\sum_{PR}$ are computed:

$$W_{PR} = U_{PR}\sum\nolimits_{PR}V_{PR}{}^{T} \tag{10}$$

- In this step, the SVs of both image watermarks are embedded inside the host medical image:

$$\sum\nolimits_{11} = \sum\nolimits_{RLL} + \beta*\sum\nolimits_{FIW} \tag{11}$$

$$\sum\nolimits_{12} = \sum\nolimits_{RLH} + \beta*\sum\nolimits_{PR} \tag{12}$$

Here, β is a scaling factor whose value is chosen as 0.01.

- Serially, inverse transformations of SVD, IWT, and HT are performed for generating the watermarked image M_W.

4.2 Extraction process

- The watermarked image M_W is transformed with HT resulting in M_{WI} as the illumination component, whereas the reflectance component is denoted by M_{WR}.
- The M_{WR} component is processed with first-level IWT resulting in several frequency sub-bands as: M_{WRLL}, M_{WRHL}, M_{WRLH}, and M_{WRHH}.
- Furthermore, the SVD of the M_{WRLL} and M_{WRLH} sub-bands is computed as:

$$M_{WRLL} = U_{WRLL}\sum\nolimits_{WRLL}V_{WRLL}{}^{T} \tag{13}$$

$$M_{WRLH} = U_{WRLH}\sum\nolimits_{WRLH}V_{WRLH}{}^{T} \tag{14}$$

- For retrieval of the image and PR watermarks, the SVD coefficients are altered as:

$$\sum\nolimits_{Recov1} = \left(\sum\nolimits_{WRLL} - \sum\nolimits_{RLL}\right)/\beta \tag{15}$$

$$\sum\nolimits_{Recov2} = \left(\sum\nolimits_{WRLH} - \sum\nolimits_{RLH}\right)/\beta \tag{16}$$

- The inverse SVD of $\sum_{Recov1}$ and $\sum_{Recov2}$ is computed for achieving altered IWT coefficients for both the watermarks. The inverse IWT is computed for extracting the image watermark, whereas the sequentially inverse IWT and AT are computed for the recovery of the PR watermark.

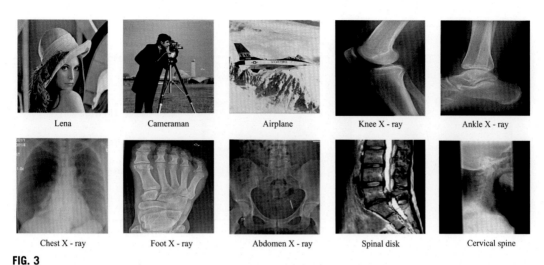

FIG. 3

Various host images used in the proposed technique.

5 Simulation results

The proposed watermarking technique is tested with standard benchmark [58] and medical images of size 512×512. "Peppers" [58] of dimension 512×512 is used as the first image watermark, whereas PR data are taken as the second image watermark of size 512×512. Medical images used in our simulation analysis are chosen from [59–65]. The simulation results for the proposed algorithm are computed using MATLAB software. Several host images used in the proposed algorithm are presented in Fig. 3, while the two image watermarks used are depicted in Fig. 4. The watermarked image and recovered watermarks are shown in Fig. 5. Moreover, we have computed several performance metrics

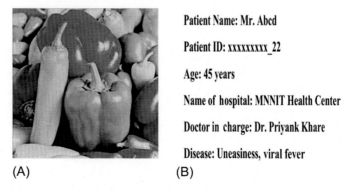

(A)   (B)

FIG. 4

Two watermarks used in our proposed scheme. (A) Peppers image. (B) PR data.

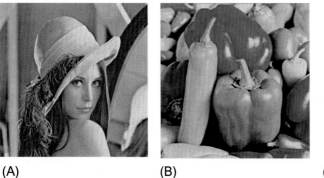

Patient Name: Mr. Abcd

Patient ID: xxxxxxxxx_22

Age: 45 years

Name of Hospital: MNNIT Health Center

Doctor in charge: Dr. Priyank Khare

Disease: Uneasiness, viral fever

(A)   (B)   (C)

FIG. 5

(A) Watermarked image. (B) Recovered image watermark. (C) Recovered PR watermark.

Table 1 Different performance parameters for the proposed technique.

Image	SSIM	PSNR (dB)	NC	BER
Lena	0.9946	46.6808	0.9998	0.0088
Knee X-ray	0.9954	46.6182	0.9999	0.0088
Ankle X-ray	0.9959	46.4052	0.9999	0.0086
Chest X-ray	0.9940	47.1455	1.00	0.0085
Foot X-ray	0.9968	45.5580	0.9999	0.0086
Abdomen X-ray	0.9965	45.1269	0.9999	0.0086
Spinal disk	0.9964	46.4748	0.9995	0.0092
Cervical spine	0.9928	47.0063	0.9993	0.0192
Cameraman	0.9983	46.5672	1.00	0.0085
Airplane	0.9973	46.5223	1.00	0.0086

BER, *bit error rate;* NC, *normalized correlation;* PSNR, *peak signal-to-noise ratio;* SSIM, *structural similarity index.*

such as structural similarity index (SSIM) [66], peak signal-to-noise ratio (PSNR) [67], BER [67], and normalized correlation (NC) [68]. Robustness is evaluated with the help of NC and BER, while imperceptibility is evaluated using PSNR and SSIM. Table 1 depicts various performance metrics for the proposed algorithm. NC is evaluated for the image watermark, while BER is calculated for the PR watermark. The average value of PSNR is above 46 dB, whereas SSIM and NC values are close to unity as tabulated in Table 1. Hence, Table 1 clearly accounts for the effectiveness of the proposed technique.

In Table 2 several watermarked images under attack as well as the recovered watermarks for the developed technique are diagrammatically demonstrated, whereas graphical variation of NC and SSIM together are presented in Fig. 6. Table 3 tabulates robustness of the proposed technique in terms of NC and BER. The highest value of NC is found to be 1.00 for Sharpening attack, while the lowest BER of 0.0094 is achieved for JPEG compression (90) + Gaussian noise (0.01, 0.0001) attack for the Foot X-ray image. Thus the proposed scheme is robust toward different attacks.

Table 2 Watermarked images exposed to several attacks and corresponding extracted watermarks obtained.

Attacks	Watermarked image	Extracted image watermark	Extracted PR watermark
Gaussian noise (0, 0.0002)			Patient Name: Mr. Abcd Patient ID: xxxxxxxx_22 Age: 45 years Name of Hospital: MNNIT Health Center Doctor in Charge: Dr. Priyank Khare Disease: Uneasiness, Viral Fever
Salt and pepper noise (0.0005)			Patient Name: Mr. Abcd Patient ID: xxxxxxxx_22 Age: 45 years Name of Hospital: MNNIT Health Center Doctor in Charge: Dr. Priyank Khare Disease: Uneasiness, Viral Fever
Gamma correction (0.9)			Patient Name: Mr. Abcd Patient ID: xxxxxxxx_22 Age: 45 years Name of Hospital: MNNIT Health Center Doctor in Charge: Dr. Priyank Khare Disease: Uneasiness, Viral Fever
Scaling (2, 0.5)			Patient Name: Mr. Abcd Patient ID: xxxxxxxx_22 Age: 45 years Name of Hospital: MNNIT Health Center Doctor in Charge: Dr. Priyank Khare Disease: Uneasiness, Viral Fever
Sharpening			Patient Name: Mr. Abcd Patient ID: xxxxxxxx_22 Age: 45 years Name of Hospital: MNNIT Health Center Doctor in Charge: Dr. Priyank Khare Disease: Uneasiness, Viral Fever
Gaussian filter (3×3)			Patient Name: Mr. Abcd Patient ID: xxxxxxxx_22 Age: 45 years Name of Hospital: MNNIT Health Center Doctor in Charge: Dr. Priyank Khare Disease: Uneasiness, Viral Fever
JPEG compression (70)			Patient Name: Mr. Abcd Patient ID: xxxxxxxx_22 Age: 45 years Name of Hospital: MNNIT Health Center Doctor in Charge: Dr. Priyank Khare Disease: Uneasiness, Viral Fever

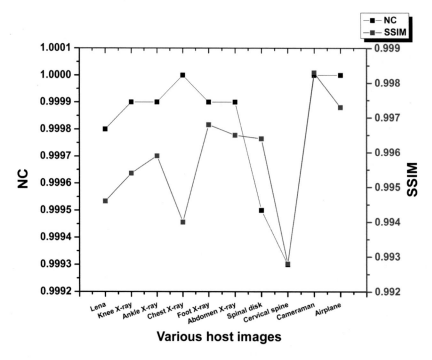

FIG. 6

Graphical analysis of normalized correlation and structural similarity index values for the proposed scheme.

Fig. 7A and B graphically depicts NC and SSIM values for several JPEG compression attacks applied to host images. In Fig. 7A, NC values are above 0.9 for all images although 0.9668 and 0.9687 are observed as the lowest NC values for Cervical spine and Spinal disk images for compression attack with a quality factor of 10. SSIM values shown in Fig. 7B are quite acceptable with the highest SSIM value of 0.9925 for the Lena image under $Q = 70$. Hence, the developed technique is found to be robust and imperceptible under compression attacks.

Imperceptibility analysis is also performed for the proposed technique as exhibited in Figs. 8 and 9. In Fig. 8 the highest PSNR is attained for the Cervical spine image under a Gaussian filter attack of 49.8058 dB, whereas a PSNR of 14.6140 dB is observed as the lowest under the Histogram equalization attack for the Knee X-ray image. The average PSNR value for the majority of attacks is above 30 dB, which strongly shows that the scheme has good perceptual invisibility, whereas from Fig. 9 it can be interpreted that the SSIM values are acceptable because they are in the proximity of 1.00 except for the Histogram equalization attack where 0.6975 is its lowest value for the Cervical spine image.

To validate the performance of the proposed method we have compared it with existing works such as: [38]ᵃ, [38]ᵇ, [13, 19], where [38]ᵃ denotes the technique using BPNN, while [38]ᵇ denotes the scheme without using BPNN as tabulated in Table 4. The symbol * signifies that NC values are not

Table 3 Computation of NC and BER metrics for robustness analysis.

Attack	Knee X-ray		Chest X-ray		Foot X-ray		Spinal disk		Cervical spine		Lena	
	NC	BER	NC	BER	NC	BER	NC	BER	NC	BER	NC	BER
Salt and pepper noise (0.001)	0.9991	0.0365	0.9953	0.0535	0.9991	0.0289	0.9973	0.0413	0.9966	0.0787	0.9994	0.0193
Salt and pepper noise (0.0005)	0.9998	0.0168	0.9960	0.0186	0.9991	0.0177	0.9990	0.0156	0.9981	0.0372	0.9998	0.0136
Gaussian noise (0, 0.0002)	0.9981	0.0430	0.9941	0.0448	0.9990	0.0218	0.9961	0.0499	0.9954	0.0666	0.9995	0.0185
Speckle noise (0.0004)	0.9998	0.0140	0.9962	0.0208	0.9994	0.0161	0.9989	0.0143	0.9986	0.0163	0.9999	0.0137
Histogram equalization	1.00	0.0878	0.9993	0.0976	0.9983	0.0974	0.9957	0.0843	0.9998	0.0712	0.9978	0.1223
Sharpening	1.00	0.0220	0.9983	0.0213	0.9995	0.0493	1.00	0.0198	1.00	0.0170	1.00	0.0537
Mean filter	0.9617	0.0296	0.9532	0.0446	0.9987	0.1077	0.9629	0.0291	0.9659	0.0291	0.9685	0.0404
Gaussian filter (3 × 3)	0.9945	0.0286	0.9943	0.0287	0.9955	0.0303	0.9896	0.0291	0.9904	0.0274	0.9922	0.0307
Median filter (3 × 3)	0.9133	0.0293	0.9576	0.0297	0.9985	0.1163	0.9596	0.0291	0.9453	0.0291	0.9584	0.0406
Wiener filter (3 × 3)	0.9924	0.0296	0.9908	0.0331	0.9935	0.0545	0.9651	0.0291	0.9721	0.0291	0.9744	0.0313
JPEG compression (70)	0.9972	0.0142	0.9868	0.0262	0.9935	0.0116	0.9771	0.0288	0.9758	0.0287	0.9866	0.0115
Rotation (90 degrees)	0.9728	0.0291	0.9296	0.0291	0.9743	0.1342	0.9642	0.0291	0.9641	0.0291	0.9696	0.0291
Gamma correction (0.9)	1.00	0.0100	0.9981	0.0101	0.9953	0.0290	0.9970	0.0209	0.9997	0.0093	0.9986	0.0236

Continued

Table 3 Computation of NC and BER metrics for robustness analysis—cont'd

Attack	Knee X-ray		Chest X-ray		Foot X-ray		Spinal disk		Cervical spine		Lena	
	NC	BER	NC	BER	NC	BER	NC	BER	NC	BER	NC	BER
Scaling (2, 0.5)	0.9931	0.0174	0.9936	0.0239	0.9957	0.0239	0.9887	0.0152	0.9881	0.0132	0.9915	0.0279
JPEG compression (70) +Salt and pepper noise (0.0002)	0.9972	0.0109	0.9869	0.0157	0.9934	0.0108	0.9771	0.0149	0.9752	0.0133	0.9865	0.0111
JPEG compression (90) +Gaussian noise (0.01, 0.0001)	0.9986	0.0124	0.9934	0.0100	0.9978	0.0094	0.9923	0.0147	0.9927	0.0176	0.9959	0.0110

BER, *bit error rate*; NC, *normalized correlation*.

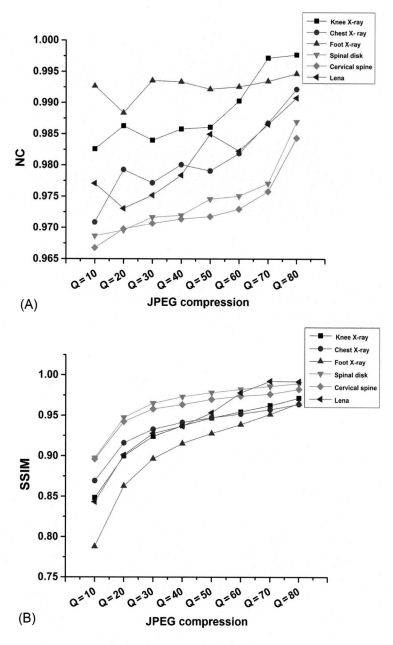

FIG. 7

JPEG compression attack analysis. (A) Normalized correlation. (B) Structural similarity index.

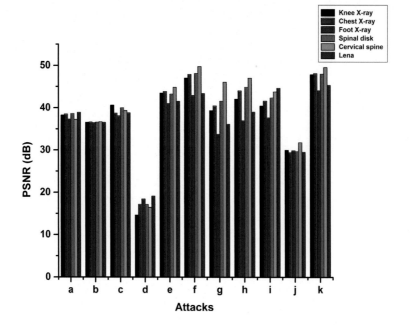

FIG. 8

Peak signal-to-noise ratio values for several cover images against numerous attacks. (a) Salt and pepper noise (0.0005). (b) Gaussian noise (0, 0.0002). (c) Speckle noise (0.0004). (d) Histogram equalization. (e) Sharpening. (f) Gaussian filter (3 × 3). (g) Median filter (3 × 3). (h) Wiener filter (3 × 3). (i) JPEG compression (70). (j) Gamma correction (0.9). (k) Scaling (2, 0.5).

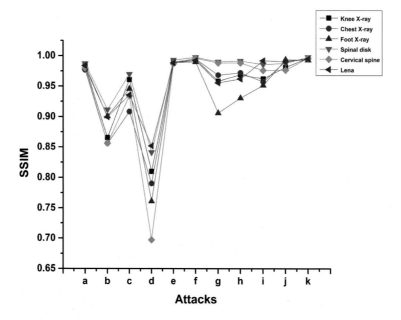

FIG. 9

Structural similarity index values for several cover images against numerous attacks. (a) Salt and pepper noise (0.0005). (b) Gaussian noise (0, 0.0002). (c) Speckle noise (0.0004). (d) Histogram equalization. (e) Sharpening. (f) Gaussian filter. (3 × 3). (g) Median filter (3 × 3). (h) Wiener filter (3 × 3). (i) JPEG compression (70). (j) Gamma correction (0.9). (k) Scaling (2, 0.5).

Table 4 Proposed technique comparison with previously reported schemes.

Attacks		[38]ᵃ	[38]ᵇ	[19]	[13]	Proposed method
JPEG compression	$Q=10$	0.2081	0.3120	0.5306	*	**0.9771**
	$Q=30$	0.9733	0.9803	0.7335	*	**0.9752**
	$Q=50$	*	*	0.7364	−0.1863	**0.9850**
	$Q=60$	0.9679	0.9703	*	*	**0.9823**
	$Q=70$	*	*	0.7394	*	**0.9866**
	$Q=80$	0.9812	0.9871	*	*	**0.9908**
Salt and pepper noise (0.001)		0.9604	0.9658	*	*	**0.9994**
Gaussian noise (0.01, 0.0005)		0.9741	0.9761	*	*	**0.9980**
Average filter		0.9824	**0.9869**	*	*	0.9685
Median filter [2 2]		*	*	0.6736	0.4585	**0.9626**
Median filter [3 3]		0.0025	0.0123	0.2216	*	**0.9584**
Sharpening (0.9)		*	*	0.7394	*	**0.9987**
Rotation (60 degrees)		*	*	*	0.5741	**0.7455**
Histogram equalization		*	*	0.7394	*	**0.9978**

*The symbol * signifies that NC values are not reported for these attacks, while boldface values denotes that these values are higher in comparison to other values for same set of attack in this table.*

reported for these attacks, while boldface values denotes that these values are higher in comparison to other values for same set of attack in Table 4. Moreover, graphical comparison between the scheme developed in this chapter and schemes in [34, 35] is demonstrated in Fig. 10A and B. The proposed technique certainly surpasses both the reported schemes in terms of NC.

6 Conclusions

A robust, imperceptible, and secure dual image watermarking technique for e-healthcare applications was proposed in this chapter. Our proposed method included attributes of HT, IWT, SVD, and AT. A reflectance component of the host image provided excellent imperceptibility and robustness, whereas security of the PR watermark was enhanced by using AT. IWT reduced rounding errors and provided reduced computational complexity as compared to conventional wavelet transform, while resistance toward several attacks was attained by using SVD. From the assessment of simulation results it was easily concluded that the proposed technique was highly robust and more imperceptible toward attacks. In addition to this, the proposed scheme was found to be predominant over other previously developed techniques [13, 19, 34, 35], [38]ᵃ, and [38]ᵇ. Hence, it is concluded that a secure medical image watermarking was developed in this work for the transmission of vital medical information. Furthermore, the proposed scheme can also be extended for a variety of applications in color and video image watermarking.

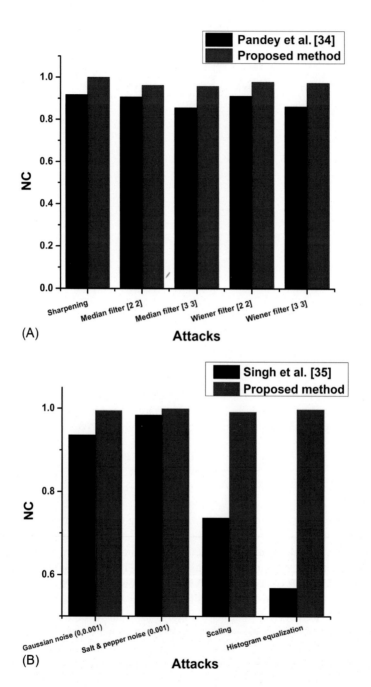

FIG. 10

Graphical comparative analysis of the proposed technique with (A) Pandey et al. [34] and (B) Singh et al. [35].

References

[1] S.P. Mohanty, A. Sengupta, P. Guturu, E. Kougianos, Everything you want to know about watermarking: from paper marks to hardware protection: from paper marks to hardware protection, IEEE Consum. Electron. Mag. 6 (3) (2017) 83–91.

[2] S.J. Horng, D. Rosiyadi, P. Fan, X. Wang, M.K. Khan, An adaptive watermarking scheme for e-government document images, Multimed. Tools Appl. 72 (3) (2014) 3085–3103.

[3] M. Agbaje, O. Awodele, C. Ogbonna, Applications of digital watermarking to cyber security (cyber watermarking), in: in: Proceedings of Informing Science & IT Education Conference (InSITE), 2015, pp. 1–11.

[4] G. Kaur, K. Kaur, Digital watermarking and other data hiding techniques, Int. J. Innov. Technol. Explor. Eng. 2 (5) (2013) 181–183.

[5] C. Kumar, A.K. Singh, P. Kumar, A recent survey on image watermarking techniques and its application in e-governance, Multimed. Tools Appl. 77 (3) (2018) 3597–3622.

[6] L. Singh, A.K. Singh, P.K. Singh, Secure data hiding techniques: a survey, Multimed. Tools Appl. (2018) 1–21.

[7] N. Agarwal, A.K. Singh, P.K. Singh, Survey of robust and imperceptible watermarking, Multimed. Tools Appl. 78 (7) (2019) 8603–8633.

[8] M. Ulutas, G. Ulutas, V.V. Nabiyev, Medical image security and EPR hiding using Shamir's secret sharing scheme, J. Syst. Softw. 84 (3) (2011) 341–353.

[9] R. Singh, Digital image watermarking: an overview, Int. J. Res. 2 (2015) 1087–1094.

[10] K. Muhammad, M. Sajjad, I. Mehmood, S. Rho, S.W. Baik, A novel magic LSB substitution method (M-LSB-SM) using multi-level encryption and achromatic component of an image, Multimed. Tools Appl. 75 (22) (2016) 14867–14893.

[11] C.H. Yang, C.Y. Weng, H.K. Tso, S.J. Wang, A data hiding scheme using the varieties of pixel-value differencing in multimedia images, J. Syst. Softw. 84 (4) (2011) 669–678.

[12] Q. Su, Y. Niu, Q. Wang, G. Sheng, A blind color image watermarking based on DC component in the spatial domain, Optik 124 (23) (2013) 6255–6260.

[13] D. Rosiyadi, S.J. Horng, N. Suryana, N. Masthurah, A comparison between the hybrid using genetic algorithm and the pure hybrid watermarking scheme, Int. J. Comput. Theory Eng. 4 (3) (2012) 329–331.

[14] A.K. Singh, M. Dave, A. Mohan, A hybrid algorithm for image watermarking against signal processing attacks, in: International Workshop on Multi-Disciplinary Trends in Artificial Intelligence, Springer, Berlin, Heidelberg, 2013, pp. 235–246.

[15] A.K. Singh, M. Dave, A. Mohan, Multilevel encrypted text watermarking on medical images using spread-spectrum in DWT domain, Wirel. Pers. Commun. 83 (3) (2015) 2133–2150.

[16] C. Das, S. Panigrahi, V.K. Sharma, K.K. Mahapatra, A novel blind robust image watermarking in DCT domain using inter-block coefficient correlation, AEU Int. J. Electron. Commun. 68 (3) (2014) 244–253.

[17] S. Fazli, M. Moeini, A robust image watermarking method based on DWT, DCT, and SVD using a new technique for correction of main geometric attacks, Optik 127 (2) (2016) 964–972.

[18] A.K. Singh, M. Dave, A. Mohan, Robust and secure multiple watermarking in wavelet domain, J. Med. Imaging Health Inform. 5 (2) (2015) 406–414.

[19] A.K. Singh, B. Kumar, M. Dave, A. Mohan, Multiple watermarking on medical images using selective discrete wavelet transform coefficients, J. Med. Imaging Health Inform. 5 (3) (2015) 607–614.

[20] A. Singh, A. Tayal, Choice of wavelet from wavelet families for DWT-DCT-SVD image watermarking, Int. J. Comput. Appl. 48 (17) (2012) 9–14.

[21] A.K. Singh, B. Kumar, S.K. Singh, S.P. Ghrera, A. Mohan, Multiple watermarking technique for securing online social network contents using back propagation neural network, Futur. Gener. Comput. Syst. 86 (2018) 926–939.

[22] P. Khare, A.K. Verma, V.K. Srivastava, Digital image watermarking scheme in wavelet domain using chaotic encryption, in: 2014 Students Conference on Engineering and Systems, 2014, pp. 1–4.

[23] A.K. Singh, Improved hybrid algorithm for robust and imperceptible multiple watermarking using digital images, Multimed. Tools Appl. 76 (6) (2017) 8881–8900.

[24] A.K. Singh, B. Kumar, M. Dave, A. Mohan, Robust and imperceptible dual watermarking for telemedicine applications, Wirel. Pers. Commun. 80 (4) (2015) 1415–1433.

[25] C. Kumar, A.K. Singh, P. Kumar, R. Singh, S. Singh, SPIHT-based multiple image watermarking in NSCT domain, Concurr. Comput. Pract. Exp. 32 (1) (2018) e4912.

[26] S. Thakur, A.K. Singh, S.P. Ghrera, NSCT domain–based secure multiple-watermarking technique through lightweight encryption for medical images, Concurr. Comput. Pract. Exp. (2018) e5108.

[27] A.K. Singh, Robust and distortion control dual watermarking in LWT domain using DCT and error correction code for color medical image, Multimed. Tools Appl. (2019) 1–11.

[28] S. Singh, V.S. Rathore, R. Singh, M.K. Singh, Hybrid semi-blind image watermarking in redundant wavelet domain, Multimed. Tools Appl. 76 (18) (2017) 19113–19137.

[29] S. Singh, V.S. Rathore, R. Singh, Hybrid NSCT domain multiple watermarking for medical images, Multimed. Tools Appl. 76 (3) (2017) 3557–3575.

[30] S. Singh, R. Singh, A.K. Singh, T.J. Siddiqui, SVD-DCT based medical image watermarking in NSCT domain, in: Quantum Computing: An Environment for Intelligent Large Scale Real Application, Springer, Cham, 2018, pp. 467–488.

[31] A. Shehab, M. Elhoseny, K. Muhammad, A.K. Sangaiah, P. Yang, H. Huang, G. Hou, Secure and robust fragile watermarking scheme for medical images, IEEE Access 6 (2018) 10269–10278.

[32] M. Elhoseny, G. Ramírez-González, O.M. Abu-Elnasr, S.A. Shawkat, N. Arunkumar, A. Farouk, Secure medical data transmission model for IoT-based healthcare systems, IEEE Access 6 (2018) 20596–20608.

[33] S. Thakur, A.K. Singh, S.P. Ghera, A. Mohan, Chaotic based secure watermarking approach for medical images, Multimed. Tools Appl. (2018) 1–14.

[34] R. Pandey, A.K. Singh, B. Kumar, A. Mohan, Iris based secure NROI multiple eye image watermarking for teleophthalmology, Multimed. Tools Appl. 75 (22) (2016) 14381–14397.

[35] A.K. Singh, M. Dave, A. Mohan, Hybrid technique for robust and imperceptible multiple watermarking using medical images, Multimed. Tools Appl. 75 (14) (2016) 8381–8401.

[36] F.N. Thakkar, V.K. Srivastava, A blind medical image watermarking: DWT-SVD based robust and secure approach for telemedicine applications, Multimed. Tools Appl. 76 (3) (2017) 3669–3697.

[37] A. Srivastava, P. Saxena, DWT-DCT-SVD based semiblind image watermarking using middle frequency band, IOSR J. Comput. Eng. 12 (2) (2013) 63–66.

[38] A. Zear, A.K. Singh, P. Kumar, A proposed secure multiple watermarking technique based on DWT, DCT and SVD for application in medicine, Multimed. Tools Appl. 77 (4) (2018) 4863–4882.

[39] A. Kannammal, S. Subha Rani, Two level security for medical images using watermarking/encryption algorithms, Int. J. Imaging Syst. Technol. 24 (1) (2014) 111–120.

[40] A. Sharma, A.K. Singh, S.P. Ghrera, Robust and secure multiple watermarking for medical images, Wirel. Person. Commun. 92 (4) (2017) 1611–1624.

[41] K. Swaraja, Medical image region based watermarking for secured telemedicine, Multimed. Tools Appl. 77 (21) (2018) 28249–28280.

[42] T. Meenpal, DWT-based blind and robust watermarking using SPIHT algorithm with applications in telemedicine, Sādhanā 43 (1) (2018) 4.

[43] J.M. Guo, H. Prasetyo, False-positive-free SVD-based image watermarking, J. Vis. Commun. Image Represent. 25 (5) (2014) 1149–1163.

[44] P. Khare, V.K. Srivastava, Image watermarking scheme using homomorphic transform in wavelet domain, in: 2018 5th IEEE Uttar Pradesh Section International Conference on Electrical, Electronics and Computer Engineering (UPCON), 2018, pp. 1–6.

[45] H.A. Abdallah, O.S. Faragallah, H.S. Elsayed, A.A. Shaalan, F.E.A. El-samie, Robust image watermarking method using homomorphic block-based KLT, Optik 127 (4) (2016) 2374–2381.

[46] R.C. Gonzalez, R.E. Woods, Digital Image Processing, second ed., 455, Publishing House of Electronics Industry, Beijing, 2002.

[47] W. Sweldens, The lifting scheme: a construction of second generation wavelets, SIAM J. Math. Anal. 29 (2) (1998) 511–546.

[48] R. Mehta, N. Rajpal, V.P. Vishwakarma, LWT-QR decomposition based robust and efficient image watermarking scheme using Lagrangian SVR, Multimed. Tools Appl. 75 (7) (2016) 4129–4150.

[49] V.S. Verma, R.K. Jha, Improved watermarking technique based on significant difference of lifting wavelet coefficients, SIViP 9 (6) (2015) 1443–1450.

[50] B. Kazemivash, M.E. Moghaddam, A robust digital image watermarking technique using lifting wavelet transform and firefly algorithm, Multimed. Tools Appl. 76 (20) (2017) 20499–20524.

[51] R. Liu, T. Tan, An SVD-based watermarking scheme for protecting rightful ownership, IEEE Trans. Multimed. 4 (1) (2002) 121–128.

[52] M.Q. Fan, H.X. Wang, S.K. Li, Restudy on SVD-based watermarking scheme, Appl. Math. Comput. 203 (2) (2008) 926–930.

[53] X.P. Zhang, K. Li, Comments on "An SVD-based watermarking scheme for protecting rightful ownership" IEEE Trans. Multimed. 7 (3) (2005) 593–594.

[54] R.S. Run, S.J. Horng, J.L. Lai, T.W. Kao, R.J. Chen, An improved SVD-based watermarking technique for copyright protection, Expert Syst. Appl. 39 (1) (2012) 673–689.

[55] Z. Tang, X. Zhang, Secure image encryption without size limitation using Arnold transform and random strategies, J. Multimed. 6 (2) (2011) 202.

[56] S. Roy, A.K. Pal, A robust blind hybrid image watermarking scheme in RDWT-DCT domain using Arnold scrambling, Multimed. Tools Appl. 76 (3) (2017) 3577–3616.

[57] S. Roy, A.K. Pal, A robust reversible image watermarking scheme in DCT domain using Arnold scrambling and histogram modification, Int. J. Inf. Comput. Secur. 10 (2–3) (2018) 216–236.

[58] https://homepages.cae.wisc.edu/~ece533/images/.

[59] https://commons.wikimedia.org/wiki/File:X-ray_of_a_normal_knee_by_lateral_projection.jpg.

[60] https://en.m.wikipedia.org/wiki/File:X-ray_of_normal_ankle_-_lateral.jpg.

[61] https://en.wikipedia.org/wiki/Pneumothorax#/media/File:Rt_sided_pneumoDWP.jpg.

[62] https://commons.wikimedia.org/wiki/File:X-ray_of_normal_right_foot_by_dorsoplantar_projection.jpg.

[63] https://en.wikipedia.org/wiki/File:X-ray_of_abdomen_with_perforated_IUD.jpg.

[64] https://commons.wikimedia.org/wiki/File:HerniatedSpinalDisk-NarrowedNerveRoot.JPG.

[65] https://commons.wikimedia.org/wiki/File:Cervical_spine_Xray.jpg.

[66] Z. Wang, A.C. Bovik, H.R. Sheikh, E.P. Simoncelli, Image quality assessment: from error visibility to structural similarity, IEEE Trans. Image Process. 13 (4) (2004) 600–612.

[67] A.K. Singh, B. Kumar, G. Singh, A. Mohan (Eds.), Medical Image Watermarking: Techniques and Applications, Springer, 2017.

[68] X.B. Kang, F. Zhao, G.F. Lin, Y.J. Chen, A novel hybrid of DCT and SVD in DWT domain for robust and invisible blind image watermarking with optimal embedding strength, Multimed. Tools Appl. 77 (11) (2018) 13197–13224.

An analysis of security access control on healthcare records in the cloud

P. Chinnasamy[a], P. Deepalakshmi[b], and K. Shankar[c]

Department of Information Technology, Sri Shakthi Institute of Engineering and Technology, Coimbatore, Tamil Nadu, India[a] Department of Computer Science and Engineering, Kalasalingam Academy of Research and Education, Srivilliputtur, Tamil Nadu, India[b] Department of Computer Applications, Alagappa University, Karaikudi, Tamil Nadu, India[c]

1 Introduction

The Healthcare Information System (HIS) preserves three basic health information and medical data including the Personal Health Record (PHR), the Electronic Medical Record (EMR), and the Electronic Health Record (EHR). Healthcare service organizations offer HIS from a private server farm/server to maintain the health data in systems such as the EHR and the EMR [1]. The PHR denotes the historical backdrop of health data about an individual, which can be normally overseen by the patients themselves. However, in earlier times, individuals usually kept track of their records [2]. With technological advancements such as cloud computing, the PHR is stored in the cloud, and it can be accessed from anyplace by any approved individual, and the knowledge is imparted among various health-service providers. The sharing of PHR demands various requirements, for instance, the sharing of only incomplete health-record data rather than complete data [3]. The HIS is anything but a different and autonomous part of the health system that should be structured by the service-delivery system. It is used for gathering, handling, putting away, recovering, and moving the required data [4]. The primary aim of the HIS is to improve the procedures of data handling to extricate the valuable data for health arrangements, basic leadership, and the asset portion through various sources to render quality services [5]. Serbia's healthcare system has the highest number of representatives in the region, yet it distributes only minimal cash for the sector. With ever-increasing healthcare costs today compared to expenses incurred in other services, the suppliers of health benefits in Serbia, particularly the emergency hospitals, are under consistent pressure [6].

2 Review of the EHR literature

Jagli et al. [7] performed an extensive search of the medical information act, which indicated that there is a precarious pattern in the utilization of the Electronic Health Record. There is a significant number of EHR software that is accessible, and these are utilized as a service comprehensively. However, many practitioners have no knowledge about the best EHR SaaS item. Henceforth, there is a need to

Intelligent Data Security Solutions for e-Health Applications. https://doi.org/10.1016/B978-0-12-819511-6.00006-6

distinguish the best EHR SaaS from a pool of software-service items. To upgrade the search to attain the ideal EHR SaaS item, researchers have proposed a novel method for utilizing predefined traits of these items and to find the connection between them.

Based on the knowledge acquired from clinicians about supporting situations, this investigation proposed German PHR systems using an open-cloud infrastructure, cell-phone access, with a concentration on trust, privacy, and interoperability [8]. Before possible usage, a multi-focus survey study was conducted to predict the aim of patients and physicians in using the system and to evaluate their trust of various suppliers that were connected in such a framework. The trust among the healthcare suppliers surpassed the trust in different establishments such as private companies, health insurance agencies, etc.

In 2018, Sahney et al. [9] mentioned that EHR is the need of the hour because it not only improves the quality but also reduces the cost of the healthcare that is already embraced in many developing countries. Despite the constructive outcomes, the selection rate for the EHR system among Indian medical practices is moderate, thanks to the clinicians who act as the main hurdle for the program. For effective reception, many steps have been started, and a few new advances must be taken. This requires an organized exertion from each one of the stakeholders. Information technologies are vulnerable so their security should is a concern and should be maintained consistently.

In 2019, Zhu et al. [10] conducted a study in which the EHR access log information was separated from the EHR system of a scholastic medical center to develop communication networks among healthcare professionals (HCPs) in every patient's virtual consideration group. The study quantified the correspondent linkages between HCPs by considering the reverse of the average time between the access events in which the "source HCPs sent data to and the goal HCPs recovered data from" the EHR system. Social network analysis was used to look at and envision the correspondence system structures, recognize chief consideration groups, and distinguish significant auxiliary contrasts crosswise over the networks.

A personally controlled Electronic Health Record (PCEHR) system maintained by the Australian government makes the nation's health system progressively agile, dependable, and sustainable, according to Mamun [11]. Their study proposed that concentrations and confinements together create powerful validations and combine to improve the security and protection of EHRs using a hybrid access-control model. A homomorphic encryption strategy was connected with storing and working with EHR in the proposed cloud-based PCEHR framework.

In 2019, Ashfaq et al. [12] conducted a study in which an Electronic Health Record (EHR)-driven prediction model was proposed to function in a solitary system utilizing both expert and machine-determined features in consolidation to consecutive patterns and to address the class-irregularity issue. The study assessed the commitment of every component toward prediction, execution (ROC-AUC, F1-measure), and cost savings.

The EMR systems empower the proficient collection of significant, accurate, and complete information to improve the clinical organization via the advancement, execution, and optimization of clinical pathways, as opined by Vimalachandran et al. [13]. This can be achieved, as per the study, by verifying the Electronic Medical Record (EMR) and Electronic Health Record Systems (EHR) via improved access control. Although its expense and time-investment funds empower the progress, it does not come without inborn difficulties. Inadequate policy improvement, in the zones of information security and protection of health data, has all the earmarks of being a major weakness. A secure access-control model must be present to access the EMR and electronic data.

3 Overview of electronic health records

The reform requires that hospitals receive interoperable Electronic Health Records (EHR) and to encourage information sharing and participation among the healthcare suppliers. These actions are expected to eventually enhance the nature of consideration and proficiency in the health system. However, there are likewise some moral issues raised by e-health professionals. Fig. 1 shows the components of HIS. The EHR of a patient can be found in his or her mobile phone along with the health card. In this manner, the assignment of supervising the healthcare data is not only connected with requirements on privacy or access, but it also exists in consolidating the information in general for a progressively comprehensive perspective [14].

3.1 Important components

3.1.1 Electronic medical records

In EMR, the patient information can be followed over an all-inclusive timeframe by multiple healthcare suppliers. It can help in the identification of individuals who are scheduled for preventive checkups and screenings, and it also helps in screening how every patient measures up to specific necessities such as immunizations and pulse readings. The quality of Electronic Medical Records is assessed by recognizing the proficiency, accessibility, satisfaction, and security. Effectiveness is measured as the availability and usability of the system [15], whereas accessibility is determined by the rightness and usefulness of EMRs. The quality of healthcare services is portrayed as the degree of healthcare benefits in improving the health results, which could be estimated by recognizing the patients' or health experts' perceptions. This will robotize and streamline the supplier work

FIG. 1

Components of HIS.

process [16]. EHR can be made and supervised by approved suppliers in an advanced configuration that is equipped to impart information to different suppliers crosswise over more than one healthcare organization like labs, specialists, medical imaging offices, pharmacies, emergency facilities, and school- and work-environment centers. This helps all the clinicians associated with a patient's consideration to store and access information from a solitary place [17].

3.1.2 Health information exchange (HIE)

The purpose of HIE is to advance the proper and secure access as well as the recovery of a patient's health data to reduce the cost and to improve the quality, safety, and speed of the patient being treated. This upgraded correspondence offers healthcare suppliers a holistic perspective on a patient's health, and it reduces the risk of errors, duplicate treatments or tests, and readmissions while improving the security and outcome for the patients [18]. HIE is critical for an effective healthcare change, empowering interoperability and significant utilization of health data and innovation. Although HIE is here to support healthcare, health data and technology professionals leverage the majority of the advancements [19].

(i) Activity-based costing (ABC)

ABC is a costing strategy proposed by Cooper and Kaplan in which various items consume the same activities, and these activities require healthcare assets in various proportions [20]. ABC methodology provides an accurate estimate of the expense of an item or administration, particularly when it is made of a segment of people-oriented activities and activities in a hospital setting. It is especially appropriate to give this careful consideration since the worth must be determined by estimating cost and results related to surgery; besides, all parts of the pre- and postoperative administration of items related to the medical condition will be considered [21].

(ii) Patient-reported outcomes

Pharmaceutical businesses perceived the significance of considering Patient-Detailed Outcomes (PROs) as close biomarkers for health improvement. The segregation between health outcomes and treatment outcomes shifted toward providing a clear picture when the investigation into health services started to concentrate on improving the patients' health-related personal satisfaction, especially when patients experience ideal medical treatment [22]. In clinical pharmacology preliminaries, PROs are used as either essential result measures or as a supplement to essential outcome measures [23].

(iii) Enterprise data warehousing

Traditionally, the best practice for examination is to make a dimensional model data warehouse that organizes the most significant undertaking information for investigation. The number of data sources is excessively assorted, whereas the information differs a lot in terms of accessibility, quality, and format to allow a complete consideration of everyday extraction into the data warehouse [24]. The sheer volume of information overloads the information distribution center and makes the capacity, memory, and scalability requirements untenable.

(iv) EHR system architecture

The architecture of the EHR system differs from one healthcare supplier to another. When all is said and done, the EHR system comprises of a few segments as shown in Fig. 2. With specific intention, these segments are delineated into different administrations that include a patient derives from different

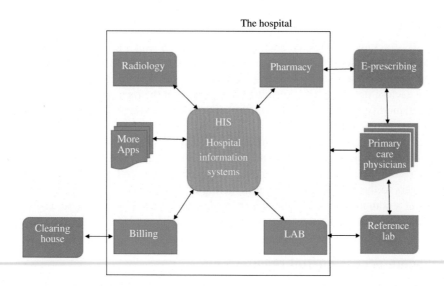

The hospital

FIG. 2

Architecture of the EHR system.

divisions such as radiology, the laboratory, the pharmacy, and the administration. These parts are likewise presented in customer server applications based on a request-reply protocol. Customer server architecture furnishes different endorsed clients with safe access [25]. An EHR plan is consequently composed of different customer-service applications. The requirements are defined to guarantee that the EHR systems are loyal to the requirements of healthcare conveyance, are clinically substantial and solid, are morally stable, meet winning lawful prerequisites, bolster great clinical practice, and facilitate information investigation for a large number of purposes. Contingent on the design, both ordering and recovery frameworks need to manage the identification of different assets, the integration of heterogeneous data models, and the mapping of distinctive patient identifiers [26].

- EHR systems should guarantee the efficiency and security of data streams while eliminating the duplicate actions, namely diagnoses, and at the same time should upgrade the speed, efficiency, and proximity of health frameworks.
- Access to data is required for performance monitoring and correlation of the actions that are needed for economic evaluation studies.
- Case-mix consolidation and data mining should support the provider's procurement.
- The Hospital Information System is a part of Health Information Systems where the hospital unit is both the environment and the healthcare institution.
- The meaning of standard Clinical Document Architecture (CDA) guarantees structure consistency to permit interpretation by both computer frameworks and end clients.
- Beyond these, one can also feature other advantages such as its ability to allow simultaneous consultation and alteration of patient information by different health professionals, space savings over the growing number of clinical records, data security, confidentiality promotion, and the integration of different information resources.

3.2 Threat model of EHR

The framework structure considers an antagonistic situation in which the capacities of the attacker's conceivable conduct are characterized. In the center assailant, the probability of an individual who approaches correspondence associations or communication equipment is considered [27]. The attacker can tune in to each of the messages transmitted or can see that the messages are moved onto the specialized gadget, modify the EHR, or infuse their own delivered messages. This model accepts that any secret data stored or uploaded in a united database on a cell phone might be vulnerable to break-ins or different sorts of spillage, and this procedure is the adversary model shown in Fig. 3. The method for "danger displaying" optimizes network security by perceiving targets and vulnerabilities in the framework, and afterward, it executes an arrangement for countermeasures to relieve the aftereffects of missing these dangers to the system [28]. Threat modeling is a helpful device for analyzing the security requirements of a computer system. Distinguishing the dangers creates reasonable and important security necessities that can be used to concoct the threat model.

3.3 Healthcare access-control requirements

Access to Personal Health Information (PHI) is restricted and should be revealed to healthcare experts under specific conditions since they are the brief custodians of data. These special conditions include the treatment of patients and the advancement of the administration and arrangement of healthcare through measurements for field researchers who utilize unencrypted/pseudonymized data for assessment. These conditions even include formal requests for law implementation. The instances of revelation enactment and well-being criteria in such a manner invites the enactment of the Canadian

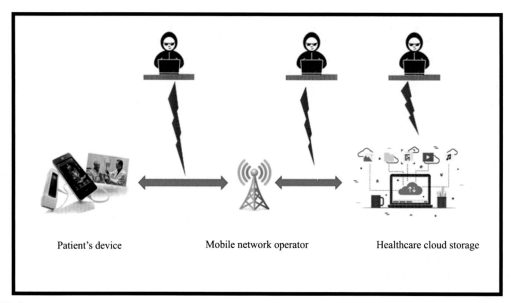

Patient's device   Mobile network operator   Healthcare cloud storage

FIG. 3

Adversary model of the EHR.

Personal Health Information Act (PHIA), the U.S. Health Insurance Portability and Accountability Act (HIPAA) Privacy and Security Rule, the English NHS-Data Protection Act, and the Brazilian Health Informatics Society (SBIS) confirmation program [29]. Access control plays a significant role in the scenario mentioned earlier in limiting the information to more actual information along with the approval strategies connected to data-framework access control. Approval is the third stage next to distinguishing the proof and validation strategies in nonexclusive access control. These things (information, framework features, and so on) are mapped to client consents during the approval procedure so they can be observed.

3.3.1 Access-control requirements

An Electronic Health Record access-control mechanism must overcome the issues of all EHR members, for example, patients, supporting staff, and medical experts. To complete their work, every member needs to access specific zones of the health record. Various members likewise should be enabled to set explicit record access controls. The following privacy and security prerequisites for healthcare conditions have been recognized as essential:

- Each healthcare system must have the privilege to design and implement its security policy.
- If necessary, healthcare professionals must have the right to define document security.
- Patients should have control over their data, including whether certain medical practitioners should have access to such data.
- Patients should be able to hide some specific information on health records from selected medical professionals.
- Under certain conditions, patients should be able to delegate control over their health records to another party (e.g., in the case of mental illness).
- It should be an easy task to manage the access-control policies to ensure that the system is used and that confidence is maintained within the system.
- The legitimate uses of health records must be allowed, such as an overall level of service availability of the system and overriding requirements for "need-to-know" access to data during an emergency.

3.4 Access-control mechanisms for EHR

EHR systems store both statistics and health data about patients. The authorization of access-control approaches is firmly incorporated because neither statistical data nor medical information should be accessed without any appropriate access rights. Supporting the approved and specific sharing of EHR frameworks among a few gatherings, with various obligations and targets, is undoubtedly an incredible challenge. It is perceived that most of the clinical and EHR systems uploaded nowadays join access-control measures, for the most part, to help with needs inside a solitary association. In any case, the number of prerequisites is ever-increasing for cutting-edge access-control strategies. One of the point-by-point approval determination structures for EHR information is put forth by the ISO 13606-4 standard. This displays a security data model to represent and convey the access strategy for the data. However, it has been purposely kept nonexclusive in consideration of the assorted variety of arrangement criteria that will be stipulated in various countries and provincial healthcare information in the cloud [30]. Authorization deploys a security arrangement based on framework possibilities by the confirmed client. It is commonly done by mapping current things and authorizations in an entrance-control matrix table. The security arrangements are connected distinctively, relying on the endorsement of access control presented on an EHR scheme.

3.4.1 Access-control policy specification for EHRs

The trustworthiness of healthcare systems is estimated to be dependent on a security approach since it is a complex mix of genuine, moral, ecological, hierarchical, mental, operational, and technical consequences. Role-based access control is a structure to control client access to assets based on jobs. It can decrease altogether the expense of access-control policy administration and can be generally progressively used in large organizations [7]. Overall, these arrangements have a place with class experience about the ill effects of the powerlessness to withstand for the entrance dynamism related with e-health applications. To be specific, it is important to consider the way that such arrangements need to change the figure content when the related access structure is altered. This brings about significant extra overhead to the framework. Moreover, the mind-boggling key administration is related to an encryption strategy.

Security requirements

- Patient privacy is critical to forecast any kind of unapproved exposure to patient's health data. Consequently, any client who does not have enough attributes to satisfy the entrance requirements must be restricted from giving access to the EHR information of patients even under attribute collusion.
- The issuer of an attribute must have the control of the delegation right, denoting that any further appointments by the client, who received the property, are attainable with the assent of the present issuer as well as the assent of the AA who administrated the thought-about attribute.
- Whenever a specific property of a client is no longer legitimate, the user should not be able to use this ascribe to access the health data that are restricted in the LHP. This property is alluded to as the attribute revocation.
- Typically, the treatment procedure of a patient may require collaborative efforts from various groups including general experts, emergency staff members, authorities in the patient's home supplier, and experts from outside suppliers in certain situations.
- Further, the security of every patient's medical information is a major issue, and, if not addressed adequately and transparently, the patient may lose trust in both the treatment and the EHR system.
- Access-control mechanisms have undergone numerous improvements in both the scholarly world and in industry to fulfill the necessities of healthcare areas. Be that as it may, advancement to date has not been adequate to meet the security requirements of a combined healthcare environment.

3.4.2 Categories of ACMs

The mechanisms for access control can be categorized into four essential gatherings including discretionary, mandatory, role-based, and attribute-based. An access-control system depicts information, profiles, or data recovery rubrics for clients. A subject demands approval for an object component. Any substance that incorporates information or measurements and assets, which a subject requires to complete an arranged errand or prerequisite, could be the article. The access-control framework, which requires a specific task, also requires the weight of responsibility to assess the subject's solicitation for access to a specific thing and produces an answer that may produce any kind of effect. ACMs provide a way for system administrators to control the types of clients and procedures that can access various records, gadgets, interfaces, and so forth, in a computer system. This is an essential thought when verifying a computer system or network of any size. This ACO in EHR procedure has six sorts and these are explained in the following segment.

Discretionary access control (DAC) for EHR

DAC is the first of these policies discussed in this section. It depends on client features as well as associations that are characterized. The right of entry is typically based on the client's approved verification, which in turn is based on the classes submitted for approval and the personality of the controller to choose whether to approve or deny access to the application. The proprietor of the object depicts the theme that can pass the object so that the complete utilization of the item can be chosen by the object's administrator [11,13]. This sort of access control is generally less secure than obligatory access control, although it is a well-known structure in operating systems of an organization. Although it is less secure, it is simple to utilize and is progressively versatile to suit the situations that don't require the severe well-being of items. The DAC structure is shown in Fig. 4. The most significant element that can cause an issue with the system is that the proprietor can move his position to someone else.

Data spillage is another issue in such a way that the control policies are resolved by requirements by an owner without checking the data of the users and it doesn't recognize articles or subject areas. This access control depends on client or gathering control. While assigning permissions and constraints to clients rather than chipping away at a single user, it characterizes bunches that are controlled by the owner and introduces certain authorizations and limitations in it. This circumstance can cause genuine security spills in a situation in which the proprietor is not dependent.

Mandatory access control (MAC) for EHR

Mandatory Access Control provides the security for a centralized and authorized server that is designed by a designated and approved security head. All users are similarly found by the access approach, and in this, no super client exists as in DAC. The requirement for a MAC component occurs when a framework's security strategy manages the security decisions that need not be chosen by the owner of the object, whereas the data protection choices must be implemented by the system. Typically, the obligatory access control occurs in military-style security. Numerous interfaces and security-mark systems are commonly used to foresee access to MAC. MAC is constantly connected with the access Multi-Level Security (MLS). After security, the wholeness and privacy of the system are its most significant features. Consequently, it can expand the security to the most astounding level in an entire system, and it possess low adaptability. The purpose behind this is framework security, and, in any case, even this does not guarantee outright protection. It is used in government and military framework upgrades because of these highlights. While MAC performs the operations, it does not consider the relationship it has with the clients into thought, and it also does not consider the security award that guarantees that every client in the working system performs the client assignments, thinking about this reality. Users and procedures must have suitable access to these classes before they can associate with these objects.

Multilevel Systems (MLS): In this system, data access is overseen by naming the subjects and objects. Before permitting the cooperation between the two, a subject's mark is assessed against the object's label. A decent comprehension of MLS would not be complete without understanding its starting points and the issues it was meant to solve. The U.S. military and insight networks have generally isolated the information based on its security classification.

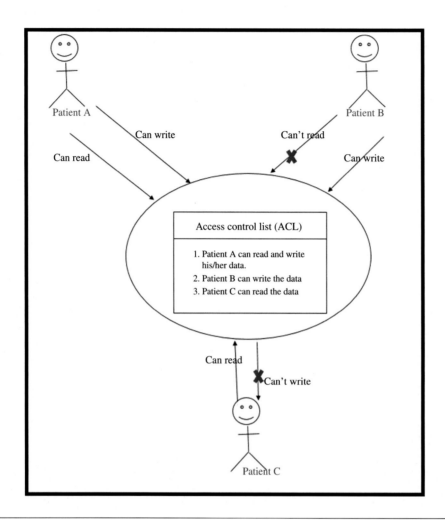

FIG. 4

DAC model for EHR.

Bell-La-Padula: In 1976, the U.S. Department of Defense developed the Bell La-Padula model to formulate the secrecy criteria. The model describes two mandatory rules for access control (Fig. 5). This module also presents a concept of a state machine, with a lot of permissible states in a computer system, characterizing a mathematical model of computation that is used to plan both computer programs and successive rational circuits.

No-Read Up: This means that an object with a higher level cannot be pursued by a subject with a specified level of safety.

No-Write Down: This means that an object with a lower level cannot be written down by a subject with a specified level of safety.

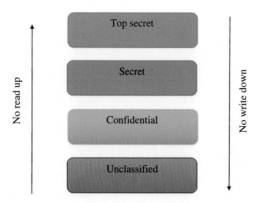

FIG. 5

The Bell-La-Padula model for MAC.

In a medical setting, for example, a doctor is given a higher level of security than a nurse. This model keeps the doctor from trading a medical record encoded at the nurse's degree of security, even though this might be earnestly required. The doctor abuses the said security policy by trading the data during emergency surgery.

Biba model

- A sort of scheme, that guarantees data integrity, is described in the Biba model. Integrity labels are given to procedures and objects inside this Biba model. The low procedures honestly are not able to write for objects of high integrity. The procedures of high integrity, at the same time, cannot peruse things of reduced integrity.
- A high integrity strategy can peruse low-honesty things that fall under the variety known as "low watermarking," which improves the adaptability of the Biba model. However, this is decreased to the safety level of the object until the manual reconfiguration.
- In EHR, the Biba model addresses the integrity issue discussed earlier by prohibiting the nurse from writing incorrect data upward.
- *The model*, be that as it may, provides a serious degree of inflexibility because the doctor cannot access the notes of the nurse. It is probable that the use of required access-control forms, in an EHR setting, will be challenging to infer from a large number of purchasers associated with these plans, a wide assortment of information types, and a readiness to provide the patients their due ownership and (partial) control over their medical records.
- However, the use of some kind of MAC approach in an EHR scheme cannot be avoided, as medical officials, in the long run, need to dole out the access rights.

Role-based access control (RBAC) for EHR

RBAC was proclaimed in 1992 and discharged in 2000 by the National Institute Standards and Technology of the United States (NIST) [2]. It is composed of core, hierarchical, and static separation of obligation connections and the dynamic partition of obligations' relationship components. Here, the choices on access are dependent on the role of individual users as the major aspect of an organization. The users accept dispensed roles (in the current study case, doctor, nurse, or receptionist). Access rights (or permissions) are collected based on the user roles, whereas the utilization of assets is confined to authorized individuals. In contrast to DAC or MAC systems, where users approach the objects based on their own and the item's authorizations, the clients must be individuals from the fitting gathering or should play a role in the RBAC framework, before they can interface with documents, catalogs, gadgets, and so forth (Fig. 6). It is otherwise termed as nonoptional access control because the user inherits their role benefits. The user does not have control over the job to which he or she is assigned. As described earlier, it is a different-leveled arrangement of classes. It is frequently utilized in association with an incredible number of clients where the distinctive work gatherings or divisions with various capacities are incorporated, such as systems, advancement, business, and service departments.

In EHR, RBAC has a special mention in providing fine-grained access control and overseeing huge numbers of customers and assets by executing the standard of "have-to-know." However, a few evaluations of access requests are quite complicated because the other relevant parameters should be considered in the evaluation too. By adding relevant parameters to RBAC, there is a chance to build the unpredictability of the EHR system. As a rule, RBAC exhibits an impression of being a superior choice over DAC and MAC, even though it is not an appropriate solution for a secure EHR scheme.

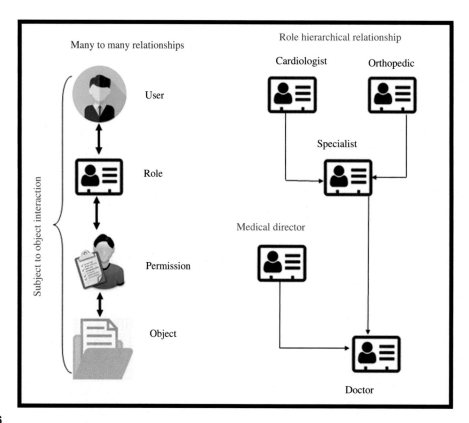

FIG. 6

Role hierarchy over an EHR.

For example, the subject attributes may be < Provider; Doctor > and < Department; Orthopedic >; whereas the object attributes might be < Patient Name; china > and < Document Type; Summary Of Medical Checking >; and the environmental attribute might be < Access IP = 192:123: **:**.**>>. The access rule statement could be written as follows: "A doctor working in Orthopedic can access China's care report overview from a desktop on a particular network subnet of the hospital." In the role assignments that are used in RBAC, the users can be shifted from one role to another in an easy manner, given that the permissions can be connected.

Benefits of RABC

- RBAC lets the associations rapidly include and change their roles. Further, it implements them across the platforms, Operating Systems (OSs), and applications to improve the efficiency of the system.
- RBAC systems meet the administrative and statutory requirements for confidentiality and privacy because the executives and IT offices can more effectively manage the data that is being accessed and utilized.
- RBAC offers a logically streamlined methodology. Instead of trying to administer lower-level access control, everyone can be aligned with the organizational structure of the business, and users can perform their jobs more efficiently and autonomously.
- Another role could be that of a customer service representative who may have read/write access to the customer database, and yet another role could be that of a customer database administrator who has full control of the customer database.
- ABAC rules can evaluate the attributes of subjects and resources that are yet to be invented by the authorization system.

Attribute-based access control (ABAC) for EHR

ABAC is a sort of open-key encryption in which the attributes of the user rely on private, significant, and mystery content. The decryption of the ciphered text can be accomplished only if the buyer's arrangement of qualities coordinates with the attributes of the figure content. The ABAC [18] model offers an access-control procedure that is progressively unique and granular. The users can distinguish access-control procedures with the help of the qualities of different organizations, for example, themes, activities, resources, and environments. The structure of ABAC is shown in Fig. 7. To summarize, none of the present models are adequate, although every model has some capacity that is urgent for an EHR safety model. DAC empowers the patients to control the data that can be viewed by the explicit medical experts, whereas MAC empowers the medical office to screen access to explicit sorts of data. In case of RBAC, it permits the access rights to be allotted according to the medical roles. The significant issue that the current article considers in the solution is the low ability of capacity and the registration of fog nodes. This model assessed an access choice based on user attributes and those of the record, whereas this work also exhibited the use of a strategy-based, semantic web approach to implement ABAC at an archive level.

Also, access control is a mechanism by which the services choose whether to accept or deny requests according to the permissions designated to users.

- *Identification*: Assigning a responsible gathering for activities. A responsible gathering might be an individual or a Non-individual Person Entity (NPE), for example, a router. The term *client* is used to cover both cases.

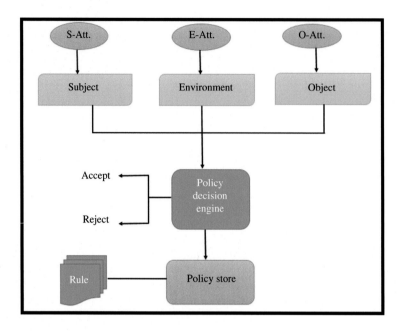

FIG. 7

Components of ABAC.

- **Authentication**: The means that are used to prove the right to use an identity, take on a role, or prove possession of one or more attributes.
- **Authorization**: The means of expressing the access policy by explicitly granting a right.
- **Access Decision**: Using some combination of the other three considerations to decide whether a request should be fulfilled.

ABAC is highly complex because of its particular support for the policies. Besides, bungling issues and befuddling properties can occur, particularly when those attributes, given by the user, do not match those utilized by the service provider of a web-based system or service.

3.5 Access-control constraints for EHRs

The members of the EHR systems need to fulfill the accompanying requirements. The access-control criteria of attendants include things the medical caretakers need to figure out, who needs to be allowed to access their Electronic Health Records, who determines what fragile information is in their EHRs, and who is allowed to access it. This case does not require any sort of constraints [30]. Access-control decision-making is possible in an ordinary way. The independent user accesses some portion of the consents or all authorizations from a delicate blend of consents: This is a solitary-free client who progressively accesses some portion of the permissions or all permissions from a touchy mix of permissions. These requirements are met by using DAC, MAC, and RBAC interfaces in the following steps:

- RBAC tries to reduce the gap by combining the forced organizational constraints with the flexibility of explicit authorization.

- In RBAC, the roles for users are assigned statically and cannot be used in a dynamic environment. It is more difficult to change the access rights of the user without changing the specified roles of the user.
- The role is nothing but the simplified version of the user behavior and their assigned duties. These are used to assign system resources to the departments and their respective members.
- Roles define the specification, whereas enforcement is required for protection while the real-world policies may need to be defined.
- Constraint specification in ABAC cannot be predicted as in the case of RBAC since there are different traits. Imperatives may exist among various values of a set-esteemed quality and also on values crosswise over various attributes.
- Patients nominate the names of particular professionals they trust, and this is achieved via the DAC interface after which the Access Control List (ACL) is created.
- With the help of security labels, data can be classified into sensitive/protected information. This can be achieved by MAC interfaces to update EHR data.
- Practically, we do not recommend utilizing the "no-read-up" and "no-record" rules that are actualized in MAC. This is because, for most of the patients, keeping track of the transitive connections, executed by a total chain of command of security levels, would be too convoluted for an assignment. Alternatively, simple access/no-access settings must be given to patients.

3.5.1 Overall performance of access controls

Dynamicity: DAC, RBAC, MAC, and ABAC do not possess this feature as they only permit the display of security policies that are restricted to static authorizations, although ABAC is strong in the powerful condition in which the users' attributes are allotted at the time of solicitation and are settled based on an access decision.

Distributed Systems: Classical models are tricky for the distributed system. The ABAC bolsters a circulated condition where the quantity of clients is very high. Furthermore, there is an assurance that the client attributes are brought together in the database in an open and disseminated environment.

Simplicity: All the access controls are administratively straightforward and the access-control model is simple to utilize in that the consents are appointed statically as per the static set-up policies. Although the ABAC model is perplexing because it is very flexible and shareable, it also bolsters worldwide understanding, whereas the client traits are heterogeneous.

Trust: Trust is one of the most significant issues in the access-control mechanism. Trust is primarily acquired in the local domain. It has been established that, in ABAC trust, the constitution is increasingly mind-boggling because of the worldwide understanding of the characteristics in the sharable environment. All the models are most appropriate for structures that work in an open domain, such as cloud computing where various organizations can guarantee both access to data and security for their resources.

As customers of EHR, medical professionals have certain significant criteria for access control. In the case of healthcare, a specialist could contain the role of a doctor and/or intern. This infers that individuals, based on expertise, are connected with the exercises related to their jobs—either doctor or intern—without the overseer listing the doctor and assistant exercises. Health professionals must:

- Access all information needed to meet the medical function under ordinary situations (e.g., standard GP consultation) except when the patient has prevented the physician from accessing the data field.

- Access all the data needed during emergencies regardless of patient access-control environments.
- Link health professionals across the globe through virtual communities of practice so that they can inform one another about effective policies and promote successful practices while at the same time hiding patient's critical medical information.
- The ratio is often skewed, resulting in fewer health providers in rural areas, which results in inefficient secondary services in smaller towns, whereas a high concentration of tertiary healthcare services is available in urban areas.

4 Conclusions

This article discussed access-control requests in the healthcare setting and the current procedures in the healthcare system for access control. We detailed the EHR architecture and the danger model for a general EHR system. The access controls for these aspects must be checked by a central management system. The asymmetric key-based methodology is reasonable in this unique circumstance, for example, in a medical clinic where pre-enrollment of the on-screen characters is plausible. However, we described the level of security features rendered by the combination of each of the four access-control models to an EHR conspire. Healthcare workers pose serious threats to electronic health-record well-being. Additionally, this system is the first to provide two suits of access-control systems for medical applications: cross-area property-based access in ordinary circumstances, and secret phrase-based break-glass access in critical circumstances. These two mechanisms guarantee not only the security of the scrambled medical records of the patients but also they promptly provide data access at critical times to save the patients' lives. Nevertheless, there are still issues related to interoperability among various models, such as legal and institutional limits to significant data. For example, medical data and the execution of a square chain-based idea over an EHR record can illuminate the above insider issue.

References

[1] V. Koufi, F. Malamateniou, G. Vassilacopoulos, Privacy-preserving mobile access to Personal Health Records through Google's Android, in: 2014 4th International Conference on Wireless Mobile Communication and Healthcare-Transforming Healthcare Through Innovations in Mobile and Wireless Technologies (MOBIHEALTH), November, IEEE, 2014, p. 347.

[2] H.M. Chao, S.H. Twu, C.M. Hsu, A secure identification access control scheme for accessing healthcare information systems, in: 4th International IEEE EMBS Special Topic Conference on Information Technology Applications in Biomedicine, April, IEEE, 2003, pp. 122–125.

[3] M.F.F. Khan, K. Sakamura, A smartcard-based framework for delegation management in healthcare Access Control systems, in: 2016 IEEE Region 10 Conference (TENCON), November, IEEE, 2016, pp. 2739–2742.

[4] H. Chi, E.L. Jones, L. Zhao, Implementation of a security access control model for inter-organizational healthcare information systems, in: 2008 IEEE Asia-Pacific Services Computing Conference, December, IEEE, 2008, pp. 692–696.

[5] A. Chryssanthou, I. Varlamis, C. Latsiou, A security model for virtual healthcare communities, in: Virtual Communities, Social Networks and Collaboration, Springer, New York, NY, 2012, pp. 75–113.

[6] K. Abouelmehdi, A. Beni-Hssane, H. Khaloufi, M. Saadi, Big data security and privacy in healthcare: a review, Proc. Comput. Sci. 113 (2017) 73–80.

[7] D. Jagli, S. Purohit, S. Chandra, Knowledge acquisition for electronic health records on cloud, Procedia computer science 112 (2017) 1909–1915.

[8] N. Ploner, M.F. Neurath, M. Schoenthaler, A. Zielke, H.U. Prokosch, Concept to gain trust for a German Personal Health Record system using Public Cloud and FHIR, J. Biomed. Inform. 95 (2019) 103212.

[9] R. Sahney, M. Sharma, Electronic health records: a general overview, Curr. Med. Res. Pract. 8 (2) (2018) 67–70.

[10] X. Zhu, S.P. Tu, D. Sewell, N.A. Yao, V. Mishra, A. Dow, C. Banas, Measuring electronic communication networks in virtual care teams using electronic health records access-log data, Int. J. Med. Inform. 128 (2019) 46–52.

[11] Q. Mamun, A conceptual framework of personally controlled electronic health record (pcehr) system to enhance security and privacy, in: International Conference on Applications and Techniques in Cyber Security and Intelligence, Edizioni della Normale, Cham, June, 2017, pp. 304–314.

[12] A. Ashfaq, A. Sant'Anna, M. Lingman, S. Nowaczyk, Readmission prediction using deep learning on electronic health records, J. Biomed. Inform. 97 (2019) 103256.

[13] P. Vimalachandran, H. Wang, Y. Zhang, Securing electronic medical record and electronic health record systems through an improved access control, in: International Conference on Health Information Science, May, Springer, Cham, 2015, pp. 17–30.

[14] H.S.G. Pussewalage, V.A. Oleshchuk, Attribute based access control scheme with controlled access delegation for collaborative E-health environments, J. Inf. Secur. Appl. 37 (2017) 50–64.

[15] S. Pal, M. Hitchens, V. Varadharajan, T. Rabehaja, Policy-based access control for constrained healthcare resources in the context of the Internet of Things, J. Netw. Comput. Appl. 139 (2019) 57–74.

[16] S. Novak, N. Djordjevic, Information system for evaluation of healthcare expenditure and health monitoring, Physica A: Statistical Mechanics and its Applications 520 (2019) 72–80.

[17] R. Gaardboe, T. Nyvang, N. Sandalgaard, Business intelligence success applied to healthcare information systems, Proc. Comput. Sci. 121 (2017) 483–490.

[18] A.G. Venier, Root cause analysis to support infection control in healthcare premises, J. Hosp. Infect. 89 (4) (2015) 331–334.

[19] Q. Chen, M.Z. Nayyer, I. Raza, S.A. Hussain, A.B. Letaifa, M.S. Ferdous, K. Biswas, M.J. M. Chowdhury, N. Chowdhury, V. Muthukkumarasamy, H.F. Atlam, Toward realizing self-protecting healthcare information systems: design and security challenges, Adv. Comput. 114 (2019) 113.

[20] L. Rostad, O. Edsberg, A study of access control requirements for healthcare systems based on audit trails from access logs, in: 2006 22nd Annual Computer Security Applications Conference (ACSAC'06), December, IEEE, 2006, pp. 175–186.

[21] M.A. de Carvalho Junior, P. Bandiera-Paiva, Health information system role-based access control current security trends and challenges, J. Healthc. Eng. 2018 (2018) 6510249. https://doi.org/10.1155/2018/6510249.

[22] E.O. Boadu, G.K. Armah, Role-based access control (RBAC) based in hospital management, Int. J. Softw. Eng. Knowl. Eng. 3 (2014) 53–67.

[23] M.S. Winchester, B. King, Decentralization, healthcare access, and inequality in Mpumalanga, South Africa, Health Place 51 (2018) 200–207.

[24] Y. Yang, X. Zheng, W. Guo, X. Liu, V. Chang, Privacy-preserving smart IoT-based healthcare big data storage and self-adaptive access control system, Inf. Sci. 479 (2019) 567–592.

[25] A. Ferreira, R.J.C. Correia, D.W. Chadwick, L. Antunes, Access Control in Healthcare: the methodology from legislation to practice, in: MedInfo, 2010, pp. 666–670.

[26] V. Kapsalis, L. Hadellis, D. Karelis, S. Koubias, A dynamic context-aware access control architecture for e-services, Comput. Secur. 25 (7) (2006) 507–521.

[27] A.M. Altamimi, Security and privacy issues in ehealthcare systems: towards trusted services. Int. J. Comput. Sci. Appl. 7 (9) (2016), https://doi.org/10.14569/IJACSA.2016.070933.

[28] M. Evered, S. Bögeholz, A case study in access control requirements for a health information system, in: Proceedings of the Second Workshop on Australasian Information Security, Data Mining and Web Intelligence, and Software Internationalisation, January, Vol. 32, Australian Computer Society, Inc., 2004, pp. 53–61

[29] F. Lega, Developing a marketing function in public healthcare systems: a framework for action, Health Policy 78 (2–3) (2006) 340–352.

[30] S. Stan, Transnational healthcare practices of Romanian migrants in Ireland: inequalities of access and the privatisation of healthcare services in Europe, Soc. Sci. Med. 124 (2015) 346–355.

Security and interference management in the cognitive-inspired Internet of Medical Things

7

Prabhat Thakur and Ghanshyam Singh

Department of Electrical and Electronics Engineering Science, Auckland Park Kingsway Campus,
University of Johannesburg, Johannesburg, South Africa

1 Introduction

Industry 4.0 (I4.0) is a key aspect for future manufacturing and industrial development, which is eagerly awaited by industrialists and researchers. Rapid progress in the field of computing, micro/nano/electromechanical systems, communication, and the internet are likely to achieve this in the very near future [1–8]. The Internet of Things (IoT) has emerged as a very prominent technology that addresses and manages communication among various things such as mobile phones, sensing nodes, industrial sensing, actuating devices, etc. [9–15]. Prominent applications of the IoT are smart homes, smart wearables, smart cities, smart grids, connected vehicles or smart cars, smart chains, smart retail, connected health, etc. All these applications are an integral part of human life these days; however, here, we are emphasizing smart health because the prime importance of a human being is to stay healthy [16–20]. In addition to this, from an I4.0 perspective, the health industry contributes hugely to the total gross domestic product (GDP) of developed countries, e.g., 16.7% and 10% in the United States and United Kingdom, respectively [21].

Moreover, as per the Organization for Economic Co-operation and Development (OECD) Observer magazine, the more that is spent on healthcare, the stronger the economy of a country [21]. It is reported that a 10% increase in life expectancy creates an economic growth of around 0.3%–0.4% a year. In addition, economists claim that healthcare spending is a positive for the growth of a country as it creates jobs and, in turn, people will spend more on the health system. This is proved by an example in the OECD Observer magazine as follows. In 2009, healthcare contribution is one-sixth of the United States' GDP. In 2010, the Patient Protection and Affordable Care Act (Obamacare) was passed and a few years later, healthcare spending increased by 3.9% and produced around 500,000 jobs in the sector. This is only one example: how important is the healthcare system to the economy and how many more systems are there in different countries? Thus it is clear that the medical industry is a major contributor to the economic and industrial growth of a country. Therefore it is worth emphasizing the connection and communication potentials of the health industry that are addressed by the Internet of Medical Things (IoMT) [22–25]. The IoMT is a subpart of the IoT, where the IoT deals with communication and always-on connectivity between devices, called things. Specifically, when these things relate to the medical industry, such as dosimeters, pulse oximeters, etc., then the IoT was renamed the IoMT. The communication channel/spectrum is an essential resource for communication, which is allocated to every kind of service such as telephony, satellite technology, military equipment, etc. and standardized by the IEEE [26]. Similarly, IEEE 802.15.6 is the standard that addresses the physical as well as medium access control spectrum allocation issues for short-range, highly reliable communication in the IoMT. Moreover, this standard defines the various types of communications such as narrowband communication, ultrawideband (UWB) communication, and human body communication with three levels of security (0, 1, 2) with authentication and encryption. These frequency bands of the IEEE 802.15.6 have to comply with applicable medical and communication regulatory authorities such as the Medical Implant Communications Service (MICS) [27–30], Wireless Medical Telemetry Services (WMTS) [31–34], Industrial, Scientific and Medical (ISM) equipment [35,36], and Ultra Wide-Band (UWB) [37,38].

The allocated spectrum bands in IEEE 802.15 in various countries are shown in Fig. 1. The allocated spectrum bands are sufficient for the current scenario as per the number of wireless-connected medical devices. However, the number of wireless-connected devices is increasing rapidly and as per the report provided by Deloitte, the business is going to increase by $52.2 bn by 2022 from $14.9 bn in 2017, as shown in Fig. 2 [24]. This means in the future that the available spectrum bands will be insufficient and this results in spectrum scarcity for the IoMT. The prominent solution in the literature that addresses the spectrum scarcity problem is dynamic spectrum access using cognitive radio (CR), where the unlicensed/cognitive users (CUs) are permitted to communicate with the licensed/primary users (PUs). CR is defined as a device which has two key properties that are cognition and reconfigurability. The cognition refers as the ability of device to know about the surrounding electromagnetic environment by using spectrum sensing. However, reconfigurability is the ability of device to regulate its operating parameters such as as power, modulation scheme, multiple access technique etc., as per the available surrounding environment. Therefore it is worthy and essential to explore the concept of dynamic spectrum access in the IoMT and in this chapter we present the cognitive-inspired IoMT.

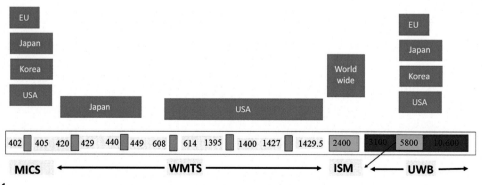

FIG. 1

Spectrum allocation for IEEE 802.15 different countries [26].

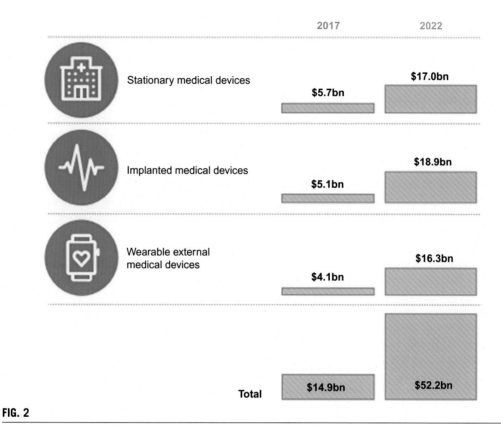

FIG. 2

The business increment in wireless-connected devices from 2017 to 2022 [24].

The key concerns for the IoMT are managing interference to human tissues due to electromagnetic emission of devices, in addition to interference between devices. Therefore the key highlights of this chapter are:

- The various constituents of the CR-inspired IoMT such as cognitive radio, the IoT, as well as the IoMT are explained briefly.
- Furthermore, the different aspects of spectrum sensing and spectrum sharing techniques in the IoMT are illustrated.
- The interference management techniques for the CR-inspired IoMT are explored and elaborated.
- Moreover, due to privacy requirements of medical health information, the security concerns for the cognitive-inspired IoMT are described.

Furthermore, this chapter is organized as follows. The next section describes the key constituents of the cognitive-inspired IoMT. Section 3 presents the different aspects of the cognitive-inspired IoMT. Additionally, interference management and security concerns for the CR-inspired IoMT are illustrated in Sections 4 and 5, respectively. Finally, Section 6 looks at future perspectives.

2 Constituents of the cognitive-inspired Internet of Medical Things

In this section, we deal with the fundamentals of cognitive radio communication systems and the IoMT.

2.1 Spectrum sharing in cognitive radio networks

In cognitive radio networks [39–43], the CU establishes communications on the PU channel in such a way that the PU communication remains unaffected by following a cognitive engine cycle, which comprises the following steps, namely, (1) spectrum sensing [44,45], (2) spectrum analysis and decision [46], (3) spectrum accessing [47,48], and (4) spectrum mobility [49,50]. Initially, the CU performs spectrum sensing on the channels to detect the status of the channel that is idle (free) or active (busy). Furthermore, the CU selects the most suitable idle channel for the communication and starts the data transmission on that channel by using the appropriate spectrum accessing technique. The reappearance of the PU communication is an important phenomenon during the CU communication, and if it happens the CU needs to switch its communication to the other available channel, and this process is termed spectrum mobility. Interference avoidance to the PU communication by the CU communication is achieved by using various spectrum accessing techniques: interweave, underlay, overlay, and hybrid spectrum accessing techniques, which are explained in detail as follows.

In the interweave spectrum accessing approach, spectrum sensing ability is essential for the CU and the entire communication uses time frames where a time frame comprises the sensing and data transmission periods. The CU senses the channel during the sensing periods and transmits the data during the data transmission period if the channel is sensed as idle, otherwise it senses another channel. The process of spectrum sensing and data transmission repeats periodically until the completion of communication. The key limitation of this accessing technique is that the CU needs to stop its communication if the channel is sensed as idle, which is undesirable in certain applications such as voice telephony. Therefore a new spectrum accessing technique is proposed where the CU establishes the communication simultaneous to PU communication; however, the interference at the PU receiver is avoided by constraining the CU transmission power so that the power received at the PU receiver is below the predefined threshold, called the interference temperature. This approach provides seamless communication; however, the key issue is the low channel capacity due to constrained power transmission even in the absence of the PU. Because both approaches have adequacies and inadequacies, to enjoy the benefits and avoid the inadequacies of both approaches, researchers have proposed a potential technique called hybrid spectrum accessing, where spectrum sensing is a prerequisite. The idle-sensed channels are accessed via interweave spectrum access; however, busy channels are accessed by using the underlay spectrum access approach. In addition to this, overlay spectrum access is a potential spectrum access technique, which allows the CU and PU to access the channel simultaneously with full power; however, interference management is achieved by using advance encoding techniques such as dirty paper coding [51]. The need for such advance encoding techniques makes this approach more complex and less popular.

2.2 Internet of Things

A thing in the IoT can be a person with sensing units implanted on the body, a sensing device installed in a forest, a farm animal with a biochip transponder, a well-equipped vehicle, a mobile, a computer, or any other natural or indigenously developed object that can be assigned an IP address and is able to transmit/receive (transceiver) data over a network [9]. The rapid evolution of the IoT has a deep economic and social impact on human life in various perspectives such as health, medical concerns, smart homes, cities, offices, retail, marketing, cars, etc. However, these things are usually resource constraints, for example: (1) energy constraints for battery-operated things whose battery is irreplaceable and unchangeable such as sensing devices installed at remote places or inside the human body, etc., (2) spectrum constraints for densely deployed devices in a particular area, and (3) maximum power transmission constraints for devices installed on the human body, etc. Various organizations in a variety of industries are using the IoT to operate more efficiently, cost-effectively, faultlessly, and have a better understanding of customers to improve customer services, improve decision-making, and increase the value of business. However, one thing is insufficient to serve these functions for industry. Therefore the IoT finds various applications in industry by exploiting different kinds of things such as the medical industry, transport industry, consumer services, etc.

2.3 Internet of Medical Things

The IoMT is an integral and highly desired but less explored constituent of the IoT. The IoMT deals with medical sensing, processing, communication, as well as actuating devices. This means IoMT devices need to be sufficient and eligible to be installed inside the human body, outside the body, or in a nearby zone; however, communication also needs to be maintained among all the installed devices as well as with the base station for connecting to internet/cloud/remote location, as shown in Fig. 3. Thus the IoMT can be further classified into the following subparts: hospitals and clinics, homes, on the body, and/or inside the body. In other ways, these are classified as biomedical devices, WBANs, telemedicine systems, and mobile hospital information systems, as shown in Fig. 4 and well illustrated by Favela et al. in [53].

   Biomedical devices are not generally designed to transmit data through wireless systems; however, their functions are affected because of electromagnetic interference. Telemedicine systems are used to monitor, diagnose, and treat patients remotely by forwarding the data collected by WBANs. Moreover, mobile hospital information systems store, retrieve, and process patients' medical health records. Here, the WBAN is an integral and very prominent aspect of the IoMT, which needs to sense (collect), process, as well as communicate that information to a suitable sink such as the base station and a central node. Therefore communication for WBANs is classified into three parts, namely, intra-WBAN, inter-WBAN, and beyond-WBAN communication. In intra-WBAN communication, the sensing nodes communicate with each other inside or on the body without any intermediate device such as a router; however, for different kinds of sensing nodes, other devices such as a router and base station come under the category of inter-WBAN communication. In beyond-WBAN communication, the sensor nodes are connected to remote locations through the base stations' access points. The key scenario for beyond-WBAN communication comprises telemonitoring of a patient or healthy person, telemedicine, telemedical database accessing, etc. [27]. Intra-WBAN communication further comprises inside-body, on-body, and inside/on-body node communication.

   Inside-body node design causes much concerned and is a challenging issue when compared with on/outside-body nodes because of size as well as power constraint. Therefore inside-body sensing nodes are further classified with and without battery, and with and without sensing ability. The battery requirement increases the size of the devices; however, batteries have limited duration that directly affects the life of a device. Moreover, spectrum sensing ability increases the need for processing power and directly affects the lifetime of battery-operated devices. Therefore without spectrum sensing and

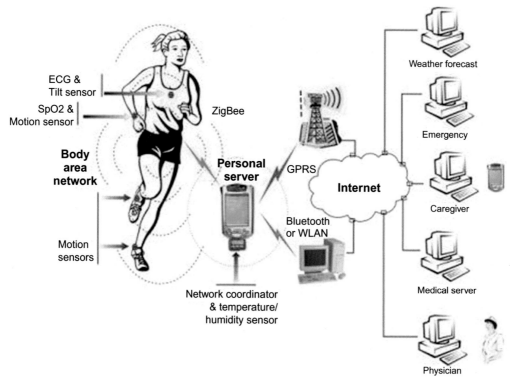

FIG. 3

A scenario of the Internet of Medical Things [52]. *ECG*, electrocardiogram; *GPRS*, general packet radio services; *SpO2*, peripheral capillary oxygen saturation; *WLAN*, wireless local area network.

From E. Jovanov, A. Milenkovic, C. Otto, et al., A wireless body area network of intelligent motion sensors for computer assisted physical rehabilitation, J. Neuroeng. Rehabil. 2 (2005) 6.

without batteries it is a suitable option for inside the body; however, the key question is how to achieve spectrum sensing- and battery-free conditions. Spectrum sensing conditions can be achieved by using data-based spectrum sensing techniques according to which a database can be created by the outside-body nodes, and on demand the spectrum can be provided to the inside-body nodes. On-body sensing node communication is less vulnerable to the challenges faced by inside-body units because the batteries are easy to replace and their size, because of the use of a battery, is not a major concern. Inter-WBANs are primarily categorized into two types that have infrastructure-based and infrastructure-less architecture. In the infrastructure-based inter-WBANs, communication is controlled by a centralized unit, which is also known as centralized architecture; however, infrastructure-less architecture devices perform all the functions of spectrum accessing individually, therefore they are also known as ad-hoc architecture devices. Beyond-WBAN also comprises ad-hoc architecture. Furthermore, potential techniques for the implementation or complete working of the IoMT are medical sensors, connectivity among sensors using the IoT, and artificial intelligence to fetch the required information from the data produced by the sensing devices.

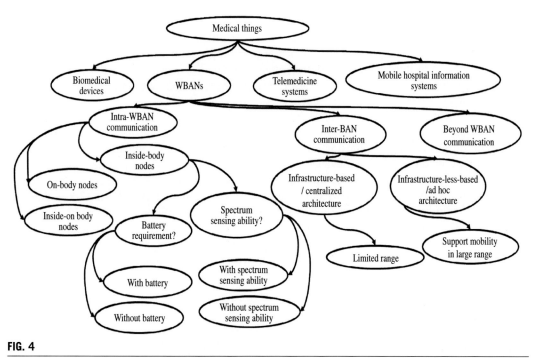

FIG. 4

Varieties of various Internet of Medical Things.

On the other hand, recent developments in the field of nanogenerators due to body organ functionalities, motivates us to think about battery-free inside-body sensing nodes. The number of energy harvesting techniques to provide complementary power to prolong battery life or fulfill complete power demand of the implanted medical electronic devices has been reported in the literature [12]. The key phenomena inside the human body used for energy harvesting are heart beating, muscle stretching, and glucose oxidation by exploiting the piezo/triboelectric, electromagnetic, thermoelectric, and electrochemical effects. Among all of the reported phenomena, mechanical movement of organs is the most abundant energy source in vivo. Quyang et al. [54] presented a symbiotic cardiac pacemaker that exploits heart beats to harvest energy so that the power demand of pacemakers can be fulfilled with any external source. It is reported that the symbiotic pacemaker improves sinus arrhythmia and successfully prevents deterioration, and the energy harvested from each cardiac motion cycle is 0.495 μJ; however, the required endocardial pacing threshold energy is 0.377 μJ. Thus it is clear that the proposed symbiotic cardiac pacemaker is a well-tested and effective solution to fulfill the demand for power supply for pacemakers. Ansari and Karami [55] proposed an energy harvester that converts myocardial motions into electricity to power leadless pacemakers, and the generated energy is stored in a battery or super-capacitor. The device is composed of a bimorph piezoelectric beam confined in a gray iron frame. The proposed system is assembled at high temperature and operated at body temperature.

In addition to this, one important aspect of the IoMT is electronic skin (e-skin), which comprises most of the properties of human or animal skin and is composed of countless neural sensors that can perceive various stimuli, such as pressure, temperature, and texture of an object [56]. In addition to its advanced sensing capability, human skin is mechanically flexible, stretchable, robust, and self-healing, therefore e-skin is an artificial smart skin, aimed at providing a similar sense of touch to robots and artificial prostheses by mimicking some of the features of human skin. To achieve this property, there is a need to develop and integrate multiple sensors on nonplanar, flexible, and conformal surfaces, first, to make it viable, and then to advance today's e-skin applications.

By using various sensors, e-skin can be used for the health monitoring of an athlete, patient, or a healthy person at home. The key flexible, stretchable, and robust nature of e-skin makes it more appropriate for monitoring, diagnosing, and treating human beings as compared to the individual deployment of medical sensing devices. E-skin similar to WBANs can collect data on the body and also transmit to a remote location through a proper communication medium. Prof. Takao Someya at the University of Tokyo has reported a very thin, nearly 3.5 μm e-skin (similar to the thread of a spider), which can monitor various health conditions as well as be displayed on a 24*16 LED array [57]. In addition, the e-skin can measure the electrocardiogram with a nano-mesh electrode combined with a wireless communication module, which makes it more suitable for remote monitoring of the patient. Some other works for the implementation of e-skin are reported in [58–60].

3 Cognitive-inspired Internet of Medical Things

As we have seen in previous sections the number of wireless-connected medical devices is increasing very rapidly and in the near future the spectrum allocated for the IoMT will not be able to serve such a large number of devices. Therefore we need to look for an efficient and effective way to resolve this problem and one prominent solution is dynamic spectrum access using the cognitive radio.

The key constituents of cognitive radio are spectrum sensing and spectrum accessing techniques, which are further elaborated in detail with their suitability in the IoMT, as shown in Fig. 5. The spectrum sensing techniques are further classified as coherent and noncoherent techniques—the word coherent refers to the need of PU activities/parameters; however, the noncoherent technique is free from such prerequisites. Furthermore, spectrum accessing techniques are classified either with or without the prerequisite of spectrum sensing ability.

3.1 Spectrum sensing techniques

Spectrum sensing techniques are broadly classified into two forms: narrowband and wideband spectrum sensing, where the narrowband comprises the coherent and noncoherent spectrum sensing techniques. There are various coherent spectrum sensing techniques, namely, feature detection (which further comprises cyclostationarity, waveform detector, corelation detector), matched filter detector, eigenvalue-based techniques, etc.; however, there is only one noncoherent technique, called energy detection spectrum sensing. In this section, we emphasize only the narrowband spectrum sensing techniques, because wideband spectrum sensing is out of the scope of this chapter due to its unsuitability for the IoMT.

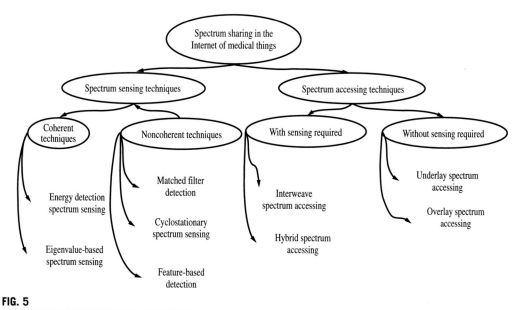

FIG. 5

Spectrum sharing techniques in the Internet of Medical Things.

3.1.1 Energy-based spectrum sensing

This is a very popular technique due to its less complex nature and no requirement for PU activity, which is noncoherent in nature. In this technique, the CU receiver receives the signal from the PU, samples it, and performs the average sum of all the samples to compute the energy level of the incoming signal [61]. Furthermore, this energy is compared with a predefined value known as energy threshold and if computed energy is greater than the threshold, the PU is assumed to be present otherwise considered as absent. However, threshold selection is a critical and prime perspective for this spectrum sensing technique because even small change in the value of threshold affects the decision drastically which means from present to absent or vice-versa. Therefore, various researchers are working to achieve the effective as well as efficient threshold selection techniques [62–64]. In addition to this, the poor performance of the energy detection technique in the low signal-to-noise ratio (SNR) makes it unsuitable for low SNR scenarios whether it is an inside- or on-body node.

3.1.2 Matched filter detection

This is the first type of noncoherent spectrum sensing that requires information on the signal transmitted by the PU [65]. This detection technique relies on the matched filter detector, which is popular in communication theory where the key aim is to maximize the SNR. The key constraint with this technique is that at the receiving end (i.e., at the CU), there should be full information available about the transmitted signal (i.e., the PU) because the correlation between the received and already available signal is computed, and if it is high the PU is assumed to be present, or absent if it is low. This technique is robust to the high noise disturbance and low SNR scenarios, and not only detects the PU signal but can also measure the power level of the PU signal. Moreover, it is worth mentioning that the performance of this technique degrades in high noise fluctuating scenarios. Therefore it is perceived that this technique is suitable for scenarios where information on PU signals can be provided and a sufficient complexity level can be handled; however, it is unsuitable for high fluctuating SNR scenarios in WBANs.

3.1.3 Feature detection

In the feature detection spectrum sensing technique, a specific signature of the PU signal such as pilots, beacon frames, cyclic prefix, hopping sequence, etc. is captured by the CU [66]. Specifically, the cyclostationary nature of a waveform differentiates it from the noise, which is a prominent example of feature detection. However, the key limitation of this approach is the requirement of the PU transmitted signal period, chirp rate, etc. Thus it is clear that similar to the matched filter detection technique, the feature detection technique is unsuitable for scenarios where the information on PU signals can be provided and a sufficient complexity level can be handled; however, it is unsuitable for the scenario where very fast spectrum sensing is desired because it is slow compared to the energy detection technique.

3.1.4 Eigenvalue-based detector

This detector comes under the class of noncoherent spectrum sensing detector, which means it does not require any information about the PU transmitted signal. This detector relies on the principle that some of the communication signals convey a specifically known structure to the covariance matrix, which can be achieved based on the correlation among the received signal samples [67]. The test statistic in the detector is the ratio of the max to min eigenvalue of the covariance matrix, which is compared with the threshold to form decisions. This spectrum sensing technique is highly reliable in such a way that it can detect the PU signal efficiently even in low SNR scenarios. However, the key limitation is high-computational complexity. This technique is most suitable for medical services due to noncoherence, high reliability, as well as its robust nature to noise uncertainty; however, high WBAN devices need to handle the high-computational complexity.

3.2 Spectrum accessing techniques

Potential spectrum accessing techniques for WBANs are illustrated as follows and key aspects for the IoMT are illustrated in Table 1.

3.2.1 Interweave spectrum accessing

For this spectrum accessing technique, the CUs/sensing nodes need to be equipped with the spectrum sensing ability in addition to their own sensing (specific parameters such as temperature, humidity, etc.) ability. The sensing devices sense the spectrum and transmit the information toward the base station via that channel if it is detected as idle, otherwise it senses another channel. This accessing technique is not suitable for battery-operated small sensing devices, which cannot tolerate the high-computational complexity and power consumption. Therefore it is worth saying that the interweave spectrum accessing technique is suitable for on-body sensing devices, which can tolerate the large size and high-computational complexity; however, it is unsuitable for inside-body sensing nodes.

Table 1 Key aspects of spectrum accessing techniques for the Internet of Medical Things.

Spectrum accessing strategy	Simultaneous transmission of CU and PU	Prerequisite	Constraints on power transmission	Interference management	Suitability for application in WBANs
Interweave	Not allowed	Spectrum sensing	–	Interference controlling	On body
Underlay	Allowed	Interference power tolerable limit of PU	Power at PU receiver due to CU transmission needs to be below the interference limit	Interference avoiding	Inside body
Hybrid	Allowed	Spectrum sensing, interference power tolerable limit of PU	Power at PU receiver due to CU transmission needs to be below the interference limit tolerable by the CU	Interference controlling and interference avoiding	On body
Overlay	Allowed	Advance interference cancellation techniques are required at PU and CU	–	Interference mitigating	Inside body, on body, base station

CU, cognitive user; PU, primary user; WBANs, wireless body networks.

3.2.2 Underlay spectrum accessing

In this spectrum accessing technique, there is no need for spectrum sensing ability as the CU transmits the data with constrained power so that the PU communication remains impervious. However, the key prerequisite for this technique is the availability of maximum tolerable interference at the PU, which is called interference temperature. This technique is suitable for inside-body sensing devices that are battery operated and irreplaceable because the low/constrained power transmission improves the life of sensing devices as well as provides seamless communication.

3.2.3 Overlay spectrum accessing

This spectrum accessing technique has a very complex nature; however, it can provide high-channel capacity due to high-power transmission even in the presence of a PU and is suitable for on-body or outside-body sensing devices that can tolerate such high complexity. The most suitable device for overlay spectrum access in the WBAN is the base station, which needs to transmit the entire data collected from all the sensing devices to the nearby or remote controlling station.

3.2.4 Hybrid spectrum accessing technique

The hybrid spectrum accessing technique is a combination of interweave and underlay spectrum accessing techniques and spectrum sensing ability is desired for the sensing device. Due to spectrum sensing ability requirements, this technique is unsuitable for inside-body devices; however, it is suitable for on-side as well as outside body devices. The key issue that the hybrid spectrum accessing technique needs to address is power switching from high to low and vice versa.

4 Interference management in the cognitive-inspired Internet of Medical Things

Interference management is an important aspect in conventional wireless networks; however, it becomes of prime importance in WBANs because even a small amount of interference can affect communication, which may directly result in the loss of human life. Therefore, in this section, we have investigated various aspects of interference management in cognitive inspired WBANs, namely, (1) spectrum sensing, (2) prediction and update of WBAN channel access and sensing times, (3) prediction of PU activities, (4) transmission below PU tolerable interference, (5) allocation of a portion of SU power to relay the PU message, and (6) spectrum monitoring, as shown in Fig. 6.

4.1 Spectrum sensing

Spectrum sensing is the prime element of the CR-inspired IoMT for interference avoidance where the channel is sensed before data transmission and data are only transmitted on the idle-sensed channel. On the emergence of the PU, the CU needs to switch the communication to another idle-sensed channel to avoid interference at the same channel. Various spectrum sensing techniques are well illustrated in Section 3.1. The key issue with the spectrum sensing technique is that it needs to provide a dedicated time slot or extra sensing units [48]. In addition to this, the complexity as well as prerequisites for the spectrum sensing technique used need to be considered during the design of IoMT. Therefore selection of the particular spectrum accessing technique for WBAN scenarios (inside body, on body, etc.) is a potential issue that is yet to be investigated.

4.2 Spectrum prediction

Spectrum prediction is a technique that exploits the historical information about the PU channel states to predict the future states of the channel [68–70].

Spectrum prediction is used for interference management in two ways: (1) as a supporter of the spectrum sensing technique and (2) for spectrum mobility by predicting the emergence time of the PU on the current communication channel. In the first approach, the CU predicts the states of channels in the high traffic environments, among which a highly idle predicted channel is selected for spectrum sensing. If that channel is sensed as idle, then data transmission starts, otherwise the second highest idle-sensed channel is sensed, and so on [71]. In the second approach, the CU predicts the emergence time of the PU during the CU transmission and enables the CU to switch its communication before emergence of the PU, which results in proactive spectrum mobility [50]. Thus it is clear that spectrum prediction enables the CU to avoid interference with the PU that occurred during the emergence and detection time of the PU. Various spectrum prediction techniques are reported in the literature, e.g., hidden Markov model-based prediction, multilayer perceptron neural network-based prediction, Bayesian inference-based prediction, moving average-based prediction, autoregressive model-based prediction, static neighbor graph-based prediction, and deep learning-based prediction [68,72].

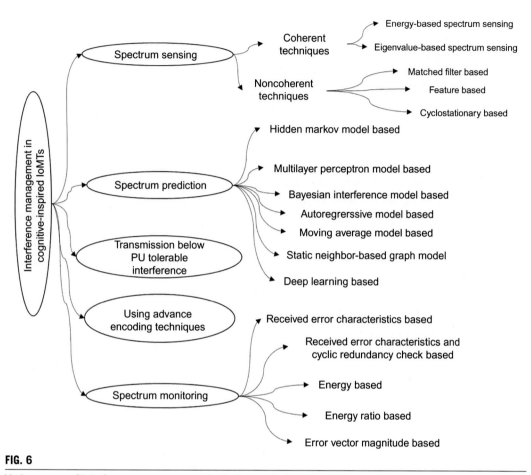

FIG. 6

Various ways of interference management in the Internet of Medical Things. *IoMT*, Internet of Medical Things; *PU*, primary user.

The key issues with the spectrum prediction technique are: (1) the need for historical information, which is not so easy to obtain, (2) the need for a storage unit as well as power requirements for the predictive analysis because for predictive analyses huge amounts of data need to be analyzed, which introduces the challenges of big data analytics, (3) moreover, the complexity of the prediction technique, which is also a prominent point that needs to be considered during the design of medical things because the more complex nature of the technique may affect power consumption as well as size of the unit.

4.3 Transmission below the PU interference tolerable limit

This is potentially a very effective way to avoid interference at the PU if we have information of the PU interference tolerable limit and high channel capacity per unit bandwidth is optional. In this technique, the CU controls its power in such a way that the power received at the PU receiver is below the already defined interference threshold. This technology is achieved by using UWB technology, where all the information is spread over a large bandwidth with low power similar to noise. This enables the CU to avoid interference at the PU by exploiting the well-explored spread spectrum technique [73].

The key issue with this technique is the availability of the interference threshold level that can be tolerated by the PU. In addition to this, the low data rate per unit bandwidth restricts the application of this technique only in scenarios where the generated data rate is less than the achieved data rate, which makes it unsuitable for high data-generated scenarios.

4.4 Using advanced encoding techniques

These techniques allow the CU to transmit data with full power even in the presence of a PU on the channel; however, for this the CU should have the ability to use advanced encoding techniques. The use of advance encoding techniques makes a system more complex and needs more power for processing. This technique is unsuitable for inside-body sensing devices because of the highly complex nature and demand for high power; however, it is suitable for on-body or surrounding medical devices where high data rates are required and because cost and complexity can be compromised with better medical facilities. The key issues that need to be addressed by researchers for this technique are complexity and power consumption; however, the practical implementation of this technique is a major milestone.

4.5 Spectrum monitoring

Spectrum monitoring is a very prominent and recently explored technique used to detect the emergence of a PU during the CU communication so that the CU can stop/switch the communication on that channel. This technique serves the same purpose as spectrum sensing; however, it does not require an extra hardware unit and time, which make it more suitable for spectrum mobility/hand-off. The CU only exploits the characteristics of the received signal for processing to know the deviation from the normal received signal that indicates the emergence of the PU. On detection of the emergence of the PU, the CU stops its communication immediately, and switches its communication to another available channel. In the literature, various spectrum monitoring techniques are reported such as received error count-based spectrum monitoring, received error count and cyclic redundancy check-based spectrum monitoring, energy-based spectrum monitoring, energy ratio-based spectrum monitoring, and error vector magnitude-based spectrum monitoring [74].

The challenge for the spectrum monitoring technique is to analyze the processing power required for a particular monitoring technique because an increase in processing power affects the total power consumption of the medical unit that makes it unsuitable for inside-body units.

5 Security concerns regarding the cognitive-inspired IoMT

The security aspects that have to be considered for healthcare services, especially for the IoMT and WBANs, are highly confidential. Therefore the data generated by the sensing devices need to be encrypted to protect against intrusion attacks. However, the small size of inside-body devices creates challenges for researchers who desire low-power and fewer overhead encryption techniques, which is a perplexing task. Moreover, the introduction of cognitive radio to the IoMT makes it more challenging for security concerns due to spectrum sensing and accessing techniques, therefore various security

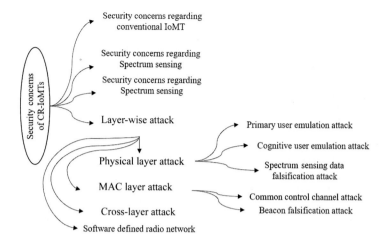

FIG. 7

Security concerns of cognitive-inspired Internet of Medical Things.

concerns for the cognitive-inspired IoMT are depicted in Fig. 7. Spectrum sensing is vulnerable to primary user emulation attacks, where the intruder mimics the primary user activities and restricts the CU/medical devices to find the idle channel even when it is idle [75]. Moreover, in the absence of a PU, if the CU is using the available spectrum, mimicking of CU activities starts the cognitive user emulation attack. The proposed solution for these attacks in conventional cognitive radio networks is to identify the intruders by differentiating legitimate users in the following ways, namely, (1) key allocation based, (2) trust based, etc. [76]. However, the small size and limited power capacity of the IoMT, especially inside-body devices, makes it a very challenging and prominent research area that is yet to be explored.

Accessing techniques also introduce security challenges for the IoMT; these are called common control channel attack and beacon falsification attack. Moreover, cross-layer design and reconfigurability with a software-defined networking introduce further challenges [77–79]. Controlled power transmission using the spread spectrum technique via the UWB is prominent and less vulnerable to security threats and is preferred for security in wireless communication.

In addition to this, the key challenge is an open research issue that is yet to be explored, e.g., (1) design of the cognitive-inspired IoMT physical parameter specifications, (2) design of medium access control protocols, (3) design of nanodevices (medical) bearing in mind flexibility, implantation, life period, and power consumption, and (4) design of minimum and maximum values of transmission parameters due to constraint on the effect on the human body organs and tissues.

6 Conclusion

The key aim of this chapter was to address the potential aspects of spectrum sharing in the IoMT. In this chapter, we started with the IoMT and its role in I4.0. Furthermore, the key constituents that are the IoT, cognitive radio and the IoMT, were explored. Moreover, the exploitation of CR in the IoMT was illustrated where the emphasis was on spectrum sensing, spectrum sharing, and interference management issues. In addition to this, by keeping in mind the security need for the IoMT, the key aspects of secure communication for the cognitive-inspired IoMT and its challenges were explored. This is only one step toward the feasibility of the cognitive-inspired IoMT; there are various open-research challenges for the design of a complete cognitive-inspired IoMT framework.

References

[1] B. Chen, J. Wan, L. Shu, P. Li, M. Mukherjee, B. Yin, Smart factory of industry 4.0: key technologies case, and challenges, IEEE Access 6 (2017) 6505–6519.

[2] M. Brettel, N. Friederichsen, M. Keller, M. Rosenberg, How virtualization, decentralization and network building change the manufacturing landscape: an industry 4.0 perspective, Int. J. Mech. Ind. Sci. Eng. 8 (1) (2014) 37–44.

[3] F. Li, J. Wan, P. Zhang, D. Li, D. Zhang, K. Zhou, Usage-specific semantic integration for cyber-physical robot systems, ACM Trans. Embed. Comput. Syst. 15 (3) (2016) 1–20.

[4] J. Zhou, Intelligent manufacturing-main direction of 'Made in China 2025', China Mech. Eng. 26 (17) (2015) 2273–2284.

[5] J. Wan, M. Yi, D. Li, C. Zhang, S. Wang, K. Zhou, Mobile services for customization manufacturing systems: an example of industry 4.0, IEEE Access 4 (2016) 8977–8986.

[6] J. Wan, S. Tang, Q. Hua, D. Li, C. Liu, J. Lloret, Contextaware cloud robotics for material handling in cognitive industrial Internet of Things, IEEE Internet Things J. 5 (4) (2018) 2272–2281.

[7] D. Zhang, J. Wan, C.-H. Hsu, A. Rayes, Industrial technologies and applications for the Internet of Things, Comput. Netw. 101 (2016) 1–4.

[8] S. Wang, J. Wan, D. Zhang, D. Li, C. Zhang, Towards smart factory for Industry 4.0: a self-organized multi-agent system with big data based feedback and coordination, Comput. Netw. 101 (2016) 158–168.

[9] A. Al-Fuqaha, M. Guizani, M. Mohammadi, M. Aledhari, M. Ayyash, Internet of Things: a survey on enabling technologies, protocols, and applications, IEEE Commun. Surv. Tutor. 17 (4) (2015) 2347–2376.

[10] D. Evans, The Internet of Things: How the Next Evolution of the Internet Is Changing Everything, CISCO, San Jose, CA, USA, White Paper, 2011.

[11] L. Atzori, A. Iera, G. Morabito, The Internet of Things: a survey, Comput. Netw. 54 (15) (2010) 2787–2805.

[12] J. Gubbi, R. Buyya, S. Marusic, M. Palaniswami, Internet of Things (IoT): a vision, architectural elements, and future directions, Futur. Gener. Comput. Syst. 29 (7) (2013) 1645–1660.

[13] A. Gluhak, S. Krco, M. Nati, D. Pfisterer, N. Mitton, T. Razafindralambo, A survey on facilities for experimental Internet of Things research, IEEE Commun. Mag. 49 (11) (2011) 58–67.

[14] Z. Sheng, S. Yang, Y. Yu, A.V. Vasilakos, J.A. Mccann, K.K. Leung, A survey on the IETF protocol suite for the Internet of Things: standards, challenges, and opportunities, IEEE Wirel. Commun. 20 (6) (2013) 91–98.

[15] F. Wang, L. Hu, J. Zhou, A survey from the perspective of evolutionary process in the internet of things, Int. J. Distrib. Sensor Netw. 2015 (2015) 1–9.

[16] Are IOT healthcare solutions the future of the healthcare industry?, iot.nxt, 2019. Available at: https://www.itweb.co.za/content/VgZey7JAdLLvdjX9. (Accessed 5 May 2019).

[17] Examples of the Internet of Things in healthcare, Ecosuitancy, 2019. Available at: https://econsultancy.com/internet-of-things-healthcare/. (Accessed 5 May 2019).

[18] R. Chouffani, Current and future applications of IoT in healthcare, TechTraget, 2019. Available at: https://internetofthingsagenda.techtarget.com/feature/Can-we-expect-the-Internet-of-Things-in-healthcare. (Accessed 5 May 2019).

[19] S. Chatterjee, S. Chatterjee, S. Choudhury, S. Basak, S. Dey, S. Sain, K. S. Goshal, N. Dalmia, S. Sirchar, Internet of Things and Body area network-an integrated future, in: 2017

IEEE 8th Annual Ubiquitous Computing, Electronics and Mobile Communication Conference (UEMCON), New-York, USA, October, 2017, pp. 1–6.

[20] G. Elhayatmy, N. Dey, A.S. Ashour, Internet of things based wireless body area network in healthcare, in: N. Dey, A. Hassanien, C. Bhatt, A. Ashour, S. Satapathy (Eds.), Internet of Things and Big Data Analytics Toward Next-Generation Intelligence, Studies in Big Data, Vol. 30, Springer, Cham, 2017.

[21] https://community.mbaworld.com/blog/b/weblog/posts/healthcare-its-influence-and-importance-in-the-economy.

[22] B. Marr, Why the internet of medical things (IoMTs) will start to transform healthcare in 2018, Available at: https://www.forbes.com/sites/bernardmarr/2018/01/25/why-the-internet-of-medical-things-iomt-will-start-to-transform-healthcare-in-2018/#717e8a0a4a3c. (Accessed 5 May 2019).

[23] K. Devis, Introduction to the Internet of Medical Things (IoMT), Digikey, 2019. Available at: https://dzone.com/articles/internet-of-medical-things-iomt. (Accessed 5 May 2019).

[24] Medtech and the Internet of Medical Things: How connected medical devices are transforming health care, Available at: https://www2.deloitte.com/global/en/pages/life-sciences-and-healthcare/articles/medtech-internet-of-medical-things.html. (Accessed 5 May 2019).

[25] H. Singh, Internet of Medical Things (IoMT): Future of the Medical World, Customer Think, 2019. Available at: http://customerthink.com/internet-of-medical-things-iomt-future-of-the-medical-world/. (Accessed 5 May 2019).

[26] K.S. Kwak, S. Ullah, N. Ullah, An overview of IEEE 802.15.6 standard, in: 2010 3rd International Symposium on Applied Sciences in Biomedical and Communication Technologies (ISABEL 2010), Rome, Italy, 2010, pp. 1–6.

[27] S. Sodagari, B. Bozorghami, H. Aghvami, Technologies and challenges for cognitve radio enabled wireless body area networks, IEEE Access 6 (2018) 29567–29586.

[28] M.N. Islam, M.R. Yuce, Review of medical implant communication system (MICS) band and network, ICT Express 2 (4) (2016) 188–194.

[29] K.Y. Yazdandoost, R. Kohno, Health care and medical implanted communications service, in: 13th International Conference on Biomedical Engineering. IFMBE Proceedings, vol. 23, Springer, Berlin, Heidelberg, 2009.

[30] T. Gee, Medical Implant Communications Service Tutorial, Available at: https://medicalconnectivity.com/2006/03/03/medical-implant-communications-service-tutorial/. (Accessed 5 May 2019).

[31] Wireless Medical Telemetry Service (WMTS), Available at: https://www.fcc.gov/wireless/bureau-divisions/mobility-division/wireless-medical-telemetry-service-wmts. (Accessed 5 May 2019).

[32] Wireless Medical Telemetry Systems, Available at: https://www.fda.gov/medical-devices/wireless-medical-devices/wireless-medical-telemetry-systems. (Accessed 5 May 2019).

[33] Wireless Medical Telemetry Services (WMTS), Available at: https://searchhealthit.techtarget.com/definition/WMTS-wireless-medical-telemetry-services. (Accessed 5 May 2019).

[34] American Hospital Association, Wireless Medical Telemetry Service (WMTS), Available at: http://www.ashe.org/wmts/, 2019. (Accessed 5 May 2019).

[35] Industrial, Scientific and Medical Radio Band (ISM Band), Available at: https://www.techopedia.com/definition/27785/industrial-scientific-and-medical-radio-band-ism-band. (Accessed 5 May 2019).

[36] Industrial, Scientific and Medical (ISM), Available at: https://celectronics.com/training/learning/product_family_standard/ISM-Industrial-Scientific-Medical-equipment.html. (Accessed 5 May 2019).

[37] S.D. Amico, M.D. Matteis, O. Rousseaux, K. Philips, B. Gyselinck, D. Neirynck, A. Baschirotto, Ultra wide band in medical applications, in: Advances in Biomedical Sensing, Measurements, Instrumentation and Systems, Lecture Notes in Electrical Engineering, Vol. 55, Springer, Berlin, Heidelberg, 2009.

[38] https://www.sciencedirect.com/topics/engineering/ultra-wide-band. (Accessed 5 May 2019).

[39] I.F. Alkyldiz, W.-Y. Lee, M.C. Vuran, S. Mohanty, NeXt generation/dynamic spectrum access/cognitive radio wireless networks: a survey, Comput. Netw. 50 (13) (2006) 2127–2159.

[40] A. Ghasemi, E.S. Sousa, Fundamental limits of spectrum-sharing in fading environment, IEEE Trans. Wirel. Commun. 6 (2) (2007) 649–658.

[41] J. Mitola, G.Q. Maguire, Cognitive radio: making software radio more personal, IEEE Pers. Commun. 6 (4) (1999) 13–18.

[42] S. Haykin, Cognitive radio: brain-empowered wireless communications, IEEE J Sel. Areas Commun. 23 (2) (2005) 201–220.

[43] P. Thakur, G. Singh, S.N. Satasia, Spectrum sharing in cognitive radio communication system using power constraints: a technical review, Perspect. Sci. 8 (2016) 651–653.

[44] A. Ali, W. Hamouda, Advances on spectrum sensing for cognitive radio networks: theory and applications, IEEE Commun. Surv. Tutor. 19 (2) (2017) 1277–1304.

[45] T. Yucek, H. Arslan, A survey of spectrum sensing algorithms for cognitive radio applications, IEEE Commun. Surv. Tutor. 11 (1) (2009) 116–130.

[46] M. Masonta, M. Mzyece, N. Ntlatlapa, Spectrum decision in cognitive radio networks: a survey, IEEE Commun. Surv. Tutor. 15 (3) (2013) 1088–1107.

[47] M.G. Khoshkholg, K. Navaie, H. Yanikomeroglu, Access strategies for spectrum sharing in fading environment: overlay, underlay and mixed, IEEE Trans. Mob. Comput. 9 (12) (2010).

[48] P. Thakur, A. Kumar, S. Pandit, G. Singh, S.N. Satasia, Advanced frame structures for hybrid spectrum accessing strategy in cognitive radio communication system, IEEE Commun. Lett. 21 (2) (2017) 410–413.

[49] W.-Y. Lee, I.F. Alkyldiz, Spectrum aware mobility management in cognitive radio cellular networks, IEEE Trans. Mob. Comput. 11 (4) (2012) 529–542.

[50] P. Thakur, A. Kumar, S. Pandit, G. Singh, S.N. Satasia, Spectrum mobility in cognitive radio network using spectrum prediction and monitoring techniques, Phys. Commun. 24 (2) (2017) 1–8.

[51] P. Thakur, G. Singh, Power management for spectrum sharing in cognitive radio communication system: a comprehensive survey, J. Electromagn. Waves Appl. 34 (4) (2020) 407–461.

[52] https://www.google.com/search?rlz=1C1GCEB_enZA837ZA837&biw=1440&bih=740&tbm=isch&sa=1&ei=XzLUXNGKBZGmaIbMj_AC&q=wireless+body+area+networks&oq=wireless+body+area+networks&gs_l=img.3..0j0i24l9.346385.353323..353524...0.0..1.899.10411.2-12j7j1j3j3......1....1..gws-wiz-img.......35i39j0i67j 0i10i67.r0Zg6LZnn4w#imgrc=NY5Mduz6sdcl1M:. (Accessed 9 May 2019).

[53] J. Favela, M. Rodriguez, A. Preciado, V.M. Gonzalez, Integrating context-aware public displays into a mobile hospital information system, IEEE Trans. Inf. Technol. Biomed. 8 (3) (2004) 279–286.

[54] H. Ouyang, et al., Symbiotic cardiac pacemaker, Nat. Commun. 10 (2019) 1821, https://doi.org/10.1038/s41467-019-09851-1.

[55] M.H. Ansari, M.A. Karami, A sub-cc nonlinear piezoelectric energy harvester for powering leadless pacemakers, J. Intell. Mater. Syst. Struct. 29 (3) (2018) 438–445.

[56] C.G. Nunez, W.T. Navaraj, E.O. Polat, R. Dahiya, Energy-autonomous, flexible, and transparent tactile skin, Adv. Funct. Mater. 27 (18) (2017) 1–12.

[57] https://www.youtube.com/watch?v=zpGujcLRHNw. (Accessed 6 June 2019).

[58] Flexible electronic skin aids human-machine interactions, Available at: https://www.acs.org/content/acs/en/pressroom/presspacs/2018/acs-presspac-november-28-2018/flexible-electronic-skin-aids-human-machine-interactions-video.html. (Accessed 6 June 2019).

[59] Artificial "Electronic Skin" Could Warn Humans of Impending Danger, Available at: https://futurism.com/artificial-electronic-skin-could-alert-danger. (Accessed 6 June 2019).

[60] Z. Ma, S. Li, H. Wang, W. Cheng, Y. Li, L. Pan, Y. Shi, Advanced electronic skin devices for healthcare applications, J. Mater. Chem. B 7 (2019) 173–197.

[61] I. Sobron, P. Diniz, W. Martins, M. Velez, Energy detection technique for adaptive spectrum sensing, IEEE Trans. Commun. 63 (3) (2015) 617–627.

[62] A. Kumar, P. Thakur, S. Pandit, G. Singh, Fixed and dynamic threshold selection criteria in energy detection for cognitive radio communication systems, in: Proceedings of 10th IEEE International Conference on Contemporary Computing (IC3), India, August, 2017, pp. 1–6.

[63] A. Kumar, P. Thakur, S. Pandit, G. Singh, Performance analysis of different threshold selection schemes in energy detection for cognitive radio communication systems, in: Proceedings of 4th IEEE International Conference on Image Information Processing (ICIIP), India, December, 2017, pp. 153–158.

[64] A. Kumar, P. Thakur, S. Pandit, G. Singh, Analysis of optimal threshold selection for spectrum sensing in a cognitive radio network: an energy detection approach, Wirel. Netw 25 (2019) 3917–3931, https://doi.org/10.1007/s11276-018-01927-y.

[65] X. Zhang, R. Chai, F. Gao, Matched filter based spectrum sensing and power level detection for cognitive radio network, in: 2014 IEEE Global Conference on Signal and Information Processing (GlobalSIP), Atlanta, USA, December, 2014, pp. 1267–1270.

[66] H. Chen, C.H. Vun, A feature-based spectrum sensing technique for cognitive radio operation compressive, Circ. Syst. Signal Process. 17 (3) (2018) 1287–1314.

[67] L. Du, M. Laghate, C. Liu, D. Cabric, Y. Chen, Improved eigen-value-based spectrum sensing via sensor signal overlapping, in: 2016 8th IEEE International Conference on Communication Software and Networks (ICCSN), Beijing, China, June, 2016, pp. 122–126.

[68] X. Xing, T. Jing, W. Cheng, Y. Huo, X. Cheng, Spectrum prediction in cognitve radio networks, IEEE Wirel. Commun. 20 (2) (2013) 90–96.

[69] I. Cristian, S. Moh, A low-interference channel states prediction algorithm for instantaneous spectrum accessin cognitive radio networks, Wirel. Pers. Commun. 84 (4) (2015) 2599–2610.

[70] S.D. Barnes, B.T. Maharaj, A.S. Alfa, Cooperative prediction for cognitive radio networks, Wirel. Pers. Commun. 89 (4) (2016) 1177–1202.

[71] P. Thakur, A. Kumar, S. Pandit, G. Singh, S.N. Satashia, Performance analysis of high-traffic cognitive radio communication system using hybrid spectrum access, prediction and monitoring techniques, Wirel. Netw 24 (6) (2018) 2005–2015.

[72] R. Mannes, M. Clayes, F.A.P.D. Figueiredo, I. Jabandzic, I. Oerman, S. Latre, Deep learning based spectrum prediction collision avoidance for hybrid wireless environments, IEEE Access 7 (2019) 45818–45830.

[73] M. Pereira, O. Postolache, P. Girao, Spread spectrum techniques in wireless communication, IEEE Instrum. Meas. Mag. 12 (6) (2009) 21–25.

[74] P. Thakur, A. Kumar, S. Pandit, G. Singh, S.N. Satashia, Spectrum monitoring techniques for spectrum mobility in cognitive radio networks: a technical reviews, China Commun. (2018) (Under review).

[75] R. Chen, J.-M. Park, J.H. Reed, Defense against primary user emulation attacks in cognitive radio networks, IEEE J. Sel. Areas Commun. 26 (1) (2008) 25–37.

[76] J. Li, Z. Feng, Z. Feng, P. Zhang, A survey of security issues in cognitive radio networks, China Commun. 12 (3) (2015) 132–150.

[77] D. Mendez, I. Papapanagiotou, B.Y. Mena, Internet of things: Survey on security, Inf. Secur. J. 27 (3) (2018) 162–182.

[78] M. Ammar, G. Russello, B. Crispo, Internet of Things: a survey on the security of IoT frameworks, J. Inf. Secur. Appl. 38 (2018) 8–27.

[79] F.A. Alaba, M. Othman, I. Abaker, T. Hashem, F. Alotaibi, Internet of Things security: a survey, J. Netw. Comput. Appl. 88 (2017) 10–28.

Access control and classifier-based blockchain technology in e-healthcare applications

Andino Maseleno[a], Wahidah Hashim[a], Eswaran Perumal[b], M. Ilayaraja[c], and K. Shankar[d]

Institute of Informatics and Computing Energy, Universiti Tenaga Nasional, Kajang, Malaysia[a] Department of Computer Applications, Alagappa University, Karaikudi, India[b] School of Computing, Kalasalingam Academy of Research and Education, Krishnankoil, Tamil Nadu, India[c] Department of Computer Applications, Alagappa University, Karaikudi, Tamil Nadu, India[d]

1 Introduction

Blockchain Technology (BT) works by storing data in account records that are disseminated in a decentralized way. It does this by registering gadgets that are part of the blockchain framework [1]. The ledger is stored in a decentralized system of nodes that are made through cryptographic procedures, accessed by all excavators inside the system [2,3]. The inborn qualities of blockchain engineering and configuration exhibit characteristics such as transparency, power, auditability, and security [4]. A blockchain can be viewed as an appropriate database, composed as a list of requested blocks, where the submitted blocks are changeless [5]. This is a scenario where patients store their information in an Electronic Health Record (EHR) framework for safeguarding and further access [6]. Patients share their health information with specialists and healthcare associations with the assistance of these EHR frameworks. Blockchain provides a decentralized digital database of transactions, otherwise known as a distributed record, which is kept up to date by a system of computers that authorize an exchange before it is affirmed and added to the record [7]. The framework stores the information in blockchain when the patient shares his or her information with the framework [8,9]. To guarantee the privacy of redistributed EHRs, the existing plan uses a cell phone-based key understanding plan to set up a safe channel between the patient and doctors [9]. Patients can give a portion of their earned parts to emergency clinics and backup plans, which can utilize these assets to treat them. This is one method of publicly supporting the subsidy programs for the poorest individuals in society [10]. The appropriated record is used here to enable an individual to demonstrate that he or she exists at a specific time and place, and this is confirmed by a gathering of people using the distributed idea of blockchain [11]. The most remarkable features of appropriated ledgers are permanence, protection from oversight, decentralized support, and disposal of the requirement for a centralized and trusted third party [12].

By carefully choosing e-healthcare information, the classifier model is used from the characterized information, which is ready to access those records, and such access should be upheld and checked [12]. The blockchain-based access-control director for health information improves the interoperability of this framework. Off the blockchain system, with the contribution of the public, the blockchain was proposed as an access-control manager of healthcare information [13].

The server part performs the prehandling task, which incorporates feature extraction, standardization, and selection as a classification task. The restrictions of the innovation incorporate high-energy utilization and the moderate speed of account exchanges, and when these emerge, they need to be protected as a changeless record that requires computationally concentrated digital marking [14]. Moreover, patient care frequently originates from health suppliers who are not part of the coordinated network of health associations. An example of this would be a case where the patients are treated in an outside country. The presentation of disseminated health records and the distribution of health data among health associations are vital variables to guarantee the selection of blockchain technologies [15]. More significantly, when trading anyone's information off the hub in the blockchain network, it does not influence the condition of the ledger since the data in it is recreated among numerous hubs in the network. In this manner, by its temperament, the blockchain can shield healthcare data from potential data loss, defilement, and security attacks, for example, a ransomware attack. Any other element that gathers digital health data remains the caretaker of the data collected and is compelled by a solemn obligation to ensure the privacy, classification, and security of such data.

2 Related works

Blockchain has a broad scope of features such as a dispersed ledger, decentralized capacity, authentication, security, and immutability. It has already moved ahead to pragmatic applications in industrial segments, for example, healthcare [16]. Indeed, even with these upgrades, there are few worries because the blockchain innovation has its vulnerabilities that should be addressed, for example, mining impetuses, mining assaults, and key administration. A complete classification of blockchain-empowered applications across different divisions, for example, supply chain, business, healthcare, IoT, protection, and data management, was performed, and the researchers proposed key topics, drifts, and rising zones for research in this area [17]. Storing and performing calculations using sensitive private healthcare information in the cloud is conceivable by decentralization and is empowered by the Peer to Peer (P2P) network. According to the study by Al Omar et al. [18], by utilizing the decentralized or distributed property, the blockchain innovation guarantees responsibility and honesty. Data security and protection are improved by the blockchain innovation in which the information is encrypted and distributed across the whole system [19]. It can guarantee both data security and protection while expanding the trust of the open areas. The pertinent parts of the blockchain innovation are discussed in the literature that explores some utilization cases in the healthcare zone that may be improved by the use of this innovation [20]. It provides security, secrecy, and information honestly without any third-party organization in control of the exchanges, and, in this manner, it makes intriguing examination zones.

An investigation of blockchain research, in the field of healthcare, is led by Marko Hölbl et al. [21]. Healthcare is one of the basic regions where blockchain advancement has huge potential, on account of its inexorable, understanding-driven method for managing social insurance structures, to interface unique systems, and to augment the precision of Electronic Healthcare Records. Studies have shown that blockchain innovation analyzed in the healthcare industry is expanding, and it is, for the most part, used for data sharing, overseeing health records, and access control. Blockchain applications in the healthcare industry essentially require a prominent degree of confirmation, interoperability, and record sharing since it demands legitimate prerequisites, for example, Health Insurance Portability and the Accountability Act of 1996 (HIPAA) [22]. These applications incorporate shrewd contracts, misrepresentation discovery, and character confirmation.

Indeed, even with these enhancements, there are still issues that persist because the blockchain innovation has its vulnerabilities and issues that should be addressed, for example, mining motivators, mining attacks, and key administration. The present condition of blockchain innovation and its applications in a few explicit qualities of this problematic innovation can reform "the same old thing" rehearses, according to Casino et al. [23]. Based on an organized, deliberate review and thematic content examination of the writing, the researchers presented a far-reaching classification of blockchain-empowered applications that are used across a wide range of sectors. In the study [24], it has been conveyed that the ledger innovation with accentuation on the highlights are pertinent to dispersed frameworks. Besides, the paper examined the utilization of coordinated noncyclic diagram globally, concerning conveyed ledgers, and contrasts it with blockchain-based arrangements. The two standards are analyzed by utilizing agent executions such as Bitcoin, Ethereum, and Nano. This procedure has a delegate arrangement regarding the connected data structures to keep up the ledger, accord systems, exchange affirmation certainty, ledger size, and adaptability.

2.1 Purpose of BT

- The essential thought behind BT is that it permits performers in a framework [19] to make use of the computerized resources utilizing a P2P network that stores these transactions in a distributed way over the system.
- The proprietors of the benefits and exchanges, including change of ownership, are enrolled on the ledger using public-key cryptography and digital signatures.
- Because of security, this program was developed so that any block or even an exchange that adds to the chain cannot be altered, which at last provides a high scope of security [25].
- A blockchain system can help in the alleviation of crosswise data fragmentation issues over healthcare substances. With blockchain usage for EHRs, the individuals from a private and distributed system can share the block substance with fitting viewership authorizations, whereas the former is held responsible for the information shared.
- Blockchain cannot scale to the levels required in the event, and it is expected to act as the foundation of the financial framework, not to mention a large chunk of data.
- Attempts are being made for the handling of wider-use cases. It might not be able to scale to fulfil the anticipated need during a time when the implicit truth is understood, which could mean that the innovation will remain unfit to fulfil the motivation for its creation.
- If an anomaly is recognized at some point along the supply chain, the blockchain framework can lead all the elements in the route to its originating place. This makes it simple for organizations to conduct examinations and to execute essential activities.
- This further guarantees that the owner of the record works on the transactions. The block encryption in the chain makes it harder for any programmer to aggravate the conventional arrangement of the chain. The prominent favorable circumstances of the blockchain innovation are the decentralization of network, straightforwardness, trustworthiness, inalterability, and indestructible innovation [26].

- Each framework has a database, and it is imperative to secure this database. This is because, when the framework works with outsider associations, there is a high chance for the database being hacked or the data may end up being accessed by unauthorized persons [27].
- Traditionally, the time taken by the transaction is high, especially during preparation and initialing into a banking association. When BT is utilized, it ordinarily reduces the ideal opportunity for preparation and initialing.

3 Methodology for security

Blockchain advancement is an approach to accomplish a dependable and user-enabled response for e-Health conditions [28–30]. Electronic Health Records (EHRs) are never made to manage lifetime records among various associations, and patients share their data among various organizations. To secure the healthcare database, essentially the classifier, a Support Vector Machine (SVM) is used to categorize e-healthcare information into sensitive and nonsensitive data [31–33]. In the process of upgrading the security of e-healthcare administration data, user-based access control is used. The basic disseminated record development in Bitcoin is also known as blockchain to differentiate it from other blockchain headways. This BT is used to support drug prescriptions, to store network (chain management), pregnancy, and the management of any other hazardous information to support access control, information sharing, and to supervise the review trail of restorative exercises. Healthcare frameworks could improve the security and reliability of patients' data since patients would have control over their social-protection records. Finally, the approval methodology discerns the portion of the data that needs to be restricted to an external requester on the security approach. This framework "Even the Secure Health" was designed to prevent an outsider from illegally accessing or tampering with the system's data; it also empowers the managers to identify misbehavior from insiders.

3.1 BT—A distributed ledger technology

This is a distributed database maintained by a consensus protocol and run by nodes in a distributed system. This consensus protocol replaces a central administrator since all the friends contribute to the maintenance of the integrity of the database. This distribution model comprises various layer works such as the fabric layer, the application layer, and the networking layer. All these layers are used for a secure communication agreement, public key foundation, and organization of the databases. In any case, ideas that exist for a decentralized administration model that sits in the application layer, which also enables the network members to have a stake in future updates to the fabric layer [24]. The ledgers are repeated with indistinguishable duplicates held by all system clients. New data are added to the ledger when all the clients concur that the data is exact. All clients will be informed of any attempt by a solitary client to adjust the data, in principle, making change impossible without the consent of others. Early-model frameworks are in development for a dedicated application inside healthcare data. The connected data structures are present for ledger upkeep, accord instruments, and exchange affirmation certainties such as the ledger size and adaptability issues.

Fig. 1 shows the graphical representation of this framework. While the distributed ledgers enable any peer to make new exchanges and access the common database, the legitimate peers identify malicious changes to authentic exchanges. In distributed ledgers, blockchain is extremely valuable not only for financial transactions but also in e-healthcare applications [20]. Distributed ledgers cut down

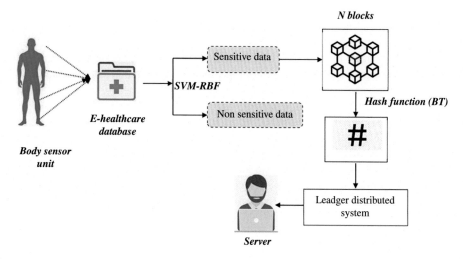

FIG. 1

Model for the distributed system.

on operational aspects. The security is tightened with high-end features because of the decentralized nature, and the records are immutable. Specialized distributed consensus protocols empower the databases to partake in a shared system in which not all the members are required to confide in one another. Distribution of databases among multiple peers without any hesitation has empowered novel decentralized applications, for example, cryptographic monetary forms. This blockchain-distributed system has a few advantages:

- When efficient frameworks such as BT are embraced for regular business forms, the requirement for third parties decreases or sometimes becomes null in obtaining a good deal on organization costs.
- The data in the BT network are ethical since the information in the system can be adjusted or included by shared agreement.
- The BT specialists use their ability in organizations to develop a morally mechanized and circulated ledger for financial trades that can be modified according to one's trade needs.
- The fundamental focus of this examination is to propose a holistic BT structure that covers all partners in the healthcare space and to investigate the chances and difficulties by uncovering the incorporated BT.
- The key reasons for circulated frameworks can be spoken by asset sharing, receptiveness, simultaneousness, adaptability, adaptation to internal failure, and transparency.
- EHR can be trusted by offering access to the conveyed ledger for all the participants while in parallel, maintaining protected and transparent tradeoff data [34].

3.2 Classifier: An SVM

E-healthcare prerequisites are related to security and protection because of extra patient data to ensure the medical data of the patients [35]. On the Internet, the sharing of records and information is becoming increasingly common with cloud storage. A set of physiological sensors with an individual server is available to collate the healthcare information from an emergency clinical condition, a heterogeneous system, and a remote social-insurance server [36]. In EHRs, the users might be the health-data owners (i.e., the patients) or the requester or servers. Thus, there could be neighborhood or cloud servers that store, process, and investigate the collected information. They follow an exceptionally clever approach to utilize the immense number of features without the need to use as much calculation as seems to be important. The prime target of this methodology is to amplify the edge between the classes and to limit the separation between the hyperplane points of the EHR process. To upgrade the security of this framework and to classify sensitive and nonsensitive data, the novel classifier Support Vector Machine (SVM) [37] was used. The technique of this classification is discussed in the later segment. The subsequent algorithm can be officially compared, after which every dot product is supplanted by a nonlinear kernel function again. This enables the algorithm to fit the maximum edge hyperplane in a transformed feature space. The training is performed using a few records of parameters about the disease, alongside the appropriate response expected for each case.

3.2.1 Pros of the proposed SVM
- SVMs are excellent when there is no clue about the data.
- The SVM works well even with unstructured and semiorganized data such as content, images, and trees.
- The kernel trick is the genuine quality of the SVM. With a proper kernel function, it is possible to tackle any complex issue.
- Selecting a reasonable kernel would cause concern about the closeness between comparative organizations because the more comparative two are, the higher the kernel values would be. Consequently, at the season of a new classification, the money-related proportion values would be compared with support vectors.
- The projection of each support vector on the hypersurface needs to be identified along the angle of decision function. After this, the summarized, generalized curvature on the hypersurface needs to be computed.

3.2.2 RBF-SVM classifier
The ideal objective of this methodology is to maximize the edge between the classes and to restrain the distance between the hyperplane focuses. To execute the nondirect procedure, the kernel functions are started in the SVM model. The RBF kernel is a capacity whose worth relies on good ways from the inception or some point. In this research, the researchers utilized the Radial Bias Function (RBF) kernel classifier to classify the e-healthcare information into two classes. The RBF network can be exploited to discover a set weight for a decent curve. The hyperplane capacity is as follows

$$\sum_{i=1}^{M} a_i . T_i . k(a, a_i) = 0 \tag{1}$$

Eq. (1) represents the hyperplane function in which $k(a, a_i)$ signifies the inner product of the two vectors induced in the feature space. "T_i" signifies the target value, and these terms are used for the kernel-based classification process.

RBF

In machine learning, the RBF or RBF kernel function is used as part of a support vector machine classification. The weights are in a dimensional gap that is superior to the innovative data. Learning is equal to the discovery of an exterior in a high-dimensional gap that supplies the greatest fit to preparation data.

$$k(a, a_i) = \exp\left(-\alpha \|a - a_1\|^2\right), \quad \alpha > 0 \tag{2}$$

The value of the RBF kernel decreases through detachment with the series between zero and one. It also incorporates a composed clarification as a correspondence to the evaluation. The attribute break of the kernel contains an unending number of measurements. In RBF systems, the hidden and output layers assume altogether different jobs, whereas the comparing weights have different implications and properties for the classification, dependent on the target class. From this classifier, the healthcare provider relies on how best the class algorithms of machine learning are adjusted to clinical data.

Input: E-healthcare database.
Model: RBF kernel-based SVM classifier.
Output: Class1 as sensitive data and Class 2 as nonsensitive data.

3.3 E-healthcare security analysis via BT

The hyper ledger is considered a BT, implying that only designated parties can access it rather than the public blockchain that is available to all. In healthcare, this kind of blockchain design is valuable because it characterizes a defined user base composed of suppliers, payers, and other subsidiary gatherings to access the blockchain. From the classified healthcare information, the sensitive information-to-security model notwithstanding, the protocol was considered, whereas extra incorporation and prohibition criteria were utilized depending on the essentialness of the theme and the frequency of BT, healthcare, or both, as referred to in the exploration. Even though there are numerous advantages provided by healthcare frameworks, in any case, they are vulnerable to a wide range of security dangers as a result of their portability and structure. In this way, the identification of security-related necessities, vulnerabilities, and dangers is key to the advancement of a dependable framework. The recognizable proof of system resources, potential vulnerabilities and dangers, and suitable countermeasures can make the related system dangers comprehensible.

3.3.1 Procedure of BTs

BT is a block that records a portion of the exchanges made in a given measure of time. A block might be understood as an individual bank statement. Blocks are connected in sequential order with the help of hashes so that no one can create a mess with this ledger, while it can also remain accessible to everybody. Each block contains the hash from the previous block [38]. Along these lines, if an individual plans to create a mess in it, he or she should first change each one of the intended hashes. The exact procedure of the blockchain process is shown in Fig. 2. The use of blockchain in healthcare structures for various attributes is divided practically, especially as related to the exclusion from records, thanks to the huge expenses incurred with the procedure. Important layers, such as texture, application, and networking layers, are discussed in the following sections.

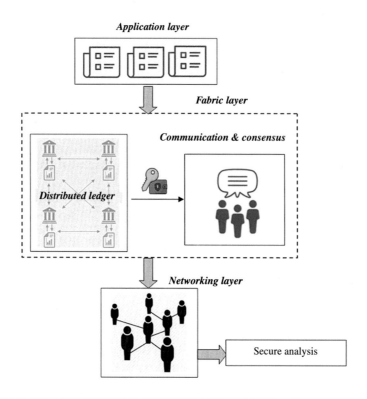

FIG. 2

Process of BT in e-healthcare.

Application Layer: Applications that are downloaded from the Play Store or Apple Store provide the client with a chance to use the BT biological system that falls under this classification. This layer is important when inefficient communications, high trust, and solid demand for data approval and agreement are desired. The health segment can use blockchain innovation comprehensively as far as the running of medical organizations, service delivery to patients, and the tracking of a supply chain for pharmaceutical products are concerned so that the application layers gain significance in this research model. The application layer fuses the health-data assets to offer the information to healthcare organizations and to satisfy the last person's needs, based on the genuine conditions of the objective inhabitants and service requirements.

Fabric Layer: The details of the new blocks must be identified by the past blocks, and a protocol must exist to confirm the similarity with the determination. Here, the blocks are important for sending money between parties as Bitcoin to encoding state transitions in a state machine such as in Ethereum. Stability is accomplished at the proliferation layer, whereas the nodes are expected to have the option for rapid dispersal of affirmed blocks to different nodes with the goal that they know to expand on the latest blocks rather than the more established stale block.

Network Layer: This is a protocol to decide how the ledger and blocks are transmitted between nodes in the network. It is the place where the guidelines set up on the protocol layer are actualized.

Nonetheless, the network layer can be isolated depending on their particular functions; the extent to which the software systems are set off BT is unbelievable and these systems work to overcome various difficulties. This layer forms and imparts the information gained by the recognition layer and provisions through specialized phases of heath records for the communication model. Well-planned transportation rules not only build transmission capability and abatement vitality consumption but also ensure data classification and security.

This BT model works depending on the Hash function idea, a single node may declare its decision about the submitted data. Different nodes in the framework simply check it. The digger, which reported both at the beginning and the end, is remunerated after the larger part of different nodes confirms it as the right one. Since confirming the outcome is a computationally low-priced task, the procedure does not consume much time. The perfect methodology for changing the blockchain information is to have over 51% of the computational force, and in that condition, it is smarter to burrow rather than to attack for focal points. The blockchain seems fitting in that it doesn't have a single purpose of failure, and this makes it amazing. One of the most significant properties of blockchain is that it can work in a distributed and decentralized style without requiring outside specialist service providers or centralized authority. Blockchain can work in a trustless system condition without any trust in companion nodes while it also looks after anonymity.

3.3.2 Important elements in BT

Distributed Ledger: Sensitive e-healthcare data are in a distributed ledger that offers a proportion of strength by restricting the effect of a digital security episode experienced by any single node. This guarantees the uprightness, as changes cannot be performed deceitfully when everyone has concurrent access to all records, which is a fundamental factor for the recognition of records and the utilization of blockchain in supply chains. This innovation, used in blockchains, offers propelled strategies for public-private encryption to the character and digitization of records. The records react well to any suspicious movement or alteration. As nobody can change the record, and everything refreshes quickly, the BT protocol for all of these nodes is simple to follow as per the record.

Hash Functions: This capacity is used to protect the data in cloud storage systems; it makes it difficult to recreate the information from the hash alone. A cryptographic hash work "h" is taken as an input for a message of arbitrary length and produces a message condensation, or "hash," of a fixed length. For cryptographically secure hash capacities, it is commonly viewed as farfetched to the point of inconceivability that two significant messages would share a hash.

- The proposed data secure approach considers the hash function with three features needs to be fulfilled for this examination.
- Past block hashes can be in multiple numbers if the blockchain is stretched and every one of them is added.
- Each block contains the block hash with the past block hash money and time stamp, block form with the nonce, and target address that incorporates the message.

3.3.3 BT toward security

Healthcare associations found that a reactive, bottom-up, and innovation-driven way to handle security decisions and privacy prerequisites may not be sufficient to ensure security for the association and its patients. Actualizing security measures remains a perplexing procedure, and the stakes are persistently raised as an approach to vanquish security controls that become increasingly refined. Healthcare associations or suppliers must guarantee that an encryption plan is productive, simple to use by both patients and healthcare experts, and effectively extensible to incorporate new Electronic Health Records. Moreover, the number of keys held by each gathering ought to be minimized. To improve security to this end, proposed solutions must adopt two strategies: prevention of tampering, followed by detection and filtering of the compromised data. Thus, giving security awareness to the projects is highly recommended in both the expansion of security and the strength of restorative gadgets and health.

(a) Encryption: Encryption is how messages or data are encoded so that they can be approved [39]. In the encryption technique, each share has a block, and each block area is encoded by the encryption strategy. This BT permits third-party service providers to perform particular kinds of activities on the encrypted data of clients without decrypting the encrypted data while maintaining the privacy of the clients' encrypted data. In encryption, if the client needs to question some data on the server, he initially scrambles the data and stores the encoded data in the server.

The blocks of information are connected in chronological order in a blockchain that uses a cryptographic hash function to safely attach each block to the past and resulting blocks. In this way, any endeavor to modify data within a block would change the hash values. This encryption is represented as follows:

$$hash(Encrypt(data, public_k), h_k) = hash(data, hash_k)$$
$$hash(Encrypt(data, public_{k1}), h_k) = hash(Encrypt(data, public_{k2}), h_k)$$

(3)

In this procedure, every two parts of the data are fed as input for the encryption procedure. The public key generation of the encryption point multiplies when the point expansion procedure is followed.

(b) Decryption: Decryption is a system that is the opposite of encryption. That is, it is the method that moves over the encrypted content into a kind of plain substance [40]. In cryptography, the ciphered images are communicated after encryption to the decryption method.

$$Decrypted\ Data = Decrypt(Cipher)$$

(c) Validation Process: There are different available models for consensus components, including proof-of-work, proof-of-stake, and verification-of-specialist. This model is ordinarily used in selected blockchains because it requires the gatherings to possess some level of trust, whereas the proof-of-work and proof-of-stake models do not expect such trust and are all normally used in public BT.

3.3.4 Access-control model for e-healthcare

The design for a control security model depends on information interoperability and supports the security basics of healthcare frameworks along with the ability to have fine-grained access control. It uses three diverse security and protection prerequisites such as identification, authentication, and approval. Identification is not a unique security issue by itself, although it aims at differentiating the users. In other terms, ensuring the security of e-health data is a big test for two principal reasons: huge computational overhead when the encryption systems are utilized, and the impact of individual medical data changes in the employing alteration strategies. Furthermore, to accomplish increasingly successful access control, a remarkable authentication certificate is presented for every client, and this was verified before accessing the data. The authorization procedure figures out the portion of data that can be confined from the outsider adhering to the security policy. A legitimate access-control component ought to guarantee patient privacy, and a decent balance should be given between the accessibility and classification. Clients can be given a specific job according to their obligations or corporate positions, and they can later be reassigned to another job without affecting the hidden access-control infrastructure.

Along these lines, the access-control model is used to influence the way a user can be validated. It is better to secure the e-health data, which is explained in the following text.

E-Healthcare Data Owner: Attribute-based access strategy, isolating their specific information into different parts and encryption of each part utilizing the symmetric encryption methods, comes under different substance keys. The healthcare supplier possesses the vehicle of capacity or transmission of such an electronic medical record.

User: The user is affirmed to access the information if the access approach, related to the cipher data portrayed by the data owner, is satisfied by the information characteristic. Access control is a component that permits the proprietors of assets to characterize, manage, and enforce the access conditions appropriate to every resource.

Service Provider: The SP comprises information servers to control the information access and information administration executives to manage the properties of users. Health specialist organizations are generally afraid of disclosing their health data, which can hurt their activity prospects or their capacity to get protection coverage. Their pattern endeavors to use ascribe-based encryption to guarantee the patient-centric control process.

Central Authority: This is a completely trusted assemblage that is accountable for entitling, denying, and refreshing the properties of clients. It produces public as well as private parameters for systems and stipends with differing access to clients based on their properties. Access-control strategies have many appealing features; they are neither hearty nor effective in key generation.

4 Result analysis

The methodology discussed earlier was executed in MATLAB2015a with an i7 processor and 4GB RAM. To assess the performance of this method, e-healthcare data was utilized. The performance was categorized in terms of throughput, energy, and encryption and decryption time. This study analyzed the healthcare data collected from hospitals.

Fig. 3 demonstrates the e-healthcare data classification exactness. Here, the chosen classifier model was compared with K-Nearest Neighbor (KNN) and Naïve Bayes (NB) classifier. The "X" hub signifies the measure of data, whereas "Y" demonstrates the accuracy dimension of the information-classification process. Nonetheless, the studies conducted earlier, which classified the data at the sensor system concentrated on the decrease in inertness as opposed to energy proficiency. For instance, the database size was 300 whereas the precision of SVM was 89.22%. When it was compared with NB, the difference was 2.5% to 6% compared to the KNN classifier. From this chart, it can be understood that the classifiers showed excellent outcomes on data classification. This reality again affirms the scourge of dimensionality in SVM processing. In other terms, it also demonstrates the reduced effectiveness of the measurement by the proposed system. The principal classification stage $\alpha 1$ fluctuates, and in this stage, the patient's state was classified as normal and abnormal based on the observed health records. These investigations exhibit the proficiency of e-health and its adaptability in expanding the

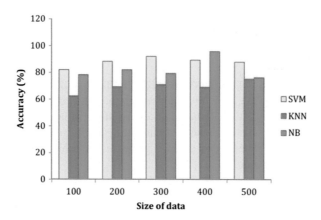

FIG. 3

Graph for e-healthcare data classifier.

Table 1 Evaluation of security measures.

E-health sensitive data size (kb)	Energy (%)	Throughput (kbps)	Memory (byte)	Execution time (sec)	Security level (%)
100	40.11	425	1304	4.5	78.22
200	49.22	568	1254	10.22	82.22
300	52.11	1052	1724	12.55	89.45
400	56.22	1078	1355	19.22	95.14
500	60	2187	1248	30.5	89.22

observation time when compared with other such studies, while it also reduces battery use regarding health records.

The measures for the proposed BT for e-healthcare information execution are shown in Table 1. Here, the researchers considered the throughput, energy, memory, and time, which are critical measures since these examine the security. It was segregated based on the database size in kb. From this diagram, one can achieve the most extreme security level, throughput, and minimum energy for e-healthcare data security. Numerically, the best execution was achieved from the database estimate 500 kb, and it was actualized from the SVM-BT approach. The throughput was reduced with increasing key size resulting from high usage of computational power and encryption attributes. There was a visible impact in changing the key size on encryption as well as decryption time in various sizes of the input file. At the same time, both throughput and packet loss through BT were estimated along with few parameters such as energy and throughput. Several inputs are present to perceive the rate of development of time for encryption changes with variable input size. Before getting access to a square in the BT, the data is organized through keen interest. One of the key terms to be guaranteed while composing brilliant contracts is block identity generation. Block-ID generation incurs a cost in terms of execution and exchange.

   The comparative analysis of security measures is shown in Fig. 4. Here, three methods were used to compare the performance, such as Advance Encryption Standard (AES), Elliptic Curve Cryptography (ECC), and the proposed model. Fig. 4 demonstrates the throughput vs. "N" of blocks, which is characterized by several encrypted bits per sec (throughput). If the block size was 10, then the throughput esteem was 3018 kbps. Its better value contrasted with different methods and the proposed structure devours less energy than the customary, conventional security strategies for healthcare. Since the security method is connected in the proposed structure, less energy is used. In this manner, the proposed BT in the healthcare structure provides a proficient asset and a secure model for medicinal data transmission among patient and remote accessible specialists. In this way, Fig. 5 demonstrates the energy

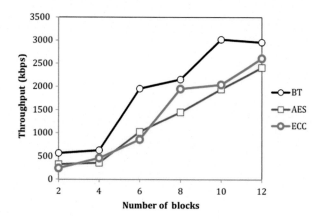

FIG. 4

Comparative analysis of throughput (kbps).

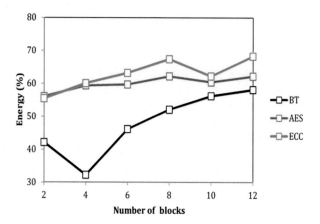

FIG. 5

Comparative analysis of energy (%).

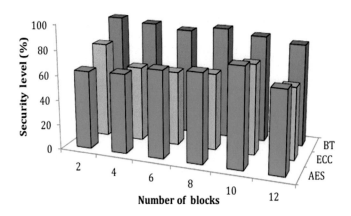

FIG. 6

Comparative analysis of security level (%).

level of the security process, how it was determined by the information in encryption and decryption processes, and how much of the energy zone was used in terms of percentage. Here, two comparison techniques were considered. In the end, Fig. 6 demonstrates the security level of the proposed framework with the number of blocks, the number of secured information in every block, for instance, when the block was "12," the security was 82.33%, and finally, the maximum level compared with different strategies. The tests were dependent on a few trial investigations to feature the prevalence of the proposed cryptosystem, which is deemed optimum compared with other class-encryption schemes.

5 Conclusion

The concept of BT was initially connected with digital currency, although it has several other potential uses such as development and inclusion of integrated applications for healthcare information, handling of multilevel healthcare systems, and recorded frameworks. This article discussed e-healthcare security in the ledger-distributed framework, and it showed signs of improvement in security level, throughput, and energy level. From this investigation, the researcher attained the most extreme scalability, security, and performance of the e-healthcare security process. Blockchain-empowered applications are more difficult to keep running with an increasing number of individuals or patients on the framework. In any case, blockchain is not considered the only compelling answer in any circumstance. Rather, one should assess the explicit blockchain issues and how they influence the healthcare business. For example, mining that forces the center component of BT has not been completely considered in the healthcare business, just because the explicit BT attacks can end the whole framework. When using BT-cipher encryption, it becomes challenging for an intruder to break the security, in comparison to that of the stream cipher. Likewise, healthcare associations ought to be specific about big-data sellers and abstain from the assumption that their big-data circulation will be secure. Different threats and attacks occur during every phase of the life cycle in big data, which must be overcome through countermeasures and practical procedures, especially in healthcare data privacy as well as security.

The smooth trade-off between security and execution helps in the advancement of real applications. In the future, the optimization systems with BT will be used for the healthcare information security model.

Acknowledgment

The authors acknowledge the financial support of RUSA–Phase 2.0 grant sanctioned vide Letter No. F. 24-51/2014-U, Policy (TNMulti-Gen), Dept. of Edn. Govt. of India, Dt. 09.10.2018.

References

[1] A. Al Omar, M.Z.A. Bhuiyan, A. Basu, S. Kiyomoto, M.S. Rahman, Privacy-friendly platform for healthcare data in cloud based on blockchain environment, Futur. Gener. Comput. Syst. 95 (2019) 511–521.

[2] C. Huang, H. Lee, D.H. Lee, A privacy-strengthened scheme for E-healthcare monitoring system, J. Med. Syst. 36 (5) (2012) 2959–2971.

[3] N. Alassaf, B. Alkazemi, A. Gutub, Applicable light-weight cryptography to secure medical data in IoT systems, J. Res. Eng. Appl. Sci. 2 (2) (2017) 50–58.

[4] D. Kamboj, T.A. Yang, An exploratory analysis of blockchain: applications, security, and related issues, in: Proceedings of the International Conference on Scientific Computing (CSC), The Steering Committee of The World Congress in Computer Science, Computer Engineering and Applied Computing (WorldComp), 2018, pp. 67–73.

[5] Y. Lu, The blockchain: state-of-the-art and research challenges, J. Ind. Inf. Integr. 15 (2019) 80–90.

[6] F. Wu, L. Xu, S. Kumari, X. Li, A.K. Das, J. Shen, A lightweight and anonymous RFID tag authentication protocol with cloud assistance for e-healthcare applications, J. Ambient. Intell. Humaniz. Comput. 9 (4) (2018) 919–930.

[7] C. Pirtle, J. Ehrenfeld, Blockchain for healthcare: the next generation of medical records? 42 (2018) 172.

[8] F. Daneshgar, O.A. Sianaki, P. Guruwacharya, Blockchain: a research framework for data security and privacy, in: Workshops of the International Conference on Advanced Information Networking and Applications, March, Springer, Cham, 2019, pp. 966–974.

[9] W. Wang, A vision for trust, security and privacy of blockchain, in: International Conference on Smart Blockchain, December, Springer, Cham, 2018, pp. 93–98.

[10] L.A. Linn, M.B. Koo, Blockchain for health data and its potential use in health it and health care related research, in: ONC/NIST Use of Blockchain for Healthcare and Research Workshop. Gaithersburg, Maryland, United States: ONC/NIST, 2016, pp. 1–10.

[11] S. Cheng, Y. Gao, X. Li, Y. Du, Y. Du, S. Hu, Blockchain application in space information network security, in: International Conference on Space Information Network, August, Springer, Singapore, 2018, pp. 3–9.

[12] G. Kumar, M. Rai, G.S. Lee, An approach to provide security in wireless sensor network using block mode of cipher, in: International Conference on Security Technology, December, Springer, Berlin, Heidelberg, 2011, pp. 101–112.

[13] C. Pei, Y. Xiao, W. Liang, X. Han, Trade-off of security and performance of lightweight block ciphers in industrial wireless sensor networks, EURASIP J. Wirel. Commun. Netw. 2018 (1) (2018) 117.

[14] E. Gökalp, M.O. Gökalp, S. Çoban, P.E. Eren, Analysing opportunities and challenges of integrated blockchain technologies in healthcare, in: EuroSymposium on Systems Analysis and Design, Springer, Cham, 2018, pp. 174–183.

[15] J. Lopes, J.L. Pereira, Blockchain technologies: opportunities in healthcare, in: The 2018 International Conference on Digital Science, October, Springer, Cham, 2018, pp. 435–442.

[16] T. McGhin, K.K.R. Choo, C.Z. Liu, D. He, Blockchain in healthcare applications: research challenges and opportunities, J. Netw. Comput. Appl. 135 (2019) 62–75.

[17] F. Casino, T.K. Dasaklis, C. Patsakis, A systematic literature review of blockchain-based applications: current status, classification and open issues, Telematics Inform. 36 (2018) 55–81.

[18] A. Al Omar, M.Z.A. Bhuiyan, A. Basu, S. Kiyomoto, M.S. Rahman, Privacy-friendly platform for healthcare data in cloud based on blockchain environment, Futur. Gener. Comput. Syst. 95 (2019) 511–521.

[19] N. Elisa, L. Yang, F. Chao, Y. Cao, A framework of blockchain-based secure and privacy-preserving E-government system, Wirel. Netw. (2018) 1–11, https://doi.org/10.1007/s11276-018-1883-0.

[20] L. Zhu, Y. Wu, K. Gai, K.K.R. Choo, Controllable and trustworthy blockchain-based cloud data management, Futur. Gener. Comput. Syst. 91 (2019) 527–535.

[21] M. Hölbl, M. Kompara, A. Kamišalić, L. NemecZlatolas, A systematic review of the use of blockchain in healthcare, Symmetry 10 (10) (2018) 470.

[22] T. McGhin, K.K.R. Choo, C.Z. Liu, D. He, Blockchain in healthcare applications: research challenges and opportunities, J. Netw. Comput. Appl. (2019).

[23] F. Casino, T.K. Dasaklis, C. Patsakis, A systematic literature review of blockchain-based applications: current status, classification and open issues, Telematics Inform. (2018).

[24] F.M. Benčić, I.P. Žarko, Distributed ledger technology: blockchain compared to directed acyclic graph, in: 2018 IEEE 38th International Conference on Distributed Computing Systems (ICDCS), July, IEEE, 2018, pp. 1569–1570.

[25] R. Wang, J. He, C. Liu, Q. Li, W.T. Tsai, E. Deng, A privacy-aware PKI system based on permissioned blockchains, in: 2018 IEEE 9th International Conference on Software Engineering and Service Science (ICSESS), November, IEEE, 2018, pp. 928–931.

[26] S. Chakraborty, S. Aich, H.C. Kim, A secure healthcare system design framework using blockchain technology, in: 2019 21st International Conference on Advanced Communication Technology (ICACT), February, IEEE, 2019, pp. 260–264.

[27] X. Zhang, R. Li, B. Cui, A security architecture of vanet based on blockchain and mobile edge computing, in: 2018 1st IEEE International Conference on Hot Information-Centric Networking (HotICN), August, IEEE, 2018, pp. 258–259.

[28] K. Shankar, M. Elhoseny, E. Dhiravidachelvi, S.K. Lakshmanaprabu, W. Wu, An efficient optimal key based chaos function for medical image security, IEEE Access 6 (1) (2018) 77145–77154, https://doi.org/10.1109/ACCESS.2018.2874026.

[29] S.K. Lakshmanaprabu, S.N. Mohanty, K. Shankar, N. Arunkumar, G. Ramireze, Optimal deep learning model for classification of lung cancer on CT images, Future Gen. Comput. Syst. 92 (2019) 374–382.

[30] E. Mohamed, K. Shankar, S.K. Lakshmanaprabu, A. Maseleno, N. Arunkumar, Hybrid optimization with cryptography encryption for medical image security in Internet of Things, Neural Comput. Appl. (2018), https://doi.org/10.1007/s00521-018-3801-x.

[31] S.K. Lakshmanaprabu, K. Shankar, A. Khanna, D. Gupta, J.J. Rodrigues, P.R. Pinheiro, V.H.C. De Albuquerque, Effective features to classify big data using social internet of things, IEEE Access 6 (2018) 24196–24204.

[32] S.K. Lakshmanaprabu, K. Shankar, D. Gupta, A. Khanna, J.J. Rodrigues, P.R. Pinheiro, V.H.C. de Albuquerque, Ranking analysis for online customer reviews of products using opinion mining with clustering, Complexity 2018 (2018) 3569351. https://doi.org/10.1155/2018/3569351.

[33] K. Shankar, S.K. Lakshmanaprabu, D. Gupta, A. Maseleno, V.H.C. de Albuquerque, Optimal feature-based multi-kernel SVM approach for thyroid disease classification, J. Supercomput. 76 (2020) 1128–1143.

[34] H. Seo, J. Park, M. Bennis, W. Choi, Consensus-before-talk: distributed dynamic spectrum access via distributed spectrum ledger technology, in: 2018 IEEE International Symposium on Dynamic Spectrum Access Networks (DySPAN), October, IEEE, 2018, pp. 1–7.

[35] E. Mohamed, K. Shankar, J. Uthayakumar, Intelligent diagnostic prediction and classification system for chronic kidney disease, Sci. Rep. 9 (2019) 9583, https://doi.org/10.1038/s41598-019-46074-2.

[36] M. Elhoseny, G.-B. Bian, S.K. Lakshmanaprabu, K. Shankar, A.K. Singh, W. Wu, Effective features to classify ovarian cancer data in internet of medical things, Comput. Netw. 159 (2019) 147–156.

[37] A. Diez-Olivan, J.A. Pagan, N.L.D. Khoa, R. Sanz, B. Sierra, Kernel-based support vector machines for automated health status assessment in monitoring sensor data, Int. J. Adv. Manuf. Technol. 95 (1–4) (2018) 327–340.

[38] D. Minoli, B. Occhiogrosso, Blockchain mechanisms for IoT security, IoT 1 (2018) 1–13.

[39] M. Elhoseny, K. Shankar, S.K. Lakshmanaprabu, A. Maseleno, N. Arunkumar, Hybrid optimization with cryptography encryption for medical image security in internet of things, Neural Comput. & Applic. (2018) 1–15, https://doi.org/10.1007/s00521-018-3801-x.

[40] K. Shankar, M. Elhoseny, E.D. Chelvi, S.K. Lakshmanaprabu, W. Wu, An efficient optimal key based chaos function for medical image security, IEEE Access 6 (2018) 77145–77154.

Machine learning algorithms for medical image security

J. Jennifer Ranjani[a] and C. Jeyamala[b]

Department of Computer Science & Information Systems, Birla Institute of Technology and Science, Pilani, India[a]
Department of Information Technology, Thiagarajar College of Engineering, Madurai, India[b]

1 Introduction

Healthcare is a high-priority industry and end users expect the maximum level of service and security irrespective of cost. A report by WHO mentions that about 58% of member states have an e-health strategy, 55% of countries have legislation to protect electronic patient data, and over 85% of countries have one or more initiatives for e-healthcare. Due to remarkable developments in image acquisition devices, medical images play a vital role in several areas of e-healthcare, such as telesurgery, telediagnosis, medical consultation between clinicians, distance learning, training, etc.

Recently, artificial intelligence (AI) and machine learning have endured a tremendous growth particularly in the field of medicine, for example, computer-assisted diagnosis and surgery, medical image interpretation, segmentation, image analysis, etc. These technologies can aid physicians in diagnosing and predicting a disease accurately, thereby the impact of a disease can be reduced or prevented. Machine learning helps the physician to make personalized diagnoses and decisions based on the comprehensive information of a patient in real time together with the lessons learned from communal knowledge. This implies that machine learning is a fundamental technology rather than a new tool to meaningfully process the medical data that is normally difficult for the human brain to comprehend. A key difference between conventional techniques and machine learning is its ability to learn from inputs and outputs, instead of being programmed with rules. Features extracted from the application are the inputs and the outputs are the labels. Machine learning algorithms create a generic model by mapping the inputs to the outputs. For example, a machine learning algorithm is built from the set of digitized slides read by pathologists [1]. The machine learning algorithm has the ability to understand the new pathology slides that were previously unread by pathologists. This is called supervised machine learning. Thus machine learning can be used in applications that require accuracy in predicting results. Traditional machine learning algorithms have a limited ability to process raw data. Until recently, applications based on machine learning required handcrafted features to transform raw data into useful representations. Deep learning is a form of representation learning that automatically draws the features required for detection or classification [2]. Different levels of representation can be obtained in deep learning methods by aggregating simple but nonlinear models. These compositions are ideally suited to learn heterogeneous and complex information generated from e-healthcare applications such as medical images, monitoring of sensor data, notes and prescriptions from physicians, etc.

Intelligent Data Security Solutions for e-Health Applications. https://doi.org/10.1016/B978-0-12-819511-6.00009-1

One of the major differences between human and machine learning is that humans can learn complex and generic associations from small datasets. However, machines require volumes of data to learn the same task. Patients' electronic health records (EHRs) are the basis for e-healthcare applications. Physicians are limited by the number of patient records they can view, whereas a machine learning model can easily be trained to view millions of EHRs.

The key challenge for the e-healthcare industry is to ensure the security of patients' EHRs. EHRs are easily targeted by cybercriminals because on an average the black market value per record is very high. Increased growth in medical imaging modalities demands extensive and tedious efforts to analyze the medical images. The motivation behind this chapter is to explore the various machine learning-based algorithms to ensure the security of EHRs in e-healthcare applications. The chapter is organized as follows: Section 2 discusses the application of deep learning for steganography, Section 3 highlights the application of machine learning for steganalysis, Section 4 focuses on machine learning for image encryption, and Section 5 details the application of machine learning in privacy-preserving computations. The chapter is concluded with the future research directions of integrating machine learning with information security.

2 Deep learning for steganography

Exchanging medical data and EPRs between remote locations is an inherent part of a typical e-healthcare system. However, transmission of medical data over insecure channels requires additional security as these channels are susceptible to interference. Steganography is the art of hiding sensitive information like EPRs on a cover media without trace. Steganalysis, on the other hand, aims to detect if the images are hidden with secret information. A good steganographic algorithm will be able to resist steganalysis and it should be undetectable even when the embedding capacity is reasonably high. Also, it should not be possible for the intruder to differentiate ordinary media and media containing secret information. Fig. 1 shows the block diagram of a basic steganographic system.

Neuroscience has inspired artificial neural networks (ANNs), a class of machine learning algorithms that can be used to approximate functions that rely on a large number of mostly unknown inputs. Over the years, ANNs were analyzed by researchers with the aim of attaining human-like performance, especially in the fields of machine learning and pattern recognition. These capabilities of ANNs to

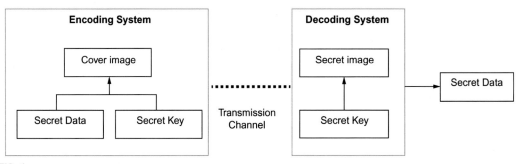

FIG. 1

Block diagram of a basic steganographic system.

approximate complex functions from unknown input make it an obvious choice for steganographic applications to determine an optimum embedding and extraction strategies. Performance of the machine learning algorithms is dependent on the efficiency of manually crafted feature extraction techniques, whereas deep learning techniques have the ability to extract features and understand the data automatically.

2.1 Brief insight into deep learning networks

Before describing the deep learning models for steganography, it is necessary to understand the overall perspective of deep learning networks. A generic structure of deep learning along with different steganography and steganalysis scenarios is discussed in [3]. Deep learning networks for images learn inherent features along with the discriminating boundaries that differentiate the classes. A computing unit in the neural network can be represented as a node in an oriented graph. The network modifies the parameters of these computing units by learning from the training samples. Pixel intensities are fed as input to these computing blocks, which then transmit the value to subsequent blocks. A convolution module is one of the important stages in any deep network. Dependent on the quality of the input images a preprocessing module can precede a convolution module. The preprocessing module can contain one or more filters to make the image suitable for the subsequent stages. The filtered image is then fed as an input to the convolution module. The convolution module comprises operations such as convolution, activation, pooling, and normalization.

The depth-wise separable convolution and inception networks contain two or more convolution layers. An activation function is applied to the filtered image after each convolution. Some of the activation functions could be $f(x) = |x|$ or $f(x) = \sin(x)$ or $f(x) = \frac{e^{-x^2}}{\sigma^2}$ or $f(x) = \max(0, x)$, etc. To perform back propagation, the activation function must be differentiable; hence, typically, those functions that require little computation to determine the derivative are chosen. However, functions like hyperbolic tangent are not chosen because they could cause the back propagation to cancel the gradient. A pooling operation computes the average or maximum within a local neighborhood. Often downsampling is coupled with pooling to reduce the size of the feature map. Normalization is required to condition the data. Types of normalization commonly used are batch normalization [4], layer normalization [5], instance normalization [6], group normalization [7], weight normalization [8], cosine normalization [9], etc. Batch normalization is mostly preferred irrespective of its dependence on batch size. Weight and cosine normalizations are used to normalize the network weight rather normalizing the input.

Different types of deep learning models are available in the literature [10] with their share of merits and demerits as indicated in Table 1.

2.2 Least significant bit substitution using a feed-forward neural network

In [11], least significant bit (LSB) substitution using a single layer feed-forward neural network (FNN) is proposed. Let the pixels in the cover and the stego image be denoted by vectors of length N as $X = \{x_1, x_2, ..., x_N\}$ and $Y = \{y_1, y_2, ..., y_N\}$, respectively. This technique replaces the LSB of each x_k with the secret binary digit m_k. The receiver can collect the secret information by extracting the LSBs of the stego image. For simplicity, the LSB of the cover and stego image can be denoted as X and Y.

Table 1 Comparison of different deep learning models.

Model name and description	Merits	Demerits
Deep neural network allows nonlinear relationship and is suitable for regression and classification problems.	Commonly used because it has high accuracy.	Learning is comparatively slow.
Convolutional neural network transforms 2D data into a 3D feature map using the convolutional filters.	Fast learning and improved performance.	Requires increased amount of labeled data.
Recurrent neural network has the ability to learn sequential events.	Time-related dependencies can be effectively modeled in sequential events.	Requires large datasets.
Deep Boltzmann machine can be used to model unidirectional connections between the hidden layers.	Robust inference is possible even if the data is ambiguous.	Parameter optimization is not possible for larger datasets.
Deep belief network makes the hidden layer of each subnetwork visible to the next layer.	The likelihood of each layer can be maximized using the greedy approach.	Computationally complex initialization process.
Deep autoencoder is used in supervised learning for feature extraction and dimensionality reduction.	Does not require a labeled dataset.	Requires a pretraining step.

LSB substitution algorithm using single layer FNN

Training phase

1. Randomly generate the cover and secret bit-pair, (x_i, m_i).
2. Generate the respective target output such that $z_i = m_i$.
3. Feed the individual training data into a single layer FNN.
4. Use the hill climbing technique to optimize the parameters of the FNN model.

Testing phase

1. Determine the output z_i for the given (x_i, m_i).
2. Set a threshold to obtain the stego bit, for instance, let $\theta = 0.5$.
3. The stego bit is set as $y_i = 1$ if $y_i \geq 0.5$.

A variant to the single layer FNN is also proposed in [11], called the multilayer FNN. It comprises a single input and output layer along with one or more hidden layers. The multilayer FNN can be easily extended for grayscale images. The secret data can be embedded onto the n-bits of the cover image by creating an identical multilayer FNN. The n-LSBs are extracted from the cover image to form disjoint pixel vectors. The encoder FNN can be modified as a decoder by providing the stego vector as the input and the message to be extracted as the target output.

2.3 Deep-stego

A deep neural network for color images is proposed in [12]. The neural network decides the bit in which the secret data is to be embedded, thus the secret data is distributed throughout the image.

Deep-stego algorithm

Encoder algorithm

1. Use the *Prep-Network* to increase the size of the secret image progressively to distribute the secret bits across the $N \times N$ pixels of the cover image.
2. Train the *Hiding Network* to create the container image by combining the cover image with the outcome of the *Prep-Network*. Five convolution layers containing filters of $\{3 \times 3, 4 \times 4, 5 \times 5\}$ patches are utilized by the hiding network.
3. The container image is formed by encoding two images so that it looks similar to the cover image.
4. Add the error $\|c - c'\| + \beta \|s - s'\|$ in the *Prep-Network* as well as the *Hiding Network*. Here, c and s are the cover and secret images, respectively.
5. Add a small amount of noise to the *Hiding Network* to avoid encoding the secret image in the LSBs of the cover image.

Decoder algorithm

1. Train the *Reveal Network* using the container image and the secret image is the target output.
2. Apply $\beta \|s - s'\|$ as the error signal to reconstruct the secret image.

ImageNet [13] dataset is used for training and testing the deep-stego algorithm. A subset of 1000 images from ImageNet that are not used during the training phase are used during the testing process. Additionally, a number of test images are created using mobile cameras and DSLRs. Traditional steganographic algorithms aim to reconstruct the secret data without error. However, the deep-stego algorithm does not aim for perfect reconstruction. Hence, it is suitable for applications where the secret message to be hidden is an image and the quality of both the cover and secret image can be compromised. The proposed deep-stego system can be improved by permuting the secret pixels using a key before hiding it on the cover image. Though this approach increases the difficulty of the intruder to detect the secret, it also increases the complexity of the encoding data using the deep neural network. Also, a trusted channel should be established between the two ends to communicate the secret key used for permutation.

2.4 Steganography using deep convolutional generative adversarial networks

Steganography without embedding (SWE) helps to avoid machine learning-based steganalysis and detection. Cover selection and cover synthesis are the two basic approaches in SWE. The cover selection method learns a dataset containing natural images and develops a relationship between the images in the dataset and the secret data. The secret map is then mapped with one or more images in the dataset. The cover synthesis approach generates a new cover image based on the secret data. In [14], SWE using deep convolutional generative adversarial networks (GANs) is proposed where is the secret data is mapped into a noise vector. A generator neural network is trained to generate the carrier image with respect to the noise vector. A separate extractor network can be trained to extract the secret information.

Steganography using deep convolutional GANs

Cover image generation phase

1. Generate a noise vector, z_i.
2. Divide the secret message into S_i segments.
3. Map each noise vector z_i to a secret segment S_i.

4. Generate the cover image from z_i. The cover image can also be called the stego image in the case of SWE algorithms.
5. One or more bits of the secret message are mapped with the noise vector using:

$$r = random\left(\frac{m}{2^{\sigma-1}} - 1 + \delta, \frac{m+1}{2^{\sigma-1}} - 1 - \delta\right)$$

Here, m denotes the bits in the secret vector and $\sigma = \frac{|S_i|}{|z_i|}$ refers to the number of secret bits stored in 1 noise bit. δ is the tolerance deviation, which is used to extract accurate information from the stego vector.

Training of the extractor

1. Divide the stego image into subimages of $64 \times 64 \times 3$ dimensions.
2. Generate the noise vector between -1 and 1 with a dimension of 1×100. Using different seeds during the noise generation eliminates overfitting.
3. The architecture of E is similar to D, but the *tanh* function is used as an output layer instead of the *softmax* function. The *tanh* function conditions the noise vector.
4. In all the other layers, use *Leak-Relu* and batch normalization. Pooling layer or dropout is not incorporated.
5. After the fourth convolutional layer, add a fully connected layer.
6. Use E to retrieve the secret information when the training loss is small or after E converges.

The generator G in the deep convolutional GANs is used to fit the training set for generating the cover image. G comprises a fully connected layer and four deconvolution layers. The discriminator D is the inverse of G. A two-class softmax layer is used as the last layer in D and is used to discriminate if the output is from the generator or the training data. Loss computed from the feedback of G and D is used to train the two convolutional neural networks (CNNs). Nonlinear learning capabilities of the network can be enhanced by including activation function, dropout operation, and pooling layer. The nonlinear features aid in learning the parameters and to fit them efficiently. A detailed algorithm for cover or stego image generation and data extractions is given in [14].

2.5 CNN-based adversarial embedding

Data extraction can fail due to the addition of noise vectors on stego images. In [15], an adversarial embedding (ADV-EMB) scheme that can fool the CNN-based steganalyzer is proposed. ADV-EMB modifies the cost function according to the gradient from the target CNN steganalyzer. This scheme utilizes JPEG images as cover images. Xu-CNN [16] is used as the target steganalyzer and is trained using the cover and stego images generated by J-UNIWARD [17]. The CNN consists of one discrete cosine transform filtering layer and 20 convolution layers.

ADV-EMB using CNNs

1. Use the conventional cost function to compute the initial embedding cost for the cover image.
2. Divide the pixels in the cover image into common elements and adjustable elements. Either fixed or random positions generated using a secret key can be used for these elements.
3. Use the initial embedding cost function to embed the secret bits into the common group.
4. Embed the bits into the adjustable elements by updating the embedding cost. According to the gradient of the steganalyzer, the cost function is either doubled or halved compared to the cost of the common group elements.
5. Apply distortion minimization coding to both common and adjustable groups.
6. Test if the resultant image can fool the steganalyzer; if yes, terminate the embedding, otherwise, repeat steps 2–5.

3 Machine learning for steganalysis

The art and science of detecting hidden data in a digital media is termed steganalysis. Steganalysis is analogous to cryptanalysis and the major objective is to defeat steganography or to determine the strength of the underlying steganographic algorithm used for hiding data. Extensive usage of steganalysis can be realized in applications like cyber forensics, cyber warfare, detection of cybercrimes, etc. Universal steganalysis [18] techniques are robust in their ability to detect hidden data irrespective of the steganographic technique. The majority of steganalysis methods reported in the literature are specific to the steganographic algorithm. Steganalysis can be broadly classified as "signature steganalysis" and "statistical steganalysis". If the signature of the steganographic algorithm is used for steganalysis, it is called signature steganalysis, and if the statistical properties of the images are used for steganalysis, it is called statistical steganalysis. Universal and statistical steganalyzers make use of machine learning algorithms, as they are capable of learning features from the available data and extending it for further classification.

3.1 Steganalysis using CNNs

Recently, CNNs were also used for analyzing innocent-looking documents for possible hidden information [19]. CNNs consist of neural networks that are hierarchically arranged. CNNs have filtering and pooling operations that are trainable. Repeated and alternating applications of filtering and pooling results in complex feature representations. The detection accuracies are high when the same key is used for generating the stego image. A single global filtering layer is used as an initial convolutional layer followed by another convolutional layer to generate high-level features.

Steganalysis using CNNs

1. Use a single 3×3 edge detection filter initially on the input image.
2. Apply a hyperbolic tangent function for activation.
3. Use another convolutional layer of 64 filters along with zero padding to extract the high-level features map of size 2×2.
4. Use the same hyperbolic tangent function as mentioned in step 2.
5. Reshape the feature vector into 64×4.
6. Determine the output from a fully connected layer consisting of two *softmax* neurons.

The proposed approach does not contain pooling layers and is able to perform steganalysis without any hidden layers. A minibatch stochastic gradient descent (SGD) approach is used to train the deep network. This algorithm processes a minibatch of samples and computes the gradient values using back propagation, which is used to update the network parameters. Stable convergence can be obtained using the minibatch SGD. The following parameters are used during the training phase: batch size and learning rate, and decay and momentum are 100, 0.5, 5×10^{-7}, and 0, respectively.

3.2 Support vector machine-based steganalyzer for LSB matching steganography

Xia et al. [20] analyzed the reliability of learning-based steganalysis with support vector machines (SVM) as the classifier. Learning-based steganalysis methods rely on the principle of binary classification. The training data consists of an equal proportion of clean and stego images. Stego images are generated with variations in payload using steganographic algorithms. From the training data, complex features are extracted using feature extraction methods. SVM classifiers are trained with the feature vectors. This research work was exclusively based on the design of steganalysis for LSB-based steganographic schemes. It has been experimentally proven that LSB matching smoothens the histograms of multiorder differences. The smoothness caused is prominently seen at the peak of the histograms. A co-occurrence matrix is created for feature extraction. Extracted features are used to train the SVM classifier. The reliability of the steganalyzer is evaluated for LSB matching and HUGO—an improvised version of LSB. Experimentation includes testing on the two image datasets, namely Natural Resources Conservation Service (NRCS) consisting of 3161 images and Break Our Steganographic System (BOSS) consisting of 9074 images. The NRCS images are converted into grayscale images and each image is divided into four subimages to increase the number of training images. There are four different payloads, namely 1, 0.5, 0.25, and 0.1 bits per pixel (bpp).

SVM-based steganalyzer for LSB matching steganography
Feature extraction
1. Generate stego images using LSB matching and HUGO algorithms in the spatial domain for the datasets NRCS and BOSS.
2. Calculate the first-order difference at an arbitrary location of the image before ($D_c^1(i.j)$) and after ($D_s^1(i.j)$) embedding. The difference is given by:

$$C_d = \left(D_s^1(i.j)\right) - \left(D_c^1(i.j)\right)$$

3. Calculate the probability density of C_d as:

$$
\begin{cases}
P\{C_d = 2\} = P\{C_d = -2\} = \dfrac{1}{16}\rho^2 \\[2mm]
P\{C_d = 1\} = P\{C_d = -1\} = \dfrac{1}{16}\rho - \dfrac{1}{4}\rho^2 \\[2mm]
P\{C_d = 0\} = 1 + \dfrac{3}{8}\rho^2 - \rho
\end{cases}
$$

where ρ represents the payload [0,1].
4. Compute the histograms of the first-order differences of the original and stego images.
5. Approximate the first-order differences of the histograms with Gaussian distribution.
6. Collect the differences with a very small absolute value because the histograms are smoothened at the peak because of LSB matching.
7. Model the differences with a co-occurrence matrix, which consists of 648 multiorder difference features.
8. Train the SVM classifier with extracted features using the radial basis function as the kernel function.
9. Test the model with the 6644 original images and 26,576 stego images of the NRCS dataset. The testing data of BOSS includes 3074 original images and 12,296 stego images. The performance reliability of the classifier is measured by:

$$\rho = 2A - 1$$

where A is the area under the receiver operating characteristic curve.

The proposed steganalyzer has a higher reliability than the previous works on subtractive pixel adjacency matrix, renormalized difference histogram feature, and amplitude of local extrema. On average, the detection reliability is 0.7293 for NRCS images and 0.9243 for BOSS images. The difference in the prediction accuracy is because the BOSS images have a lower noise component than the NRCS images.

4 Machine learning for medical image encryption

Telemedicine essentially involves large volumes of storage and exchange of EHRs among physicians, patients, and healthcare professionals for better health services. Health records involve extensive usage of multimedia, especially images, which are generated from various imaging technologies like conventional X-rays, ultrasound imaging, digital mammography, computed axial tomography, positron emission tomography, and magnetic resonance imaging. These medical images are highly sensitive as they contain the confidential data of patients. Hence, encryption is essential for the secure transmission and storage of medical images. The process of a medical image encryption system is shown in Fig. 2.

A substantial amount of work has been carried out in the application of chaotic maps for medical image encryption. Recent exponential advancements in the field of machine learning have shown promising directions in its application to cryptography. This section highlights the application of CNNs and SVMs for the encryption of medical images.

4.1 Iris image encryption using CNN

An image encryption and decryption process based on iris features using deep learning has been proposed by Li et al. [21]. Iris has been recognized as the best choice of biometric technology, especially in the field of banking, because of strong uniqueness, strong biological activity, strong anticounterfeiting ability, and lifelong stability. Deep learning has been integrated with iris encryption to handle voluminous data and to enhance accuracy in feature extraction from iris images. Experimentation has been carried out on the iris dataset in the CASIA iris database public version, which includes 400 images of iris under 10 different categories.

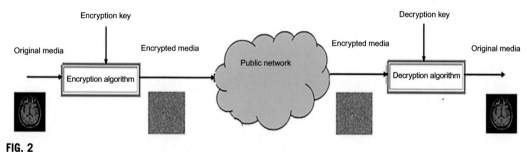

FIG. 2

Block diagram of medical image encryption.

Iris image encryption using CNN
Feature extraction
1. Perform preprocessing on the CASIA iris dataset to remove the effects of iris dryness and localization.
2. Use CNN to extract features of the iris images present in the dataset. The CNN structure includes five layer networks, a 5×5 convolution filter, and a 2×2 pooling filter for sampling. In the forward-propagation phase, the input weight matrix is multiplied by each phase point. In the back-propagation phase, the weight matrix is adjusted using a gradient descent algorithm to minimize the error.
3. The extracted iris features are represented in the output matrix.

Iris image encryption

1. Input the image to be encrypted to the trained CNN model to extract the feature vector $V1$.
2. Use Reed-Solomon error correcting code to encode the feature vector $V1$. The encoded result $VK1$ becomes the encryption key.
3. Convert the iris image to be encrypted into grayscale. Perform an XOR operation on $VK1$ and the gray value of the iris image to generate its encrypted version.
4. Send the encrypted image and Reed-Solomon error correcting code to the receiver.

Iris image decryption

1. Input the image to be decrypted to the trained CNN model to extract the feature vector $V2$.
2. Apply Reed-Solomon error correction code to correct the feature vector $V2$ to map exactly with the dimensions of the feature vector $V1$. The encoded result $VK2$ becomes the decryption key.
3. Perform an XOR operation on $VK2$ and the gray value of the encrypted iris image to recover the original image.

The feasibility of the algorithm has been evaluated using the accuracy of decryption. On average, the false acceptance rate is 0.003% and the false rejection rate is 1.043%, which is well within the satisfactory limits.

4.2 Combined encryption and data hiding using SVMs

Reversible data hiding methods are widely used in telemedicine applications because the electronic records of the patient can be directly embedded into the medical images. The correspondence between the health records and associated medical images can thus be easily maintained. Manikandan et al. [22] proposed a reversible data hiding scheme combined with encryption based on machine learning. An SVM, one of the widely used classification algorithms, is used at the receiver side for data extraction and recovery of hidden messages.

Combined encryption and data hiding using SVMs

Data hiding and encryption

1. Split the image I of size $m \times n$ to be encrypted into nonoverlapping square blocks of a predefined size.
2. Initialize a matrix Z of order $m \times n$ with zeros.
3. Select any three keys for encryption: K_1, K_2, and K_3. Any standard text-based algorithm can be used for encryption.
4. Repeat until all sub-blocks are encrypted:
   - Select an unencrypted sub-block of the image C based on a pseudorandom sequence.
   - If the message bit to be embedded is 1, encrypt C with K_1.
   - Otherwise encrypt C with K_2.
   - In the case where no embedding is required, encrypt C with K_3.
   - Copy the encrypted sub-block to Z at the appropriate positions.
5. The undivided regions of the mage after splitting are encrypted using K_3; copy the encrypted regions to Z.

Training of SVMs

1. Train the SVM model using six different features, namely Standard deviation, Peak in the histogram after quantization, Maximum vote from histogram bins, Entropy, Correlation between adjacent pixels, and Smoothness measure. The training set includes 1000 natural image blocks and 1000 encrypted image blocks.
2. The trained SVM is a binary classifier that includes two class labels: Class 0: natural or Class 1: encrypted.

Data extraction and decryption

1. Split the image I of size $m \times n$ to be decrypted into nonoverlapping square blocks of a predefined size.

2. Initialize a matrix Z' of order $m \times n$ with zeros.
3. Repeat until all sub-blocks are decrypted:
   * Decrypt the sub-blocks with keys K_1, K_2, and K_3 to generate C_1, C_2, and C_3.
   * Classify C_1, C_2, and C_3 as natural or encrypted using the trained SVM model.
   * Copy the decrypted sub-block with class label 0 to Z' at the appropriate positions.
4. Decrypt the undivided regions with K_3 and copy the decrypted regions to Z'.

The proposed algorithm has been tested with 5000 standard medical images of the OsriX dataset and was found to have satisfactory performance in terms of bit error rate and embedding rate. On average, the bit error rate is 1.72×10^{-1} and the embedding rate is 0.01234 bpp, which confirm the satisfactory performance of the proposed algorithm.

5 Machine learning for privacy in medical images

Machine learning techniques have proliferated in many areas of image processing such as segmentation, image analysis, texture analysis, and image reconstruction. Comparatively, application of machine learning in the field of medical imaging is limited because of the unavailability of large numbers of medical images for training. Though machine learning algorithms support training with millions of images, datasets in medical imaging are on the order of hundreds of subjects. Due to the patient privacy data regulations, the medical images, though generated in large volumes, are not available for research. Hence, three major privacy-preserving techniques have been developed to exploit the advantages of machine learning in medical imaging.

* **Federated learning:** No direct access to data, but machine learning models can be trained using the data.
* **Differential privacy:** Ensures privacy protection through mathematical and formal procedures.
* **Encrypted computation:** Facilitates machine learning even when the dataset is encrypted.

These techniques will not only secure the training models by providing large volumes of training data but also have the capability to provide accurate data for training. This section discusses the application of machine learning for preserving privacy in medical images.

5.1 CNN for homomorphic inference on encrypted medical images

The majority of classification tasks involved in medical imaging are outsourced to third-party cloud because of high computational requirements. Because of the sensitivity of the healthcare data, the privacy of the training and test data is to be preserved. These applications demand computational ability over encrypted data, especially in the absence of a decryption key. Homomorphic encryption seems to be a viable solution. Although CNN can extract features from encrypted data, it is limited by the large volume of CNN computations for high-resolution images. A new resource-efficient homomorphic encryption strategy CaRENet is proposed by Chao et al. [23]. The major objective of the research work is to reduce the computational requirements of CNN by developing a library that supports all homomorphic computations.

CNN for homomorphic inference on encrypted medical images

Image packing
1. Digitize the image into a three-dimensional tensor.
2. Flatten the three-dimensional tensor to a one-dimensional vector.
3. Map each individual one-dimensional vector to multiple ciphertexts.
4. When one ciphertext is filled with the maximum amount of values, switch to the next ciphertext.

Design of layers
1. Design the convolutional layer and fully connected layer with matrix-based operations supporting homomorphic functions like additions and multiplications of ciphertexts.
2. Construct the weight matrix of the convolution layer with all possible shifted locations of filters. Construct the weight matrix of the fully connected layer in such a way that the number of rows is equal to the number of output neurons and the weights in each row correspond to the input neurons.
3. Compute the dot product by parallelizing the multiplication of each row of weight matrix with a one-dimensional vector. Skip all zero row segments to eliminate unnecessary multiplications.

The performance of CNNs in the classification of encrypted data has been analyzed for retinopathy of prematurity and diabetic retinopathy images. Experimental results report a reduction in memory by a factor of 45.9%. Also, the proposed system supports high-resolution images.

5.2 Random forest for privacy preserving and disease prediction

Disease predictors based on machine learning demand a large amount of training data. This training data is to be collected across various medical labs, hospitals, and research institutions. Disease prediction is normally offered as a cloud service, wherein a patient or a doctor can submit the medical health record to obtain a prediction. Since the data related to health records of an individual is processed in an untrusted cloud environment, privacy and security of data have become major concern. Machine learning algorithms seem to be a viable solution as it can learn from hidden and encrypted data during the training phase. Ma et al. [24] studied the effect of using random forest (RF), not only as a classifier, but also for securing data shared by multiple sources. Data is stored in the cloud with no privacy leakage as the data is encrypted. The system facilitates multiple owners to encrypt their individual data and collaboratively train the RF classifier. Also, secure outsourced rational computation is supported to enhance accuracy and to overcome the limitation of integer-only arithmetic in Pailier homomorphic schemes. Any authorized user can use the RF predictor by uploading the health data to obtain a prediction in a privacy-preserving way.

RF for privacy preserving and disease prediction

Key generation
1. The key center generates keys for data owners, cloud service providers, operation platforms, and authorized users.

Data owner
1. Convert the data from rational format to integer format.
2. Encrypt the data in integer format and upload the data to the cloud service for training the RF classifier.

Construction of RF

1. Construct the training encrypted dataset D, which has d tuples $(x_1, y_1), (x_2, y_2), \ldots (x_n, y_n)$. Each instance (x_i) contains m features $\{fi_1, fi_2, fi_3, \ldots fi_n\}$ and a class label $y_i \in [0, 1]$.
2. Use a bagging sample on D to obtain the encrypted dataset for the construction of random trees. Randomly choose a subset f_i from the feature set F.
3. Create a random tree over the ciphertexts. Compute the best split of each internal node by leveraging secure rational computation protocols. A Gini index of each feature is used to identify the best split. Create the root node corresponding to the selected feature.
4. Repeat step 3 to construct a left and right subtree until all the instances are covered.
5. Store the root node in the cloud for constructing the RF.

Disease prediction

1. Encrypt the instance for which the prediction is to be made.
2. Search all the random trees in the RF by matching the encrypted data with the root node.
3. Recursively travel left and right of the random trees based on the value of the encrypted instance until the leaf node is reached to obtain the class label.
4. The class with the maximum frequency count is the predicted result.

The heart disease dataset from UCI Machine Learning Repository is used to evaluate the performance of the proposed model. The accuracy of the RF classifier over encrypted data is just 0.023 less than the RF classifier over natural data.

6 Conclusion

The majority of applications of machine learning in the broader domain of information security focus on cryptanalysis, steganalysis, malware analysis, encrypted traffic analysis, and machine learning-based intrusion detection systems. Analysis involves searching a very large space of possible solutions. Finding the optimal solution in such a huge space is made easier and possible by machine learning algorithms. This chapter covered the application of machine learning techniques for securing medical images especially in the sub-domains of data hiding, encryption, and privacy preservation. Future directions of research in integrating machine learning and information security include:

- Design symmetric and asymmetric cryptosystems based on machine learning.
- Use machine intelligence to create a personal cryptosystem between two communicating AI-based agents.
- Enhance accuracy of machine learning training models for encrypted data.
- Improve cryptanalysis of chaos-based medical image encryption through machine learning.
- Use deep learning to extract decryption keys from blocks of ciphertexts.
- Integrate machine learning with differential and linear cryptanalysis for improving the efficiency of cryptanalysis.
- Develop machine learning models to interpret homomorphic and multiparty computation.

In spite of the enormous advantages of using machine learning for security, it must always be ensured that the trained machine learning model is resistant to adversarial settings. Machine learning models must be protected from revealing statistical information on training data to attackers. The benefits of integrating machine learning with medical imaging can be broadened to a greater extent with proper cooperation and collaboration among academic and research institutions, hospitals, and cloud service providers. Research work confirms that machine learning can revolutionize the healthcare industry by enhancing the healthcare services for future generations.

References

[1] A. Rajkomar, J. Dean, I. Kohane, Machine learning in medicine, N. Engl. J. Med. 380 (14) (2019) 1347–1358.

[2] Y. LeCun, Y. Bengio, G. Hinton, Deep learning, Nature 521 (2015) 436–444.

[3] M. Chaumont, Deep learning in steganography and steganalysis from 2015 to 2018, in: Digital Media Steganography: Principles, Algorithms, Advances, Elsevier, 2020.

[4] S. Ioffe, C. Szegedy, Batch normalization: accelerating deep network training by reducing internal covariate shift, in: Proceedings of the 32nd International Conference on Machine Learning, vol. 37, 2015, pp. 448–456.

[5] J. Ba, J.R. Kiros, G.E. Hinton, Layer Normalization, 2016. arXiv:1607.06450 [stat.ML].

[6] D. Ulyanov, A. Vedaldi, V. Lempitsky, Instance Normalization: The Missing Ingredient for Fast Stylization, 2016. arXiv:1607.08022 [cs.CV].

[7] Y. Wu, K. He, Group normalization, in: Proceedings of the European Conference on Computer Vision (ECCV), 2018, pp. 3–19.

[8] T. Salimans, D.P. Kingma, Weight normalization: a simple re-parameterization to accelerate training of deep neural networks, in: Proceedings of the 30th Conference on Neural Information Processing Systems, 2016, pp. 901–909.

[9] C. Luo, J. Zhan, X. Xue, L. Wang, R. Ren, Q. Yang, Cosine normalization: using cosine similarity instead of dot product in neural networks, in: Proceedings of the International Conference on Artificial Neural Networks, Lecture Notes in Computer Science, vol. 11139, 2018, pp. 391–392.

[10] M.I. Razzak, S. Naz, A. Zaib, Deep learning for medical image processing: overview, challenges and future, classification in bioapps, in: Springer Lecture Notes in Computational Vision and Biomechanics, vol. 26, 2018, pp. 323–350.

[11] H.-Z. Wu, H.-X. Wang, Y.-Q. Shi, Can Machine Learn Steganography? – Implementing LSB Substitution and Matrix Coding Steganography with Feed-Forward Neural Networks, CoRR, 2016. abs/1606.05294.

[12] S. Baluja, Hiding images in plain sight: deep steganography, in: Proceedings of the 31st Conference on Neural Information Processing Systems, 2017, pp. 2069–2079.

[13] O. Russakovsky, J. Deng, H. Su, J. Krause, S. Satheesh, S. Ma, Z. Huang, A. Karpathy, A. Khosla, M.S. Bernstein, A.C. Berg, F.-F. Li, ImageNet Large Scale Visual Recognition Challenge, CoRR, 2014. abs/1409.0575.

[14] L. Hu, W. Wang, S. Jiang, B. Zheng, Li, a novel image steganography method via deep convolutional generative adversarial networks, IEEE Access 6 (2018) 38303–38314.

[15] W. Tang, B. Li, S. Tan, M. Barni, J. Huang, CNN based adversarial embedding for image steganography, IEEE Trans. Inf. Foren. Secur. 14 (8) (2019) 2074–2087.

[16] G. Xu, Deep convolutional neural network to detect J-UNIWARD, in: Proceedings of the 5th ACM Workshop on Information Hiding Multimedia Security, 2017, pp. 67–73.

[17] V. Holub, J. Fridrich, T. Denemark, Universal distortion function for steganography in an arbitrary domain, EURASIP J. Inf. Secur. 2014 (1) (2014) 1–13.

[18] A. Nissar, A.H. Mir, Classification of steganalysis techniques: a study, Digital Signal Process. 20 (2010) 1758–1770.

[19] M. Salomon, R. Couturier, C. Guyeux, J.-F. Couchot, J.M. Bahi, Steganalysis via a convolutional neural network using large convolution filters for embedding process with same stego key: a deep learning approach for telemedicine, Eur. Res. Telemed. 6 (2) (2017) 79–92.

[20] Z. Xia, X. Wang, X. Sun, B. Wang, Steganalysis of least significant bit matching using multi-order differences, Secur. Commun. Netw. 7 (8) (2014) 1283–1291.

[21] X. Li, Y. Jiang, M. Chen, et al., Research on iris image encryption based on deep learning. EURASIP J. Image Video Process. 2018 (1) (2018), https://doi.org/10.1186/s13640-018-0358-7.

[22] V.M. Manikandan, V. Masilamani, Reversible data hiding scheme during encryption using machine learning, Proc. Comput. Sci. 133 (2018) 348–356.

[23] J. Chao, A.A. Badawi, B. Unnikrishnan, J. Lin, C.F. Mun, J.M. Brown, J.P. Campbell, M. Chiang, J. Kalpathy-Cramer, V.R. Chandrasekhar, P. Krishnaswamy, K.M.M. Aung, CaRENets: Compact and Resource-Efficient CNN for Homomorphic Inference on Encrypted Medical Images, 2019. arXiv:1901.10074 [cs.CR].

[24] Z. Ma, J. Ma, Y. Miao, X. Liu, Privacy-preserving and high-accurate outsourced disease predictor on random forest, Inf. Sci. 496 (2019) 225–241.

Genetic algorithm-based intelligent watermarking for security of medical images in telemedicine applications

10

Rohit Thanki

C. U. Shah University, Wadhwan, Gujarat, India

1 Introduction

In today's e-era, which mainly includes e-commerce, e-banking, e-health, and e-learning, information can be effectively downloaded with no authorization from the proprietor. Once in a while, these circumstances produce different issues, for example, copyright security and proprietor verification. In such cases, assurance and verification of advanced information are required before it is exchanged over the open-source transmission medium. In response to these issues, analysts have proposed different information concealing strategies: cryptography, steganography, and watermarking [1,2]. Watermarking is primarily utilized for the assurance and validation of information. This method beats the constraints of steganography by embedding a watermark into the host content such that even the basic client cannot discover the hidden watermark. As per the literature [1–5], the watermarking framework has three components: a watermark embedder, a correspondence channel, which might be wired or wireless, and a watermark extractor. The watermark embedder embeds a watermark into host images to generate the watermarked image, while the watermark extractor extracts the watermark from the test image, which can be the watermarked image with or without attacks. The major requirements of digital image watermarking are recalled here [1–5]:

1. **Robustness:** The watermarking technique must protect owners' data against any manipulations and has to be robust.
2. **Imperceptibility:** After watermark insertion into host data, the visual quality of the host data should not be affected, i.e., the watermark should be imperceptible.
3. **Embedding capacity:** The watermarking technique should allow the hiding of large size watermarks [3].

Watermarking techniques are mainly developed in three processing domains: spatial domain, transform domain, and hybrid domain [2,6]. Spatial domain techniques are easy to implement but provide less imperceptibility as the host image pixels are directly modified. Transform domain watermarking is complex but provides increased robustness compared to spatial domain watermarking. In all the transform domain techniques, the host image is converted into the frequency domain using various image transforms such as discrete Fourier transform, discrete cosine transform (DCT), and discrete wavelet transform (DWT) before watermark embedding and is inverse transformed later. In all the hybrid domain techniques, the host image is converted into the hybrid coefficients of frequency using various image transforms before watermark embedding and is inverse transformed later. Recently, new transforms such as fast discrete curvelet transform (FDCuT)- [7], nonsubsampled contourlet transform- [8], and finite ridgelet transform- [9] based watermarking schemes have been proposed by various researchers.

Most of the existing watermarking schemes are based on additive and multiplicative properties where the scaling factor plays an important role in the generation of watermarked images [1–9]. In many schemes, this scaling factor is a fixed value or user-defined value. Due to this, sometimes watermarks do not fulfill the basic requirements for a given dataset. Therefore to tackle this problem, researchers have introduced the concept of optimized scaling factor with the help of optimization algorithms and bioinspired algorithms [10]. Here, based on evaluation parameters of imperceptibility and robustness, the optimized scaling factor is calculated with the help of the fitness function. Different types of algorithms such as simulated annealing, tabu search, particle swarm optimization (PSO), genetic algorithm (GA), etc. are widely used for this purpose [10]. Also, fewer medical image watermarking schemes based on optimization algorithms are proposed in the literature [11]. These two points are the motivation to develop new medical image watermarking schemes based on an optimization algorithm in this chapter.

The medical image watermarking scheme based on hybridization of DCT-SVD (singular value decomposition) and a GA is proposed for the security of medical data in telemedicine applications in this chapter. Here, the singular value of DCT coefficients accords with the watermark bits and optimized scaling factor, which is generated with the help of a GA. The main points in this chapter: (1) provide detail of various image watermarking schemes based on a GA; (2) develop a blind, robust, and optimized watermarking scheme for the security of medical images; and (3) improve the robustness of many existing watermarking schemes available in the literature.

The rest of the chapter is organized as follows: details of a GA-based watermarking scheme are given in Section 2. The technical background of terminology used in this proposed scheme is given in Section 3. The technical detail of the proposed scheme is discussed in Section 4. The experimental results of the proposed scheme and comparison of obtained results with existing studies are discussed in Section 5. Finally, conclusion of the proposed scheme is discussed in Section 6.

2 Genetic algorithm-based image watermarking

Information on various GA-based image watermarking schemes is given in this section. Here, a GA is used to find the optimized scaling factor or optimized transform coefficients for hiding a watermark logo. Details of the schemes are as follows.

Shieh et al. [12] proposed a DCT and GA-based blind and robust image watermarking scheme. In this scheme, DCT coefficients were modified using a watermark logo and optimized scaling factor. Here, the optimized scaling factor was generated using a GA and fitness function, which was generated with the help of evaluation parameters such as peak signal-to-noise ratio (PSNR) and normalized correlation (NC). Kumsawat et al. [13] proposed a discrete multiwavelet transform and GA-based blind and robust image watermarking scheme. In this scheme, the watermark logo is inserted into selected wavelet coefficients of the image with the help of a scaling factor. The selection of coefficients took place with the help of a GA. Shih et al. [14] proposed a DCT-based blind and robust image watermarking scheme along with a GA. In this scheme, a GA was used for proper detection of the watermark logo at the detection side. Huang et al. [15] proposed two image watermarking schemes based on transformation coding and a GA. In these schemes, transformation coding based on DCT and DWT (which are used in JPEG and JPEG 2000 compression standards) is used for embedding the watermark logo. While a GA was generated optimized scaling factor with the help of PSNR and NC of obtained results.

Chu et al. [16] proposed a blind image watermarking scheme based on DWT and a GA. Here, the selection of proper wavelet coefficients was done with the help of a GA. Lai et al. [17] proposed a nonblind image watermarking scheme based on SVD and a GA. In this scheme, singular values of the host image were modified by an optimized scaling factor and watermark logo. The proper value of the scaling factor was obtained with the help of a GA in this scheme. Aslantas et al. [18] proposed a nonblind and robust image watermarking scheme based on a GA and SVD. In this scheme, singular values of the cover image were modified by the optimized scaling factor and watermark logo.

Maity et al. [19] proposed two image watermarking schemes in the spatial domain with the help of a GA. In these schemes, a GA was used to improve the detection of the watermark at the detection side and find the optimal value to achieve a good-quality watermarked image. In the first scheme, a GA was used to find the optimal value for the embedding of the watermark logo into wavelet coefficients of the cover image. In the second scheme, a GA was used to find optimal coefficients of the cover image to achieve a good-quality watermarked image. Boato et al. [20] proposed an image watermarking scheme based on quantization index modulation and a GA. In this scheme, the modulation index value was optimized by the GA using performance parameters of the watermarking scheme. Fakhari et al. [21] proposed a wavelet and GA-based blind watermarking scheme for the security of a medical image. This was the first watermarking scheme along with a GA for a medical image. In this scheme, the approximation wavelet sub-band of the medical image was modified by the watermark logo and optimized scaling factor, which was generated with the help of a GA.

Loukhaoukha [22] proposed a nonblind watermarking scheme using SVD and a GA. In this scheme, singular values of the cover image were modified by an optimized scaling factor. The optimized scaling factor was generated using a GA. Vahedi et al. [23] proposed a blind color image watermarking scheme using DWT and a GA. In this scheme, a GA was used to find suitable approximation wavelet coefficients of the color image where the watermark logo was inserted into it. Agarwal et al. [24] proposed a blind watermarking scheme using hybridization of DCT and DWT along with a GA. In this scheme, a GA was used to find suitable hybrid coefficients of the cover image and a watermark logo was inserted into it. Maity et al. [25] proposed an image watermarking scheme based on a wavelet transform and a GA. In this scheme, a GA was used to find the best wavelet coefficients where the watermark logo was inserted.

Naheed et al. [26] proposed a medical image watermarking scheme using interpolation and a GA. In this scheme, embedding locations for the watermark were calculated with the help of interpolation and a GA. After obtaining the best locations, the watermark logo was inserted into those locations of the cover image to achieve the watermarked image. Bahrushin et al. [27] proposed an image watermarking scheme based on DCT and a GA. In this scheme, the best DCT coefficients were obtained with the help of a GA. The fitness function of the GA was calculated with the help of PSNR and NC in this scheme. Hardisal et al. [28] proposed a color image watermarking scheme based on DWT and a GA.

Table 1 Fitness function used in existing watermarking schemes based on a genetic algorithm.

Schemes	Fitness function
Shieh et al. [12]	$f = PSNR + \lambda \cdot \sum_{i=1}^{N} NC\left(w, w_i^*\right)$
Huang et al. [15]	$f = PSNR + \lambda_1 \cdot \frac{1}{N} \sum_{i=1}^{N} BCR\left(w, w_i^*\right) + \lambda_2 \cdot Bits_N$
Chu et al. [16]	$f = PSNR + \lambda \cdot BCR(w, w^*)$
Aslantas et al. [18]	$f = \left[1 \middle/ \left(\frac{1}{N} \sum_{i=1}^{N} corr\left(w, w_i^*\right) - corr(I, WI) \right) \right]$
Maity et al. [25]	$f = \frac{3MSSIM \times (1-PG) \times CC}{[MSSIM + (1-PG)CC + MSSIM(1-PG)]}$
Hardisal et al. [28]	$f = \frac{\sum_{c=1}^{3} PSNR_c}{3} - \sum_{i=1}^{22} (1 - NC_i) + 5$

After reviewing the research work on GA-based watermarking schemes, the following points were noted: (1) most researchers used their own fitness function, which is summarized in Table 1; (2) most schemes do not show effectiveness of the quality of extracted watermark logos or images; and (3) fewer schemes are available for medical images.

3 Technical background

The use of image transformation in the proposed scheme and basic details of the GA are discussed in this section. Also, the selection of hybrid coefficients for watermark embedding is also discussed in this section.

3.1 Image transformation

In this proposed scheme, the hybridization of DCT and SVD is used. The selection of these hybrid coefficients is done in such a way that blind detection of the watermark logo is possible at the detector side. Therefore, first, basic information regarding DCT and SVD and then selection of hybrid coefficients are discussed.

- *Discrete cosine transform*

This is one of the well-known image transformations that converts an image from the spatial domain to the frequency domain. This transform converts pixel values of the image into its cosine frequency coefficients. This transform can be applied to the image in two ways: as a block-wise DCT and a direct DCT [29]. In the block-wise DCT approach, the image converts into nonoverlapping blocks and then DCT is applied to these blocks to obtain its frequency coefficients. In the direct DCT approach, DCT is directly applied to image pixels to obtain its frequency coefficients. DCT decomposes any image into three different frequencies: low, middle, and high. The low- and high-frequency coefficients are largely affected by attacks; therefore middle-frequency coefficients are used for watermark embedding [29].

The forward DCT and inverse DCT for any image can be calculated with the help of Eqs. (1), (2), respectively [29]. Fig. 2 shows the original medical image along with block-wise DCT.

$$I(u,v) = \alpha(u) \cdot \alpha(v) \sum_{x=0}^{M-1} \sum_{y=0}^{N-1} i(x,y) \cdot \cos\left[\frac{(2x+1)u\pi}{2M}\right] \cdot \cos\left[\frac{(2y+1)v\pi}{2N}\right] \tag{1}$$

$$i(x,y) = \sum_{u=0}^{M-1} \sum_{v=0}^{N-1} \alpha(u) \cdot \alpha(v) \cdot \cos\left[\frac{(2x+1)u\pi}{2M}\right] \cdot \cos\left[\frac{(2y+1)v\pi}{2N}\right] \tag{2}$$

where:
$$\alpha(u) = \sqrt{\frac{1}{M}} \text{ for, } u=0; \alpha(u) = \sqrt{\frac{2}{M}} \text{ for, } u=1,2,3,...,M-1$$
$$\alpha(v) = \sqrt{\frac{1}{N}} \text{ for, } v=0; \alpha(v) = \sqrt{\frac{2}{N}} \text{ for, } v=1,2,3,...,N-1$$
$, x=0, 1, 2, ..., M-1; y=0, 1, 2, ..., N-1.$

- *Singular value decomposition*

This is a linear algebra operation that decomposes any image into three matrices: U matrix, V matrix, and S matrix. The U and V matrices are called orthonormal matrices, while the S matrix is called a singular matrix. The size of these matrices depends on the size of the actual image. If the size of the image is $M \times N$ then the sizes of U and V are $M \times M$ and $N \times N$, while the size of S is $M \times N$. The values in the U matrix and V matrix are real or complex numbers, while values in the S matrix are real positive numbers. The values of the S matrix are represented by various properties of the image such as brightness and geometric features. This matrix also has an important role in watermarking due to the arrangement of values in it [8].

- *Selection of hybrid coefficients*

In the proposed watermarking scheme, the hybridization of DCT and SVD is used for the embedding of the watermark logo into the cover medical image. Here, first, the cover medical image is divided into nonoverlapping blocks with a size of 8×8. Next, the block-wise DCT is applied to image blocks to obtain its DCT coefficients. The SVD is applied to these DCT coefficients to obtain values of the U matrix, S matrix, and V matrix. After obtaining the hybrid coefficients of medical image blocks, it is observed that the values of $U(3,2)$ and $U(5,2)$ near to each based on characteristics of the input medical image. Therefore these two values are used for embedding of the watermark logo into the cover image. Fig. 1 shows the values of the U matrix for a magnetic resonance imaging (MRI) image [30] after application of SVD on DCT blocks of these images, respectively.

3.2 Genetic algorithm

The GA was developed using a biological concept such as the genetic structure and behavior of chromosomes of the human population [31,32]. This algorithm is used for various optimization and searching problems in real life. The detailed working of this algorithm is as follows [33]: (1) the set of individuals is maintained in the population. In this population, each individual represents a solution for the given problem. Each individual gives the finite length vector of components as a solution. The components of the solution are analogous to genes. The combination of several genes creates a chromosome. (2) A fitness score is assigned to each individual, which has the ability to complete.

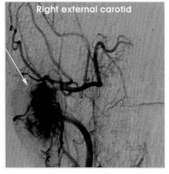

(A)

(B)

−0.992	0.121	0.031	0.002	0.006	0.000	0.000	−0.002
−0.119	−0.969	−0.002	−0.191	−0.089	−0.025	0.033	−0.017
−0.032	−0.073	−0.860	0.166	0.470	0.049	−0.024	0.042
0.000	0.164	−0.496	−0.472	−0.701	−0.068	0.076	−0.053
−0.013	−0.073	−0.063	0.375	−0.335	−0.028	−0.734	0.445
−0.014	−0.092	−0.089	0.749	−0.406	0.097	0.405	−0.290
0.001	−0.003	−0.001	−0.085	−0.004	0.624	−0.449	−0.634
0.001	0.001	−0.021	0.070	0.053	−0.770	−0.295	−0.558

(C)

FIG. 1

(A) Original magnetic resonance imaging (MRI) image. (B) MRI image block with a size of 8 × 8. (C) Values for the U matrix of the MRI image block.

From A. Al-Haj, A. Mohammad, Crypto-watermarking of transmitted medical images, J. Digit. Imaging 30 (1) (2017) 26–38.

(3) Once the initial generation is created, the algorithm evolves the generation with the help of different operations: (a) Selection—this operator selects the individual that has a good fitness score and allows them to pass their genes to the successive operations. (b) Crossover—this operation represents mating between individuals. Here, two randomly selected individuals at crossover sites exchange their genes and create a completely new individual, which is referred to as the offspring. An example of the crossover operation is shown in Fig. 2A. (c) Mutation—this operation adds random genes to the offspring to maintain diversity in the population to avoid premature convergence. An example of this operation is shown in Fig. 2B. (4) Finally, the algorithm terminates when the population has converged. The flowchart is shown in Fig. 3.

Parent string 1: ABDEGFHG	Parent string 1: EHGAGFHG
Parent string 2: EHGADBGB	After mutation operation: **EHMACFGN**
After crossover operation: **EHGAGFHG** (offspring)	

(A)   (B)

FIG. 2

(A) Crossover operation. (B) Mutation operation.

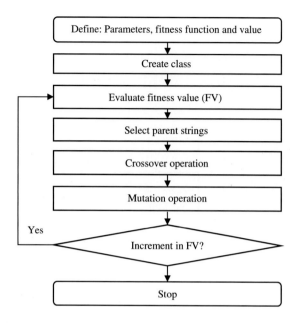

FIG. 3

Flowchart of a genetic algorithm.

4 Proposed scheme

In [34,35], a robust and blind medical image watermarking algorithm is presented, but the scaling factor in these algorithms is taken as a fixed value. Therefore the analysis of these algorithms is limited. For the solution to this limitation, the new watermarking algorithm is proposed. This scheme is based on block-based DCT-SVD and a GA, in which the U matrix values of DCT coefficients of the medical image are modified by an optimized scaling factor according to watermark bits. For watermark embedding, hybrid coefficients of the medical image are given better imperceptibility and provided robustness against attacks. The GA adaptively selects a proper value of the scaling factor. A block diagram of this proposed scheme is shown in Fig. 4. This scheme has three processes: embedding, extraction, and selection of proper scaling factor using a GA.

4.1 Embedding process

The steps for this process are:

Step 1: Take a cover medical image and watermark logo. Calculate the spatial resolution of these images.

Step 2: The cover medical image converts into nonoverlapped blocks with a size of 8×8.

Step 3: The block-wise DCT is applied to medical image blocks to obtain its DCT frequency coefficients. Then, SVD is applied to DCT frequency coefficients to obtain its matrices such as U, S, and V.

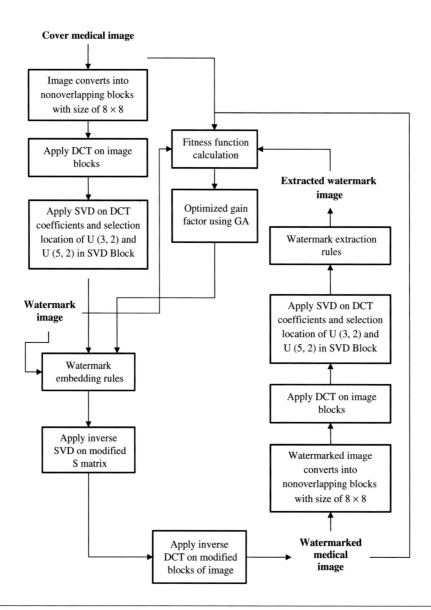

FIG. 4

Working of the proposed scheme. *DCT*, discrete cosine transform; *GA*, genetic algorithm; *SVD*, singular value decomposition.

Step 4: Next, the values of $U(3,2)$ and $U(5,2)$ are taken for embedding of the watermark bits. The watermark bits are embedded into the coefficients of the cover medical image using the following conditions:

- If the value of the watermark bit is 0, then:

$$U_{New}(3,2) = U(3,2) - \left(\alpha_{Optimized}/2\right)$$
$$U_{New}(5,2) = U(5,2) + \left(\alpha_{Optimized}/2\right) \quad (3)$$

- If the value of the watermark bit is 1, then:

$$U_{New}(3,2) = U(3,2) + \left(\alpha_{Optimized}/2\right)$$
$$U_{New}(5,2) = U(5,2) - \left(\alpha_{Optimized}/2\right) \quad (4)$$

where U_{New} is a modified value of specific coefficients of the U matrix, U is the original value of specific coefficients of the U matrix, and $\alpha_{Optimized}$ is an optimized value of the scaling factor.

- This process performs for all values of watermark bits.

Step 5: After obtaining the modified U matrix, inverse SVD is applied to it along with the original matrices of U and V to obtain modified DCT frequency coefficients of the cover medical image.

Step 6: Finally, inverse block-wise DCT is applied to the modified DCT frequency coefficients to obtain the watermarked medical image.

4.2 Extraction process

The steps for this process are:

Step 1: Take a watermarked medical image and calculate its spatial resolution.

Step 2: The watermarked medical image converts into nonoverlapped blocks with a size of 8×8.

Step 3: The block-wise DCT is applied to the watermarked medical image blocks to obtain its DCT frequency coefficients. Then, SVD is applied to the DCT frequency coefficients to obtain its matrices such as U, S, and V.

Step 4: Next, the value of U (3,2) and U (5,2) are taken for extraction of the watermark bits. The watermark bits are extracted from these coefficients of the watermarked medical image using the following conditions:

- If U (3,2) $> U$ (5,2)

  watermark bit $= 0$;

  else

  watermark bit $= 1$

Step 5: Finally, reshaping of the watermark bit is done to obtain the watermark logo at the detector side.

4.3 Selection of proper scaling factor using GA

The selection of scaling factors plays an important role in the performance of any watermarking scheme based on additive qualities. The value of this factor is mainly used to assess the visible quality of the watermarked image and robustness of the extracted watermark logo. If the value of this factor is low, then the quality of the watermarked image is ideal and vice versa. In most algorithms, the selection of this factor is done manually by the user, which depends on the nature of the cover image. For standardization of the watermarking algorithm for different types of medical images, some optimization algorithms are used for selecting the scaling factor. Thus, in this chapter, a bioinspired algorithm, GA with hybridization of a DCT+SVD-based watermarking scheme, can provide an optimized scaling factor.

To incorporate GA into the medical watermarking scheme, an initial population is generated using a random function. Next, operations such as selection, crossover, and mutation are performed on the generated population for the given fitness function. The output of this algorithm gives a best fitness function. The value of this function is used as the optimized scaling factor during the embedding process. This value is added to hybrid coefficients of the medical image according to watermark bits. Calculation of the fitness function for this scheme is given in Eq. (5). The minimum value of the fitness function is taken as the optimized scaling factor assigned to the next iteration. This process continues until population convergence is achieved. In this scheme, minimum fitness is obtained at the end of each iteration. The equation of the fitness function is:

$$f = 1 - \max \left(\frac{NC(w, w^*) + NC(MI, MI^*)}{2} \right) \tag{5}$$

where NC indicates normalized correlation, w and w^* indicate the original watermark logo and extracted watermark logo, respectively, and MI and MI^* indicate the cover medical image and watermarked medical image, respectively.

5 Results and discussion

The performance of the proposed algorithm is analyzed using different types of medical images such as MRI, computed tomography, and ultrasound with a size of 512×512 pixels, whereas the hospital logo as watermark logo with a size of 64×64 pixels (shown in Fig. 5). The medical images are taken from different medical image databases [30,36].

The PSNR [37] is used as a measure of imperceptibility of the watermarked medical image, whereas NC [37] and the structural similarity index measure (SSIM) [38] are used to measure robustness of the extracted watermark logo. The mathematical equation of PSNR, NC, and SSIM is:

$$PSNR = 10 \times \log_{10} \left(\frac{255^2}{MSE} \right) \tag{6}$$

$$MSE = \frac{1}{i \times j} \sum_{x=0}^{i-1} \sum_{y=0}^{j-1} (MI(x, y) - MI^*(x, y))^2 \tag{7}$$

where MI is an original cover medical image and MI^* is a watermarked medical image, respectively.

$$NC = \frac{\sum_{x=1}^{M} \sum_{y=1}^{N} w(x, y) \times w^*(x, y)}{\sum_{x=1}^{M} \sum_{y=1}^{N} w^2(x, y)} \tag{8}$$

where w is the original watermark logo and w^* is the extracted watermark logo.

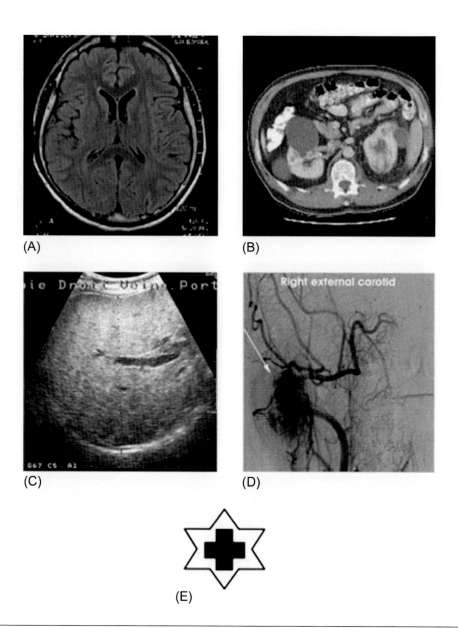

FIG. 5

Test cover medical images. (A) Brain computed tomography (CT). (B) Body CT. (C) Ultrasound. (D) Magnetic resonance imaging. (E) Watermark logo.

$$\text{SSIM} = \frac{\left(2\mu_w\mu_{w*} + C_1\right)\left(2\sigma_{ww*} + C_2\right)}{\left(\mu_w^2 + \mu_{w*}^2 + C_1\right)\left(\sigma_w^2 + \sigma_{w*}^2 + C_2\right)}$$

(9)

where μ_w is the average of the original watermark logo, μ_{w*} is the average of the recovered watermark logo, σ_{ww*} is the covariance of the original watermark logo and recovered watermark logo, and C_1, C_2 are constant values.

5.1 Imperceptibility test

In the proposed scheme, a cover medical image with a size of 512×512 is converted into 4096 blocks with a size of 8×8. The watermark logo with a size of 64×64 is converted into a bit vector with a size of 4096. Block-wise DCT followed by SVD is applied to image blocks to obtain the hybrid frequency coefficients of the medical image. Next, according to the value of the watermark vector, the optimized scaling factor is added to the $U(3,1)$ coefficient and the $U(5,2)$ coefficient of the hybrid frequency coefficients of the medical image to obtain its modified version. After embedding of the watermark, inverse SVD and inverse block-wise DCT are applied to the modified coefficients to obtain the watermarked medical image. The resultant watermarked medical image using the proposed scheme is shown in Fig. 6A–D.

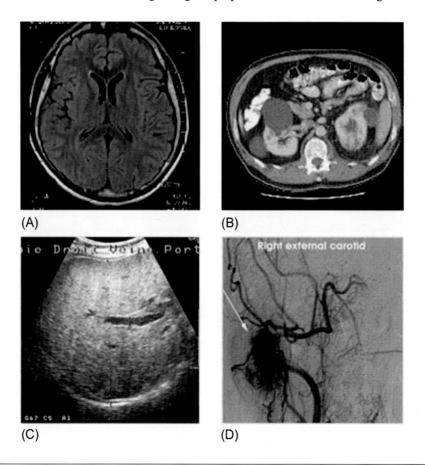

(A)　　　　　　　　(B)

(C)　　　　　　　　(D)

FIG. 6

Watermarked medical images obtained using the proposed watermarking scheme. (A) Brain computed tomography (CT). (B) Body CT. (C) Ultrasound. (D) Magnetic resonance imaging.

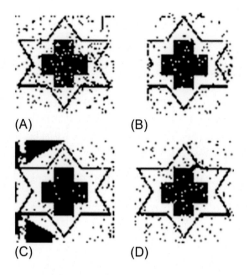

FIG. 7

Extracted watermark logo obtained using the proposed watermarking scheme. (A) Brain computed tomography (CT). (B) Body CT. (C) Ultrasound. (D) Magnetic resonance imaging.

For the extraction side, the watermarked image is extracted from the watermarked medical image using the comparison process. Here, first, block-wise DCT and SVD are applied to the watermarked medical image to obtain coefficient values of U (1,1) and U (2,2). Next, comparison of these coefficients is performed to obtain the extracted watermark bits. Finally, the reshaping process is applied to these bits to obtain the watermark logo at the extraction side. The resultant extracted watermark image using this proposed scheme is shown in Fig. 7A–D.

The obtained PSNR (dB) values between the cover medical image and the watermarked medical image, and NC and SSIM values between the original watermark image and the extracted watermark image, are summarized in Table 2. The obtained values indicate that PSNR values are higher than 32 dB for all types of images. So, the proposed algorithm fulfills the requirement of invisibility and provides a good-quality watermarked medical image. The obtained NC and SSIM values indicate that the quality of the extracted watermark images is near to the quality of the original version.

Table 2 Obtained PSNR (dB) and NC values of the proposed scheme without attacks.

Types of medical image	PSNR (dB)	NC	SSIM
Brain CT	38.0616	0.9202	0.9484
Body CT	35.5274	0.9493	0.9588
US	33.9335	0.8034	0.8931
MRI	39.4061	0.9480	0.9662

CT, *computed tomography;* MRI, *magnetic resonance imaging;* NC, *normalized correlation;* PSNR, *peak signal-to-noise ratio;* SSIM, *structural similarity index;* US, *ultrasound.*

Table 3 Obtained NC values and SSIM values of proposed scheme against watermarking attacks.

Watermarking attacks	Brain CT		Body CT		US		MRI	
	NC	SSIM	NC	SSIM	NC	SSIM	NC	SSIM
Blurring	0.5825	0.6876	0.6592	0.7358	0.5584	0.6760	0.5214	0.6463
JPEG ($Q=25$)	0.8563	0.8627	0.9005	0.9105	0.8801	0.9161	0.8360	0.8730
JPEG ($Q=40$)	0.8551	0.8775	0.9127	0.9260	0.9061	0.9365	0.8463	0.8959
Sharpening	0.9399	0.9590	0.9624	0.9656	0.9449	0.9657	0.9415	0.9622
Salt and pepper noise (0.01)	0.8451	0.8872	0.8638	0.9018	0.8561	0.9407	0.8319	0.8899
Gaussian noise (0.01)	0.6317	0.7415	0.6423	0.7577	0.6905	0.7898	0.6504	0.7533
Rotation (20 degrees)	0.6119	0.7041	0.6582	0.7335	0.5897	0.6908	0.5728	0.6763
Rotation (10 degrees)	0.6003	0.7007	0.6651	0.7377	0.5790	0.6801	0.5471	0.6630
Cropping (10%)	0.9427	0.9599	0.9684	0.9696	0.9590	0.9756	0.9537	0.9697
Cropping (13%)	0.9421	0.9592	0.9674	0.9688	0.9577	0.9747	0.9521	0.9686
Scaling (512–256–512)	0.8266	0.8806	0.8845	0.9120	0.8704	0.9179	0.8629	0.9089
Intensity adjustment	0.9387	0.9570	0.9565	0.9598	0.9424	0.9589	0.9387	0.9626
Histogram equalization	0.8930	0.9235	0.9424	0.9508	0.9405	0.9626	0.8983	0.9334
Low-pass filter	0.9258	0.9482	0.9527	0.9603	0.9421	0.9661	0.9446	0.9649
Median filter	0.8698	0.9108	0.9105	0.9301	0.9077	0.9427	0.8551	0.9065

CT, *computed tomography;* MRI, *magnetic resonance imaging;* NC, *normalized correlation;* SSIM, *structural similarity index;* US, *ultrasound.*

5.2 Robustness test

The robustness of the proposed scheme is tested against standard watermarking attacks such as JPEG compression, the addition of noise, filtering, blurring, histogram equalization, and geometric attacks such as rotation and cropping. The robustness of the algorithm is measured using NC and SSIM, and if these values are near to 1 then this indicates that the robustness of the scheme is good and vice versa. The NC and SSIM values of the proposed scheme against watermarking attacks are summarized in Table 3. Fig. 8 shows the watermarked body CT image and extracted watermark image after different applications of watermarking attacks on the watermarked body CT image. Fig. 8 and Table 3 indicate that this scheme is less robust against rotation attack and blurring attack.

5.3 Performance comparison

The performance of the proposed scheme is evaluated by comparing it with existing similar watermarking schemes [21,39,40] in the literature. The NC values of the proposed scheme are compared to the GA-based medical watermarking scheme proposed by Fakhari et al. [21] and summarized in Table 4.

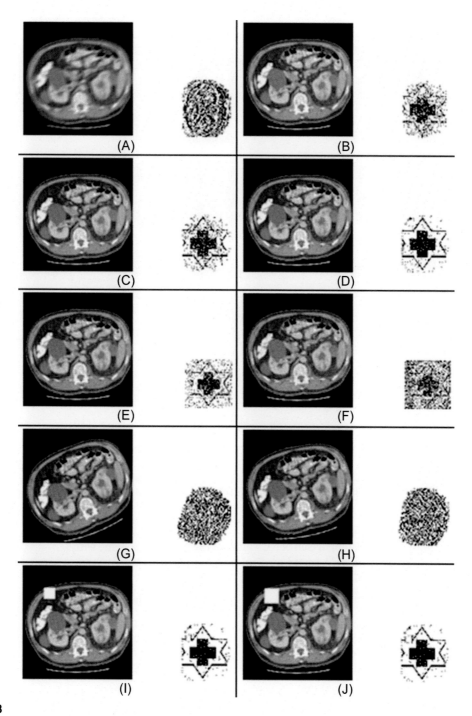

FIG. 8

Performance of proposed watermarking algorithm against watermarking attacks. (A) Blurring. (B) JPEG (Q=25). (C) JPEG (Q=40). (C) Gaussian noise. (D) Sharpening. (E) Salt and pepper noise (0.01). (F) Gaussian noise (0.01). (G) Rotation (20 degrees). (H) Rotation (10 degrees). (I) Cropping (10%). (J) Cropping (13%).

(Continued)

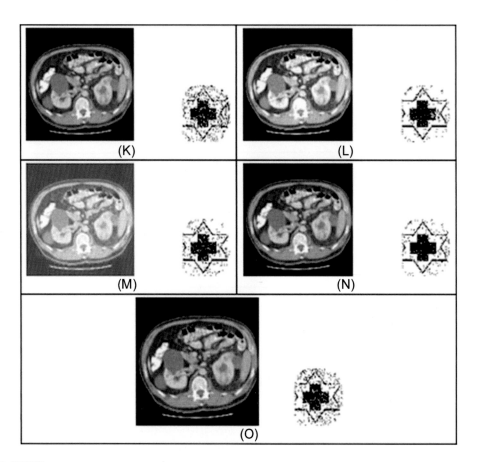

FIG. 8, CONT'D

(K) Scaling. (L) Intensity adjustment. (M) Histogram equalization. (N) Low-pass filter. (O) Median filter.

Table 4 Comparison of NC values of the proposed scheme with the existing GA-based medical image watermarking scheme [21].

Attacks	Fakhari scheme [21]	Proposed scheme
JPEG ($Q=40$)	0.9172	0.9127
Gaussian noise (0.01)	0.9181	0.6905
Rotation (10 degrees)	0.9162	0.6651
Cropping (10%)	**0.9195**	**0.9684**

GA, *genetic algorithm;* NC, *normalized correlation.*

Table 5 Comparison of normalized correlation values of the proposed scheme with the Thakkar scheme [39].

Attacks	Thakkar et al. [39]		Proposed	
	Cameraman	Lena	Cameraman	Lena
Rotation (20 degrees)	0.148	0.108	**0.5376**	**0.4979**
Rotation (10 degrees)	0.174	–	**0.5129**	**0.5063**
Cropping (10%)	0.1774	–	**0.8910**	**0.9079**
Cropping (13%)	0.177	0.107	**0.8886**	**0.9073**
Intensity adjustment	0.881	0.838	**0.8862**	**0.9067**

Table 6 Comparison of normalized correlation values of the proposed scheme with the Tao scheme [40].

Attacks	Tao et al. [40]	Proposed
	Lena	Lena
Rotation (10 degrees)	0.7554	0.5063
Scaling	**0.8127**	**0.8170**
Cropping (10%)	0.8029	0.9079
JPEG ($Q=40$)	0.9524	0.8098
Salt and pepper noise (0.01)	0.8916	0.7887
Low-pass filter (3×3)	**0.7849**	**0.9001**

Table 7 Features comparison of the proposed scheme with existing schemes [20,39,40].

Features	Fakhari scheme [21]	Tao scheme [40]	Thakkar scheme [39]	Proposed scheme
Nature of algorithm	Blind	Blind	Blind	Blind
Size of cover image	512×512	256×256	512×512	512×512
Size of watermark	10 bits	32×32	64×64	64×64
Used optimization	Genetic algorithm	Hybrid particle swarm optimization	Particle swarm optimization	Genetic algorithm
Used transform	Block DWT	Block SVD	Block DWT	Block DCT+SVD
PSNR range	50–51 dB	Not reported	10–37 dB	33–39 dB

DCT, *discrete cosine transform;* DWT, *discrete wavelet transform;* PSNR, *peak signal-to-noise ratio;* SVD, *singular value decomposition.*

The comparison in Table 4 shows that the robustness of the proposed scheme is better than the Fakhari scheme [21] for cropping attack.

The performance of the proposed scheme is compared to two intelligent image watermarking schemes [39,40] and summarized in Tables 5 and 6, respectively. In this scheme, an optimized scaling factor is generated using PSO. The comparison in Tables 5 and 6 shows that the proposed scheme provides better robustness than these two schemes against attacks such as rotation, cropping, scaling, and low-pass filter. The various features of existing intelligent watermarking schemes are also compared with the proposed scheme and summarized in Table 7. This comparison shows how the proposed scheme differs compared to existing schemes.

6 Conclusions

This chapter presented a blind and intelligent medical image watermarking algorithm based on hybridization of DCT+SVD and a GA. In this algorithm, the values of the U matrix of the DCT frequency coefficients of the medical image were modified by an optimized scaling factor according to the watermark bits. The optimized scaling factor was generated with the help of the GA. The experimental results showed that the proposed scheme fulfilled all the requirements of medical image watermarking. Comparative analysis also showed that the performance of the proposed scheme was better than (in term of robustness) many existing schemes in the literature. In the future, other optimization algorithms such as simulated annealing and PSO can be used with the scheme to compare the performance of this approach, which may improve the usefulness of the scheme in telemedicine applications.

References

[1] S. Borra, H.R. Lakshmi, Visual cryptography based lossless watermarking for sensitive images, in: International Conference on Swarm, Evolutionary, and Memetic Computing, December, Springer, Cham, 2015, pp. 29–39.

[2] R.M. Thanki, A.M. Kothari, Digital watermarking: technical art of hiding a message, in: Intelligent Analysis of Multimedia Information, IGI Global, 2017, pp. 431–466.

[3] S. Banerjee, S. Chakraborty, N. Dey, A.K. Pal, R. Ray, High payload watermarking using residue number system, Int. J. Image Graph. Signal Process. 3 (2015) 1–8.

[4] B. Surekha, G.N. Swamy, A spatial domain public image watermarking, Int. J. Secur. Appl. 5 (1) (2011) 1–12.

[5] A.S. Ashour, N. Dey, Security of multimedia contents: a brief, in: Intelligent Techniques in Signal Processing for Multimedia Security, Springer, Cham, 2017, pp. 3–14.

[6] A.K. Singh, B. Kumar, G. Singh, Mohan, A. (Eds.)., Medical Image Watermarking: Techniques and Applications, Springer, 2017.

[7] R. Thanki, S. Borra, V. Dwivedi, K. Borisagar, An efficient medical image watermarking scheme based on FDCuT–DCT, Eng. Sci. Technol. 20 (4) (2017) 1366–1379.

[8] S. Singh, R. Singh, A.K. Singh, T.J. Siddiqui, SVD-DCT based medical image watermarking in NSCT domain, in: Quantum Computing: An Environment for Intelligent Large-Scale Real Application, Springer, Cham, 2018, pp. 467–488.

[9] R. Thanki, S. Borra, A color image steganography in hybrid FRT–DWT domain, J. Inf. Secur. Appl. 40 (2018) 92–102.

[10] S. Borra, R. Thanki, N. Dey, Digital Image Watermarking: Theoretical and Computational Advances, CRC Press, 2018.

[11] H.C. Huang, F.C. Chang, Y.H. Chen, S.C. Chu, Survey of bio-inspired computing for information hiding, J. Inf. Hiding Multimedia Signal Process. 6 (3) (2015) 430–443.

[12] C.S. Shieh, H.C. Huang, F.H. Wang, J.S. Pan, Genetic watermarking based on transform-domain techniques, Pattern Recogn. 37 (3) (2004) 555–565.

[13] P. Kumsawat, K. Attakitmongcol, A. Srikaew, A new approach for optimization in image watermarking by using genetic algorithms, IEEE Trans. Signal Process. 53 (12) (2005) 4707–4719.

[14] F.Y. Shih, Y.T. Wu, Enhancement of image watermark retrieval based on genetic algorithms, J. Vis. Commun. Image Represent. 16 (2) (2005) 115–133.

[15] H.C. Huang, J.S. Pan, Y.H. Huang, F.H. Wang, K.C. Huang, Progressive watermarking techniques using genetic algorithms, Circuits Syst. Signal Process. 26 (5) (2007) 671–687.

[16] S.C. Chu, H.C. Huang, Y. Shi, S.Y. Wu, C.S. Shieh, Genetic watermarking for zerotree-based applications, Circuits Syst. Signal Process. 27 (2) (2008) 171–182.

[17] C.C. Lai, H.C. Huang, C.C. Tsai, Image watermarking scheme using singular value decomposition and micro-genetic algorithm, in: 2008 International Conference on Intelligent Information Hiding and Multimedia Signal Processing, August, IEEE, 2008, pp. 469–472.

[18] V. Aslantas, A singular-value decomposition-based image watermarking using genetic algorithm, AEU Int. J. Electron. Commun. 62 (5) (2008) 386–394.

[19] S.P. Maity, M.K. Kundu, Genetic algorithms for optimality of data hiding in digital images, Soft. Comput. 13 (4) (2009) 361–373.

[20] G. Boato, V. Conotter, F.G. De Natale, C. Fontanari, Watermarking robustness evaluation based on perceptual quality via genetic algorithms, IEEE Trans. Inf. Forensics Secur. 4 (2) (2009) 207–216.

[21] P. Fakhari, E. Vahedi, C. Lucas, Protecting patient privacy from unauthorized release of medical images using a bio-inspired wavelet-based watermarking approach, Digital Signal Process. 21 (3) (2011) 433–446.

[22] K. Loukhaoukha, On the security of digital watermarking scheme based on SVD and tiny-GA, J. Inf. Hiding Multimedia Signal Process. 3 (2) (2012) 135–141.

[23] E. Vahedi, R.A. Zoroofi, M. Shiva, Toward a new wavelet-based watermarking approach for color images using bio-inspired optimization principles, Digital Signal Process. 22 (1) (2012) 153–162.

[24] C. Agarwal, A. Mishra, A. Sharma, Gray-scale image watermarking using GA-BPN hybrid network, J. Vis. Commun. Image Represent. 24 (7) (2013) 1135–1146.

[25] S.P. Maity, S. Maity, J. Sil, C. Delpha, Collusion resilient spread spectrum watermarking in M-band wavelets using GA-fuzzy hybridization, J. Syst. Softw. 86 (1) (2013) 47–59.

[26] T. Naheed, I. Usman, T.M. Khan, A.H. Dar, M.F. Shafique, Intelligent reversible watermarking technique in medical images using GA and PSO, Optik 125 (11) (2014) 2515–2525.

[27] A. Bahrushin, G. Bahrushina, R. Bazhenov, K. Kim, R. Tsoy, Robust image watermarking technique based on genetic algorithm optimization and even odd modulation, in: DOOR (Supplement), 2016, pp. 415–427.

[28] N. Hardisal, M. Zarlis, E. Nababan, Adaptive watermarking technique using micro genetic algorithm, J. Inotera 1 (1) (2017) 64–70.

[29] F.Y. Shih, Digital Watermarking and Steganography: Fundamentals and Techniques, CRC Press, Boca Raton, FL, 2017.

[30] R.M. Thanki, V.J. Dwivedi, K.R. Borisagar, Multibiometric Watermarking with Compressive Sensing Theory: Techniques and Applications, Springer, Germany, 2018.

[31] D. Whitley, A genetic algorithm tutorial, Stat. Comput. 4 (2) (1994) 65–85.

[32] M.D. Vose, The Simple genetic Algorithm: Foundations and Theory, Vol. 12, MIT Press, 1999.

[33] Working of Genetic Algorithms, https://www.geeksforgeeks.org/genetic-algorithms/. (Accessed June 2019).

[34] S. Borra, R. Thanki, A FRT-SVD based blind medical watermarking technique for telemedicine applications, Int. J. Digital Crime Forensics 11 (2) (2019) 13–33.

[35] R. Thanki, S. Borra, V. Dwivedi, K. Borisagar, An efficient medical image watermarking scheme based on FDCuT–DCT, Eng. Sci. Technol. 20 (4) (2017) 1366–1379.

[36] MedPix™, Medical Image Database, Available at:http://rad.usuhs.mil/medpix/medpix.html, 2019. https://medpix.nlm.nih.gov/home. (Accessed June 2019).

[37] M. Kutter, F.A. Petitcolas, Fair benchmark for image watermarking systems, in: Security and Watermarking of Multimedia Contents, Vol. 3657, International Society for Optics and Photonics, 1999, April. pp. 226–240.

[38] Z. Wang, A.C. Bovik, H.R. Sheikh, Structural similarity based image quality assessment, in: Digital Video Image Quality and Perceptual Coding, 2005, pp. 225–241.

[39] F. Thakkar, V.K. Srivastava, A particle swarm optimization and block-SVD-based watermarking for digital images, Turk. J. Electr. Eng. Comput. Sci. 25 (4) (2017) 3273–3288.

[40] H. Tao, J.M. Zain, A.N. Abdalla, M.M. Ahmed, Hybrid particle swarm optimization for robust digital image watermarking, Int. J. Phys. Sci. 6 (31) (2011) 7222–7232.

Data security for WBAN in e-health IoT applications

K.V. Arya[a] and Rajasi Gore[b]

Information and Communication Technology, ABV-Indian Institute of Information Technology and Management Gwalior, Gwalior, India[a] Computer Science and Engineering Department, Motilal Nehru National Institute of Technology Allahabad, Prayagraj, India[b]

1 Introduction

The Internet of Things (IoT) is an emerging technology consisting of interconnected objects for ubiquitous service. IoT has the potential to enhance business opportunities as each device and object serves information that has huge benefits to various domains. Domains include agriculture, healthcare, waste management, traffic management, electricity management, pollution management, and many more [1]. These objects communicate with each other and produce suitable solutions for high-scale applications. Medicine and healthcare have been two of the most promising business applications in the field of IoT. IoT has enhanced healthcare applications and produced e-health applications such as individual fitness, care of the elderly, remote monitoring of patient's health and detection and handling of chronic diseases. Home treatments, automatic ambulance booking, and online medical facilities are other achievements in the healthcare domain that have been helped with IoT. All these facilities are nowadays available due to a varied range of medical and diagnostic sensors that collect data from patients' bodies and the environment [2]. The data collected are termed IoT data, which are passed on to the IoT framework for healthcare. The data are then analyzed by domain experts and medical assistance is provided to the patient in real time. IoT has enhanced user understanding and quality of human life for e-health applications at minimum cost.

According to health assistance providers, e-health applications can save diagnosis time and free up hospital space. The last decade has seen IoT solving real-world problems in the healthcare domain. The IoT framework used for e-health application is the IoT network for healthcare (IoThNet) [3]. It provides communication of health information support for real-time decision making and allows personalized communication between system and patients. In IoThNet, wearable sensors use 6LoWPAN as a communication protocol and Internet Protocol version 6 addressing as a network layer to be able to connect to the Internet. User datagram protocol is used as a transport layer to transfer data to the end application of IoThNet. A huge amount of sensor data are collected by the framework. Sensors for body temperature, respiration rate, and blood pressure form a wireless body area network (WBAN). The IoThNet framework then shares the data from these heterogeneous devices over a grid of mobile and static electronic devices having good storage capacity, such as smartphones, laptops, and nearby hospital systems.

Intelligent Data Security Solutions for e-Health Applications. https://doi.org/10.1016/B978-0-12-819511-6.00011-X

In addition to IoT services, IoT healthcare applications require experts' attention [4]. The services provided by e-health applications are supervised by doctors and are user centric. Decisions made by the domain experts and doctors are totally based on users' data. Hence, data security is vital in the healthcare domain as it carries useful information from patient to application and back to patient with suggestions for remedial action. Furthermore, the sensors and devices are connected to the Internet, which is globally accessible by anyone at any time and from anywhere. This makes e-health application an easy target for hackers. Security of WBAN data is important as decisions are totally based entirely on the body data of the patient. If there is any change in the value, it can have a huge impact on diagnosis, and a disease will be falsely predicted. This chapter covers e-health applications and use of WBAN technology, security challenges in WBAN, and currently proposed solutions to safeguard patients' information. Providing security to WBANs is an essential aspect for any application as it gives the user correct information according to the user's correct details.

Later sections deal with IoT healthcare applications, WBAN, and its data security. Section 2 will provide existing IoT applications in healthcare. Section 3 will discuss WBAN technologies being used in these applications to gather data. In Section 4, we will discuss the need for data security in WBANs. Section 5 describes various attacks on WBANs in detail. Section 6 discusses current security solutions proposed to secure WBAN data.

2 E-health applications

Various solutions based on IoT have been proposed for tackling real-world problems in the healthcare domain. These real-world problems are mainly confined to inaccessible hospitals, doctors, and medical support at critical times. IoT monitors noncritical patients remotely and also provides assistance in real time. Patients are not required to make appointments on a daily basis. As shown in Fig. 1, the data are collected via the WBAN and other medical technologies and are sent to nearby hospitals and specific doctors for remote diagnosis. E-health applications save bed space and doctors' time for critical patients at hospitals. It is important to know that IoT is not replacing hospitals. It is just providing support and is an aid that can handle more patients via sensors and the Internet. It is mainly used to provide medical assistance to people living in rural areas or people who are diagnosed with long-term illnesses and the elderly. These applications can provide people with the necessary help without going to hospital. Due to the huge benefits of remote health monitoring, many researchers have used IoT as a solution for healthcare. IoT e-health applications have been developed for specific purposes such as rehabilitation, diabetes management, assisted ambient living for elderly persons, and many more. All these applications have different aims but use similar technology for serving users. Rehabilitation after physical injury has been a popular area for several researchers.

In [5], an expert system has been developed that provides habitation plans based on individuals' symptoms. The system learns from previous patient records stored in the database and provides corresponding solutions. A patient's condition is matched with old records of symptoms and treatment. A doctor manually checks system response and then the system provides an approved solution to the patient. In 87.9% of cases, a plan proposed by the system completely matched the doctor's plan and no modifications were made. In [6], the authors proposed mathematical models for the measurement of joint angles in physical hydrotherapy systems. It provided better accuracy in tracking improved joint movement through therapy.

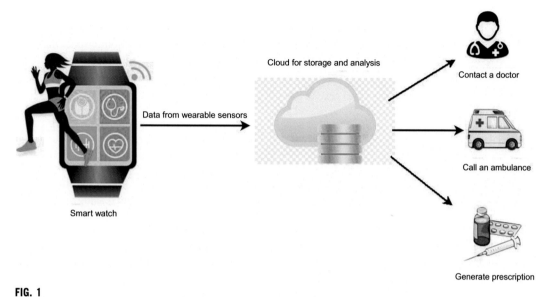

Data from wearable sensors

Smart watch

Cloud for storage and analysis

Contact a doctor

Call an ambulance

Generate prescription

FIG. 1

E-health application model.

The authors in [7] proposed an e-health application that remotely monitored patients suffering from Parkinson's disease with the help of IoT. Data were collected from wearable sensors that observed gait patterns, tremors, and general activity levels. These data combined with vision-based technologies such as a camera inside the home provided efficient monitoring. Furthermore, the authors suggested the application can provide treatment plans to patients remotely with the help of machine learning in the future.

In [8], a system was proposed that monitored blood-glucose levels in diabetic patients. Patients were required to take blood-glucose readings manually at set time periods. The data were passed on to the system where it dealt with two kinds of data abnormalities. The first was misreading of blood-glucose levels and the second was misreading of the data. The system removed the abnormalities and analyzed the data. According to the severity of the patient's condition, it decided whom to notify. If the condition was not critical, the patient was informed directly. If the patient was critical and needed assistance, family members and a doctor were notified. This system has been completely realized and is further improved through automated blood-glucose level readings captured by smart watches.

The authors in [9] proposed a system that detected an upcoming heart attack by tracking patients' heart rate in real time. An electrocardiogram (ECG) sensor was used to collect heart rate data and was forwarded via Bluetooth to the user's smartphone. ECG data were analyzed and a decision was provided to the user application. During the last decade, the number of people dying from heart attacks at early age has increased. That is why such a system that predicts heart attacks is much needed. Furthermore, system prediction can be improved by taking respiratory rate data into account with heart rate [10].

SPHERE [11] is an activity and health monitoring system that takes data from WBANs, camera, and the environment. This system is proposed for people with chronic illnesses who can be remotely monitored by doctors without the need to leave home for a check-up. Machine learning can be beneficial to make SPHERE an expert system that can monitor health in real time without the need of doctors. The learning algorithm is designed according to domain experts to provide accurate medical assistance. All these applications use data from WBAN technology to remotely monitor patients with different health issues. We will discuss various sensors that constitute WBANs and their usage in the next section.

3 WBAN technology

WBAN is a known network of sensors implanted over the body for monitoring patients' health. These sensors are in physical contact with and measure movements inside the body [12]. Different sensors have been developed in recent years targeting different areas of the body and are increasing as the technology advances in the medical field. These sensors generate accurate data and collectively form a body area network (BAN). This network is capable of forwarding the data to remote locations for processing. Thus monitoring of patients' health via e-health applications has been possible only because of WBAN technology. There are many existing sensors in WBANs. These sensors are classified in two types based on their operations. The two types are shown in Fig. 2.

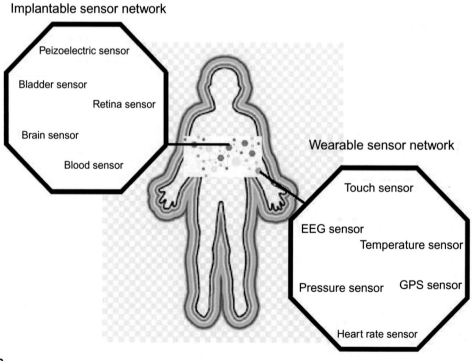

FIG. 2

WBAN technology.

- Wearable sensors: These sensors are worn outside the patient's body. They collect data through physical contact. They are easily adjustable, removable, and controlled. These sensors need no medical assistance during usage. For example, ECG, electroencephalogram, blood pressure sensor, and pulse rate sensor are used to monitor a critical patient. A global positioning system sensor is used to gather the locations of mobile patients. Motion sensor, temperature sensor, and many other sensors are used to monitor the activity of patients.
- Implantable sensors: These sensors are used in critical patients and are under continuous observation by doctors. These are attached to the skin or inside the body. Their working is not observable by the patient and the data are directly sent to hospitals for analysis. These sensors are specific types of biosensors for specific purposes. They have the ability to continuously measure metabolism rates without the need for personal intervention regardless of the person's physiological state. The implantable biosensors have great impact on diabetes and trauma care patients, as well as soldiers in action. They provide more detailed human health information and their data are critical. The data from these sensors have to be secured, because the patient is unaware of its presence and working.

4 WBAN architecture

The sensors used in WBANs are low powered. They cannot directly communicate their data to remote locations. Thus they form a network within themselves to work as one unit [13]. The body cannot have a wired network of sensors as it can hamper the daily routine of the patient. Thus the sensors used in WBANs are embedded devices having sensing as well as communication capabilities. Data from these sensors are collectively sent to a base station. The base station is the one that serves as a gateway, between the BAN and the Internet, for accessing healthcare services. The WBAN has a specific architecture as shown in Fig. 3. There are BAN nodes and a BAN network coordinator. These BAN nodes are located at different places of the body, and communicate their data to a network coordinator.

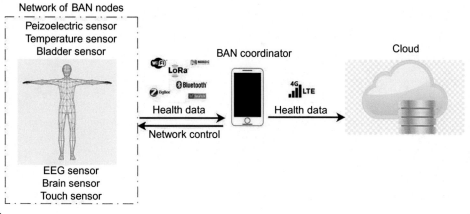

FIG. 3

WBAN architecture.

Low-range communication protocols such as Bluetooth and ZigBEE are used to communicate data to the BAN network coordinator. The network coordinator manages the network by checking whether all BAN nodes are active and working properly. After receiving the data from each node, the network coordinator uses high-range communication protocols such as WiFi and General Packet Radio Service to communicate with the base station. Other sensors that gather data about environmental conditions around the patient send their data directly to the base station. Data from the body as well as the environment are used in e-health applications to perform better remote monitoring of patients' health. Since all the communication is wireless, data are prone to attack. Hence, WBAN architecture should provide security for possible attacks that can happen during data collection and communication to e-health applications. The traditional security solutions cannot be used in the case of WBANs for various reasons, which are discussed in the next sections.

5 Security challenge in WBAN

As shown in Fig. 4, data from WBANs are collected and transmitted via a wireless medium. These health data collected from various WBAN sensors need to reach the cloud of the e-health application safely. Thus security should be provided for WBAN health data during data collection and transmission. Major security requirements in standard communication environments are similar to e-health applications' security requirements. The proposed application to be secured should satisfy the following conditions:

- Confidentiality: Medical data should be safe and inaccessible by malicious users and attackers.
- Integrity: Transferred medical data are not tampered with by attackers and are the same at both ends of the transmission.
- Authentication: Data being transferred should belong to the same person as the data that have been recorded.

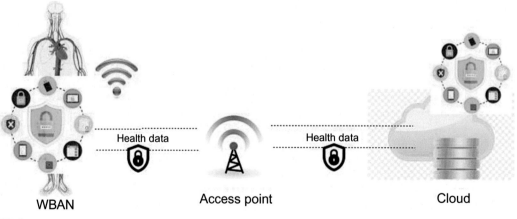

FIG. 4

Secure WBAN data transmission.

- Availability: Service to the user will be guaranteed irrespective of attacks.
- Fault tolerance: Service to the user is provided in the presence of system failures.

These five points are fundamental security requirements to make any application 100% secure. In the case of WBAN, these will not guarantee complete security [14]. Other challenges that are specific to WBAN are as follows:

- Computational limitations: WBAN devices have very low computation power and cannot analyze data at they are collected. The data have to be sent to a nearby device having good processing power to compute the data. Thus data need to be forwarded via a channel that makes them in vulnerable to attack during transmission.
- Memory limitations: WBAN devices have less storage power and their data need to be stored on nearby devices such as smartphones or laptops. Thus data have to be transmitted. Data are vulnerable to attack.
- Mobility limitations: WBAN devices have to work well in case of mobile activity by patient such as outdoor exercise. These devices need to switch networks to send the collected data. Thus data are insecure and vulnerable to attack when they pass through different networks.

The security of WBAN data from attacks is a prominent and required challenge to be solved by e-health applications. The data if stolen or modified can lead to false service to patients, which can trigger risks to health. Various attacks [15] that are possible on WBANs are discussed in the next section.

6 Security attacks in WBAN

An e-health application is supposed to have comprehensive perception, reliable transmission, and intelligent processing. WBAN sensors are prone to attacks during perception and transmission of data through a wireless medium. Possible attacks should be kept in mind while designing a secure application.

6.1 Attacks at the data collection level

1. Jamming attack: The radio frequency channel used by WBANs to communicate is used by intruders who start sensing packets through this wireless channel by blocking other communications. Jamming signals are returned to the sender when their packets collide with the packets from the intruders. No data communication happens as the channel is fully occupied by intruders from both ends.
2. Data collision attack: When collision occurs in a network, the packet is lost. Packets are retransmitted when a negative acknowledgment arrives. The attacker deliberately sends packets that collide with data packets, and packets are continuously retransmitted. The data packets never reach their destination. If a data packet does reach its destination, then erroneous activity must be suspected.
3. Data flooding attack: The intruder sends a high number of connection requests to the target node until resources of the target node are completely wasted. The target node denies service after a period of time and wastes its time serving connection requests only.

4. Desynchronization attack: The intruder intercepts the information between sensor nodes and duplicates it a number of times using a forged sequence number to multiple receivers of an active connection. This would end in an infinite cycle in a WBAN, which will make the sensor nodes transmit the information again and thus waste their energy.
5. Spoofing attack: In this attack, an intruder falsifies its identity and replays or modifies the message. The intruder is in the network without other network nodes, and it attacks the information.
6. Selective forwarding attack: In this attack, the nodes are attacked such that they forward only selected packets and the rest are dropped. If any base station is attacked, the number of packet drops will be increased, harming a huge amount of critical source data.
7. Sybil attack: In this attack, a malicious node has multiple identities and changes routing information from target identity to its address. The data destined to different entities are collected by a single malicious node behaving as a different entity. This attack generally happens in peer-to-peer networks.

6.2 Attacks at transmission level

At transmission level, there is a high risk of attack. Attacks generally include modifying data, spying on data, changing network topology, tampering with data, and producing false network traffic to keep the network busy and unavailable for service [16]:

1. Eavesdropping: This is the most common type of attack where an attacker listens to all the communications happening over the wireless channel.
2. Man-in-the-middle attack: Attackers create their own access point and request that patient data are routed to them. All the traffic can be manipulated via an access point.
3. Data tampering attack: In this attack, an attacker is aware of the encryption/decryption key and tampers with patients' data during communication by authorizing nodes in the network.
4. Scrambling attack: In this attack, the radio frequency channel for wireless transmission is kept busy for a short period of time. This affects normal operation of data transmission and causes an availability issue in the network whereby patients' data are unable to be transferred at the required time. The attacker prevents data from reaching the base station by attacking the wireless channel.
5. Signaling attack: Initially, when the WBAN begins data transmission, a synchronization operation takes place though signaling. The sender and receiver need to signal each other using the public/private key, authenticate with each other, establish a secure connection, and then register before actual data transmission. The intruder attacks the base station by signaling with false packets. Thus the base station is made to handle only incoming signaling processes. After some time, the station becomes unavailable for patients' data due to heavy loads.
6. Denial of service attack: The attacker receives an IP address and port of destination processing node. The node is bombarded with false packets from different locations. Due to this attack, the node is busy capturing false packets and becomes unavailable to WBAN data. Finally, the WBAN is not able to forward patient data due to node unavailability.
7. Unfair allocation: An attacker distributes a medium access control channel for wireless communication that has low bandwidth and high noise. Due to this, incoming patient's data packets are either lost or contain a lot of errors when they reach the processing unit of the application.

8. Message modification attack: In this attack, the patient's data are intercepted via a wireless channel by a third party. Data are modified with false details and replayed to the destination.
9. Hello flood attack: An intruder adds a malicious node to the network. This node requests the routing path of every data-sending node. Once this node is connected with every other node on the network, it floods a hello message continuously. The buffers are occupied through hello messages making the network drop patients' critical data.
10. Data interception attack: An attacker captures the data from wireless traffic coming from the WBAN. This happens when a deployed wireless access point has no encryptions. The data are open and easy to capture by attackers through the wireless channel.
11. Wormhole attack: In this attack, patient data from a particular location are collected at another location that is not an application-specific target location. Many nodes are deployed in the network for the attack. The intruder changes the network route for the packets by creating paths to these malicious nodes that are shorter than the original packet routing path. This path is known as a wormhole tunnel, which leads to another location. Due to the change in network topology, the routing decision is changed and packets are forwarded to another location via the tunnel.

7 Data security advancements

Data are captured by the WBAN and transmitted via wireless channels. Three points need attention for a secure transmission. First, the data should reach only the intended receiver. Second, the data should be the same at both ends. Third, the data being transmitted have not been read or copied by an unintended party. These three cases are the security challenges corresponding to authentication, integrity, and confidentiality, respectively. For the first case, both ends need to authenticate their identity. For the second and third case, the authenticated data should be sent in encrypted form and decrypted at the intended receiver's end.

- Authentication: This is a process of verifying or proving that something is true and genuine. Authentication is of two types. First is user authentication for using the services of the application. This provides proof of identity of data sources so that no other user can access the services. The other type is message authentication. There is a message authentication code with a message to authenticate that the message is the same as sent by the sender. User authentication is either password based or biometrics based. The problem in password-based authentication is that the password can be duplicated and anybody can access the application. Biometrics-based authentication, on the other hand, is unique for every user. It is based on distinct biological features of the user such as a signature, figure print, voice modulation, etc.
- Encryption: This is an algorithm designed to hide the data by converting them into cipher text. Cipher text can only be read by the intended recipient. The conversion can be performed either by hashing or using keys or both. Two schemes are required for this conversion to happen, symmetric and asymmetric, as shown in Fig. 5. The first scheme is symmetric key encryption. In this encryption, the algorithm uses the same key at both sender and receiver ends. The sender encrypts the data into cipher data using a key and the receiver decrypts the cipher data using the same key. The key is shared before communication happens. The most used algorithms

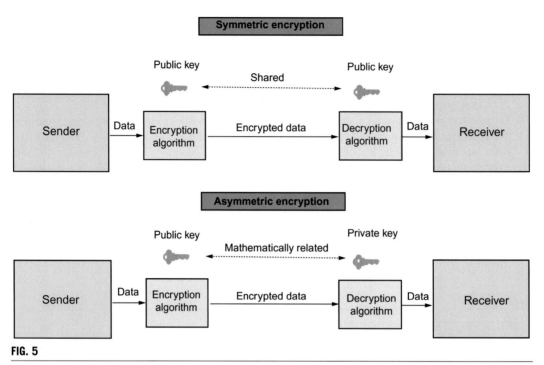

FIG. 5

Types of encryption.

of the first scheme are Data Encryption Standard and Advance Encryption Standard. This scheme is less secure as key can be intercepted by attackers during its transmission. The second scheme is public key encryption. The sender and receiver use a pair of keys, private and public, to encrypt and decrypt the data at both ends of communication. Both the keys are mathematically related to each other. This is more secure than the first scheme because attackers cannot decrypt with a single key only. The most used algorithms of the second scheme are Digital Signature Algorithm and Rivest Shamir Adleman. Security of public keys has been implemented using the public key infrastructure technique. For prevention purposes, the key length is very large making it impossible for the attacker to guess. The keys are changed frequently so that all the transmitted data cannot be attacked.

These algorithms are combined to make authenticated encryption algorithms provide complete security. But the existing authentication and encryption algorithms are designed for traditional systems and are not suitable for resource-constrained devices. To make a WBAN-based e-health application secure, the encryption and authentication procedures should be designed based on computational and storage limitations of the devices. Algorithms having less time and space complexity are more efficient in the case of IoT applications. The algorithm should not compromise security at any cost with its decrease in complexity. The next section will surveys recent works in the authentication and encryption of data in WBANs for e-health applications.

8 Survey on encryption algorithms

An encryption algorithm provides increased security when keys are randomly generated and have a large bit size that cannot be easily decoded by an attacker. But transmitting such a huge key size will consume device energy and network bandwidth. A huge number of body sensors collectively sending such large sequences of keys before real communication is very demanding on WBANs. Thus key management algorithms have been created to decrease the key size and still make the encryption algorithm highly secure [17]. The first lightweight encryption algorithm on generating a random key for resource-constrained devices was developed by authors in [18]. The author in [19] developed a key generation scheme using a fuzzy vault scheme. The vital values coming from the data sensors were used as a key for communication. In [20, 21], the authors developed a secure key generation technique for ECG systems. The key is generated during the RR interval. The RR interval is the time between the calculation of two heartbeats. The authors have assumed continuous sensing of ECG sensors in the RR interval. They have not considered the possibility of no ECG data in the RR interval. The other challenge in this work is that the RR interval is not fixed in real-time applications.

The author in [22] used frequency domain analysis of a photoplethysmogram (PPG) signal for generating a random key. They used a fuzzy vault scheme [23] for transmitting the data. A combined form of chaff point and fifth-order polynomial increased the security of the system. The drawback of this work is chaff point generation. In [24], the authors proposed a secret key agreement based on physiological values from ECG and PPG signals. The authors in [25] proposed an improved fuzzy vault method for key generation. They eliminated the issue of chaff point generation in ECG signals. However, a working model was not provided to justify its improvement. Finally, the authors in [26] proposed an algorithm known as the one time padding (OTP) algorithm. The algorithm generated a key to encrypt a secret key for implantable devices. Implantable devices once inside the body cannot be controlled from outside. Thus the random key generation process is removed to save energy and increase longevity. The results proved that it is safe from brute force attack. The only drawback is the memory issue of OTP generation on WBANs.

Researchers are still developing new algorithms for efficient random key generation for resource-constrained devices used in WBANs.

9 Survey on authentication algorithms

Lightweight authentication algorithms have been proposed in the area of e-health applications for WBAN technology. In recent decades, many studies have focused on methods for improving the ecurity performance of authentication schemes with fewer problems. The author in [27] proposed a requirement for three-factor authentication schemes for WBANs. The first factor is a password, pin, and secret key. The second factor is a device supporting the first factor such as smart cards and smartphones. The third factor is a biometric such as a thumbprint, iris recognition, user's voice, etc.

The authors in [28] proposed an authentication scheme having a static password, a smart card, and a biometric. A combination of these increased security compared to systems using only one of these factors. They used a one-way hash function for authentication. The system using this authentication scheme was vulnerable to insider and man-in-the-middle attacks. To safeguard, the proposed three-factor authentication scheme from attacks, the authors in [29] proposed an efficient uniqueness-and-anonymity-preserving user authentication scheme. Their proposed scheme could safeguard the system from insider and man-in-the-middle attacks but caused vulnerability to disclosure and tracing attacks. The author in [30] proposed an anonymity-preserving authentication scheme for mobile devices with fewer problems. This scheme was vulnerable to disclosure attack and had no three-factor authentication. In [31], the authors proposed a smartcard-based authentication scheme for WBANs. It used a symmetric encryption algorithm and thus was vulnerable to attack. This proves that authentication alone cannot safeguard the system. A good encryption algorithm is also needed.

The authors in [32] proposed a solution using a low-entropy password in an anonymous authentication scheme. They provided third-party authentication to the system. However, including a third party compromises the privacy of personal information. A third party cannot provide three-factor authentication, which makes the system vulnerable. The authors in [33] proposed a multilayer authentication scheme for one-to-many groups. It established a session key between personal data aggregator and body area sensor network using elliptic curve cryptography. The scheme was prone to privacy breech and tracing attack. They did not take into account the communication issue. The authors in [34] proposed a three-factor authentication scheme assisted by a trusted authority. The trust issue resolves the privacy breach attack but cannot guarantee 100% safety.

Most authentication schemes adopt a static password in their three factors. The authors in [35] stated that static passwords are chosen that are easy to remember. They are also easy to duplicate as passwords are generally created using user's personal information such as date of birth. The authors in [36, 37] claimed that static passwords are used in attacks like social engineering attacks, phishing attacks, and Trojan attacks. The authors started generating passwords that have a combination of special keys and numerics that provide stronger security compared to human-generated passwords [38, 39]. The authors in [40] showed that passwords stored on cloud or on any other third-party software are not at all safe and can be accessed by external sources with their permission. Thus the data need to be stored in encrypted form on cloud.

The authentication algorithms being developed do not guarantee prevention from all types of attack. If they can handle one attack, the system becomes vulnerable to other attacks. If the algorithm is less computational, it is using a third party to do the maximum of tasks. Third parties are vulnerable to attacks. Thus an approach is needed that does not use third parties, data are encrypted, and the sender is authenticated to use the system and send the data. All this will lead to a solution that may be safe from existing attacks.

10 Conclusion

The WBAN is the most used technology in e-health applications. The data from resource-constrained devices are collected and transmitted over wireless channels. Security of WBAN data is an ongoing challenge due to attacks during data collection as well as transmission. Traditional encryption and authentication schemes cannot be applied to WBANs. Solutions are proposed that can be implemented by WBAN sensors. These algorithms need to be more efficient compared to traditional algorithms in terms of time and space complexity. Since e-health applications are user centric, health data are critical. Any attack on the system may cause serious impacts on the analysis of the model and in turn on the user. Thus authentication and encryption are both necessary features to completely safeguard the applications. Many algorithms have been proposed but still there is a need for new and efficient algorithms that are 100% safe from any attacks. Hopefully in future, e-health applications will adopt these systems to counter new unforeseen attacks.

References

[1] M.T. Lazarescu, Design of a WSN platform for long-term environmental monitoring for IoT applications, IEEE J. Emerg. Sel. Top. Circuits Syst. 3 (1) (2013) 45–54.

[2] S. Sarkar, S. Misra, From micro to nano: the evolution of wireless sensor-based health care, IEEE Pulse 7 (1) (2016) 21–25.

[3] Z. Pang, Q. Chen, J. Tian, L. Zheng, E. Dubrova, Ecosystem analysis in the design of open platform-based in-home healthcare terminals towards the internet-of-things, in: 2013 15th International Conference on Advanced Communications Technology (ICACT), IEEE, 2013, pp. 529–534.

[4] S.T.U. Shah, H. Yar, I. Khan, M. Ikram, H. Khan, Internet of things-based healthcare: recent advances and challenges, Applications of Intelligent Technologies in Healthcare, Springer, 2019, pp. 153–162.

[5] Y.J. Fan, Y.H. Yin, L. Da Xu, Y. Zeng, F. Wu, IoT-based smart rehabilitation system, IEEE Trans. Ind. Inf. 10 (2) (2014) 1568–1577.

[6] R.C.A. Alves, L.B. Gabriel, B.T. de Oliveira, C.B. Margi, F.C.L. dos Santos, Assisting physical (hydro) therapy with wireless sensors networks, IEEE Internet Things J. 2 (2) (2015) 113–120.

[7] C.F. Pasluosta, H. Gassner, J. Winkler, J. Klucken, B.M. Eskofier, An emerging era in the management of Parkinson's disease: wearable technologies and the internet of things, IEEE J. Biomed. Health Inform. 19 (6) (2015) 1873–1881.

[8] S.-H. Chang, R.-D. Chiang, S.-J. Wu, W.-T. Chang, A context-aware, interactive M-health system for diabetics, IT Prof. 18 (3) (2016) 14–22.

[9] G. Wolgast, C. Ehrenborg, A. Israelsson, J. Helander, E. Johansson, H. Manefjord, Wireless body area network for heart attack detection [Education Corner], IEEE Antennas Propag. Mag. 58 (5) (2016) 84–92.

[10] M.A. Cretikos, R. Bellomo, K. Hillman, J. Chen, S. Finfer, A. Flabouris, Respiratory rate: the neglected vital sign, Med. J. Aust. 188 (11) (2008) 657–659.

[11] N. Zhu, T. Diethe, M. Camplani, L. Tao, A. Burrows, N. Twomey, D. Kaleshi, M. Mirmehdi, P. Flach, I. Craddock, Bridging e-health and the internet of things: the sphere project, IEEE Intell. Syst. 30 (4) (2015) 39–46.

[12] M.M. Dhanvijay, S.C. Patil, Internet of things: a survey of enabling technologies in healthcare and its applications, Comput. Netw. 153 (2019) 113–131.

[13] M.R. Yuce, Implementation of wireless body area networks for healthcare systems, Sens. Actuators A Phys. 162 (1) (2010) 116–129.

[14] A. Tewari, P. Verma, Security and privacy in E-healthcare monitoring with WBAN: a critical review, Int. J. Comput. Appl. 136 (11) (2016) 37–42.

[15] P. Niksaz, M. Branch, Wireless body area networks: attacks and countermeasures, Int. J. Sci. Eng. Res. 6 (19) (2015) 565–568.

[16] R. Nidhya, S. Karthik, Security and privacy issues in remote healthcare systems using wireless body area networks, Body Area Network Challenges and Solutions, Springer, 2019, pp. 37–53.

[17] S. Saleem, S. Ullah, K.S. Kwak, A study of IEEE 802.15. 4 security framework for wireless body area networks, Sensors 11 (2) (2011) 1383–1395.

[18] M. Ebrahim, C.W. Chong, Secure force: a low-complexity cryptographic algorithm for Wireless Sensor Network (WSN), in: 2013 IEEE International Conference on Control System, Computing and Engineering, IEEE, 2013, pp. 557–562.

[19] K.K. Venkatasubramanian, A. Banerjee, S.K.S. Gupta, EKG-based key agreement in body sensor networks, IEEE INFOCOM Workshops 2008, IEEE, 2008, pp. 1–6.

[20] C.C.Y. Poon, Y.-T. Zhang, S.-D. Bao, A novel biometrics method to secure wireless body area sensor networks for telemedicine and m-health, IEEE Commun. Mag. 44 (4) (2006) 73–81.

[21] S.-D. Bao, C.C.Y. Poon, Y.-T. Zhang, L.-F. Shen, Using the timing information of heartbeats as an entity identifier to secure body sensor network, IEEE Trans. Inf. Technol. Biomed. 12 (6) (2008) 772–779.

[22] K.K. Venkatasubramanian, A. Banerjee, S.K.S. Gupta, Plethysmogram-based secure inter-sensor communication in body area networks, Military Communications Conference, 2008, pp. 1–7.

[23] A. Juels, M. Sudan, A fuzzy vault scheme, Des. Codes Crypt. 38 (2) (2006) 237–257.

[24] K.K. Venkatasubramanian, A. Banerjee, S.K.S. Gupta, PSKA: usable and secure key agreement scheme for body area networks, IEEE Trans. Inf. Technol. Biomed. 14 (1) (2010) 60–68.

[25] Z. Zhang, H. Wang, A.V. Vasilakos, H. Fang, ECG-cryptography and authentication in body area networks, IEEE Trans. Inf. Technol. Biomed. 16 (6) (2012) 1070–1078.

[26] G. Zheng, G. Fang, R. Shankaran, M.A. Orgun, Encryption for implantable medical devices using modified one-time pads, IEEE Access 3 (2015) 825–836.

[27] M.U. Aslam, A. Derhab, K. Saleem, H. Abbas, M. Orgun, W. Iqbal, B. Aslam, A survey of authentication schemes in telecare medicine information systems, J. Med. Syst. 41 (1) (2017) 14.

[28] L. Xu, F. Wu, Cryptanalysis and improvement of a user authentication scheme preserving uniqueness and anonymity for connected health care, J. Med. Syst. 39 (2) (2015) 10.

[29] A.K. Das, A. Goswami, A secure and efficient uniqueness-and-anonymity-preserving remote user authentication scheme for connected health care, J. Med. Syst. 37 (3) (2013) 9948.

[30] R. Amin, S.K.H. Islam, G.P. Biswas, M.K. Khan, N. Kumar, A robust and anonymous patient monitoring system using wireless medical sensor networks, Futur. Gener. Comput. Syst. 80 (2018) 483–495.

[31] A.K. Das, A.K. Sutrala, V. Odelu, A. Goswami, A secure smartcard-based anonymous user authentication scheme for healthcare applications using wireless medical sensor networks, Wirel. Pers. Commun. 94 (3) (2017) 1899–1933.

[32] F. Wei, P. Vijayakumar, J. Shen, R. Zhang, L. Li, A provably secure password-based anonymous authentication scheme for wireless body area networks, Comput. Electr. Eng. 65 (2018) 322–331.

[33] J. Shen, S. Chang, J. Shen, Q. Liu, X. Sun, A lightweight multi-layer authentication protocol for wireless body area networks, Futur. Gener. Comput. Syst. 78 (2018) 956–963.

[34] D. Mao, L. Zhang, X. Li, D. Mu, Trusted authority assisted three-factor authentication and key agreement protocol for the implantable medical system, Wirel. Commun. Mob. Comput. 2018 (2018) 1–16.

[35] Y. Li, H. Wang, K. Sun, Personal information in passwords and its security implications, IEEE Trans. Inf. Forensics Secur. 12 (10) (2017) 2320–2333.

[36] F. Mouton, L. Leenen, H.S. Venter, Social engineering attack examples, templates and scenarios, Comput. Secur. 59 (2016) 186–209.

[37] S. Deyati, B.J. Muldrey, A. Chatterjee, Targeting hardware Trojans in mixed-signal circuits for security, in: 2016 IEEE 21st International Mixed-Signal Testing Workshop (IMSTW)IEEE, 2016, pp. 1–4.

[38] J. Blocki, M. Blum, A. Datta, S. Vempala, Towards human computable passwords, in: 8th Innovations in Theoretical Computer Science Conference (ITCS), 2017, pp. 1–47.

[39] R. Nithyanand, R. Johnson, The password allocation problem: strategies for reusing passwords effectively, Proceedings of the 12th ACM Workshop on Workshop on Privacy in the Electronic Society, ACM, 2013, pp. 255–260.

[40] M. Ahmadian, F. Plochan, Z. Roessler, D.C. Marinescu, SecureNoSQL: an approach for secure search of encrypted NoSQL databases in the public cloud, Int. J. Inform. Manag. 37 (2) (2017) 63–74.

Cloud-based computer-assisted diagnostic solutions for e-health

12

Shailesh Kumar, Rohini Srivastava, Shashwat Pathak, and Basant Kumar

Department of ECE, Motilal Nehru National Institute of Technology Allahabad, Prayagraj, India

1 Introduction

Early diagnosis of various fatal diseases can greatly reduce mortality risk and medical treatment expenditure. The ratio of doctors and medical experts to patients is less in middle-income countries, and it is severe in low-income countries. The Internet of Things (IoT) provides a solution for this type of problem. IoT not only offers the answer in rural areas, but is also helpful for primary and secondary healthcare centers in terms of receiving better assistance from specialist doctors in tertiary hospitals. IoT can be recognized as a "network of networks" that consists of thousands of academic, industry, and public and private institutions, health centers, and local and global government bodies, which are connected by various communication media [1,2]. Nowadays, most countries are using the internet to exchange information like media, data, opinions, and information from intelligence agencies. According to the latest assessment of the Internet World Statistics, approximately 4.5 billion out of a 7.7 billion population are internet users worldwide [3,4]. Therefore it is easier nowadays to use IoT devices, and it is cost effective as well [5]. With the rapid advancements in information and communications technology (ICT), telemedicine is being seen as a tool for bridging the gap between urban and rural healthcare facilities. Telemedicine provides healthcare facilities to far-away and rural places through the internet or image/audio transmission and videoconferencing, where a patient in the remote village may get better medical treatment from specialist consultants/doctors [6]. These telemedicine systems are based on wireless technologies that can sufficiently deliver healthcare services to short-staffed remote health centers, ambulances, ships, trains, aircraft, and home patients. Mobile telemedicine exploits the latest advances in mobile communication technologies to deliver the potential for better medical services, which is not possible with standard telephone services [7–9]. In recent years, the global system for mobile communication, General Packet Radio Service, satellite systems, 3G/4G systems, wireless LAN, Bluetooth, and wireless access protocol are the primary wireless technologies used in telemedicine. Using medical sensor networks, patients in critical care and bedridden intensive care units can be monitored efficiently. These networks can alert medical staff to an emergency in advance, together with portable devices and intelligent algorithms. Detection of many diseases such as diabetes, risk of falling, heart attack, and cataract can be analyzed from the signal or image acquired from biomedical sensors or different imaging modalities. These devices can help to set up a customized telemedicine network to carry out teleophthalmology, telecardiology, teledermatology, and teleradiology [8]. There are no straightforward solutions to India's healthcare requirements. However, the use of advances in

Intelligent Data Security Solutions for e-Health Applications. https://doi.org/10.1016/B978-0-12-819511-6.00012-1

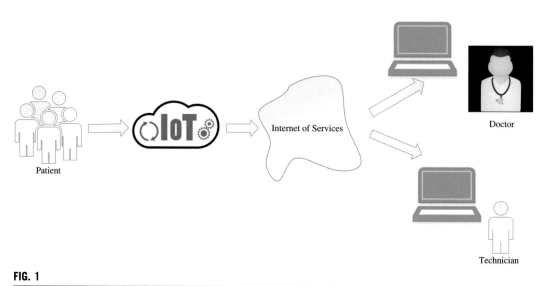

FIG. 1

The architecture of an Internet of Things (IoT)-driven e-healthcare system.

the field of ICT in healthcare delivery is an innovative idea to tackle healthcare disparity. The widespread use of ICT in medicine has opened new horizons to improve healthcare in India as well as in other developing countries [9,10]. The architecture of a mobile telemedicine system is shown in Fig. 1. This model shows that the typical telemedicine system consists of a multifunctional telemedicine unit at the patient's end and a base unit at the doctor's end. The telemedicine unit is responsible for collecting and transmitting vital physiological signals and medical images of the patient to the base unit. At the base unit, a doctor can retrieve the physiological signals and other vital information from the telemedicine unit in a continuous manner. When the base unit is stationed within a hospital (especially in emergency handling or in-home telecare), a hospital database unit can be integrated with the system to maintain routine digital health records. Doctors can retrieve medical history on demand from this archive.

According to a survey, approximately 10 million people in the United States use smartphones to search for health information and facilities, and 27% of people use smartphones for online activities. Today, there are several application platforms to manage prescriptions, promote alternative treatment options, provide price comparison, and validate orders. Applications are also available for tracking exercise, diet, and blood pressure; hence, enabling smartphones to play a vital role in the health sector.

2 Enabling techniques for IoT-based early diagnostic systems

Early detection of various diseases such as diabetes, risk of falling, heart attack, cancerous tumors, and eye diseases such as cataract, diabetic retinopathy (DR), glaucoma, etc., can significantly improve the healthcare scenario and prevent loss of life. Diabetes is a group of metabolic diseases in which the sugar level in blood increases. A high level of blood glucose can damage organs in the human body. It can produce many complications to the human body if blood sugar is abnormally high and in type 1 diabetes the condition is lifelong [11]. There are many complications associated with diabetes, including stroke, neuropathy, DR, skin disease, depression, and dementia. Hence, early detection of diabetes is needed to prevent these various diseases.

Risk of fall is more probable in the elderly population; fall is accountable for approximately 40% of all injuries related to death [12]. The leading cause of falling may be heart problems, elder age, loss of balance, and loss of consciousness. Falls in the elderly are significant problems for modern-day society. From the latest report, approximately 30% of people 65 years or older suffer from falls every year. Hence, early detection of the risk of falling is necessary for prevention from many complications.

When the flow of blood is partially or entirely blocked through the heart, a heart attack takes place. Fat and cholesterol are the leading causes of blockages in the coronary arteries [13,14]. Many complications arise during a heart attack, which can damage the heart, namely abnormal heart rhythms, heart failure, and sudden cardiac arrest. There are many symptoms such as shortness of breath, cold sweat, nausea, indigestion, heartburn, and abdominal pain. Early detection of heart attacks and other heart-related problems can save the patient from further complications and life-threatening situations. Therefore early detection of a heart attack is necessary [15,16].

The development of an early diagnostic tool/system can be based on techniques of digital signal/ image processing, artificial intelligence (AI) and machine learning (ML), medical sensor networks, cloud computing, etc.

2.1 Digital signal/image processing

A block diagram of a biomedical signal/image processing-based diagnostic model is shown in Fig. 2. Digital image processing/signal processing-based techniques contain many steps, namely image acquisition/signal acquisition, preprocessing/image enhancement, segmentation/extraction of the region of interest (ROI), and feature extraction [17,18]. Image acquisition is accomplished using various imaging modalities, and an electrocardiogram (ECG) signal or electroencephalogram (EEG) signal is acquired using an ECG and EEG, respectively. Preprocessing is performed to remove impulse noise, which appears while capturing an image or signal. To improve the contrast between foreground and background, image enhancement techniques are used. Histogram equalization is a simple image enhancement technique, which increases the contrast by stretching grayscale value [19]. Segmentation is performed for extracting the area of interest from a given image. Features are extracted from the ROI for grading diseases into classes such as healthy, mild, moderate, and severe [20,21].

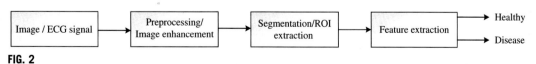

FIG. 2

Block diagram of a digital image processing-based detection system. *ECG*, electrocardiogram; *ROI*, region of interest.

2.2 Artificial intelligence/machine learning/deep learning

AI is a growing field with a variety of daily life practical applications and currently active research topics. When programmable computers were first conceived, people wondered whether such machines might become intelligent, over a hundred years before one was built. These days, people use intelligent software to automate daily routines, for audio or photo recognition, to make diagnostic decisions in the medical field, and for many research fields in science [22,23]. Trouble arises when the system depends on hard-coded knowledge that recommends that an AI system needs the capacity to obtain its understanding by extracting patterns from raw data. This ability is known as ML. ML enables a computer program to solve problems acquiring knowledge of the real world and make a decision that appears subjective [24]. To solve objective problems, complicated concepts of the program could be learned by a computer using a hierarchy of many simple concepts. If a graph were drawn to show how these concepts are assembled on top of each other, with several layers, the graph would be deep. For this reason, this is known as AI deep learning [25,26].

AI/ML-based diagnostic support is shown in Fig. 3. Primarily, it consists of three steps, namely image/signal acquisition, image processing, and AI model. Image acquisition is accomplished using a camera, and EEG signals are acquired using an EEG. The acquired signals may be corrupted by salt and pepper noise during capturing. The image-processing block takes care of this. It mainly contains preprocessing, image enhancement, segmentation, and feature extraction. An AI/ML model is applied to the extracted features of the disease.

2.3 Medical sensor based

A medical sensor-based detection system is shown in Fig. 4. There are many biomedical sensors used for the detection of different types of diseases, as follows: an *ECG sensor* is used to measure heart rate (PQRST wave) for the detection of various heart diseases. ECG acquisition can be done using three-lead, 10-lead, or 12-lead sensors. Three-lead sensors can be used for home patients, and a technician might operate it. It is a cost-effective sensor. Trained paramedic staff or medical experts only can operate 10-lead and 12-lead sensors. An *EEG sensor* is used for neurological signal acquisition. It measures brain signals to find clotting in the brain, which indicates a sign of stroke. An *accelerometer* measures the walking pattern of the human body in a three-axis motion. The risk of falling is calculated using an accelerometer. A *sphygmomanometer* sensor is used for blood pressure measurement.

FIG. 3

Block diagram of an artificial intelligence (AI)-based detection system.

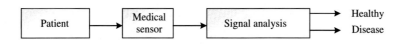

FIG. 4

Block diagram of a medical sensor board-based diagnostic system.

A *glucometer* is used to measure glucose level (diabetes) in the human body. An *SPO$_2$* measures the pulse rate of the heart along with oxygen saturation of the patient and is used by a cardiologist.

2.4 Internet of Medical Things

Most deaths can be avoided if a disease like bradycardia, tachycardia, blockage of arteries, or fall detection in the elderly, are diagnosed earlier. The basic need for using IoT-based medical devices is the lack of medical facilities as compared to the population. In rural and remote areas, people do not have quality healthcare facilities. Most of the diagnostic devices like a 10-lead ECG machine, ophthalmoscope, and spirometer require trained medical professionals. To visit hospitals for this kind of diagnosis, especially for the people living in rural areas, is very expensive [27]. Therefore IoT-based diagnostic solutions are becoming popular. IoT-based devices also have the advantage of diagnosing more than one disease; therefore it is cost effective. IoT-based diagnosis devices can also be used for mass screening, regular check-ups, and home patient monitoring [28,29]. Various biomedical sensors are available for IoT-based systems like an ECG sensor, electromyography (EMG) sensor, oxygen saturation sensor, blood pressure sensor, respiratory rate sensor, blood glucose sensor, etc.

IoT is a novel technique that provides a platform for the global network of machines to interact with the devices. IoT is also known as the Internet of Everything or the Industrial Internet. IoT is acknowledged to be one of the best technologies for global communication in the next few decades and is gaining much attention from corporations and industries globally. The significance of IoT for industries will be appreciated when all the machines can interconnect with each other and integrate with vendor-managed inventory systems, customer support systems, business intelligence applications, and business analytics [28].

2.5 IoT hardware design

Hardware design of a complete e-healthcare system provides ease of access to home patients. A complete healthcare module can be implemented on some IoT boards. These boards are very cost effective and compatible with biosensors. Arduino and Raspberry-Pi boards are the most popular boards for medical purposes. IoT-based hardware system architecture involves various diagnostic analytics, a sensor platform, connectivity with a cloud server, an application platform, product infrastructure, etc. Arduino Uno is a highly popular board for the beginner as well as professionals. Arduino Uno R3 is very simple and is based on the ATmega328P, yet it has the most powerful prototyping environment and is considered to be the first microcontroller-based development board. ATmega328P has six analog inputs and 14 digital input/output pins. It has 32 kb of flash memory; however, it deals with complex operations and difficult logic. All prototyping environments try to be compatible with the Arduino pin breakout. The Arduino Uno board is most popular because it is based on C language, the code is easy to learn, and the open-source IDE can develop sketches [30]. Raspberry Pi is a very useful platform for IoT-based applications. This board is also useful for configuring multimedia processing and transmission. It is based on BCM2837 SoC with a 1.2 GHz 64-bit quad-core ARM Cortex-A53 processor; Raspberry Pi is a sturdy board. It also includes Wi-Fi and Bluetooth, which make it compact and standalone. This board is popular as it allows installation of several packages, including Python, Java, LAMP stack, etc. [30].

3 Cloud-based intelligent diagnostic system

A generic framework for the automated detection and diagnosis of various diseases using a cloud-based smart diagnostic system is shown in Fig. 5. This cloud-based diagnostic system is used for automated early detection of multiple diseases such as cardiovascular diseases, risk of falling, blood pressure, cataract, glaucoma, etc. This is achieved by intelligent classification and analysis of physiological signals (ECG, EEG, EMG) or radiological images using computational tools such as support vector machine, artificial neural networks, etc. Early detection and timely medical intervention in life-threatening cases are the primary purposes of this cloud-based intelligent diagnostic system. Various sensors' data are acquired from patients and sent to the cloud server using IoT boards. An AI-based algorithm is used for the classification of various diseases using the received diagnostic data available on the cloud. A variety of diagnostic features is extracted from the acquired medical sensor data. These diagnostic features will assist in speedy and accurate learning of disease classification models using neural networks, support vector machines, and deep learning algorithms. The developed detection model is trained using a large number of disease-affected diagnostic parameters such as ECG, EEG, oxygen saturation, and accelerometer data. For each disease, a separate dataset will be required for the training of the subsequent diagnostic model. For validation of the proposed ML-based detection model, the output of the developed model will be compared with the ground truth data as well as the diagnostic opinion from

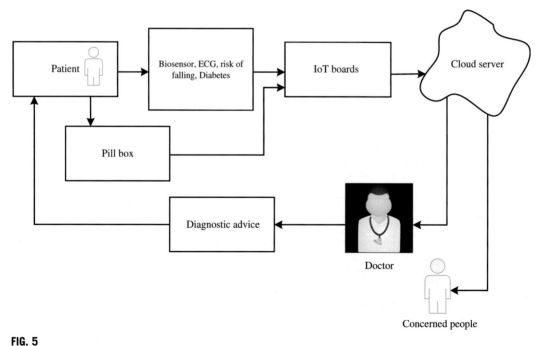

FIG. 5

Internet of Things (IoT)-enabled generic cloud-based e-health management system. *ECG*, electrocardiogram.

the concerned specialist. A suitable IT platform, along with graphical user interface, can be developed to facilitate various data acquisition, patient database management, and cloud interfacing. Multiple data of the patient can be captured at the primary healthcare center/patient's home; it is uploaded to the cloud server, where cardiovascular diseases, risk of falling, and other disease detection algorithms will perform diagnostic evaluation of the data. The system will finally generate a comprehensive diagnostic report indicating the presence/absence of each type of disease along with a prescription for the future course of action.

4 Cloud-based early diagnostic systems

4.1 Cataract

Cataracts are responsible for approximately 51% of blindness (20 million people) around the world and is also the leading cause of blindness, as per a study in 2010. According to WHO, 53.8 million individuals are affected by mild to severe disability caused by cataracts, and more than 96% of individuals are from poor and developing countries [31]. For example, it has been reported that cataract prevalence in Chinese people over 40 years old in Singapore is 35% [32]. A cataract is the most prevalent age-related ocular disease, which affects those in developing and poor countries. Clouding or opacity of the lens of the natural eye is known as a cataract, which results in blurring and finally loss of vision if it is left untreated. Protein and water are the primary building blocks of the lens of the human eye. As age increases, proteins clump together and are stored in a capsule-like structure, which forms clouding within the lens. A cataract may affect one or both eyes. There are three types of cataracts based on their location: typical cataract, cortical cataract, and subcapsular cataract [33]. A typical cataract occurs around the focal center and it is the most common type of cataract [34,35]. This type of cataract affects primarily older age people because aging proteins and other constituents of the eye lens are clumped together. A cortical cataract causes the focal point cortex (external edge) to become murky. This happens when variations in the water content in the encompass of the focal point cause fissuring [36,37]. A cortical cataract develops when variations in the water content surrounding the focal point occur which causes a crack in eye lenses [38]. Individuals with diabetes or those taking high measurement steroid solutions are at greater risk of building up this kind of cataract [39].

A teleophthalmology model is depicted in Fig. 6, where the automated cataract detection model is positioned as software in a server, placed at a remote location. The patient visits a nearby primary eyecare center and has access to a screening facility on a mobile phone through mobile app registration. The acquired image is uploaded by paramedic staff or by the patient through the mobile app. Further acquired images combined with the affected person's details are sent to the primary eyecare center through a cloud server. A document related to disease analysis is created using an automatic system and sent to the patient. The document is also sent to an ophthalmologist for a second opinion and to make a conclusion. A web platform for common health monitoring is combined with an appropriate imaging system, which can help specialist consultants to inspect the patient from remote locations and make conclusions. This way, a more reliable detection and diagnosis facility will be achieved. A cataract eye and class of eye detected by the proposed system are shown in Fig. 7A and B, respectively [40].

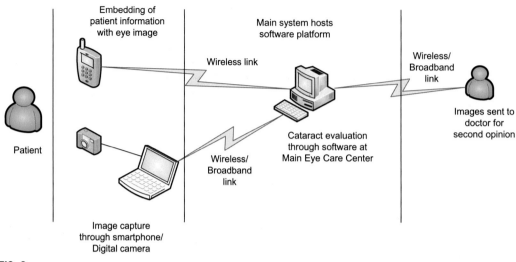

FIG. 6

Network architecture of Internet of Things-enabled cataract detection system.

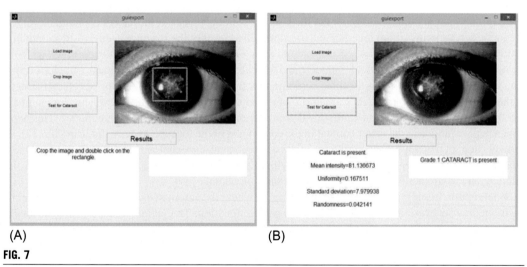

(A)   (B)

FIG. 7

(A) Cataract eye and (B) decision making by the proposed system.

4.2 Diabetic retinopathy/glaucoma [21]

DR is a major complication due to diabetes mellitus (DM) [41,42]. DR affects the retinal surface of the eye and partial blindness or permanent loss of vision may occur if not treated at an early stage. Normally, adult age individuals are affected due to DR. If one has suffered from DM for more than 15 years, then the chance of the occurrence of DR is approximately 78%. Many lesions appear on the retinal surface due to DR. Microaneurysms and hemorrhages are primary and early lesions that are present due to DR. Microaneurysms are the very first sign of DR and gradually increase as the disease progresses [43,44]. Hemorrhages are second lesions that appear after microaneurysms. Blood leakage from blood vessels is known as a hemorrhage [45,46]. Hence, recognition of both lesions, namely microaneurysms and hemorrhages, plays a vibrant role in automated DR detection at the very first stage [47,48].

A block diagram of the detection model is shown in Fig. 8. Preprocessing, feature extraction, and classification are the main steps of the suggested model for DR detection. Digital image processing is used for preprocessing of retinal fundus images. In the literature, many techniques have been proposed to enhance the contrast and remove noise, which might be added during image acquisition [48]. Acquired fundus images suffer from uneven illumination and less contrast due to eye anatomies like opaque media of the interior part of the eyeball, pupil size, and movement of the eyeball while image capturing. So, preprocessing is necessary to analyze the color fundus images. Preprocessing and

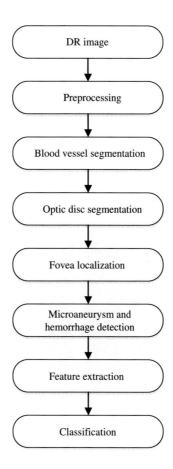

FIG. 8

Block diagram of automatic detection of diabetic retinopathy (DR) from fundus images.

contrast enhancement techniques increase the probability of disease detection by using digital image processing or by visual inspection. The green channel has better contrast between foregrounds like blood vessels and backgrounds, and it has a better contrast between the disc and other tissues on the retinal surface. Blood vessels, optic disc, and fovea have been extracted using morphology operations. Mathematical morphology is a nonlinear operation extensively used as preprocessing techniques and segmentation techniques. Improved vascular tree segmentation and extraction is accomplished using a series of morphological operations. Watershed transform is a morphological operation used for optic disc recognition and segmentation. A series of morphological operations are used for fovea segmentation. After removal of all pathological structures, namely blood vessel, optic disc, and fovea from color fundus images, white spots with a circular shape are left in the fundus images; these are known as microaneurysms and hemorrhages. Furthermore, features such as area, perimeter, circularity, number of lesions, major axis length, minor axis length, and aspect ratio have been extracted from microaneurysms and hemorrhages. The classification model, called the radial basis function neural network (RBFNN), is used to classify DR or non-DR. It is a special kind of neural network, which has only one hidden layer. RBFNN has three parameters such as weights, center, and standard deviation. These three parameters are trained using the seven features of microaneurysms and hemorrhages. The proposed model classifies the color fundus image into a healthy and DR image. The suggested automated DR detection model exploits the combined benefits of morphology operation (for blood vessel segmentation), watershed transformation (optic disc segmentation), and RBFNN (for DR classification). A retinal color fundus image and detected microaneurysms and hemorrhages by the proposed algorithm are shown in Fig. 9A and B, respectively [21].

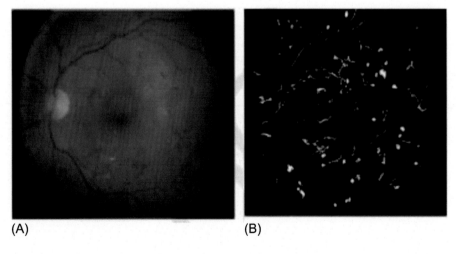

(A)   (B)

FIG. 9

(A) Retinal color fundus image. (B) Detected microaneurysms and hemorrhages.

4.3 M-cardiac care platform

Deaths due to cardiovascular diseases in India increased from 1.3 million in 1990 to 2.8 million in 2016, and more than half of deaths caused by heart ailments in 2016 were in those less than 70 years of age [49]. Cardiovascular diseases are a collective of various kinds of heart ailments, stroke, and conditions of blood vessels nourishing the limbs, therefore early diagnosis plays a crucial role in avoiding the risk of any critical situation like a heart attack [50]. The major reason behind these situations is the lack of continuous monitoring of the health of the heart. Any of these critical situations will always show early symptoms like pain in hands, nausea, light-headedness, shortness of breath, etc. If at this early stage the health of the heart is monitored by a doctor and timely medical intervention made, then several fatal heart-related issues can be avoided. An ECG of the patient can easily be acquired from a three-lead sensor or a 10-lead sensor and can be uploaded to the cloud server using Bluetooth or Wi-Fi through an IoT device like Arduino or Raspberry Pi. Figs. 10 and 11 present three-lead ECG acquisition and transmission, respectively.

The three electrodes, which are placed over the body, acquire raw ECG signals. For the removal of various noises, the preprocessing of raw ECG signals is done using an AD8232 ECG acquisition module. The electrodes make the ECG data available on the output pin of the AD8232 module. The microcontroller (Arduino) checks whether the signal is present or not. If the signal is not present, then the Bluetooth will receive zero from the microcontroller device. If the signal is present, the microcontroller acquires the analog ECG data, converts it to an 8-bit signal, and transmits it via Bluetooth to the Android phone of the patient. Android phones have an application to receive these data on a professional ECG graph and upload it to a cloud server. The cloud server contains a managed database on the

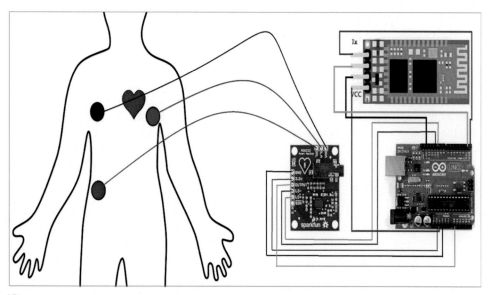

FIG. 10

Electrocardiogram acquisition and transmission system.

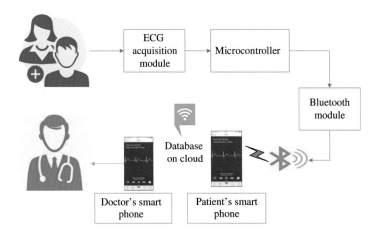

FIG. 11

Cloud based M-cardiac management system architecture. *ECG*, electrocardiogram.

patient and doctors in such a way that a particular patient can send the ECG to the doctor with whom he or she wants to consult. At the doctor's end, the application should allow the doctor to send his or her valuable diagnostic advice to the patient [51].

However, in some cases, a three-lead ECG is not fully conclusive; therefore a 10-lead ECG acquisition system is used instead. ADS1298 is an analog front end (AFE) 10-lead ECG module used to acquire an accurate ECG of the patient. An AFE is a 10-lead, eight-channel ECG acquisition board for the acquisition of an accurate ECG, and a Raspberry Pi is a single board computer used for data processing and transmission to the cloud server. The AFE board is a low-power, multichannel, 24-bit, delta-sigma, analog-to-digital converter with integrated programmable gain amplifiers. This device incorporates various ECG-specific functions that make it well suited for scalable ECG applications. The device is also used in high-performance, multichannel data acquisition systems by powering down the ECG-specific circuitry. ECG data are acquired on the computer by using an AFE board and the ECG data are converted into image format. ECG in image form is transmitted to the cloud using microcontrollers and transceiver modules [52]. Fig. 12 presents an IoT-enabled cloud-based M-cardiac management system.

4.4 Risk of fall detection

Falls are responsible for 40% of all injury-related deaths and need immediate medical attention. The reason for a fall may be heart problems, loss of consciousness, fatigue, old age, and loss of balance. Falls in the elderly are a major problem for today's society. Approximately one in every three 65-year-old adults falls every year [53,54]. Therefore primary healthcare providers should screen older adults for risk of falling at least once a year. Clinical practice guidelines on fall risk assessment involves many steps that consider falls history, medication review, physical examination, and functional and environmental assessments [55]. With the advancements in ICT and evolution of the IoT era, it is possible to develop a low-cost, IoT-enabled system for assessing the risk of falling. This system will involve medical sensors with networking capability, medical data acquisition and

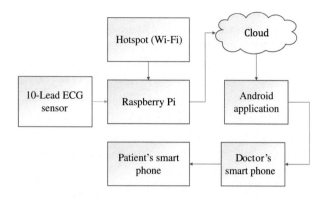

FIG. 12

Cloud-based 10-lead M-cardiac management system.

transmission module integrated with a telemedicine platform, a cloud-based server, and a deep learning/ML-based diagnostic tool. The Internet of Medical Things (IoMT) along with telemedicine is being explored in a big way to provide timely and good-quality healthcare service at remote locations. An accelerometer with communication capability can be placed on a suitable body part of the subject under observation. A telemedicine platform can facilitate the transmission of accelerometer sensor data as well as the walking pattern video of the subject to a cloud server where a deep learning-based diagnostic tool analyses the risk of falling. Therefore a telemedicine platform, supported by an IoT-enabled medical sensor, can be easily installed at primary healthcare centers located in remote and rural areas. The fall detection system will also be able to transmit the subject's video allowing pattern of walking, proper placement, working of the device, etc. to be monitored. Fig. 13 shows the framework of cloud-based early detection for the risk of falling.

An accelerometer-based sensing device, which could be placed near the body's center of gravity, can provide data regarding risk of falling. For IoT, various available modules such as Wi-Fi modules, Zigbee protocol, Ethernet shields, etc. can be employed. A microcontroller (Arduino), an accelerometer (Arduino based), and Wi-Fi-enabled IoT board can be combined in one unit for this. The Arduino

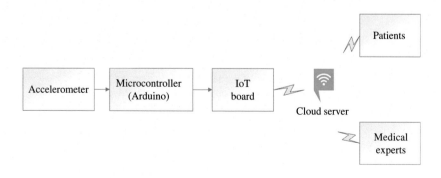

FIG. 13

Cloud-based early detection of risk of falling. *IoT*, Internet of Things.

with accelerometer will be used for data transmission and reception. The IoT board will transmit the data to the cloud server. This system will provide clinicians with a reliable framework to provide fast and accurate rehabilitative protocols to patients.

5 Challenges in cloud-based e-health systems

Cloud-based e-health computing has several advantages; however, challenges like security, privacy, data management, etc. can also be found in this healthcare management system. Table 1 presents various challenges in cloud-based e-health computing.

6 Chapter summary

This chapter presented a cloud-based generic framework for the early detection and monitoring of various diseases. Enabling concepts and technologies such as telemedicine and e-health, various aspects of IoT, various diagnostic technique models involving image/signal analysis, AI and ML were also discussed in brief. A model of a cloud-based cataract detection system for mass screening was presented. The chapter also discussed image processing and ML-based techniques for the early detection of DR using fundus images. Early detection of risk of falling and cardiovascular disease using IoT-enabled cloud-based systems have also been discussed. In spite of having numerous advantages, cloud-based computer-assisted systems for e-health have certain limitations like data security, integrity, privacy, management, and authentication. In future, advancement in various technologies can be used to overcome the limitations of cloud-based e-healthcare systems and make them more secure, reliable, and user friendly.

Table 1 Challenges in cloud-based e-health computing.

Challenges	Description
Data security, integrity, and privacy	• Merging of patient data • Bad supervision of encryption key • Uncertainty of interfaces and application programming interfaces uncertain • Insecurity of account or service • Data loss or leakage
Management	• Healthcare professional distrust and governance failure • Lack of trust for provider's compliance
Technology	• Uncertainty in performance and reliability • Bugs in large-scale distributed cloud systems • Shared technology and data
Legal	• Data authority and secrecy issues • Faith and accountability issues • Guarantee of better services

References

[1] S. Madakam, R. Ramaswamy, S. Tripathi, Internet of Things (IoT): a literature review, J. Comput. Commun. 03 (05) (2015) 164–173.

[2] S. Smagulov, V. Smagulova, Internet of Things in healthcare, Intellect. Arch. 8 (1) (2019) 1–11.

[3] W. Internet, U. Statistics, The Internet Big Picture World Internet Users and 2016 Population Stats, 4, (2016), pp. 1–6.

[4] S. Banka, I. Madan, S.S. Saranya, Smart healthcare monitoring using IoT, Int. J. Appl. Eng. Res. 13 (15) (2018) 11984–11989.

[5] G. Started, How the Internet of Things can benefit your business, 2019, pp. 1–12.

[6] B. Kumar, S. Pathak, A novel, low-cost, flexible network architecture and its performance evaluation for remote eye care solutions shashwat, Telemed. e-Health 23 (9) (2017) 1–10.

[7] D. Kim, et al., Preliminary communication mobile telemedicine system for remote consultation in cases of acute stroke, 2009, pp. 102–107.

[8] S. Chattopadhyay, J. Li, L. Land, P. Ray, A framework for assessing ICT preparedness for e-health implementations, in: 2008 10th IEEE Intl. Conf. e-Health Networking, Appl. Serv. Heal. 2008, 2008, pp. 124–129.

[9] D.P. Conradie, N.L. Ruxwana, M.E. Herselman, ICT applications as e-health solutions in the rural eastern Cape Province of South Africa, Health Inf. Manag. J. 39 (1) (2010) 17–29.

[10] H.K. Andreassen, L.E. Kjekshus, A. Tjora, Survival of the project: a case study of ICT innovation in health care, Soc. Sci. Med. 132 (2015) 62–69.

[11] WHO, Diabetes 30, 30 Oct. 2018, no. October 2018, p. 5, (2018).

[12] S. Watson, Everything You Need to Know About Diabetes, 2019, pp. 1–19.

[13] P.M. Ridker, Cardiology patient page. C-reactive protein: a simple test to help predict risk of heart attack and stroke, Circulation 108 (12) (2003) 1–5.

[14] S.C. Smith, et al., Preventing heart attack and death in patients with coronary disease, J. Am. Coll. Cardiol. 26 (1) (1995) 292.

[15] G. Affleck, H. Tennen, S. Croog, S. Levine, Causal attribution, perceived benefits, and morbidity after a heart attack: an 8-year study, J. Consult. Clin. Psychol. 55 (1) (1987) 29–35.

[16] K. Dracup, D.K. Moser, M. Eisenberg, H. Meischke, A.A. Alonzo, A. Braslow, Causes of delay in seeking treatment for heart attack symptoms, Soc. Sci. Med. 40 (3) (1995) 379–392.

[17] B. Kumar, S. Kumar, Diabetic retinopathy detection by extracting area and number of microaneurysm from colour fundus image, in: 2018 5th Int. Conf. Signal Process. Integr. Networks, 2018, pp. 359–364.

[18] D. Marin, M.E. Gegundez-Arias, A. Suero, J.M. Bravo, Obtaining optic disc center and pixel region by automatic thresholding methods on morphologically processed fundus images, Comput. Methods Prog. Biomed. 118 (2) (2015) 173–185.

[19] S. Kumar, S. Choudhary, R. Gupta, B. Kumar, Performance evaluation of joint filtering and histogram equalization techniques for retinal fundus image enhancement, in: 2018 5th IEEE Uttar Pradesh Sect. Int. Conf. Electr. Electron. Comput. Eng. UPCON 2018, 2018.

[20] B. Antal, A. Hajdu, Improving microaneurysm detection in color fundus images by using context-aware approaches, Comput. Med. Imaging Graph. 37 (5–6) (2013) 403–408.

[21] A.K. Singh, S. Kumar, A. Adarsh, B. Kumara, An automated early diabetic retinopathy detection through improved blood vessel and optic disc segmentation, Opt. Laser Technol. 121 (1994), 105815 https://doi.org/10.1016/j.optlastec.2019.105815.

[22] I. Goodfellow, Y. Bengio, A. Courville, Deep Learning, 2016, pp. 1–3.

[23] C.M. Bishop, Pattern Recognition and machine Learning, Springer, 2006.

[24] T.M. Mitchell, Machine learning and data mining, Predict. Toxicol. 42 (11) (2005) 223–254.

[25] I. Goodfellow, A.C.Y. Bengio, Deep Learning, MIT Press, 2016.

[26] D.S. Richard Duda, P. Hart, Pattern Classification, second ed., 1973.

[27] A. Das, P. Rad, K.R. Choo, B. Nouhi, J. Lish, J. Martel, Distributed machine learning cloud teleophthalmology IoT for predicting AMD disease progression, Futur. Gener. Comput. Syst. 93 (2019) 486–498.

[28] K.N. Sanjay, L.P. Shahadev, P. Sandhyakarande, Healthcare management and monitoring system using Internet-of-Things (IoT), Int. J. Adv. Sci. Res. Eng. Trends 3 (2) (2018) 27–30.

[29] S. Patil, S. Pardeshi, Human health monitoring system using IOT, Int. J. Rec. Trends Eng. Res. 4 (4) (2018) 425–432.

[30] M. Janakiram, 10 DIY development boards for IoT prototyping – the new stack, Thenewstack (2016) 1–19.

[31] R.R.A. Bourne, et al., Magnitude, temporal trends, and projections of the global prevalence of blindness and distance and near vision impairment: a systematic review and meta-analysis, Lancet Glob. Health 5 (9) (2017) e888–e897.

[32] H. Li, L. Ko, J.H. Lim, J. Liu, D.W.K. Wong, T.Y. Wong, Image based diagnosis of cortical cataract, Embc 2008 (2008) 3904–3907.

[33] H. Shen, H. Hao, L. Wei, Z. Wang, An image based classification method for cataract, in: 2008 Int. Symp. Comput. Sci. Comput. Technol, 2008, pp. 583–586.

[34] T.Y. Wong, H. Li, J.H. Lim, P. Mitchell, A.G. Tan, J.J. Wang, A computer-aided diagnostic system of nuclear cataract, IEEE Trans. Biomed. Eng. 57 (2010).

[35] R. Srivastava, et al., Automatic nuclear cataract grading using image gradients, J. Med. Imaging 1 (1) (2014).

[36] T. Kuroda, T. Fujikado, T. Oshika, Y. Hirohara, T. Mihashi, Wavefront analysis in eyes with nuclear or cortical cataract, Am. J. Ophthalmol. 134 (1) (2002) 1–9.

[37] C.J. Hammond, et al., The heritability of age-related cortical cataract: the twin eye study, Investig. Ophthalmol. Vis. Sci. 42 (3) (2001) 601–605.

[38] Y.C. Chow, X. Gao, H. Li, J.H. Lim, Y. Sun, T.Y. Wong, Automatic detection of cortical and PSC cataracts using texture and intensity analysis on retro-illumination lens images, in: 2011 Annual International Conference of the IEEE Engineering in Medicine and Biology Society, 2011.

[39] A.U. Patwari, et al., Detection, categorization, and assessment of eye cataracts using digital image processing, in: The First International Conference on Interdisciplinary Research and Development, 31 May–1 June 2011, Thailand, 2011, pp. 1–5.

[40] S. Pathak, B. Kumar, A robust automated cataract detection algorithm using diagnostic opinion based parameter thresholding for telemedicine application, Electronics 5 (3) (2016) 57.

[41] D.K. Prasad, et al., Early detection of diabetic retinopathy from digital retinal fundus images, in: 2015 IEEE Recent Advances in Intelligent Computational Systems (RAICS), 2015, pp. 240–245.

[42] M. Niemeijer, et al., Retinopathy online challenge: automatic detection of microaneurysms in digital color fundus photographs, IEEE Trans. Med. Imaging 29 (1) (2010) 185–195.

[43] S.S. Rahim, V. Palade, J. Shuttleworth, C. Jayne, Automatic screening and classification of diabetic retinopathy fundus images, Commun. Comput. Inf. Sci. 459 (2014) 113–122.

[44] K.M. Adal, D. Sidibé, S. Ali, E. Chaum, T.P. Karnowski, F. Mériaudeau, Automated detection of microaneurysms using scale-adapted blob analysis and semi-supervised learning, Comput. Methods Prog. Biomed. 114 (1) (2014) 1–10.

[45] R. Inbarathi, R. Karthikeyan, Detection of retinal hemorrhage in fundus images by classifying the splat features using SVM, Int. J. Innov. Res. Sci. Eng. Technol. 3 (3) (2014) 1979–1986.

[46] P. Jitpakdee, P. Aimmanee, B. Uyyanonvara, A survey on hemorrhage detection in diabetic retinopathy retinal images, in: 2012 9th Int. Conf. Electr. Eng. Comput. Telecommun. Inf. Technol. ECTI-CON 2012, 2012, pp. 12–15.

[47] J.P. Bae, K.G. Kim, H.C. Kang, C.B. Jeong, K.H. Park, J.M. Hwang, A study on hemorrhage detection using hybrid method in fundus images, J. Digit. Imaging 24 (3) (2011) 394–404.

[48] A.D. Fleming, S. Philip, K.A. Goatman, J.A. Olson, P.F. Sharp, Automated microaneurysm detection using local contrast normalization and local vessel detection, IEEE Trans. Med. Imaging 25 (9) (2006) 1223–1232.

[49] T. Lancet, Heart Disease, Stroke Among Top Killers in India, 2019, pp. 1–6.

[50] M.B. Liu, Cardiovascular diseases, Chin. Med. J. (Engl). 127 (2014) 6–7.

[51] D. Sen, R. Srivastava, N. Sahai, R. P. Tewari, B. Kumar, Development of IoT Enabled Low Cost Management System for m-Cardiology Introduction, n.d. pp. 2–8.

[52] N. Kumar, A. Kumar, P. Gupta, R. Srivastava, R. P. Tewari, Development of Cloud Based Multi Modal m-Cardiac Management System Proposed Methodology: m-Cardiac Care Management System, n.d. pp. 1–8.

[53] S. Prevention, J.M. Simpson, Ageing Soc. 21 (5) (2015) 667–675.

[54] A. Salvà, I. Bolíbar, G. Pera, C. Arias, Incidence and consequences of falls among, Med. Clin. (Barc.) 122 (5) (2004) 172–176.

[55] E.A. Phelan, J.E. Mahoney, J.C. Voit, J.A. Stevens, Assessment and management of fall risk in primary care settings, Med. Clin. North Am. 99 (2015) 281–293.

Progressive advancements in security challenges, issues, and solutions in e-health systems

Ritu Gothwal, Shailendra Tiwari, Shivendra Shivani, and Manju Khurana

Computer Science and Engineering Department, Thapar Institute of Engineering and Technology (TIET), Patiala, India

1 Introduction to e-health systems

To reduce excessive healthcare expenditure in remote areas a distributed and effective medical care system is required. Remote health monitoring or e-health or telemedicine is considered to be a rising technology in the domain of research [1–6]. These technologies are used to provide healthcare services to remote areas by using telecommunication and information technology. These technologies have now overcome the barriers of distance in rural areas and remote communities. In the case of emergencies and in war-like situations when physical access to healthcare services is limited, telehealth plays an essential role in saving lives. E-health provides convenience and friendly communication between patient and medical staff by using medical imaging, data sharing, resource sharing, and distance monitoring. These technologies also offer an extensive database for future research. Telehealth also includes smart devices, wearable medical devices, and various types of medical equipment connected through the internet. These devices can provide data in real time to the doctor. For different end users and age groups, multiple trends are available (Fig. 1).

1.1 Telehomecare

Telehomecare services [7] provide easy-to-use healthcare equipment and services. Patients can learn about their condition with the help of devices and for further assistant a telenurse is available for patient monitoring. Patients can learn how to manage their daily diet, medication, and exercise routine. Each day patients can check their vital signs such as blood pressure, weight, heart rate, and oxygen level.

1.2 Telerehabilitation

Telerehabilitation [8] provides services to patients with disabilities because it may be difficult for them to travel to receive treatment. Various applications are available in this field such as smart wheelchairs, braces, artificial limbs, speech language pathology, teleaudiology, etc.

Intelligent Data Security Solutions for e-Health Applications. https://doi.org/10.1016/B978-0-12-819511-6.00013-3

FIG. 1

Trends in telemedicine.

1.3 **Remote physiological monitoring**

This technology uses a mobile medical device and other equipment to gather patient-generated health data and send the data to professionals [9]. Patient data such as vital signs, blood pressure, and heart rate can be monitored by these mobile devices.

1.4 **Telenursing**

Telenursing is very useful when nurses are not available physically, especially in the case of natural disasters where immediate help cannot be provided to patients [10]. In these cases, telecommunication services and telemedicine can enable well-equipped ambulances to administer life care services. Tele-nurses are available to monitor vital signs, blood pressure, and provide first aid treatment to patients. Telenursing is also important in the presurgical and postsurgical care of patients.

1.5 **Remote patient monitoring**

Remote patient monitoring [3] is very helpful when checking patients with serious conditions who require immediate care. This is also beneficial for senior patient care. Healthcare organizations can monitor patient health issues and keep track of patient medical data using handheld medical devices and online platforms that allow communication with healthcare professionals. This is very useful, for example, for the continuous monitoring of dementia patients and Alzheimer's patients.

1.6 Telehealthcare

Telehealthcare includes the application of information and communication technology to help patients manage their own illnesses through mobile devices, self-care education, and support systems [11]. These mobile devices provide the necessary information and guidance to patients, such as what to eat, when to take medicine, etc.

1.7 Teleconsultation

By using videoconference and phone calls, patients can directly consult with doctors remotely. If a hospital needs specialist doctor services then it can directly connect to a doctor via the internet. Teleconsultation [12] can save time, money, and effort.

2 Applications of telemedicine

Telemedicine has been applied to the various fields of medical science and technology, although the scope of utilization varies from area to area. Here, we summarize some of the applications of telemedicine.

2.1 Telestroke

Telestroke [4] is also known as stroke telemedicine. It is a web-based approach for the treatment of stroke patients who have yet to be admitted to hospital. Acute stroke causes the death of brain cells due to lack of oxygen. Time plays a crucial role while treating a stroke patient and delay in treatment can cause death, brain hemorrhage, or paralysis of the patient. The 90 min following a stroke are very important; if the patient receives proper treatment then the risk of permanent damage and death are significantly lower. Telestroke services are beneficial for rural areas because specialized hospitals may be hours away. It can link countryside hospitals and underresourced hospitals to a dedicated hospital providing stroke treatment. In its primary form, the telestroke system requires a neurologist, attending nurse, telemedicine ambulance, high-speed internet connection, videoconferencing through a laptop or phone, electronic health record (EHR) [13], and practice management system applications.

The use of a telemedicine ambulance provides more precise and rapid prehospital, emergency medical services for acute stroke patients. Tele-BAT (i.e., mobile telemedicine for the brain attack team) [14] is a novel approach used to provide treatment in a short time. During the emergency, medical technicians transmit their assessment and EHR to the physicians and neurologist. Patient neurological data, vital signs, blood data, and many components of the clinical pathway (except head computed tomography scanning) are sent through the network. By analyzing these components, recombinant tissue plasminogen activator therapy [15] can be performed in a prehospital setting. The rapid response system is required for acute stroke treatment.

2.2 Telemedicine in the management of gestational diabetes management (GDM)

Patients with gestational diabetes [16] suffer from high blood sugar concentrations developed during pregnancy but which usually disappears after giving birth. It is most common in the second half of pregnancy when the body is not able to produce enough insulin. Due to the deficiency of insulin the body is not able to control blood sugar levels to compensate for the increased needs of pregnancy. Diabetes is categorized into three main groups: diabetes type 1 (T1D), diabetes type 2 (T2D), and gestational diabetes.

Artificial intelligence (AI) gives us new insights into GDM. It provides us with tools that are capable of offering medical assistance to GDM [16]. Diabetes management has been reformed by new technologies such as continuous glucose management [17] devices and the development of the artificial pancreas [18]. The MobiGuide project [19] provides guidelines for clinical practice, blood pressure, and can access data from EHRs and activity sensors. It can run on Android-based devices and provides personalized decision support for GDM patients. It uses a body area network (BAN) [20] at the front end and a decision support system at the back end.

PubMed is a database that is used for medical research and clinical applications [21]. Various AI techniques are applied to investigate multiple critical diabetes management issues. Also, MD Logic is a fuzzy controller-based glycemic control system.

2.3 Telemedicine in diabetes retinopathy

Telemedicine provides us with highly visual and image-intensive ophthalmology. Diabetes retinopathy (DR) [22] is a complication caused by diabetes mellitus. Patients slowly lose their vision causing visual disability. Medical imaging provides an efficient screening strategy for DR. New technologies such as stereoscopic imaging, nonmydriatic cameras, and mobile-based fundus cameras provide specificity for diagnosing DR. These devices can screen DR by using imaging. Diabetes patients are usually not aware of the DR problem. Therefore they do not consult an ophthalmologist unless they have visual defects. Diabetologists can capture fundus images during regular diabetic check-up. The fundus pictures are obtained from the nonmydriatic digital retinal camera. These images are transmitted through the internet to a grading center where a retinal expert reads the images. Information regarding the status of the retinopathy is generated based on these pictures, and follow-up suggestions are made by an ophthalmologist at a remote location. This information is then returned to the diabetologists. A patient log file is then created, and the doctor can keep track of the records of DR.

2.4 Telemedicine in surgery or telesurgery

For patients who are not able to travel long distances, telesurgery [23] provides safe and accurate surgical procedures. It uses robotics and wireless networking technology to connect patients and surgeons who are separated by a significant geographical distance. This technology provides technical accuracy and safety to both patients and surgeons. This system overcomes the shortage of surgeons, geographical inaccessibility, and provides immediate and high-quality surgical care. The development of the robotic surgical system will improve precision. The small robotic system enables deep-tissue procedures such as surgical exploration through natural body puncture.

2.5 Telemedicine in the management of chronic liver disease

Chronic liver disease [24] consists of a wide variety of liver pathologies such as chronic hepatitis, liver cirrhosis, and hepatocellular carcinoma. "D-LIVER" is a project developed by IBMT developed for the European Union [25]. It consists of sensor technologies that measure the condition of liver cells in a cell-based management system. Sensors are important tools for conventional biochemical analyses. Sensors in this system are able to continuously monitor the vitality and intensity of the cells using a bioreactor. Sensors are able to analyze the cells directly and develop a patient management system at a very advanced stage, which further assists with decision making. This system is known as a care flow engine. For this system an information technology application has also been developed known as a personal health manager. Patients can access this app on their computer or on a smartphone. It gathers data from all the devices that measure heart rate, blood pressure, weight, temperature, liver values, and treatment plans from the care flow engine. The main purpose of this app is to ensure optimum treatment for typical complications that are most likely to occur. This system is effective in that it automatically evaluates the results, suggests the medication dose, and recommends courses of action that are then discussed between doctor and patient.

2.6 Telemedicine for finding nucleosome positioning

To obtain accurate diagnostic results, information should be available from the gene level. Many diseases are due to abnormal reactions associated with biological processes. A nucleosome is basic unit of eukaryotes. It provides important information for remote diagnosis, for example, gene base diagnosis can be quickly determined. In recent years, finding remote nucleosome positioning has become a hot topic of research [26]. Many methods have been proposed for this, for example, the hidden Markov model, the probabilistic graphical model, fractal entropy increment of diversity [27], and many software and R packages [11], which are applied for finding the position of a nucleosome.

2.7 Telemedicine in postsurgical care

Telemedicine provides services for the postoperative period [28], which is mainly divided into three parts: (1) scheduled follow-up, (2) routine and ongoing monitoring, and (3) management of issues. Follow-up clinic visits can be avoided with a telephone call or by online videoconferencing either from the patient's home or from a remote clinic site. The routine and ongoing monitoring of patients' symptoms can be collected by interview either by phone, videophone, or using text messages.

3 Security attacks and solutions

Attackers target healthcare systems to gain profit from users. These systems are vulnerable to penetration by malicious attacks. This decreases the efficiency and performance of the systems. Personal health data can be stolen by malicious users, specifically from hospital networks and insulin pump sensors. Security attacks are performed mainly on three levels: (1) attacks at the data collection level, (2) attacks at the transmission level, and (3) attacks at the storage level [6]. A generalized diagram for a telemedicine system is given in Fig. 2.

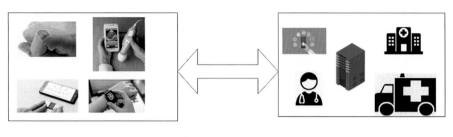

Data collection level Data transmission level Data storage level

FIG. 2

Generalized diagram for a telemedicine system.

3.1 Attacks at the data collection level

At the data collection level, several threats and attacks may cause the loss of important data, tempering information, or denial of services using buffer flow attacks. Some of the common attacks at this layer are discussed here.

3.1.1 Jamming attack

In a jamming attack, there is interference between radio signals and frequencies of the BAN [20]. This results in isolation of the sensor node from other sensor nodes. The attack prevents the sensor node from giving and receiving any messages as long as the jamming signal continues.

3.1.2 Data collision attack

When two or more nodes attempt to transmit data simultaneously, a collision attack takes place. The attacker strategically generates repeated messages on the channel. Due to the collision, the data header of the message is changed. At the receiving end, the error check mechanism detects this message as an error and rejects the received data. Thus the change in data frame header is a serious threat for the availability of the BAN.

3.1.3 Desynchronization attack

In a desynchronization attack, the attacker uses a fake sequence or control flag and copies the message between one or more endpoints of the active connection. The attacker desynchronizes the endpoints so that sensor nodes transmit the message again and again. This repeated transmission of the same packets wastes the energy of sensor nodes.

3.1.4 Spoofing attack

In a spoofing attack the attacker directly attacks a routing protocol. The attacker can cause several disruptions in the network such as spoofing, creation of routing loops, generation of fake error messages, alteration or replaying of routing information, network partitioning, attracting or repelling network traffic from selected nodes, extending or shortening source routes, and increasing end-to-end delay.

3.1.5 Selective forwarding attack
In this attack the malicious node drops the packets it likes and forwards the selected packets to cause minimum suspicion to neighboring nodes. This attack causes serious damage when the malicious node is located close to the base station.

3.1.6 Sybil attacks
The malicious attacker node pretends that the system has multiple identities of the authentic users in the network. Machine-to-machine connections using wireless and ad-hoc networks are most vulnerable to Sybil attack [29]. This type of attack has an adverse effect on geographic routing protocols, which are connected to exchange information between the nodes and their neighbors to route the geographically addressed packets efficiently. Tempering or resending the routing information can lead to denial of the services of the network by buffer overflows or creating routing self-loops. Due to these unpredictable and complex paths with high mobility of the attacker, it is challenging to detect the attack.

3.2 Attacks at the transmission level
Attack at the transmission level includes altering information, spying, and sending more signals to block the base station and networking traffic.

3.2.1 Man-in-the-middle attack
The attacker captures the communication process between the endpoints and exchanges the information between them. The attacker has full control over the communication and can read, insert, and modify the data in the hijacked communication.

3.2.2 Data tampering attack
The attacker can damage the encrypted data by authorized network nodes causing serious damage to the traffic.

3.2.3 Scrambling attack
A scrambling attack is a kind of jamming attack. It is made on a radio frequency for a short interval of time during transmission of control or management information WiMAX frames to affect the normal operation of the network. It can prevent a patient's smartphone from sending data, causing availability issues.

3.2.4 Signaling attack
The preliminary signaling operation is required before the patient's smartphone starts transmitting the data. Signaling operations contain key management, registration, and authentication IP-based connection establishment. The attacker can initiate a signaling attack on a serving base station by actuating other state signals that block the base station. The extra load on the base station results in a denial of service attack. Because the base station is unavailable, the patient's smartphone is not able to send data.

3.2.5 Unfairness in allocation
Network performance is reduced by interrupting the medium access control priority schemes.

3.2.6 Message modification attack

The attacker captures the patient's wireless channels. The attacker extracts the patient's medical data, which are then altered, misleading the involved users (doctors, nurses, family).

3.2.7 Hello flood attack

The attacker sends hello packets with powerful radio transmissions to the network. All the nodes are convinced to choose the attacker for routing their messages.

3.2.8 Data interception

The patient's information is intercepted by the attacker while exchanging it between computers of the healthcare system through the hospital local area network.

3.2.9 Wormhole attack

The aim of this attack is to change network topology and traffic flow. Two attackers can transmit their information through the tunnel that is created by this attack. This is the most severe type of attack. The attacker copies the packets at one location and replays them to another location or within the same network without changing the contents.

3.3 Attacks at the storage level

These attacks can modify the patient's medical information at the storage level, and can change the configuration of system monitoring servers.

3.3.1 Inference of patient's information

The attacker targets the patient's information by combining available data and authorized information. The attacker is then able to access the patient's information. Ideally the patient's data should be kept anonymous before publishing/posting to hide their identity.

3.3.2 Malware attack

Malware is a malicious program that is specially designed to perform harmful actions via infecting the whole system or machine. This program is so powerful that it can infect a whole hospital server. A malware attack causes unavailability and disruption in the system. Malware is able to change and update the configuration of patient monitoring servers. As a result, the system becomes unstable, which further results in malfunctioning and communication interruption.

3.3.3 Social engineering attacks

These kinds of attack are performed to benefit third parties such as insurance companies or unethical individuals. Access to the system is gained by a third-party attacker fooling either the authorized user or the patient. In this type of attack there is a high risk of disclosure of a patient's identity and personal information. Here, a patient's anonymity is at high risk.

3.3.4 Removable distribution media attack

This kind of attack is related to the hardware of the system and can result in theft or loss of data storage media such as a hard disk, computer, or USB flash drive. The hardware can also be used to propagate viruses and steal information from the telehealth system.

3.3.5 Security challenges and issues in telemedicine

Telemedicine is a new and advanced technology for healthcare systems. It is a cluster of many technologies, for example, the Internet of Things (IoT), big data, fog computing, medical imaging, machine learning, etc. These technologies are helpful in generating patient's EHRs [13]. A clinical decision support system and decision predict system are key aspects in the treatment and diagnosis of patients. The system is highly vulnerable and has many security issues due to new enhancements of technologies such as medical sensors and IoT.

For diagnosis, a patient's EHR [30] plays a significant role. This contains a large amount of multimedia information such as X-rays, CT and magnetic resonance imaging images, real-time information retrieved from body sensors, heart rate, etc. Such a large amount of data is kept on cloud systems or dedicated servers. These data are vulnerable to many threats such as inadequate medical information, data threats, privacy threats, misdiagnosis, security threats, etc.

The most significant issues that can occur in a health monitoring system are:

1. *Unauthorized access to patient medical data*: In e-health systems, privileges, access rights, integrity, and confidentiality should be clearly defined. If these essential parameters are not clearly defined, it means any malicious actions can be performed in the system, for example, a severe security threat, and patient health records can fall into the wrong hands.
2. *Attacks established at host estates*: Attacks on a host estate can occur in three forms: (a) hardware concession, (b) software concession, and (c) user concession. When hardware is faulty, this can generate serious security issues for users. It can read patient data incorrectly and data integrity can be lost. When patients are installing third-party applications on their devices, this application can contain viruses, or it can share patient information with the third party. The third party can attack the system resulting in the system malfunctioning. In a user concession, the attacker masquerading as the patient has unauthorized access to the patient network, resources, and devices. When there is any threat from the host end data, integrity cannot be assured.
3. *Internet security issues*: The internet is a primary source for transmitting medical data. These data are vulnerable to various security threats. The URL of some websites cannot be trusted because when patients use these websites, the medical information is open to a number of system vulnerabilities. In telemedicine network mostly we are using the public networks for data transmission. Most of the medical data is highly prone to various security attacks such as unauthorized attacks, alteration of patient records, theft of medical data, etc. So there is a high probability that patient receivers incorrect information or wrong prescription for drugs.
4. *Tracking user activity*: In an e-healthcare system, it is very easy to detect a user's activity through the analysis of data records from the system. One can easily deduce the activity performed by a user simply by examining the user's vital signs. Insurance companies could restrict access to insurance benefits. For patients who are using GPS-enabled devices, it is very easy for service providers to track their location.
5. *System security issues*: These issues include standard security protection related to hardware, software, human factors, storage, power failure, logical problems, network problems, natural disasters, secure processing, etc., and medical information should be transmitted securely. This secure transmission should have integrity, confidentiality, identification, authentication, authorization, and nonrepudiation.

6. *Alteration of medical data*: If an intruder attacks a system, patient information can be altered. Doctors can then misdiagnose a patient, which may result in life-threating conditions.

The next sections summarize some of the security solutions provided by many authors regarding the latest state-of-the-art for tackling the aforementioned attacks and issues in telemedicine.

3.4 Security solutions

1. Fragopoulos et al. [31] proposed a framework or architecture that fulfills the security gaps for medical devices because these devices and the data collected by them are vulnerable to security threats. The authors used MPEG-21 security standards in their framework to select and control access to medical data sent to hospital servers. For the protection of digital content, they used symmetric encryption algorithms like AES, RC4, or T-DES. Their proposed architecture has three entities: (1) the patient has a wearable embedded monitoring device (WEMD) that generates digital content, (2) a personal server collects data from the WEMD and prepares it for transfer (according to user directives it also generates valid licenses, which are MPEG-21 compatible), and (3) the digital rights management client has a software application that runs on the end user's device.

2. Maw et al. [32] proposed an adaptive access control model for medical data in body sensor networks and wireless sensor networks. In this paper, prevention and detection mechanisms are developed in a Ponder2 framework. The additional features of this framework are adapted with unexpected events by using privilege overriding; it is also capable of adjusting its decision according to the user's behavior trust value. The main limitations of this model are when a critical situation occurs, because the model lacks a prevention and detection mechanism to check it.

3. Sajedi and Jamzad [33] proposed various novel techniques for integrity, image authentication, and data hiding in medical images. To achieve their goals, they used a tree-based steganography technique. This tree-based approach provides effective and threat-free transmission over open and vulnerable networks. In the proposed method, the authors considered a medical image as having two parts: a region of interest and a region of noninterest (RONI). As a RONI does not contain any relevant information the medical data and checksum or watermark are embedded in it.

4. Hazzaa et al. [34] proposed a discrete wavelet-based digital watermarking technique that can detect any attempt at medical data theft. It uses blind detection for this purpose. This algorithm consists of two parts: an embedder and an extractor. The embedder is responsible for embedding a watermark in the medical image and the extractor is responsible for confirming the authentication of the medical image after it is sent through the network.

5. Rezaeibagha et al. [30] proposed a protocol that ensures confidentiality of patient information, mutual authentication, patient anonymity, and data integrity when patients and doctors are in transit. This protocol is based upon symmetric key schemes and also preserves the patient's anonymity.

6. Li et al. [35] proposed an efficient privacy-preserving protocol for sink node location in telemedicine networks (PSNL-TNs). Sink nodes are vulnerable to security threats because these nodes collect medical data in the network. In this paper, the authors also discussed energy consumption, safe time, evaluation metric, and delivery time in telemedicine networks (PSNL-TNs). The authors found that their schemes can reduce delivery time by 22.86%–27.61% and also safe time can be improved by 28.57%–52.70%.

7. Tan [36] proposed a secure delegation-based authentication protocol by using identity-based cryptography. The author proposed this protocol in answer to Kim et al.'s and Huang et al.'s delegation-based authentication protocols, which were based upon elliptic curve cryptography. The author has shown that Kim et al.'s and Huang et al.'s schemes are not secure for key attacks.

4 Limitations of telemedicine

Our purpose is to summarize the factors that are affecting telemedicine. We will discuss them in a convenient way to understand the limitations of telemedicine as follows.

Geography: If you are located in one geographical location, the virtual provider is located in another location, and there is a bad connection, you can claim for grievance or malpractice. However, there are no standards for physicians who are providing medical advice virtually, and there is no legal solution for service providers [37,38].

Malpractice: This area is related to sophisticated technologies, and these technologies are growing rapidly in the field of telemedicine. Examples of malpractice are inadequate signal strength, bad audio connection, signal distortion, and many other service problems that can occur in the system.

Standard of care: For in-patient visits, the standards for care are clearly defined. But the standards for telemedicine are not determined yet.

Data breaches: There is always a risk of data breach with any internet-based service.

Technical training and equipment: It takes a lot of efforts to train IT staff and purchase new technology. Training is a crucial part of the establishment of telemedicine services. It mainly depends upon the region of interest of the team. All staff must be fully trained.

Reduced care continuity: Patients who are using on-demand telemedicine services can connect to a random healthcare service provider. However, that service provider may not have a complete health record; this can reduce continuous care. They may not allow access to previous health records from the primary healthcare provider. Therefore virtual visits end up having an incomplete history. This shuffling of service providers may increase the possibility that the doctor does not know the patient history. Reduced care continuity can decrease the quality of care and customer satisfaction.

Tricky policies and reimbursement rules: Telemedicine is a fast-growing industry, yet it struggles with reimbursement policies, privacy protection rules, and healthcare laws [38]. Healthcare providers should be approached for the best telemedicine practices. Reimbursement policies are a standard stumbling block for healthcare providers. Hence, providers should first have some knowledge of reimbursement policies.

Fragmentation and alienation: Many healthcare professionals and doctors have some skepticism of telemedicine solutions. The main focus is concerned with the technology rather than the patient. In telemedicine, we treat the cases not the patients. Telemedicine splits patients into different categories, and each should be addressed separately with specialized, technical solutions. In telemedicine, there is a risk of losing the "whole patient." Sometimes patients may feel alienated from the treatment procedure. Patients' rights can be violated by fragmentation and alienation processes. Therefore patients' personal integrity should be respected by considering the patient as a whole living entity rather than just a technical case.

Security and confidentiality: Security and privacy are significant concerns of the telemedicine environment. This is the most discussed area of this technology [5,6,39,40]. The unlawful dissemination of patient information is a considerable concern. Confidentiality is essential for doctor-patient interaction, so technology should not jeopardize privacy. The doctor should protect patient information and patients' rights.

5 Role of IoT and cloud in telemedicine

IoT is a new area of the internet. The physical and digital worlds can be integrated by using IoT. IoT also plays an essential role in the field of telemedicine for the delivery of health services [41]. Various devices can be connected through the internet by IoT. Some examples are smart home-based telemedicine services, smart wheelchairs, GPS positioning applications for patients with heart diseases, mobile medicine, real-time health monitoring of a patient after discharge, monitoring Alzheimer's patients in their day-to-day life, body sensors, etc.

IoT can be considered an emerging network of physical devices or entities that contains an IP address for network connectivity. Communication takes place between the physical devices and internet-facilitated gadgets and frameworks. In the current scenario, automation can be done in nearly every field. IoT provides a cluster of benefits, along with enhanced and improved connectivity that is superior to node-to-node scenarios. High-quality e-health services can be provided to patients by IoT via remotely accessed technologies. For example, a doctor can offer prescriptions to his/her patients with medical facilities from a remote location. The patient can be situated in a distinct location (i.e., in the countryside, in a war zone, or in some remote location). Globally, healthcare services are a challenging issue in most developing and impoverished countries due to poor transportation infrastructure, limited numbers of services or doctors, etc. However, in some locations, medical services are insubstantial. In such situations, distributed and advanced healthcare services are provided by potential telemedicine technologies using the IoT infrastructure.

Hence, numerous healthcare devices, sensors, and diagnostic and scanning tools are smart gadgets that play a vital part in IoT. The design and development of the latest applications to serve the medical services in remote healthcare systems have been accelerated by wearable sensors. IoT-based healthcare services help reduce costs, provide patient satisfaction, and can upgrade the user's experience. IoT-based services could be beneficial for medical service providers by diminishing device downtime through remote acquisition. In brief, IoT-based healthcare applications can minimize cost, increase the quality of life, provide better efficiency of healthcare services, and provide corrective and preventive action on time. However, in the healthcare system, devices and applications handle patients' confidential, sensitive, and personal information. These smart devices are connected to the internet to facilitate medical services at anytime and anywhere. In such a scenario, these devices are targets for attackers. Therefore security and privacy are significant challenges in IoT-enabled devices.

6 Future of telemedicine

The large gap between patients and doctors has now been bridged by telemedicine services. These services provide more time for doctors to review cases, and the external support of physicians and specialists now make patients feel more in control of their health check-ups. A paper by Mordor Intelligence predicts that global telemedicine will be worth more than $66 billion by the end of

2021 [42]. The future of telemedicine includes disease heterogeneity, drug safety and development, precision medicine, and the cost effectiveness of care, epidemiology, and public health. Also decentralized care will become commonplace, patient-centered medical homes will become a reality, and there will be better investment opportunities and better healthcare apps [43].

6.1 Disease heterogeneity

Telemedicine approaches are instrumental in dealing with disease heterogeneity, for example, in inflammatory bowel disease (IBD) [44] and autoimmune diseases [45]. There are two types of IBD: ulcerative colitis and Crohn's disease. Ulcerative colitis affects only the colon (large intestine), whereas Crohn's disease affects the whole digestive system or any part of the digestive system. Around 60%–70% of people who have Crohn's disease need surgery to repair their digestive system [44]. A wide range of clinical phenotypes of IBD is possible regarding disease location, behavior, age, common symptoms, and other immune-mediated conditions. Big data approaches are constructive in classifying these clinical phenotypes. Big data approaches are hypothesis free in nature, therefore big data is helpful in identifying the various subgroups of patients. Data mining and other methodologies have a large number of variables from multiple sources and patients. Some studies are used in phenomapping to define distinct groups of patients with the help of big data approaches.

6.2 Precision medicine

In the past decade, there have been rapid advancements in the therapeutic pipeline. In the next few years, several new biologic and small compounds will be available [46]. For the sensible use of these therapeutics, it is very important for biomarkers to identify which patients will be benefit or be harmed by a particular drug. For the treatment of inflammatory conditions such as rheumatoid arthritis, psoriatic arthritis, juvenile arthritis, IBD, ankylosing spondylitis, and psoriasis, the tumor necrosis factor (TNF) inhibitor group of medications is used worldwide. Disease progression is stopped by these medications by reducing inflammation and targeting an inflammation-causing substance called TNF [47].

In healthy individuals an excess of TNF in the blood is automatically blocked. But in patients with rheumatic conditions, higher concentrations are found in the blood, which further results in inflammation and persistent symptoms. The disease effects on the body can be controlled by medications. These medications control the inflammation in the joints, gastrointestinal tract, and skin.

Various studies have been made to predict the response of anti-TNF therapy based on clinical information, such as disease duration, smoking status, and phenotype. Also, numerous retrospective studies have been made by post hoc analysis of clinical trials and by studying TNF gene polymorphisms, but the results are inconsistent, and there is a paucity of tools to predict anti-TNF response in clinical practice.

So, to provide proper medication to patients, the data should be taken from various sources. Integration of multiple data sources in big data studies will be helpful in the development of precision medicine for IBD. Also, different machine learning approaches can be applied to the available data sources to identify various disease phenotypes.

6.3 Drug safety

Safety concerns are always related to the discovery of new therapies. However, clinically relevant adverse events are difficult to trace under randomized controlled trials; such adverse events usually take years or decades to occur. Clinical trials are not able to predict adverse events. The study of these events currently depends upon postmarketing studies and increased risk. Various safety concerns related to these diseases are not clear yet because investment in time and money is needed. By using big data tools applied to drug safety [48] we can detect drug safety without using currently available tools.. For instance, pharmacovigilance can be improved by using text mining. Meaningful information is extracted from unstructured textual data sources to obtain data on adverse drug events from medical notes.

6.4 Decentralized care system

Decentralized clinical services provide specialists around the world with the possibility of seeing their patients without having to be present in person [49]. Today, we see examples of specialty telemedicine healthcare moving away from large settings to more community-based and cost-effective locations. Many hospitals are turning to decentralized care, especially for teleradiology services. These services are implemented with the help of community extension services or by partnering with an emergency care unit; they also attract younger physicians who enjoy flexible working hours.

6.5 Patient-centric medical homes will become a reality

Telemedicine is successful due to an increase in customer satisfaction because it is very convenient and easy to use for both doctors and patients. So, a rise in the number of customers receiving treatment in the comfort of their own homes, or being part of a medical home where patients with similar diseases are kept together [4,7,10], is to be expected. All facilities related to the treatment will be available at that medical home, for example, assistance with medicines, diet, measuring of vital signs, continuous care and support activities, etc.

6.6 Assistive technologies will become cheaper

Today, various assistive technologies are available for elderly and disabled people. For example, electric-powered wheelchairs for obstacle avoidance, robots for assisting older people, sensors for cognitively impaired persons, assist nurses, and technologies developed for assisting Alzheimer's patients with their with day-to-day life. As these technologies are in their infant phases, but when they are fully available, these technologies will become relatively cheaper.

6.7 Wearable, implantable, and microcapsule devices

Wearable, implantable, and microcapsule devices are a new range of technologies [50,51]. Patients wear these technologies or they are embedded in their dwellings. These devices provide real-time data to doctors in remote locations, and are connected to the service center or hospitals via wired or wireless networks. These devices can access patients' vital signs (blood pressure, respiration, body temperature, heart rate, fat, blood oxygenation, electrocardiogram [ECG] readings), as well as sleep parameters,

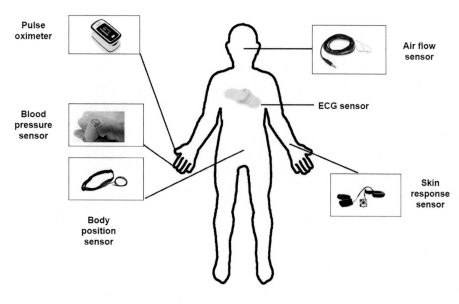

FIG. 3

Various wearable devices. *ECG,* electrocardiogram.

daily activities, and social interactions. The software embedded in these devices can detect emergency situations on the basis of the user's physical and physiological patterns, and data collected from motor activities. These devices are also helpful for older people suffering from chronic disease management such as heart attack, diabetes, and pulmonary disease. Usually, these devices are in the form of wearable devices like smart shirts or wearable healthcare assistants. For example, a smart shirt measures heart rhythm and respiration using a three-lead ECG shirt. Sense-Wear is a wearable device for physiological sign measurement. Life Reminder is a wearable healthcare assistant; it consists of a personal digital assistant, a biaxial accelerometer, a digital compass sensor, and an angular velocity sensor [50,51]. This system uses the nearest neighbor approach to locate the patient. Basically, it is used for tracking and measuring the activity of the patient. There are many more devices available. These devices are a new revolution in telemedicine networks. Various wearable devices are shown in Fig. 3.

6.8 Smart-based healthcare network

In general, smart homes provide devices for home appliance control (heating, air conditioning, bath water control, windows, doors, etc.) [51], as well as assistive devices (e.g., robotic assistant, companion robot, autonomous wheelchair, stair lift, etc.). In the future, the home-based system will become the basis of the healthcare system. These systems will be able to provide:

1. Teleconsultations and virtual visits by hospital-based health professionals.
2. Healthcare services, optimizing resources, diagnoses, and decision making for high-risk patients.

3. Treatment for most ailments except acute illness or investigations that require treatment in hospitals.

4. Postoperative, chemotherapy, asthma, chronic obstructive pulmonary disease, and diabetes treatment from health professionals at their homes.

Smart homes are designed to transmit patients' health status and data to dedicated centers. Vital sign measurement devices and mobility/activity sensors at home can transmit the data of some vital physiological signs such as blood pressure, respiration, body temperature, heart rate, glucose rate, body weight, blood oxygenation, ECG, and activity assessment. These parameters are used to build personalized data or a chart to warn the families or doctors in an adverse situation. The smart home can become part of a home-based healthcare system linked to the hospital, which is the center of the system.

7 Conclusion

Telemedicine is a new technological idea that "move the information, not the patient." This means we can get the right information at the right time. We are capable to treat the patients immediately without any delay. Moving the patient from one location to another location is always a time-consuming process. Sometimes the patient died because of not getting the proper treatment immediately. Telemedicine provides a technological revolution in healthcare services by providing emergency services immediately to the patient at his or her current location. It saves time, money and life of the patients. In telemedicine we exchange information by using image processing and video processing from patient to doctor. Whenever a patient needs to consult a doctor the information can be gathered locally and transmitted through the channel. In telemedicine, data are transmitted through the internet so there are security concerns related to patient privacy and anonymity.

References

[1] B. Klaassen, B.J. van Beijnum, H.J. Hermens, Usability in telemedicine systems—a literature survey, Int. J. Med. Inform. 93 (2016) 57–69.

[2] World Health Organization, Telemedicine: Opportunities and Developments in Member States. Report on the Second Global Survey on eHealth, World Health Organization, 2010.

[3] A. Vegesna, M. Tran, M. Angelaccio, S. Arcona, Remote patient monitoring via non-invasive digital technologies: a systematic review, Telemed. E Health 23 (1) (2017) 3–17.

[4] R. Sharma, K.S. Zachrison, J. Estrada, A. Viswanathan, L.H. Schwamm, Trends in telestroke care delivery: a 15-year experience, Stroke 50 (Suppl 1) (2019) A172.

[5] Z. Tan, Secure delegation-based authentication for telecare medicine information systems, IEEE Access 6 (2018) 26091–26110.

[6] C.X. Wang, Security issues to telemedicine system design, in: Proceedings IEEE Southeastcon'99. Technology on the Brink of 2000 (Cat. No. 99CH36300), IEEE, 1999, pp. 106–109.

[7] S.M. Finkelstein, S.M. Speedie, G. Demiris, M. Veen, J.M. Lundgren, S. Potthoff, Telehomecare: quality, perception, satisfaction, Telemed. J. E Health 10 (2) (2004) 122–128.

[8] D. Theodoros, T. Russell, R. Latifi, Telerehabilitation: current perspectives, Stud. Health Technol. Inform. 131 (2008) 191–210.

[9] J.T. Kilcoyne, R. Tsukashima, G.M. Johnson, C. Klecher, Remote physiological monitoring system, U.S. Patent 6,285,897, issued September 4, 2001.

[10] M.M. Lorentz, Telenursing and home healthcare: the many facets of technology, Home Healthc. Now 26 (4) (2008) 237–243.

[11] I. Torre Díez, S.G. Alonso, S. Hamrioui, M. López-Coronado, E.M. Cruz, Systematic review about QoS and QoE in telemedicine and eHealth services and applications, J. Med. Syst. 42 (10) (2018) 182.

[12] C. Boissin, L. Blom, W. Lee, L. Laflamme, Image-based teleconsultation using smartphones or tablets: qualitative assessment of medical experts, Emerg. Med. J. 34 (2) (2017) 95–99.

[13] M.L. Graber, D. Siegal, H. Riah, D. Johnston, K. Kenyon, Electronic health record-related events in medical malpractice claims, J. Patient Saf. 15 (2) (2019) 77–85.

[14] M.P. LaMonte, J. Cullen, D.M. Gagliano, R. Gunawardane, P. Hu, C. Mackenzie, Y. Xiao, TeleBAT: mobile telemedicine for the brain attack team, J. Stroke Cerebrovasc. Dis. 9 (3) (2000) 128–135.

[15] J.M. Roth, Recombinant tissue plasminogen activator for the treatment of acute ischemic stroke, Proc. (Baylor Univ. Med. Cent.) 24 (3) (2011) 257–259.

[16] M. Rigla, I. Martínez-Sarriegui, G. García-Sáez, B. Pons, M.E. Hernando, Gestational diabetes management using smart mobile telemedicine, J. Diabetes Sci. Technol. 12 (2) (2018) 260–264.

[17] D. Rodbard, Continuous glucose monitoring: a review of successes, challenges, and opportunities, Diabetes Technol. Ther. 18 (S2) (2016) S2–S3.

[18] V. Piemonte, M. Capocelli, L. De Santis, A.R. Maurizi, P. Pozzilli, A novel three-compartmental model for artificial pancreas: development and validation, Artif. Organs 41 (12) (2017) E326–E336.

[19] M. Peleg, Y. Shahar, S. Quaglini, Making healthcare more accessible, better, faster, and cheaper: the MobiGuide project, Eur. J. ePractice Issue Mobile eHealth 20 (2014) 5–20.

[20] M.M. Hassan, K. Lin, X. Yue, J. Wan, A multimedia healthcare data sharing approach through cloud-based body area network, Futur. Gener. Comput. Syst. 66 (2017) 48–58.

[21] K. Canese, S. Weis, PubMed: the bibliographic database, in: The NCBI Handbook (Internet). 2nd ed., National Center for Biotechnology Information, USA, 2013.

[22] S. Franc, Telemedicine and diabetes, in: Handbook of Diabetes Technology, Springer, Cham, 2019, pp. 95–110.

[23] P.J. Choi, R.J. Oskouian, R.S. Tubbs, Telesurgery: past, present, and future, Cureus 10 (5) (2018) e2716.

[24] M. Serper, M.L. Volk, Current and future applications of telemedicine to optimize the delivery of care in chronic liver disease, Clin. Gastroenterol. Hepatol. 16 (2) (2018) 157–161.

[25] S. Kiefer, M. Schäfer, M. Bransch, P. Brimmers, D. Bartolomé, J. Baños, J. Orr, D. Jones, M. Jara, M. Stockmann, A novel personal health system with integrated decision support and guidance for the management of chronic liver disease, MIE (2014) 83–87.

[26] M. Lu, S. Liu, A.K. Sangaiah, Y. Zhou, P. Zheng, Y. Zuo, Nucleosome positioning with fractal entropy increment of diversity in telemedicine, IEEE Access 6 (2017) 33451–33459.

[27] M. Lu, S. Liu, A.K. Sangaiah, Y. Zhou, P. Zheng, Y. Zuo, Nucleosome positioning with fractal entropy increment of diversity in telemedicine, IEEE Access 6 (2017) 33451–33459.

[28] S. Canon, A. Shera, A. Patel, I. Zamilpa, J. Paddack, P.L. Fisher, J. Smith, R. Hurtt, A pilot study of telemedicine for post-operative urological care in children, J. Telemed. Telecare 20 (8) (2014) 427–430.

[29] B.N. Levine, C. Shields, N.B. Margolin, A Survey of Solutions to the Sybil Attack, 7, University of Massachusetts Amherst, Amherst, MA, 2006, p. 224.

[30] F. Rezaeibagha, K.T. Win, W. Susilo, A systematic literature review on security and privacy of electronic health record systems: technical perspectives, Health Inf. Manag. J. 44 (3) (2015) 23–38.

[31] A.G. Fragopoulos, J. Gialelis, D. Serpanos, Imposing holistic privacy and data security on person centric eHealth monitoring infrastructures, in: The 12th IEEE International Conference on e-Health Networking, Applications and Services, IEEE, 2010, pp. 127–134.

[32] H.A. Maw, H. Xiao, B. Christianson, J.A. Malcolm, BTG-AC: break-the-glass access control model for medical data in wireless sensor networks, IEEE J. Biomed. Health Inform. 20 (3) (2015) 763–774.

[33] H. Sajedi, M. Jamzad, Secure steganography based on embedding capacity, Int. J. Inf. Secur. 8 (6) (2009) 433.

[34] H.M. Hazzaa, S.K. Ahmed, Watermarking algorithm for medical images authentication, in: 2015 4th International Conference on Advanced Computer Science Applications and Technologies (ACSAT), IEEE, 2015, pp. 239–244.

[35] T. Li, Y. Liu, N.N. Xiong, A. Liu, Z. Cai, H. Song, Privacy-preserving protocol for sink node location in telemedicine networks, IEEE Access 6 (2018) 42886–42903.

[36] Z. Tan, Secure delegation-based authentication for telecare medicine information systems, IEEE Access 6 (2018) 26091–26110.

[37] S. Gardiner, T.L. Hartzell, Telemedicine and plastic surgery: a review of its applications, limitations and legal pitfalls, J. Plast. Reconstr. Aesthet. Surg. 65 (3) (2012) e47–e53.

[38] S.A. Haque, S.M. Aziz, M. Rahman, Review of cyber-physical system in healthcare, Int. J. Distrib. Sensor Netw. 10 (4) (2014) 217415.

[39] M. Hussain, A.-H. Ahmed, A.A. Zaidan, B.B. Zaidan, M. Kiah, S. Iqbal, S. Iqbal, M. Abdulnabi, A security framework for mHealth apps on android platform, Comput. Secur. 75 (2018) 191–217.

[40] E. Guillen, P. Estupiñan, C. Lemus, L. Ramirez, Analysis of security requirements in telemedicine networks, in: Proceedings of the International Conference on Security and Management (SAM), The Steering Committee of the World Congress in Computer Science, Computer Engineering and Applied Computing (World-Comp), 2011, p. 1.

[41] M. Talal, A.A. Zaidan, B.B. Zaidan, A.S. Albahri, A.H. Alamoodi, O.S. Albahri, M.A. Alsalem, et al., Smart home-based IoT for real-time and secure remote health monitoring of triage and priority system using body sensors: multi-driven systematic review, J. Med. Syst. 43 (3) (2019) 42.

[42] R.M. Marcoux, F.R. Vogenberg, Telehealth: applications from a legal and regulatory perspective, Pharm. Ther. 41 (9) (2016) 567.

[43] M. Serper, M.L. Volk, Current and future applications of telemedicine to optimize the delivery of care in chronic liver disease, Clin. Gastroenterol. Hepatol. 16 (2) (2018) 157–161.

[44] J. Burisch, P. Munkholm, The epidemiology of inflammatory bowel disease, Scand. J. Gastroenterol. 50 (8) (2015) 942–951.

[45] A. Lerner, P. Jeremias, T. Matthias, The world incidence and prevalence of autoimmune diseases is increasing, Int. J. Celiac Dis. 3 (4) (2015) 151–155.

[46] C. Jobin, Precision medicine using microbiota, Science 359 (6371) (2018) 32–34.

[47] L.J. Old, Tumor necrosis factor, Science 230 (1985) 630–633.

[48] W. Raghupathi, V. Raghupathi, Big data analytics in healthcare: promise and potential, Health Inf. Sci. Syst. 2 (1) (2014) 3.

[49] E.-L. Nelson, D.M. Yadrich, N. Thompson, S. Wright, K. Stone, N. Adams, et al., Telemedicine support groups for home parenteral nutrition users, Nutr. Clin. Pract. 32 (6) (2017) 789–798.

[50] S. Pirbhulal, O.W. Samuel, W. Wu, A.K. Sangaiah, G. Li, A joint resource-aware and medical data security framework for wearable healthcare systems, Futur. Gener. Comput. Syst. 95 (2019) 382–391.

[51] M. Chan, E. Campo, D. Estève, J.-Y. Fourniols, Smart homes—current features and future perspectives, Maturitas 64 (2) (2009) 90–97.

Despeckling of ultrasound images based on the multiresolution approach and Gaussianization transform

Sima Sahu[a], Amit Kumar Singh[b], Harsh Vikram Singh[c], and Basant Kumar[d]

St. Martin's Engineering College, Secunderabad, India[a] Department of Computer Science and Engineering, NIT Patna, Patna, Bihar, India[b] Department of Electronics, Kamla Nehru Institute of Technology (KNIT), Sultanpur, Uttar Pradesh, India[c] Department of ECE, Motilal Nehru National Institute of Technology Allahabad, Prayagraj, India[d]

1 Introduction

Image processing contributes to the diagnosis of diseases. Image processing has been effectively used for the mass screening of diseases. Image enhancement and continuous monitoring of diseases are possible using digital image processing. Due to noise and poor contrast of the acquired image, image enhancement is required for human interpretation, proper visual inspection, and automatic analysis [1,2].

Ultrasound imaging is a noninvasive method for imaging tissues and internal body parts for humans. This modality is economical and highly portable, and thus widely used compared to other imaging modalities. Medical ultrasound imaging suffers from speckle noise and thus for correct diagnosis and analysis, removal of noise is essential [3,4]. A transducer produces an ultrasonic wave that is used to send human tissues and another transducer transforms the returned wave into an electrical signal. Furthermore, the electrical signal is transformed into a digital signal using a scanner [5]. Noise in an ultrasound image occurs due to the produced air gap between the human body and the transducer. An ultrasound image is affected by speckle noise, which results in inaccurate interpretation of the data [6]. Fig. 1 shows speckle noise removal techniques for an ultrasound image.

Ultrasound image denoising methods can be classified as an algorithmic approach and a statistical approach. Filtering methods based on the algorithmic approach are designed using their spatial and frequency behaviors. Different mathematical transforms such as wavelet and contourlet transform the image into coefficients and thresholds to obtain noise-free coefficients and thus a noise-free image.

Statistically approached denoising methods are based on a probabilistic model. The probability distribution function (PDF) plays an important role in finding the statistical behavior of an image. Approximating a suitable PDF for the transform coefficients, the statistical characteristics of an image can be discovered.

Intelligent Data Security Solutions for e-Health Applications. https://doi.org/10.1016/B978-0-12-819511-6.00014-5

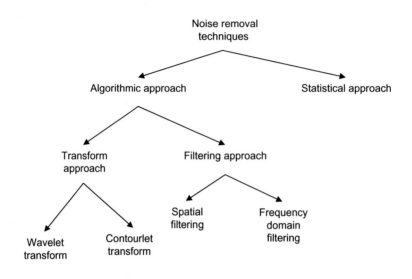

FIG. 1

Classification of noise removal techniques for an ultrasound image.

Statistical parameters can be estimated using Bayesian estimators such as maximum a posteriori (MAP), minimum mean square error (MMSE), maximum likelihood, etc. Other nonparametric estimation methods such as histogram equalization or K-nearest neighbor (KNN) are also used for estimating parameters.

Parameters can be estimated using different techniques such as parametric, nonparametric, and semiparametric. Semiparametric methods such as a scale mixture of Gaussian and a scale mixture of Laplace are used for parameter estimation. The computational complexity of semiparametric methods is better than parametric methods. Nonparametric methods are mathematically complex and costly in terms of memory and computation.

Spatial domain filters (average, adaptive weighted, median) and frequency domain filters such as Wiener filters, etc. can effectively reduce additive noise but are inefficient at reducing speckle noise. Frost filters, Lee filters, and Kuan filters are spatially adaptive filters used to reduce speckle noise. But these methods fail to preserve information. In the literature, diffusion filters [7], bilateral filters [8], and nonlocal mean filters [9] have been proposed to denoise ultrasound images. The transform domain approach is proven to remove speckle noise more efficiently than the filtering approach [10,11].

Table 1 shows the different state-of-the art speckle denoising methods. The estimators and priors used by those methods are also discussed.

This chapter introduces a new and improved despeckling method using the statistical approach. Along with the statistical approach, another procedure called the Gaussianization procedure is also introduced to correctly model the ultrasound image and estimate the unknown parameters.

In the literature, the Gaussianization procedure was implemented by many authors for different applications as shown in Fig. 2.

This chapter is organized as follows. Section 2 discusses the background and basic principles of the proposed method. Wavelet transform is discussed in Section 2.1. Section 2.2 discusses the statistical

Table 1 State-of-the art speckle removal techniques.

References	Method
Rabbani et al. [12]	• MAP and MMSE estimators • Gaussian and Laplace mixture prior • Assumed Gaussian PDF and Rayleigh PDF for noise
Achim et al. [13]	• MMSE estimator • Alpha-stable estimator
Bhuiyan et al. [14]	• MMSE estimator • Normal inverse Gaussian prior
Sadreazami et al. [15]	• MAP estimator • Cauchy prior to model contourlet coefficient
Ranjani and Chithra [16]	• Levy PDF
Bhuiyan et al. [17]	• MMAE estimator • Cauchy prior
Bibalan and Amindava [18]	• Mixture ratio estimator • Rayleigh and Rayleigh PDFs
Jafari and Ghofrani [19]	• MAP estimator • Levy PDF to recover nonsubsampled shearlet transform
Lu et al. [20]	• MAP estimator • Laplace mixture prior
Chang et al. [21]	• Generalized Gaussian prior

MAP, *maximum a posteriori;* MMAE, *minimum mean absolute error;* MMSE, *minimum mean square error;* PDF, *probability density function.*

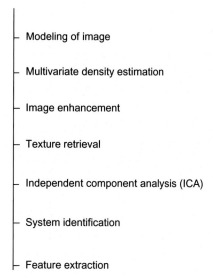

Applications of Gaussianization procedure

├ Modeling of image

├ Multivariate density estimation

├ Image enhancement

├ Texture retrieval

├ Independent component analysis (ICA)

├ System identification

├ Feature extraction

FIG. 2

Applications of the Gaussianization procedure.

modeling of an ultrasound image. The goodness-of-fit analysis is discussed in Section 2.3. Section 2.4 explains the Gaussianization procedure applied to ultrasound data. Section 2.5 explains about the Bayesian MMSE estimator. The proposed despeckling algorithm is discussed in Section 3. Numerical and visual results are presented in Section 4. Section 5 concludes the chapter.

2 Background and basic principles

Major operations and their basic principles are discussed in this section. This section gives a brief idea about discrete wavelet transform (DWT), its modeling, and Bayesian estimator.

2.1 Discrete wavelet transform

The DWT of a two-dimensional image can be found by applying one-dimensional DWT to all rows and then to all columns. A single-level DWT is shown in Fig. 3.

In Fig. 3, $I_{p,\,q}$ is the two-dimensional image. The wavelet coefficients $W(p,q)$ are given by:

$$W(p,q) = \frac{1}{\sqrt{PQ}}\left[\sum_{i=1}^{M}\sum_{j=1}^{N}f_L^A(i,j)\Phi_L^A(p,q,i,j) + \sum_{l=1}^{L}\sum_{K\in H,V,D}\sum_{i=1}^{P}\sum_{j=1}^{Q}f_l^K(i,j)\Psi_l^K(p,q,i,j)\right] \quad (1)$$

where $f_L^A, f_l^{K\in V}, f_l^{K\in H}$, and $f_l^{K\in D}$ denote approximation coefficients, vertical coefficients, horizontal coefficients, and diagonal coefficients, respectively. Ψ and Φ are the two-dimensional wavelet coefficient and scaling coefficient, respectively. In this figure, horizontal, vertical, diagonal, and approximation sub-bands are denoted by LH1, HL1, HH1, and LL1, respectively [22]. For an ultrasound image the third-level decomposition is shown in Fig. 4. A second-level decomposition is obtained by decomposing the approximation sub-band from the first level. For the next higher levels, the aforementioned procedure is repeated.

Inverse discrete wavelet transform (IDWT) is the reverse operation of DWT. Fig. 5 shows the one-level IDWT procedure. Here, two synthesis filters, low pass (h_φ) and high pass (h_ψ), are used for the reconstruction of the image [23].

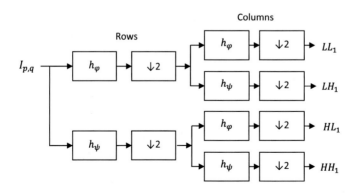

FIG. 3

One-level two-dimensional discrete wavelet transform.

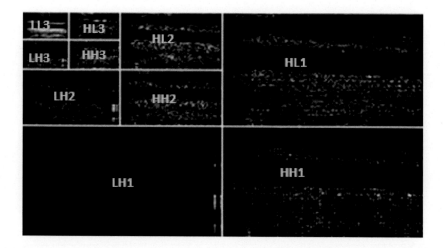

FIG. 4

Three-level sub-band representation of a two-dimensional discrete wavelet transform.

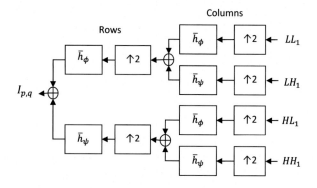

FIG. 5

One-level two-dimensional inverse discrete wavelet transform.

2.2 Distribution of wavelet coefficients and their statistical modeling

The wavelet coefficient distribution is shown in Fig. 6. Fig. 7 shows the PDF for the approximation sub-band. Fig. 8 shows the PDF for the horizontal sub-band. Vertical and diagonal sub-band coefficient distributions are shown in Figs. 9 and 10, respectively. From the density graph it can be seen that the distribution of wavelet coefficients in these sub-bands is heavy tailed in shape. To properly define the density, a long tail behavior PDF is required. In the literature, the various PDFs proposed are Levy, Cauchy, and normal inverse Gaussian, etc. In this chapter a Cauchy PDF is proposed to define the density function of wavelet coefficients due to its symmetric and unimodal property. Cauchy PDF is a stable distribution, so the parameters of the Cauchy distribution can thus be analytically tractable. The distribution of wavelet coefficients is heavy tailed at zero, so a Cauchy PDF assuming zero location parameter is applied for modeling the generated wavelet coefficients.

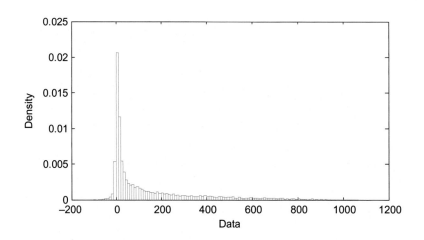

FIG. 6

Wavelet coefficient distribution in an ultrasound image.

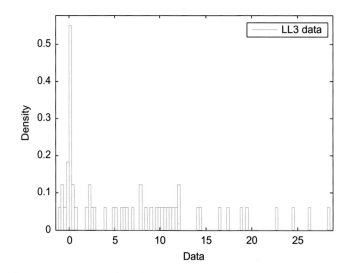

FIG. 7

Probability density function for an approximation sub-band.

The PDF of a Cauchy PDF is given by:

$$f_x(X) = \left(\frac{1}{\pi}\right)\left(\frac{\gamma}{x^2 + \gamma^2}\right) \tag{2}$$

where X defines the random variable (Cauchy) and the scaling parameter γ indicates half width at half maximum. Fig. 11 shows a Cauchy density function for various values of the scaling parameter and here the location parameter is assumed to be of zero value.

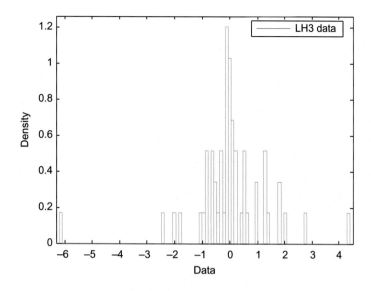

FIG. 8

Probability density function for a horizontal sub-band.

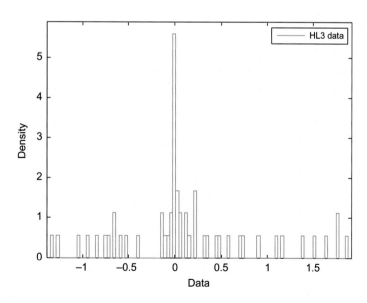

FIG. 9

Vertical sub-band coefficient distribution.

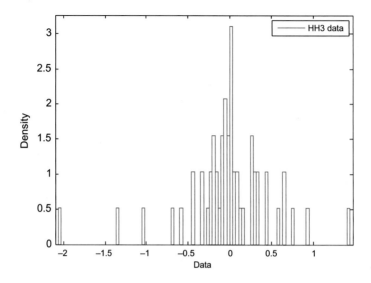

Diagonal sub-band coefficient distribution.

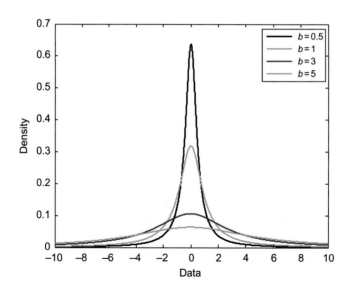

Cauchy density function.

2.3 Goodness-of-fit analysis

To retrieve the statistical measure from the wavelet coefficients, they must be suitably modeled. The goodness-of-fit analysis for a Cauchy PDF is shown in Figs. 12 and 13. Fig. 12 shows the goodness-of-fit for normal and Cauchy PDFs for a vertical sub-band at level 3. Fig. 13 shows the goodness-of-fit for a normal and Cauchy PDF and for a horizontal sub-band at level 3.

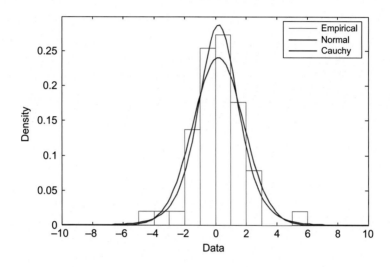

FIG. 12

Goodness-of-fit for Cauchy and normal PDFs for a vertical sub-band at level 3.

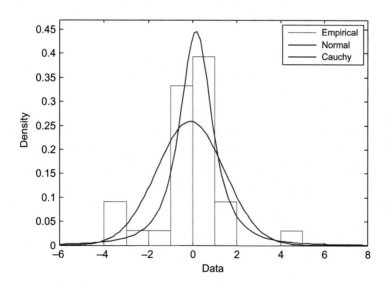

FIG. 13

Goodness-of-fit for Cauchy and normal PDFs for a horizontal sub-band at level 3.

2.4 Gaussianization transformation

Gaussianity and stationarity play a vital role in signal processing [24–26]. This chapter utilizes the Gaussianity property for accurate density estimation. The best denoising result is achieved if the density of the original signal is retrieved effectively. Gaussianization transformation Gaussianizes the dataset by transforming to a Gaussian PDF and hence maps the wavelet coefficients in a wide range. So, a sharp estimation of density is possible. This results in the correct density estimation of the noise-free wavelet coefficients. The procedure of Gaussianization transform is explained as follows:

1. Obtain the cumulative distribution function (CDF) of the wavelet coefficients.
2. Equalize the CDF of the empirical distribution with the Gaussian CDF.
3. Obtain the Gaussian PDF.

Consider a Cauchy random variable X_1 whose CDF and PDF are given by $F_{X_1}(x_1)$ and $f_{X_1}(x_1)$. Let PDF and CDF of a Gaussian random variable, X_2, be defined as:

$$f_{X_2}(x_2) = \frac{1}{\sigma\sqrt{2\pi}} e^{-\frac{(x_2-\mu)^2}{2\sigma^2}} \tag{3}$$

$$F_{X_2}(x_2) = \frac{1}{2}\left[1 + \operatorname{erf}\left(\frac{x_2-\mu}{\sigma\sqrt{2}}\right)\right] \tag{4}$$

where σ is the standard deviation and μ is the mean of the distribution. To Gaussianize the empirical data, the PDFs are equalized:

$$F_{X_2}(x_2) = F_{X_1}(x_1) = \frac{1}{2}\left[1 + \operatorname{erf}\left(\frac{x_2-\mu}{\sigma\sqrt{2}}\right)\right] \tag{5}$$

where *erf* is the error function defined as:

$$\operatorname{erf}(p) = \frac{2}{\sqrt{\pi}} \int_0^p e^{-t^2} dt \tag{6}$$

The Gaussianized data are given by [27]:

$$\hat{X}_2 = \mu + \sqrt{2}\sigma . erfinv(2F_{X_1}(x_1) - 1) \tag{7}$$

where *erfinv* is the inverse error function such that $erf(erfinv(p)) = p$ and $\hat{X}_2$ is the Gaussianized random variable containing the Gaussianized data. Replacing X_2 with $\hat{X}_2$ in Eq. (3) results in a Gaussianized density function.

2.5 Bayesian MMSE estimator

In this chapter, an MMSE estimator is used for estimating the signal parameters. MMSE is a Bayesian estimator and follows the Bayesian rule. Let A and B be two random variables with PDF $f(A)$ and $f(B)$. Bayes rule is defined as:

$$f(A|B) = \frac{f(B|A)f(A)}{f(B)} \tag{8}$$

where $f(A|B)$ is the posteriori or conditional density function of A given B, $f(B|A)$ is the likelihood of the observed signal, and $f(B)$ is known as the normalizing factor. The Bayesian estimator aims to reduce the Bayesian risk function. The Bayesian risk function is defined as:

$$
\begin{aligned}
\mathcal{R}(\hat{A}) &= E\left[L(\hat{A}, A)\right] \\
&= \int_{-\infty}^{\infty} \int_{-\infty}^{\infty} L(\hat{A}, A) f(A, B) dB dA
\end{aligned}
\tag{9}
$$

where E is the expectation operation, L is the loss function, and $f(A,B)$ is the joint density function of A and B. The joint PDF is defined as:

$$
f(A, B) = f(A|B) f(B)
\tag{10}
$$

Substituting the value of the posteriori density function, Eq. (9) can be written as:

$$
\mathcal{R}(\hat{A}) = \int_{-\infty}^{\infty} \int_{-\infty}^{\infty} L(\hat{A}, A) f(A|B) f(B) dB dA
\tag{11}
$$

The conditional risk function is defined as:

$$
\mathcal{R}(\hat{A}|B) = \int_{-\infty}^{\infty} C(\hat{A}, A) f(A|B) dA
\tag{12}
$$

The Bayesian estimation of parameter vector A can be discovered by minimizing the Bayesian risk function and is given by:

$$
\begin{aligned}
\hat{A}_{Bayesian} &= \arg \min_{\hat{A}} \mathcal{R}(\hat{A}|B) \\
&= \arg \min_{\hat{A}} \left[\int_{-\infty}^{\infty} C(\hat{A}, A) f(A|B) dA \right]
\end{aligned}
\tag{13}
$$

The Bayesian risk function can be minimized in several ways. MMSE estimation results by minimizing the mean square error of the cost function. It can be written as:

$$
\begin{aligned}
\mathcal{R}_{MMSE}(\hat{A}|B) &= E\left[\left((\hat{A} - A)^2 | B\right)\right] \\
&= \int_{-\infty}^{\infty} (\hat{A} - A)^2 f(A|B) dA
\end{aligned}
\tag{14}
$$

MMSE estimation can be obtained by minimizing the gradient risk function to zero as shown here:

$$
\begin{aligned}
\frac{d\mathcal{R}_{MMSE}(\hat{A}|B)}{d\hat{P}} &= 2\hat{A} \int_{-\infty}^{\infty} f(A|B) dA - 2 \int_{-\infty}^{\infty} A f(A|B) dA \\
2\hat{A} &- 2 \int_{-\infty}^{\infty} A f(A|B) dA = 0
\end{aligned}
\tag{15}
$$

$$
\Rightarrow \hat{A}_{MMSE} = \int_{-\infty}^{\infty} A f(A|B) dA
\tag{16}
$$

3 Methodology

The proposed despeckling is obtained by combining the Gaussianization procedure with statistical modeling. Initially, the wavelet coefficients are generated using the wavelet transform and modeled using Cauchy PDF. Furthermore, the wavelet coefficients are Gausssianized to find the noise and signal parameters. The image is recovered by estimating the optimum threshold value. The block diagram is shown in Fig. 14 and the complete procedure is summarized here.

Step 1: Application of a homomorphic approach to convert the image from spatial domain to logarithmic domain.
Step 2: Generate wavelet coefficients by using the DWT.
Step 3: Fit the Cauchy model to the data.
Step 4: Generate Gaussianized data.
Step 5: Calculate the variance of signal and noise.
Step 6: Generate the threshold value by using the MMSE estimator.

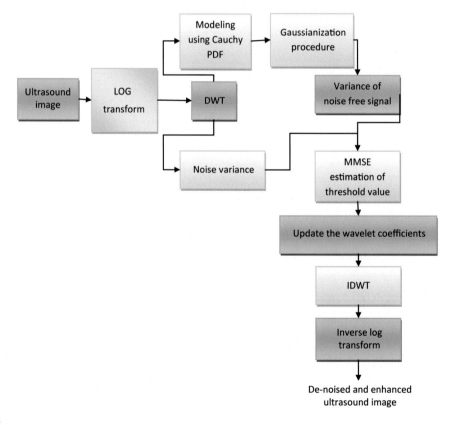

FIG. 14

Block diagram of the proposed despeckling algorithm. *DWT*, discrete wavelet transform; *IDWT*, inverse discrete wavelet transform; *MMSE*, minimum mean square error; *PDF*, probability density function.

Step 7: Threshold the wavelet coefficients.

Step 8: Application of IDWT to the updated wavelet coefficients.

Step 9: Application of inverse log transform to obtain the denoised image.

4 Simulation results

This section presents the simulation results performed on the real ultrasound image (538×340) and synthetic phantom image (256×256). The proposed method is simulated using third-level 8 dB (Daubechies group) wavelet decomposition. The algorithm is realized both qualitatively and quantitatively using a Matlab environment. The denoising performance of the combined denoising method is provided qualitatively and quantitatively. Through comparison with the state-of-the-art methods, the need for introducing a Gaussianization procedure and benefit is proved. The proposed ultrasound despeckling algorithm for an ultrasound image is compared with Cauchy-shrink [28], Cao et al. [29], and Zaki et al. [30]. The performance comparison and proposed method's efficacy is verified and proved through performance measurement parameters such as structural similarity index (SSIM), peak signal-to-noise ratio (PSNR), correlation coefficient (CoC), and edge preserving index (EPI). The qualitative comparison of the proposed method for real and synthetic images is shown in Figs. 15 and 16, respectively.

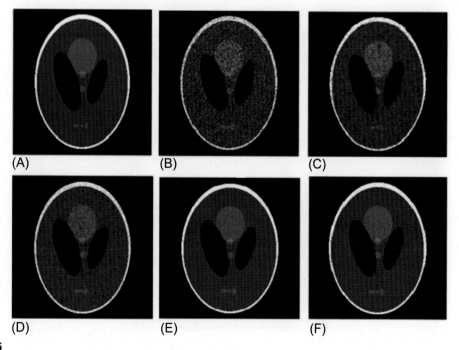

FIG. 15

Denoising results in the phantom image. (A) Original image. (B) Noisy image with variance 0.2. (C) Image denoising using Cauchy-shrink [28]. (D) Image denoising using Cao et al. [29]. (E) Image denoising using Zaki et al. [30]. (F) Proposed method.

The performance parameter comparisons for various methods for synthetic phantom images are shown in Tables 2–5. The performance comparison of various parameters for an ultrasound image is shown in Table 6. A detailed explanation of performance parameters is as follows.

(i) PSNR: For a good-quality image, a high value of PSNR is required

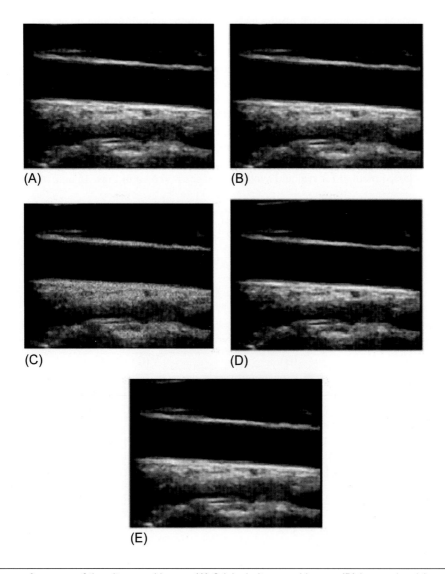

FIG. 16

Denoising performance of the ultrasound image. (A) Original ultrasound image. (B) Image denoising using Cauchy-shrink [28]. (C) Image denoising using Cao et al. [29]. (D) Image denoising using Zaki et al. [30]. (E) Proposed method.

Table 2 Peak signal-to-noise ratio (dB) result for the phantom image.

Techniques	Noise variance (σ_n^2)		
	$\sigma_n^2 = 0.1$	$\sigma_n^2 = 0.3$	$\sigma_n^2 = 0.5$
Noisy	22.12	16.45	14.63
Cauchy-shrink [28]	26.22	21.36	18.35
Cao et al. [29]	27.54	25.22	23.46
Zaki et al. [30]	33.67	32.99	25.75
Proposed method	33.97	33.83	32.58

Table 3 Structural similarity index result for the phantom image.

Techniques	Noise variance (σ_n^2)		
	$\sigma_n^2 = 0.1$	$\sigma_n^2 = 0.3$	$\sigma_n^2 = 0.5$
Noisy	0.737	0.633	0.582
Cauchy-shrink [28]	0.853	0.746	0.680
Cao et al. [29]	0.874	0.839	0.721
Zaki et al. [30]	0.947	0.917	0.835
Proposed method	0.967	0.942	0.934

Table 4 Correlation coefficient result for the phantom image.

Techniques	Noise variance (σ_n^2)		
	$\sigma_n^2 = 0.1$	$\sigma_n^2 = 0.3$	$\sigma_n^2 = 0.5$
Noisy	0.855	0.758	0.645
Cauchy-shrink [28]	0.977	0.854	0.828
Cao et al. [29]	0.959	0.881	0.835
Zaki et al. [30]	0.987	0.959	0.867
Proposed method	0.990	0.978	0.943

Table 5 Edge preserving index result for the phantom image.

Techniques	Noise variance (σ_n^2)		
	$\sigma_n^2 = 0.1$	$\sigma_n^2 = 0.3$	$\sigma_n^2 = 0.5$
Noisy	0.325	0.276	0.188
Cauchy-shrink [28]	0.545	0.534	0.422
Cao et al. [29]	0.664	0.585	0.448
Zaki et al. [30]	0.751	0.613	0.648
Proposed method	0.776	0.694	0.663

Table 6 Ultrasound image quality metrics.

Methods	Noise standard deviation ($\sigma_n = 0.4$)			Noise standard deviation ($\sigma_n = 0.5$)		
	SSIM	CoC	EPI	SSIM	CoC	EPI
Without filtering	0.488	0.287	0.224	0.412	0.244	0.189
Cauchy-shrink [28]	0.767	0.946	0.678	0.651	0.954	0.665
Cao et al. [29]	0.774	0.956	0.743	0.659	0.943	0.731
Zaki et al. [30]	0.782	0.966	0.775	0.702	0.955	0.746
Proposed method	0.795	0.977	0.829	0.737	0.960	0.814

CoC, *correlation coefficient;* EPI, *edge preserving index;* SSIM, *structural similarity index.*

$$PSNR = 20 \log_{10} \frac{255}{\sqrt{mse}} \tag{17}$$

The mean squared error (*mse*) is defined as:

$$mse = \frac{1}{r \times c} \sum_{i=1}^{r \times c} \left(\hat{I}_{p,q} - I_{p,q} \right)^2 \tag{18}$$

where $r \times c$ is the image size and $I_{p, q}$ and $\hat{I}_{p,q}$ are original and despeckled image, respectively:

$$S/mse = 10 \log_{10} \left(\sum_{i=1}^{r \times c} I_{p,q}^2 \bigg/ \sum_{i=1}^{r \times c} \left(\hat{I}_{p,q} - I_{p,q} \right)^2 \right) \tag{19}$$

(ii) CoC defines the interdependence between the true image and recovered image. The CoC of a perfect image is 1. CoC is defined as:

$$CoC = \frac{\text{cov}\left(I_{p,q}, \hat{I}_{p,q} \right)}{\sigma_{I_{p,q}} \sigma_{\hat{I}_{p,q}}} \tag{20}$$

where $\sigma_{\hat{I}_{p,q}}$ and $\sigma_{I_{p,q}}$ are the standard deviations of expected image and noise-free image, respectively. *cov* denotes covariance operation and is expressed as:

$$\text{cov}\left(I_{p,q}, \hat{I}_{p,q} \right) = E \left[\left(I_{p,q} - E[I_{p,q}] \right) \left(\hat{I}_{p,q} - E[\hat{I}_{p,q}] \right) \right] \tag{21}$$

where $E[.]$ defines expectation or mean operation.

(iii) SSIM is an image quality index parameter. The similarity between recovered image and original image can be measured using this parameter. Mathematically, it is defined as:

$$SSIM = \left(2\overline{I_{p,q}\hat{I}_{p,q}} + 2.55 \right) \left(2\sigma_{I_{p,q}\hat{I}_{p,q}} + 7.65 \right) \bigg/ \left(\overline{I_{p,q}}^2 + \overline{\hat{I}_{p,q}}^2 + 2.55 \right) \left(\sigma_{I_{p,q}}^2 + \sigma_{\hat{I}_{p,q}}^2 + 7.65 \right) \tag{22}$$

where $\overline{\hat{I}_{p,q}}$ and $\overline{I_{p,q}}$ define the expectation of the reconstructed image and original image, respectively. $\sigma_{I_{p,q}\hat{i}_{p,q}}$ is the covariance between the reconstructed image and original image. $\sigma_{\hat{I}_{p,q}}^2$ and $\sigma_{I_{p,q}}^2$ are the variance of recovered image and observed image, respectively. The SSIM value is 1 for a good visual quality image.

(iv) **EPI** is a performance parameter that defines the preservation of edges. Both despeckling and preservation of edges are required in medical science. The EPI value is 1 for perfect edge preservation. Mathematically, EPI is expressed as:

$$\text{EPI} = \left.\sum \left(\Delta I_{p,q} - \overline{\Delta I_{p,q}}\right)\left(\Delta \hat{I}_{p,q} - \overline{\Delta \hat{I}_{p,q}}\right) \middle/ \sqrt{\sum \left(\Delta I_{p,q} - \overline{\Delta I_{p,q}}\right)^2 \sum \left(\Delta \hat{I}_{p,q} - \overline{\Delta \hat{I}_{p,q}}\right)^2} \right. \tag{23}$$

where the high-pass-filtered output using 3×3 pixel approximation of a discrete Laplacian operator of $I_{p,\ q}$ is $\Delta I_{p,\ q}$.

From Tables 2–6, it is clear that the performance parameters of the proposed method are better than the state-of-the-art methods. This method is an improvement of the Cauchy-shrink method by adding the properties of Gaussianity to the dataset. The effect of Gaussianization is proved here. PSNR parameter comparison of various state-of-the-art methods and proposed methods is shown in Table 2. Artificial speckle noise is added to the phantom image of variances 0.1, 0.3, and 0.5. For each noise variance the PSNR parameter is calculated. For σ_n^2 of value 0.1, 0.3, and 0.5, the PSNR value is 33.97, 33.83, and 32.58, respectively. PSNR improvements of the proposed method are 22.81%, 18.92%, and 0.88% compared to Cauchy-shrink [28], Cao et al. [29], and Zaki et al. [30], respectively, for noise variance of value 0.1. PSNR improvements of the proposed method are 22.49%, 18.51%, and 0.47% compared to Cauchy-shrink, Cao et al., and Zaki et al. methods, respectively, for noise variance of value 0.3. PSNR improvements of the proposed method are 43.67%, 27.99%, and 20.96% compared to the Cauchy-shrink, Cao et al., and Zaki et al. methods, respectively, for noise variance of value 0.5.

SSIM parameter comparison of various state-of-the-art methods and the proposed method is shown in Table 3. For σ_n^2 of value 0.1, 0.3, and 0.5, the SSIM value is 0.967, 0.942, and 0.934, respectively. SSIM improvements for the proposed method are 11.78%, 9.64%, and 2.06% compared to Cauchy-shrink, Cao et al., and Zaki et al. methods, respectively, for noise variance of value 0.1. SSIM improvements of the proposed method are 20.80%, 10.93%, and 2.65% compared to Cauchy-shrink, Cao et al., and Zaki et al. methods, respectively, for noise variance of value 0.3. SSIM improvements of theproposed method are 27.19%, 22.80%, and 10.59% compared to Cauchy-shrink, Cao et al., and Zaki et al. methods, respectively, for noise variance of value 0.5.

CoC parameter comparison of various state-of-the-art methods and the proposed method is shown in Table 4. For σ_n^2 of value 0.1, 0.3, and 0.5, the CoC value is 0.990, 0.978, and 0.943, respectively. CoC improvements of the proposed method are 1.31%, 3.13%, and 0.30% compared to Cauchy-shrink, Cao et al., and Zaki et al. methods, respectively, for noise variance of value 0.1. CoC improvements of the proposed method are 12.67%, 9.91%, and 1.94% compared to Cauchy-shrink, Cao et al., and Zaki et al. methods, respectively, for noise variance of value 0.3. CoC improvements of the proposed method are 12.19%, 11.45%, and 8.05% compared to Cauchy-shrink, Cao et al., and Zaki et al. methods, respectively, for noise variance of value 0.5.

EPI parameter comparison of various state-of-the-art methods and the proposed method is shown in Table 5. For σ_n^2 of value 0.1, 0.3, and 0.5, the EPI value is 0.776, 0.694, and 0.663, respectively. EPI improvements of the proposed method are 29.76%, 14.43%, and 3.2% compared to Cauchy-shrink, Cao et al., and Zaki et al. methods, respectively, for noise variance of value 0.1. EPI improvements of the proposed method are 23.05%, 15.7%, and 11.67% compared to Cauchy-shrink, Cao et al., and Zaki et al. methods, respectively, for noise variance of value 0.3. EPI improvements of the proposed method are 36.34%, 32.42%, and 2.26% compared to Cauchy-shrink, Cao et al., and Zaki et al. methods, respectively, for noise variance of value 0.5.

Performance and quality parameter comparison for various state-of-the-art methods and the proposed method for an ultrasound image is given in Table 6. For σ_n^2 of value 0.4, the SSIM, CoC, and EPI improvements for the proposed method are 3.5%, 3.27%, and 18.21% compared to the Cauchy-shrink method. For σ_n^2 of value 0.4, the SSIM, CoC, and EPI improvements for the proposed method are 2.6%, 2.1%, and 10.3% compared to the Cao et al. method. For σ_n^2 of value 0.4, the SSIM, CoC, and EPI improvements for the proposed method are 1.6%, 1.1%, and 6.5% compared to the Zaki et al. method. For σ_n^2 of value 0.5, the SSIM, CoC, and EPI improvements for the proposed method are 11.66%, 0.62%, and 18.30% compared to the Cauchy-shrink method. For σ_n^2 of value 0.5, the SSIM, CoC, and EPI improvements for the proposed method are 10.58%, 1.77%, and 10.19% compared to the Cao et al. method. For σ_n^2 of value 0.5, the SSIM, CoC, and EPI improvements for the proposed method are 4.74%, 0.52%, and 8.3% compared to the Zaki et al. method.

5 Conclusion and discussion

This chapter introduced a developed despeckling method to remove speckle noise from ultrasound images. A statistical method with benefits of wavelet transform and Gaussianization transform was proposed. The main issue of the proposed method is the accurate selection of suitable PDF and estimation of signal parameters. The proposed denoising method is based on wavelet transform and estimation of threshold value by statistical modeling. For estimation of threshold value, a Gaussianization procedure and estimator were implemented. A Cauchy model is fitted on the wavelet coefficient dataset. To estimate the signal variance the Cauchy-modeled PDF was transformed to Gaussian PDF through a Gaussianization procedure. The obtained numerical results show that the threshold value is estimated accurately and noise removed effectively. In future, a mixture prior can be replaced by Cauchy PDF to obtain better results.

References

[1] T. Walter, J.C. Klein, P. Massin, A. Erginay, A contribution of image processing to the diagnosis of diabetic retinopathy-detection of exudates in color fundus images of the human retina, IEEE Trans. Med. Imaging 21 (10) (2002) 1236–1243.

[2] A. Srivastava, V. Bhateja, A. Gupta, A. Gupta, Non-local mean filter for suppression of speckle noise in ultrasound images, in: Smart Intelligent Computing and Applications, Springer, Singapore, 2019, pp. 225–232.

[3] S. Gai, Multiresolution monogenic wavelet transform combined with bivariate shrinkage functions for color image denoising, Circ. Syst. Signal Process. 37 (3) (2018) 1162–1176.

[4] Y. Zhou, H. Zang, S. Xu, H. He, J. Lu, H. Fang, An iterative speckle filtering algorithm for ultrasound images based on bayesian nonlocal means filter model, Biomed. Signal Process. Control 48 (2019) 104–117.

[5] F. Benzarti, H. Amiri, Speckle noise reduction in medical ultrasound images; 2013, (2013)arXiv preprint arXiv:1305.1344.

[6] A. Baghaie, R.M. D'souza, Z. Yu, Application of independent component analysis techniques in speckle noise reduction of retinal OCT images, Optik 127 (15) (2016) 5783–5791.

[7] G. Ramos-Llorden, G. Vegas-Sanchez-Ferrero, M. Martin-Fernandez, C. Alberola-Lopez, S. Aja-Fernandez, Anisotropic diffusion filter with memory based on speckle statistics for ultrasound images, IEEE Trans. Image Process. 24 (1) (2015) 345–358.

[8] H. Li, J. Wu, A. Miao, P. Yu, J. Chen, Y. Zhang, Rayleigh-maximum-likelihood bilateral filter for ultrasound image enhancement, Biomed. Eng. Online 16 (1) (2017) 46.

[9] P.V. Sudeep, S.I. Niwas, P. Palanisamy, J. Rajan, Y. Xiaojun, X. Wang, Y. Luo, L. Liu, Enhancement and bias removal of optical coherence tomography images: an iterative approach with adaptive bilateral filtering, Comput. Biol. Med. 71 (2016) 97–107.

[10] A. Wong, A. Mishra, K. Bizheva, D.A. Clausi, General Bayesian estimation for speckle noise reduction in optical coherence tomography retinal imagery, Opt. Express 18 (8) (2010) 8338–8352.

[11] A.S. Leal, H.M. Paiva, A new wavelet family for speckle noise reduction in medical ultrasound images, Measurement 140 (2019) 572–581.

[12] H. Rabbani, M. Vafadust, P. Abolmaesumi, S. Gazor, Speckle noise reduction of medical ultrasound images in complex wavelet domain using mixture priors, IEEE Trans. Biomed. Eng. 55 (9) (2008) 2152–2160.

[13] A. Achim, P. Tsakalides, A. Bezerianos, SAR image denoising via Bayesian wavelet shrinkage based on heavy-tailed modeling, IEEE Trans. Geosci. Remote Sens. 41 (8) (2003) 1773–1784.

[14] M.I.H. Bhuiyan, M.O. Ahmad, M.N.S. Swamy, Wavelet-based image denoising with the normal inverse Gaussian prior and linear MMSE estimator, IET Image Process. 2 (4) (2008) 203–217.

[15] H. Sadreazami, M.O. Ahmad, M.N.S. Swamy, Ultrasound image despeckling in the contourlet domain using the Cauchy prior, in: Proceedings of the IEEE International Symposium on Circuits and Systems (ISCAS), Canada, May 22–25, 2016, 2016, pp. 33–36.

[16] J.J. Ranjani, M.S. Chithra, Bayesian denoising of ultrasound images using heavy-tailed levy distribution, IET Image Process. 9 (4) (2014) 338–345.

[17] M.I.H. Bhuiyan, M.O. Ahmad, M.N.S. Swamy, Spatially adaptive wavelet-based method using the Cauchy prior for denoising the SAR images, IEEE Trans. Circ. Syst. Video Technol. 17 (4) (2007) 500–507.

[18] M.H. Bibalan, H. Amindavar, Non-Gaussian amplitude PDF modeling of ultrasound images based on a novel generalized Cauchy-Rayleigh mixture, EURASIP J. Image Video Process. 1 (2016) 48.

[19] S. Jafari, S. Ghofrani, Using heavy-tailed levy model in nonsubsampled shearlet transform domain for ultrasound image despeckling, J. Adv. Comput. Res. 8 (2) (2017) 53–66.

[20] Y. Lu, Q. Gao, D. Sun, Y. Xia, D. Zhang, SAR speckle reduction using Laplace mixture model and spatial mutual information in the directionlet domain, Neurocomputing 173 (3) (2016) 633–644.

[21] S.G. Chang, B. Yu, M. Vetterli, Adaptive wavelet thresholding for image denoising and compression, IEEE Trans. Image Process. 9 (9) (2000) 1532–1546.

[22] S. Sahu, H.V. Singh, B. Kumar, A heavy-tailed levy distribution for despeckling ultrasound image. in: Fourth IEEE International Conference on Image Information Processing (ICIIP), Himachal Pradesh, India, December 21–23, 2017, 2017, pp. 1–5, https://doi.org/10.1109/ICIIP.2017.8313674.

[23] G. Strang, T. Nguyen, Wavelets and Filter Banks, Wellesley-Cambridge Press, Wellesley, 1996.

[24] Z. Amini, H. Rabbani, Optical coherence tomography image denoising using Gaussianization transform, J. Biomed. Opt. 22 (8) (2017) 086011.

[25] S. Sahu, H.V. Singh, B. Kumar, A.K. Singh, A Bayesian multiresolution approach for noise removal in medical magnetic resonance images. J. Intell. Syst. 29 (1) (2018) 189–201, https://doi.org/10.1515/jisys-2017-0402.

[26] S. Sahu, H.V. Singh, B. Kumar, A.K. Singh, Statistical modeling and gaussianization procedure based de-speckling algorithm for retinal OCT images. J. Ambient Intell. Human Comput. (2018)https://doi.org/10.1007/s12652-018-0823-2.

[27] Z. Amini, H. Rabbani, Statistical modeling of retinal optical coherence tomography, IEEE Trans. Med. Imaging 35 (6) (2016) 1544–1554.

[28] S. Sahu, H.V. Singh, B. Kumar, A.K. Singh, De-noising of ultrasound image using Bayesian approached heavy-tailed Cauchy distribution, Multimed. Tools Appl. 78 (2017) 4089–4106.

[29] J. Cao, P. Wang, B. Wu, G. Shi, Y. Zhang, X. Li, Y. Zhang, Y. Liu, Improved wavelet hierarchical threshold filter method for optical coherence tomography image de-noising, J. Innov. Opt. Health Sci. 11 (3) (2018) 1850012.

[30] F. Zaki, Y. Wang, X. Yuan, X. Liu, Adaptive wavelet thresholding for optical coherence tomography image denoising, in: Computational Optical Sensing and Imaging, Optical Society of America, 2017 pp. CTh4B-4.

Wireless medical sensor networks for smart e-healthcare

Abhinav Adarsh and Basant Kumar

Department of ECE, Motilal Nehru National Institute of Technology Allahabad, Prayagraj, India

1 Introduction

For many decades, wireless communication networks have enjoyed continuous success in the scientific and industrial communities. This is because of valuable benefits offered by them; this technology has been able to establish its dominance in the field of network architectures. The wireless medium has unique advantages, which can be summed up in three points: the convenience of deployment, the ubiquity of information, and the low cost of installation. During its evolution, the wireless paradigm has seen the emergence of numerous evolving architectures, such as cellular networks, wireless local area networks, and others. During the last decade, a new architecture has emerged: wireless sensor networks (WSNs). This type of network is the result of a fusion of two fields of modern technology: embedded systems and wireless communications. A WSN consists of a set of on-board processing units communicating via wireless links. The general purpose of a WSN is the collection of a set of environmental parameters around conditions, such as temperature or atmospheric pressure, to route them to target points. WSNs are often considered as successors of ad hoc networks. In fact, the WSN shares several common properties with mobile ad hoc networks (MANETs), such as lack of infrastructure and wireless communications. However, one of the key differences between the two architectures is the field of application. Unlike the MANETs, which have not been able to achieve real success, WSNs have attracted an ever-growing communication sector, given their pragmatism and capabilities. A wireless communication network operating on battery power and with a lower energy requirement makes these networks simple to implement and provides nodes with multiple sensors and easy portability. These characteristics along with the ability to sense, collect, process, and communicate data make WSNs usable in a very wide range of fields and applications. Disaster management [1], healthcare [2], agriculture [3], environmental and structural study [4], wildlife monitoring [5], urban administration and automation, surveillance for security purposes [6], and fire detection and control [7] are some areas where WSNs are a great help. To give an instance out of many, for space exploration, multiple sensor nodes are placed all around the rocket and explorer (astronaut or satellite or rover). These nodes start communicating the sensed and collected data from sensors, using a control center, through a multiple-layer network. Nodes are provided with very competent and tiny sound, temperature, and vibration sensors to discover any indication of system failure as well as the presence of target phenomena or chemical or life signs. Sensor units are manufactured in accordance with the need and compatibility

Intelligent Data Security Solutions for e-Health Applications. https://doi.org/10.1016/B978-0-12-819511-6.00015-7

of the specific systems. The main feature of sensor nodes is their small size, low cost, energy efficiency, and high sensing capability. Every requirement cannot be fulfilled at once so there is a trade-off.

Taking into account the tiny size, low budget, and minimal power supply of nodes, energy efficient microcontrollers or embedded processors are employed for computation purposes, providing simple computation and storage abilities unlike hi-tech and fast multicore processor systems. Thus the requirement for processing work at the sensor node must be very limited. Also, due to the limited power of radio transceivers attached to the nodes, they have a short communication range. Thus nodes are not able to communicate very far from the central control unit. Therefore a "multihop data dissemination" tactic is often employed in WSNs, where each node only has to communicate to reach its nearest-placed nodes in the network (its neighboring nodes). Despite the limitations of sensors in WSNs, different areas of applications have their own demands and condition-based requirements. They need a robust and secure system executing their desired work with limited installation and maintenance cost. There is a need for a fast and reliable data acquisition WSN system able to assure minimum throughput with the help of a number of low-cost sensor nodes having a reasonable lifetime. The network specifies a minimal Quality-of-Service (QoS) requirement that must be met during data transfer. Researchers are working continuously on the development of sensors and network protocols to fulfill all the requirements.

Technological development in recent years has brought about important advances in meeting the needs of humans, particularly in the field of health. The available technology to which networks, sensors, and data analysis techniques can contribute together by using sensor networks and data analysis applications can help toward the development of better services for medicine, provide tools to monitor diseases, identify patterns for supporting medical diagnoses, and detect abnormal conditions to raise the alarm. Recently, a growing curiosity has been seen among researchers around the world to use WSN technology in the field of healthcare applications. E-healthcare visualizes a wide range of scenarios that requires remote 24-h supervision and guidance. The main objectives are improvement in the quality of life, enhancement of patients' well-being, early detection of health issues, provision of quick diagnoses, and reduction in healthcare cost. In many health practices, multiple sensing units are planted on a patient's body to supervise their biosignals. A proper wireless body area network (WBAN) [8] is established for these sensors to work together and share their data through common channels without interference. This establishment eases a patient's life in many ways. It dispenses with annoying wired design. Most importantly, it makes long-range extensive health monitoring of a subject (human or animal) realistic. Development in sensor design in terms of size, power requirement, and accuracy makes it possible and highly convenient to implant a WSN on a living being.

The general benefits of WSNs are very helpful in applications that are directly related to medicine and healthcare:

Ko et al. [9] presents the state of the art of WSN applications in health and medicine, and the challenges and difficulties encountered in the design of WSNs for this type of application.

Cheng [10] proposes a design for the technological application of the utilization of sensors in medical situations. This paper establishes a new trend in e-healthcare applications by using machine to machine, which refers to direct communication between devices without human intervention.

Kresimir et al. [11] present a detailed study of the status of the development of WSN applications for remote patients and healthcare in general. It also points out future challenges in this area.

Min et al. [12] describes a WSN application for remote monitoring of cardiac signals with smartphones active 24 h a day. This specific application is helpful to a group of patients with heart problems.

The paper also refers to the necessary infrastructure needed to act in a certain critical moment. The architecture of this system incorporates the use of smartphones and mainly electrocardiogram (ECG) sensors.

Zhang and Zhang [13] present a platform that intends to implement a real-time system of patient monitoring and guidance; it uses a Bluetooth network for data transmission, where each patient has a smartphone acting as a gateway for medical signal detector sensors.

Varona et al. [14] study a range of patients with cardiovascular problems over a period of 3 years with periodic assistance from a research center. The novelty of this system is that it captures wirelessly up to eight patient signals at the same time and processes the information in a database for subsequent analysis. It utilizes a local area network (LAN) for data transfer.

Becerra et al. [15] look at an application that proposes data capture with an ECG sensor for cardiac signal analysis, in which sensor data are sent to the user's cell phone. This has very large scope, and in the future researchers expect that the cellular telephone network will be used to broadcast the captured information.

Carvalho et al. [16] describe an application that proposes the use of two sensors to monitor patients from different medical aspects; with the first sensor it gathers physiological data and the other sensor is used to collect data of movement. This application relies on the internet network for sending data to a remotely located center and a LAN network for sending data to a local gateway. A cell phone or computer is used as the gateway.

2 Typical medical body sensors in a WSN

A lot of researchers are developing sensors for WSN-based healthcare systems. For instance, sensors that are easily implanted on the human body have been designed through the Code Blue [17] project at Harvard University to track biological signals. A wearable wireless node has been developed by the Ubimon group at Imperial College [18], which contains an interface to implant the body sensors. In a WSN, the sensors are implanted at different locations on/inside the body as per requirements to measure different signals emitting from different parts of the body (Fig. 1) [19].

In the field of medicine and healthcare a series of sensors has been developed that can be associated with different aspects that affect humans. This set of sensors is called the body area sensor network. The list of sensors is very large and new ones are being continuously developed by both industry and in scientific research. Referring to Hanson et al. [20], three large sensors can be applied in medicine and healthcare:

Physiological sensors: This group is related to those that measure blood pressure, amount of glucose in the blood, electrocardiograms, electroencephalograms, etc.

Biokinetic sensors: This group records movements of the human body.

Ambient sensors: This group consists of sensors that measure environmental phenomena such as humidity, light, sound pressure level, and temperature.

According to the foregoing, the following are related to examples of these groups of sensors that are found in Pantelopoulos et al. [21]:

Electrocardiogram sensor (ECG): This is a sensor electrode that is located in the chest and performs the task of sensing and sending heart signals.

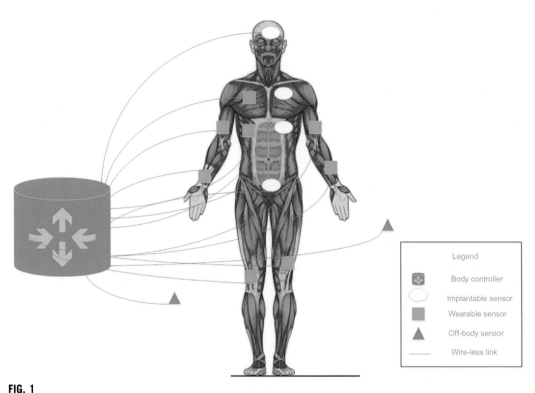

FIG. 1

Different biomedical sensors deployed on the human body.

Blood pressure sensor: This sensor is located in the arm and measures the force exerted by the circulation of blood on blood vessel walls, especially the arteries.

Sensor to measure body temperature or skin: This works as a thermometer for the body.

Sensor to measure respiration rate: This sensor indicates the amount of inspiration and expiration per unit of time.

Sensor to measure oxygen saturation: This is a sensor that works with human blood and determines the levels of oxygen.

Sensor to measure heart rate: This measures the frequency of the cardiac cycle.

Skin perspiration sensor: This shows the behavior of the body regarding sweat.

Sensor to detect heart sounds: This works like a cardiogram phone.

Sensor to measure blood glucose: This is a complementary sensor that works with blood. It measures the amount of blood glucose.

Electromyogram sensor (*electromyography*): This sensor measures the physical capacity of human body muscles.

Electroencephalogram sensor (*electroencephalogram [EEG]*): This sensor records the electrical signals generated by the brain.

Motion sensor (body movements): Records the movements of the human body in a certain area.

In recent years these devices have been increasing considerably and are custom-made to meet the needs of the patient's physique. For this reason a new generation of sensors for the human body can be categorized into four groups [22]:

Nonobtrusive devices: This is a necessary improvement in current sensors because some devices are annoying to the human body, either because of their size, weight, or radiation of energy. In the process of development of a new generation of sensors, it is a challenging task to make them smaller, with longer lifespan and improved reach. Although in specific areas that require certain performance standards to be followed, some devices may not be that small.

Parasitic devices: These are sensors that are already used in body area sensor networks, but still require further evolution. These devices must not be felt by the user (patient), and must allow normal movement of the individual. Their size should be very small and the energy consumption of these devices must be a few milliwatts.

Symbiotic devices (symbiotic nodes)**:** These sensors are placed inside the human body and are already very advanced. Their size must therefore be very small to microscopic. In the future, these devices will be biocompatible with the body.

Bioinspired devices (bioinspired nodes)**:** This is the expected progress of sensors of the future, which will be more intelligent and powered by the body that contains them. Such devices will make use of nanotechnology and molecular biology for their development. These devices will work autonomously, fueled by chemical reactions that occur in biological systems.

3 Different scenarios in WSN-based e-healthcare

Supervision during daily life: Patients with many particular health issues need to be monitored during their daily life. For example, chronic obstructive pulmonary disease limits the air flow from and to the lungs, resulting in quick and short breaths. Thus the patient's daily routine must be wisely and watchfully organized and supervised during the entire day. An appropriate WSN setup can identify the patient's activity and offer useful feedback to him/her, so that he/she may organize his/her daily life. Also, supervision through sensors, which generally provide the biosignal reading, gives more privacy to patients, unlike live video monitoring.

In-hospital monitoring: In many instances, it is necessary to keep patients in hospital for a longer duration to provide extensive care and observation. During this period all concerned medical parameters are regularly recorded and studied by specialists. This requires a large number of sensors attached to the patient's body throughout the day and night. Attachment of a large number of wired sensors to a patient is very uncomfortable, as it limits their freedom of movement. Using WSN technology and by establishing a WBAN reduces patient stress and delivers freedom of movement with ease. In such scenarios, hospitals deploy a static node through which patients wearing the WSN remain connected to the monitoring center while walking around.

Postsurgery in-home recovery monitoring: This scenario can be explained through examples of a heart surgery and epilepsy diagnostic. Once the heart patient is operated on by a surgeon, he/she is kept in hospital for recovery and postoperation complication monitoring. Then, she/he is sent home, but the doctor will need to take regular readings that reflect the progress of the patient's condition over time. Thus patients have to visit the doctor regularly. A WSN can be very useful in this situation by making follow-up of the patient's condition safe, trouble free, and inexpensive. More importantly, use of WSN technology can deliver regular readings of different biomedical parameters, unlike periodic examinations of patients by doctors. Hence, use of WSN technology provides a fast and more accurate indication of heart disorders and raises an alarm if necessary.

Epilepsy is a widespread prolonged brain disease with seizures as the main set of symptoms. Approximately 50 million people around the globe suffer from epilepsy [23]. Different categories of epilepsy have been detected; the precise distinction between them is very significant to provide the proper treatment procedure. Examination of EEG signals during a seizure is very useful to determine the type of epilepsy. Seizures are random and might occur once a week. To obtain the reading of brain signals during seizures, continuous EEG monitoring and recording is compulsory. A WBAN can provide a capable solution to the problem of continuous monitoring allowing the patient to continue his/her general life routine.

Sports training: Records of the continuous observation of athletes are a new resource to enhance their progress. With the help of sensors, all motions of an athlete can be recorded and the action of specific muscles can be evaluated. These data are examined and then training is organized accordingly. However, optimal performance is unlikely with an array of wired sensors fastened to the body. Sportsmen and women can perform more normal movements when the implanted sensors are tiny and there is no wiring attached to them. Various sensors and devices that can be useful in sport are shown in [24] and presented in Fig. 2.

The features of wireless channel links are in general of poor quality and are more time variant compared to wired ones. Healthcare deployment needs better QoS due to the significance of human health and the necessity for early detection of health disorders. Therefore to design and implement a WSN for healthcare, the advantages and limitations of WSN must be considered thoroughly.

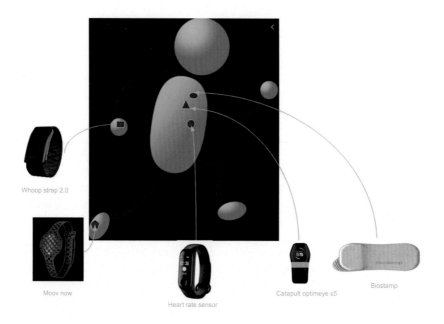

FIG. 2

Wireless sensor network sensors that can be utilized in sport [25].

4 Framework for WSN enabled e-healthcare

In networks that consist of one or more WSNs, data collected by sensors through continuous sensing of biosignals emitting from the body must be transported to specific stations for necessary analysis and/or storage. Two methods (communications network architecture) can be used to deliver data to the target. In the first method, a network architecture is designed in which the wireless sensor nodes can transfer data to the delivery center directly; this is also termed a flat network architecture and is shown in Fig. 3. In this architecture, each sensor node senses and communicates autonomously. However, the requirement for this type architecture is that each sensor must be attached to a powerful and robust radio device capable of transmitting the data to the nearest static node. In networks having a closely placed static node throughout the network setup area, this network architecture works very effectively. In some healthcare scenarios, where networks do not contain closely placed static nodes over the whole coverage area, implementation of a flat network architecture for WSN is not possible. In this case, gateway-based architecture is a promising substitute. In gateway-based architecture an intermediate node known as a gateway is placed near the body, as shown in Fig. 3. This gateway node may be portable or static in nature and equipped with a powerful radio transceiver of very large transmission range and a processor with heavy computations capability and bigger storage ability than other sensors' nodes. In this architecture, data from different body sensor nodes are transferred to the gateway node. The gateway node then forwards the received data to a target station directly or through a peripheral network. For example, imagine a scenario in which the patient is equipped with a WSN connected to a WBAN and is outside the range of a static node supporting direct communication between sensors and target station. In this case the sensor's data may be transferred to the person's cell phone [26] that can act as a gateway. This phone (having internet connection or other means of long-distance communication) sends the data to a specific base station with the help of cell-phone communication infrastructure. In a particular scenario in which even a gateway is not able to communicate due to the absence of a network, then data are stored in the memory of the available gateway and are transferred as soon as network connection is established.

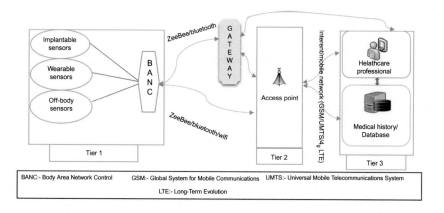

FIG. 3

Three-tier network architecture for wireless sensor network-based e-health with intermediate gateway and without intermediate gateway.

A gateway-based approach is very useful in a network where ultra-ow-power body nodes [27] may be used. The communication range of these sensors has an outreach of barely 1–2 m. In some cases, the role of the gateway node is not limited to just storing and forwarding the data from sensors but has to do computation work for information processing and data aggregation [28]. In this instance, the gateway may accumulate the data from different sensors and process them to figure out the health issues of the individual. Transmission of only a small amount of data in terms of seriousness of health issues can considerably reduce network traffic compared to transmitting the completely sensed data to base stations. Design and implementation of a three-tier network architecture with an intermediate gateway in e-healthcare applications is practical in deployment and efficient in practice. Thus most of the WSN designs developed for e-healthcare applications utilize the presence of an intermediate gateway node. Some of the research in this area is as follows:

Bakhsh [29] looks at an application model that proposes architecture that uses multiple protocols. It works with physiological sensors and biokinetic sensors. By the deployment of multiple gateways, one can provide services to several patients at the same time.

Rehunathan and Bhatti [30] propose a pilot application that uses the Bluetooth protocol, a smartphone as a gateway, and works with a patient's physiological sensors.

Aloi et al. [31] propose a novel technique that utilizes a smartphone as a gateway cooperating with different short-range communication protocols, physiological sensors, and the internet network for transmitting data to distant centers or to cloud storage.

Felisberto et al. [32] develop an application to track user movement. It uses physiological and biokinetic sensors working with the Bluetooth protocol and ZigBee (802.15.4) to provide multisensor hardware solutions for fall detection.

Gogate and Bakal [33] propose an application research that works with physiological sensors. It utilizes ESP8266 NodeMcu WiFi technology integrated on Arduino Nano boards and a personal computer as a gateway.

Min et al. [34] propose an application of wireless sensor networks for remote monitoring of cardiac signals with smartphones and the system remains active for 24 h a day. This system considers a variety of patients with heart problems and all the necessary infrastructure needed to act at a certain moment. The architecture of this system incorporates the use of smartphones and ECG sensors.

Hu et al. [35] propose one of the classic applications that, along with others such as "Codeblue" of Harvard University and MEDiSN [36], were the pioneers of medical treatments and disease control with the help of technology and mainly the use of sensors. This application has kept evolving and its approach to real-time communication by incorporating different protocols and different sensors makes it very significant.

Becerra-Luna et al. [37] propose an application designed for the treatment and monitoring of a cardiac patient. Signals are captured in real time and information is displayed on a cell phone. This application works with the Bluetooth protocol and physiological sensors.

Mohan and Sinciya [38] propose an application that proposes the capture of real-time data using different sensors and the information is transferred to a desired point using a smartphone or personal computer as an intermediated gateway.

Wang et al. [39] propose is another wireless application prototype developed for cardiac signal monitoring of a patient with WSN networks. It works with physiological sensors with IEEE 802.11 family network protocols; such a network uses smartphones as a gateway.

Almarashdeh et al. [40] propose an application aimed at the detection of vital signs in elderly patients and uses biomedical sensors that are integrated on a smart bracelet worn by the patient. The bracelet is connected to a database server and LAN connects the database server to a medical center and also to a personal assistant.

Not all previous applications have been designed to work in real time or meet the needs required by e-healthcare systems. There is great scope for future improvement in this area. There is also a need for a system that can not only capture and transfer the real-time data but also be able to perform data analysis and generate specific alerts or suggest basic treatment until help arrives. One can observe that there is a trend toward use of smartphones as a gateway to capture and transmit data from WSN sensors, as well as the use of the Bluetooth protocol, ZigBee, and Wi-Fi for local BAN.

5 Real-time application of WSN networks in e-healthcare

There are some aspects within medicine and healthcare that require more attention than others, since a person's life may depend on them; for example, patients with heart problems who need constant monitoring of the heart signal, the monitoring of patients suffering from memory problems, and the general monitoring of seniors—all these are situations that may endanger people's lives if not treated on time. The following are medical aspects that can be treated by applications of telemedicine by deployment of WSN networks for monitoring in real time and also problem-specific applications that already exist. One could say that every medical aspect is susceptible and thus needs to be controlled and monitored with the help of technology, but there are specific health issues that require more technological help than others. There are a number of problems where it is essential to refer patients to the most relevant doctors very quickly to get help to save lives.

Care of elderly patients and children: This type of care is very important and requires specific superintendence in certain areas; in some cases they simply require supervision. The mobility of this type of patient is questionable due to their elderly age and need for constant monitoring.

Alzheimer's disease (AD) and mental situations: AD is a chronic, progressive, degenerative disease of the brain. The course of treatment is variable and lasts between 5 and 20 years. It is one of the most common brain diseases and represents between 60% and 80% of all cases diagnosed with dementia [41]. Patients who suffer from bipolar personality problems can be violent at times. This is another important category of brain patients who are suitable candidates for monitoring.

Cardiovascular diseases: Cardiovascular diseases are a set of disorders of the heart and blood vessels. They are classified as arterial hypertension (high pressure), coronary heart disease (myocardial infarction),

vascular brain disease (stroke), peripheral vascular disease, weak heart, rheumatic heart disease, congenital heart disease, and cardiomyopathy [42].

Parkinson's disease: This is a neurodegenerative pathology caused by the loss of dopaminergic cells. It reflects multiple symptoms that create dangerous situations for patients, e.g., loss of control of speech due to basal ganglia dysfunction, tremor, loss of automatic movements, stiffness and impaired posture and balance, etc. [43].

Cancer: Cancer is one of the great challenge in the field of modern medicine. It's detection and control in time is necessary for saving the life of the patients.

The development of new sensors could help to detect it even without the need for biopsies.

Asthma: Asthma is a chronic respiratory disorder characterized by recurrent attacks of dyspnea and wheezing. Some causes and triggers are common to all people who suffer from the disease, but it differs from individual to individual. Although the ultimate causes of asthma are not known, what is important are inhaled substances. The following are triggers: allergens in closed spaces (for example, dust mites present in bed clothing, carpets, and upholstered furniture, pollution, and animal domestic animals); outdoor allergens (like pollens and molds); tobacco smoke; and irritating chemicals in the workplace. Other triggers may be cold air, extreme emotion, anger or fear, and physical exercise [42].

The foregoing may be considered the most relevant, but not the only, ones in the medical field that currently have help from supervision technology or tend to include technologies such as WSN networks, sensors, and data transmission in real time for continuous monitoring and guidance. In line with the previous requirements, applications that need attention and help from doctors with the help of technology for optimal guidance and monitoring are listed next regarding the aforementioned topics:

5.1 WSN applications for cardiovascular diseases

Llamoca and Kioko [44] look at an application that allows transmission of heart rate measurements of a pediatric patient in a wireless manner. The research is concerned more with electronics improvement and focuses on the development of the pulse meter. It is for local use and does not allow remote patient supervision in real time.

Dobrescu et al. [45] concern a hybrid application that uses fixed sensors in the house and sensors in the patient's body. The main focus is the real-time transmission of data related to the condition of the patient, which is being monitored during their daily routine. This is particularly aimed at monitoring sleep apnoea and supervising heart rate.

Rivera-Rodríguez et al. [46] propose the creation of a remote assistance center for patients in emergency medical situations. Again, the main focus of this proposal is to monitor vital signs from the heart with real-time transmission of ECG signals and store forward transmission of echo diagrams.

Rincón et al. [47] describe an application for real-time monitoring of cardiac signals with ECG sensors.

5.2 WSN applications for the care of children and people of an elderly age

Wendt and Potkonjak [48] review an application that uses a series of sensors in a patient's shoes to monitor their movements.

Alemdar et al. [49] look at a remote surveillance system for elderly patients using WSN and radio-frequency identification networks for continuous monitoring.

5.3 WSN applications for Alzheimer's disease and other mental illnesses

Paradiso et al. [50] review an application that provides monitoring of patients with disorders of mood, specifically bipolar disorders. The application collects information through sensors that are located in the patient's body and also in their clothes to analyze the data and understand the possible trend of the patient's condition, as well as advances in the treatment applied to the disease.

Avvenuti et al. [51] analyze a monitoring system for patients who suffer from Alzheimer's. It allows to follow up on patient's movements and generates alerts in a predetermined way.

As one can see, the union of technology and healthcare is evolving in favor of users; nevertheless, there are challenges and problems that remain to be solved, so it is important to come up with better research and make developments faster in this area to enhance the quality of patients' care. It can also be identified that most medical applications that use WSNs are mainly focused on the monitoring of cardiovascular and mobility-related diseases. Thus further improvements in this field are desired and the development of sensors is also important. In other fields of healthcare like that of dementia and Parkinson's, development is still slow, but there are already antecedents that can mark the route for further development.

6 MAC layer protocol design for e-health applications

There are a variety of protocols have been proposed and presented to support the communication at all networking layers and levels of WSNs. A medium access control (MAC) protocol for BANs to establish a wireless network among sensors and gateways needs to be designed according to application requirements. There are different parameters that need to be considered for the design and development of MAC layer protocols. Size of network and density of nodes presents in the network, mobility of nodes (static or mobile), sensing specification and traffic load, QoS requirements, surrounding environment, node features or limitation of nodes, and heterogeneity and dynamics (defined by variation of parameter with time) are main factors that influence application-specific protocol design.

The design of a MAC protocol for channel access in an emergency intrahospital real-time patient monitoring scenario has been presented and employed [52]. Different protocols exist in short-range real-time critical care monitoring and continuous surveillance of the patient in the BAN domain, which offer a patient monitoring service and focus on improved QoS parameters for targeted services. ZigBee is a very popular standard in this sector because of its low energy consumption, sufficient data rate capabilities for real-time vitals monitoring, and high scalability. However, a critical care scenario offers continuous monitoring of many physiological parameters together with varying data rates and respective priorities, e.g., ECG data have priority over temperature data. The present work deals with the development of a short-range MAC protocol that aims at prioritizing the critical physiological data and offers better QoS parameters. In a practical scenario of a critical care patient unit, performance of the proposed protocol has been tested through simulations and shows considerable improvement in network throughput and reduced end-to-end delay with guaranteed channel access to critical patient vitals.

6.1 Contention-based MAC protocols

In this class of protocol, medium is distributed and all nodes contend for the transmission slots. Central coordination in between the nodes is absent, which means that there is no scheduling of the medium access. All nodes are assumed to be saturated with data and all contend with a defined back-off timer to regulate the retransmission attempt in case of collision. Prominent examples of such protocols are: (1) sensor MAC (S-MAC): In this protocol a node listens to the medium and sends a SYNC packet in case of a clear medium [53]. This packet contains a schedule defining wake-up and sleep periods. All neighboring nodes maintain a table containing schedules of one or more transmitting nodes. During the listen period a node with a packet to send transmits a request-to-send frame and the receiver node answers with a clear-to-send frame. All other nodes except the communicating nodes enter into the sleep state, and exchange of data packets in between communicating nodes is assisted through acknowledgment messages. The sleeping mechanism alleviates energy consumed at the cost of increased latency since communication with a sleeping node may only begin after it wakes up [54]. (2) Berkeley media access control for low-power sensor networks (B-MAC): An adaptive preamble reduces idle listening in this protocol, which is a major source of energy usage in many protocols [55]. A node with a packet waits during a back-off time before checking the channel. Transmission begins on a clear channel, otherwise a second (congestion) back-off begins. Each node checks the channel using low-power listening periodically. In case the idle channel node is devoid of data to transmit, the node returns to sleep [56]. The B-MAC preamble sampling scheme adjusts the interval in which the channel is checked to equal the frame preamble size. (3) Predictive wake-up MAC (PW-MAC): PW-MAC [57] is an improvement over S-MAC and B-MAC due to use of pseudorandom schedules. All the nodes have different wake-up and transmit times, avoiding collisions. An active node requiring medium access sends a short notifying beacon to all other nodes. This node can further transmit data packets as well as request further channel statistics from the receiver, such as current time and current seed for the pseudorandom schedule used by the receiver. By using the seed in a linear congruential generator, the sending node here can predict the wake-up of the receiver. This mechanism allows a little bit more sleep time to the node before the receiver is awake.

6.2 Schedule-based MAC protocols

Protocols falling in this category access the medium in a one-by-one defined order known as a schedule. This implies that each node is active only during specific time slot(s) and enters a sleep state for the rest of the duration. The following approaches are used as protocols under this variety of medium access mechanism. (1) Low-energy adaptive clustering hierarchy (LEACH): This includes the complete set of protocol standardization, including application, routing, MAC, and physical characteristics for communication in the single hop short range wireless sensor networks [58]. In the remote monitoring of patient applications, medical data gathered by neighboring nodes are often redundant. It assumes synchronization in between the nodes of a given network with adaptive transmission power control to reach a base station, which is essentially a sink for the data. Sufficient processing capability is rendered to each node to implement different MAC protocols and accomplish the required signal processing functions to aggregate all the data in a single message. Nodes form clusters within a network, a cluster head (CH) is chosen for each such cluster, and information transmission starts. A direct sequence spread spectrum is used by each such cluster for tackling the interference [59]. (2) Power-efficient and delay-aware medium access protocol (PEDAMACS): This assumes a single access point (AP) in between the whole network, which is capable of reaching all sensor nodes in a single hop; the rest of the sensor nodes may reach the AP in multiple hops [60]. It harnesses the salient features of physical and network layers and proves to be advantageous. One of the key features includes event-driven sensing, in which the nodes wake-up only on the occurrence of that particular event, in the absence of any such event nodes remain in sleep state. The protocol can cover a larger network area by choosing multiple APs, which enables a larger network size. (3) Priority-based MAC protocol for wireless sensor networks (PRIMA): This is essentially similar in procedure to the LEACH protocol [61] as it follows a similar mechanism of creating clusters and choosing CHs for each such cluster [62]; the difference lies in the mechanism that ensures CH status is rotated at 15-min intervals. By adding 2 bits at the end of each packet, this protocol introduces four different priorities. MAC layer adds each data packet to one of these four defined priority queues as per the priority information received in the case of classifier MAC (C-MAC). Another MAC protocol used by this is channel access MAC (CAMAC), which uses carrier sense multiple access/collision avoidance (CSMA/CA) and time division multiple access (TDMA) slots for data transmission. Contention for medium access results in requests for a time slot and the CH to broadcast its schedules. TDMA slots ensure zero collisions during this scheduled data transfer. In case of CHs to base station, a similar mechanism ensures collision-free data transfer in schedules.

6.3 Hybrid MAC protocols

Shaswat Pathak [52] discussed different MAC protocols used in the BAN part of wireless medical sensor networks and proposed an energy efficient node priority-based MAC protocol for BANs. IEEE 802.15.4, or ZigBee, is a hybrid MAC protocol that aims to utilize the advantages of both these classes of MAC protocol by incorporating a contention- as well as schedule-based structure. It has a contention-based slotted CSMA/CA interval in which nodes contend for medium access and transmit a maximum of seven guaranteed time slots for the emergency data, which is allotted on a schedule-based TDMA scheme. However, this protocol lacks the prioritized access given to nodes that sometimes carry important medical information. For example, a cardiac patient in a critical care unit requires the continuous monitoring of ECG rather than temperature and blood pressure data. Assuming node capability to raise an alarm in case of emergency, a prioritized access of medium is required by these nodes. Abhiav Adarsh et al. [63] proposed a MAC protocol that incorporates a data sensitivity-based priority mechanism.

DSA-MAC [63]: This paper presents a data-sensitive adaptive medium access control (DSA-MAC) protocol for an intrahospital scenario. The main feature of this protocol is to prioritize the node, based on sensitivity of the data it has to communicate. The standard protocol such as IEEE 802.15.4 for BANs cannot fulfill all the requirements as it does not assist or maintain prioritized and varied data transfer requirements of various medical sensor nodes. This paper proposes a DSA-MAC protocol by prioritizing the available medical sensor data for channel allocation. Performance analysis of DSA-MAC shows that it outperforms other conventional MAC protocols in terms of throughput, data collision ratio, energy consumption, and average transmission time.

7 Challenges and research issues for WSN-based healthcare

Apart from advantages there are also challenges for sensors to achieve optimum performance in healthcare and disease control. As per Ashraf and Hassanien [22], these challenges are physical, mainly in relation to the size of the sensors, improvement of their sensitivity, optimal and efficient management of the energy needed for their operation, improvement in capturing and transmitting data, greater compatibility between sensors regardless of the manufacturer, and bandwidth management. In the link layer part the challenge is to improve the QoS; in the network layer the challenge is the improvements that can be made in terms of routing, which could be better optimization of consumption of energy and processing speed; and in the transport layer the challenge is to create a reliable protocol of information delivery. The challenges of WSN-based healthcare and disease control can be summarized as the development of intelligent, automatic systems that allow self-learning and assist in delivering and analyzing information correctly. Ashraf and Hassanien [22] highlight the improvements required in the field of information security, data privacy, ease of use, ease of implementation, ease of scalability, and ease of mobility. These are general challenges associated with any communication network but a general optimum solution based on the trade-off between multiple requirements may not be able to deal with the complications that arise in the field of healthcare. Thus application-specific design is needed in this area. As one can see, the topic of sensors is very extensive, and so far this chapter has discussed the categories that exist, the most common sensors, the new generation of sensors that are being proposed, and the challenges they are now facing and will face in the future.

Challenges related to WSN-based healthcare systems can be categorized in three parts. First, hardware challenges deal with sensor design issues; second, communication-related challenges concern data transfer; and third, independent challenges consider the general practicality and privacy issue.

Hardware-level challenges: Unobtrusiveness, sensitivity and calibration, energy, and data acquisition efficiency are a few parameters that rate the hardware used in a WSN [24]. The hardware device that is mounted on or placed inside the human body must be very light, such that it cannot be felt as a burden and also does not interfere with the patient's daily routine. Sensitivity is another important hardware-related issue as a sensor's reading must not be altered by minor changes in the surrounding environment. Sometimes hardware needs to be recalibrated according to conditions such as sweat and temperature variation, thus development of self-calibrating devices is required. Accuracy and energy efficiency are the main features of hardware deployed in a WSN. Hence, improvement in accuracy at low power consumption is necessary.

Communication challenges: Protocol related to different layers of data transmission are designed to manage three main tasks. First is to manage the task corresponding to the layer. Second is to deal with relative mobility and change in location of nodes. Third is to regulate power consumption. Based on their work, different layers present different challenges for WSN-based e-health.

Physical layer-related challenges: Physical layers of communication have challenging tasks to provide error-free transmission from one node to another with the help small antenna operated by a low-power supply. Different devices working with different frequencies create interoperability problems, and low bandwidth availability is desirable for better scheduling of data packets [64].

MAC layer-related challenges: This challenge is mainly limited to the BAN of a first tier of communication, where multiple sensors may share a common channel with very low bandwidth. In this case, data periodization and periodization-based channel allocation regarding biomedical signals are open to research [63,65].

Network layer-related challenges: Energy-aware routing protocols generally create congestion at nodes closer to the base station [66]. Thus there is a need to balance routing protocol.

Transport layer and application layer challenges: Cross-layer designs of protocols are very significant for end-to-end communication in case data have to go through different transmission media and network architectures. Cross-layer protocol design is a promising research issue in the area of WSN-based e-health.

Independent challenges: Apart from hardware design and data transfer there are other issues that need to be dealt with. Security of the stored data must be ensured and privacy of patients must be maintained in e-health [67]. User-friendliness, ease of deployment, scalability, and mobility of systems need to be improved to a large extent.

8 Conclusions

WSN networks constitute a new viable alternative for process monitoring; development in this field promises new advances and applications that will allow better healthcare and effective administration from doctors to patients. Likewise, the development of WSNs is complemented on two fronts: sensor development and applications for monitoring and analysis of the collected data. Sensors are getting smaller, more intelligent, and diversified. It is expected that in the future, integration of medical sensors with medical applications will be more transparent and effective in healthcare and disease control. Telemedicine applications using WSN solutions in real time are being continuously developed by exploiting emerging technologies/concepts such as data mining, AI, IoT, etc. The future is expected to be more innovative in this field, which has not yet been fully developed, because there are other problems that need to be solved. The problems of energy, routing, real-time data transmission, and security of WSN still exist.

References

[1] S.M. George, W. Zhou, H. Chenji, M. Won, Y.O. Lee, A. Pazarloglou, R. Stoleru, P. Barooah, Distress Net: a wireless adhoc and sensor network architecture for situation management in disaster response, IEEE Commun. Mag. 48 (3) (2010) 128–136.

[2] A.D. Wood, J. Stankovic, G. Virone, L. Selavo, Z. He, Q. Cao, T.T. Doan, Y. Wu, L. Fang, R. Stoleru, Context-aware wireless sensor networks for assisted living and residential monitoring, J. Neuro Eng. Rehabil. 22 (4) (2008) 26–33.

[3] J.A. Lpez Riquelmea, F. Sotoa, J. Suardaza, P. Sncheza, A. Iborraa, J.A. Verab, Wireless sensor networks for precision horticulture in southern Spain, Comput. Electron. Agric. 68 (1) (2009) 25–35.

[4] F. Ingelrest, G. Barrenetxea, G. Schaefer, M. Vetterli, O. Couach, M. Parlange, Sensor scope: application-specific sensor network for environmental monitoring, ACM Trans. Sens. Netw. 6 (2) (2010) 17:1–17:32.

[5] P. Juang, H. Oki, Y. Wang, M. Martonosi, L.S. Peh, D. Rubenstein, Energy efficient computing for wildlife tracking: design trade-offs and early experiences with zebra net, ACM SIGOPS Operat. Syst. Rev. 36 (5) (2002) 96–107.

[6] T. He, S. Krishnamurthy, L. Luo, T. Yan, L. Gu, R. Stoleru, G. Zhou, Q. Cao, P. Vicaire, J.A. Stankovic, T. F. Abdelzaher, J. Hui, B. Krogh, VigilNet: An integrated sensor network system for energy-efficient surveillance, ACM Trans. Sens. Netw. 2 (1) (2006) 1–38.

[7] A. Khadivi, M. Hasler, Fire detection and localization using wireless sensor networks, Sens. Appl. Exp. Logist. 29 (2010) 16–26.

[8] G.-Z. Yang, G.-Z. Yang (Ed.), Body Sensor Networks, Vol. 1, Springer, London, 2006.

[9] J.G. Ko, C. Lu, M.B. Srivastava, J.A. Stankovic, A. Terzis, M. Welsh, Wireless sensor networks for healthcare, Proc. IEEE 98 (2010) 1947–1960.

[10] K. Cheng, Machine-to-machine communications for healthcare, J. Comput. Sci. Eng. 6 (2012) 119–126.

[11] G. Kresimir, Z. Drago, K. Visnja, Medical applications of wireless sensor networks current status and future directions, Medicinski Glasnik 9 (2012) 23–31.

[12] G. Min, Z. Qian, N. Lionel, L. Yunhuai, T. Xiaoxi, Cardiosentinal: a 24-hour heart care and monitoring system, J. Comput. Sci. Eng. 6 (2012) 67–78.

[13] J. Zhang, Q. Zhang, E-doctor: a real time home monitoring and mobile healthcare plataform, IEEE COMSOC MMTCE Lett. 6 (2011).

[14] M.M.R. Varona, E.R. Estany, M.E.C. Lopez, J.V. Cruz, G.M. González, S.H. Garcia, N.B. Armas Rojas, Assessment of a telemetry monitoring system (movicorde) developed in Cuba, Cuban Mag. Cardiol. Cardiovasc. Surg. Organ Cuban Soc. Cardiol. 18 (2012).

[15] B. Becerra-Luna, R. Dávila-García, P. Salgado-Rodríguez, R. Martínez-Memije, O. Infante-Vázquez, Electrocardiography signal monitor and heart rate using a mobile phone with The Bluetooth communication protocol, Arch. Cardiol. Mex. 82 (2012) 197–203.

[16] S.T. Carvalho, M. Erthal, D. Mareli, A. Sztajnberg, A. Copetti, O. Loques, Monitoring remote patient in home environment. Institute of Computacao Federal University Fluminense (UFF), Institute of Informatics Federal University of Goiás (UFG) –Universidade of the State of Rio de Janeiro (UERJ), 2011.

[17] M. Welsh, Codeblue: Wireless sensors for medical care, [Online]. Available at: http://fiji.eecs.harvard.edu/codeblue.

[18] G.-Z. Yang, Ubimon – ubiquitous monitoring environment for wearable and implantable sensors, [Online]. Available at: http://www.doc.ic.ac.uk/vip/ubimon/research/index.html.

[19] F. Ullah, A. Abdullah, O. Kaiwartya, M. Arshad, Traffic priority-aware adaptive slot allocation for medium access control protocol in wireless body area network, Computers 6 (1) (2017) 9.

[20] M.A. Hanson, H.C. Powell Jr., A.T. Barth, K. Ringgenberg, B.H. Calhoun, J.H. Aylor, J. Lach, Body area sensor networks: Challenges and opportunities, Computer 42 (1) (2009) 58–65.

[21] A. Pantelopoulos, N.G. Bourbakis, A survey on wearable sensor-based system for health monitoring and prognosis, IEEE Trans. Syst. Man Cybern. C: Appl. Rev. 40 (2010).

[22] A. Darwish, A.E. Hassanien, Wearable and implantable wireless sensor network solutions for healthcare monitoring, Sensors 11 (6) (2011) 5561–5595.

[23] World Health Organization (WHO), Fact sheet 999. Epilepsy, http://www.who.int/mediacentre/factsheets/fs999/en/, 2019.

[24] R.P. Searcy, J. Summapund, D. Estrin, J.P. Pollak, A. Schoenthaler, A.B. Troxel, J.A. Dodson, Mobile health technologies for older adults with cardiovascular disease: current evidence and future directions, Curr. Geriatr. Rep. 8 (1) (2019) 31–42.

[25] T. Ray, J. Choi, J. Reeder, S.P. Lee, A.J. Aranyosi, R. Ghaffari, J.A. Rogers, Soft, skin-interfaced wearable systems for sports science and analytics, Curr. Opin. Biomed. Eng. 9 (2019) 47–56.

[26] E. Jovanov, A. Milenkovic, C. Otto, P. Groen, A wireless body area network of intelligent motion sensors for computer assisted physical rehabilitation, Network 2 (1) (2005) 6.

[27] E. Strmmer, M. Hillukkala, A. Ylisaukkooja, Ultra-low power sensors with near field communication for mobile applications, in: Proc. International Conference on Wireless Sensor and Actor Networks (WSAN), Springer, 2007, pp. 131–142.

[28] J. Ren, G. Wu, L. Yao, A sensitive data aggregation scheme for body sensor networks based on data hiding, Pers. Ubiquit. Comput. (2012).

[29] S.T. Bakhsh, Multi-tier mobile healthcare system using heterogeneous wireless sensor networks, J. Med. Imaging Health Inform. 7 (6) (2017) 1372–1379.

[30] D. Rehunathan, S. Bhatti, Application of virtual mobile networking to real-time patient monitoring, in: 2010 Australasian Telecommunication Networks and Applications Conference, IEEE, 2010, pp. 124–129.

[31] G. Aloi, G. Caliciuri, G. Fortino, R. Gravina, P. Pace, W. Russo, C. Savaglio, Enabling IoT interoperability through opportunistic smartphone-based mobile gateways, J. Netw. Comput. Appl. 81 (2017) 74–84.

[32] F. Felisberto, R. Laza, F. Fdez-Riverola, A. Pereira, A distributed multiagent system architecture for body area networks applied to healthcare monitoring. Biomed. Res. Int. 2015 (2015) 192454. https://doi.org/10.1155/2015/192454.

[33] U. Gogate, J. Bakal, Refining healthcare monitoring system using wireless sensor networks based on key design parameters, in: Information and Communication Technology for Intelligent Systems, Springer, Singapore, 2019, pp. 341–349.

[34] G. Min, Z. Qian, N. Lionel, L. Yunhuai, T. Xiaoxi, Cardiosentinal: a 24-hour heart care and monitoring system, J. Comput. Sci. Eng. 6 (2012) 67–78.

[35] F. Hu, M. Jiang, L. Celentano, X. Yang, Robust medical ad hoc sensor networks (MASN) with wavelet-based ECG data mining, Ad Hoc Netw. 6 (7) (2008) 986–1012.

[36] E.E. Egbogah, A.O. Fapojuwo, A survey of system architecture requirements for health care-based wireless sensor networks, Sensors 11 (5) (2011) 4875–4898.

[37] B. Becerra-Luna, R. Dávila-García, P. Salgado-Rodríguez, R. Martínez-Memije, O. Infante-Vázquez, Electrocardiography signal monitor and heart rate using a mobile phone with The Bluetooth communication protocol, Mex. Cardiol. Arch. 82 (2012) 197–203.

[38] G. Mohan, P.O. Sinciya, Real time healthcare system for patients with chronic diseases in home and hospital environments, Int. J. Sci. Eng. Technol. Res. 2 (4) (2013).

[39] H. Wang, D. Peng, W. Wang, H. Sharif, H.-H. Chen, A. Khoynezhad, Resource-aware secure ECG healthcare monitoring through body sensor networks, IEEE Wirel. Commun. 17 (1) (2010) 12–19.

[40] I. Almarashdeh, M. Alsmadi, T. Hanafy, A. Albahussain, N. Altuwaijri, H. Almaimoni, F. Asiry, et al., Real-time elderly healthcare monitoring expert system using wireless sensor network, Int. J. Appl. Eng. Res. 13 (2018) 973–4562.

[41] M. Handy, M. Haase, D. Timmermann, Institute of Applied Microelectronics and Computer Science University of Rostock, Richard-Wagner-Str. 31, 18119 Rostock, Germany(2005).

[42] WHO, Cardiovascular Diseases; 2013, (2013).

[43] O.M. Aguilar, C.A. Soto, M. Esguerra, Neuropsychological changes associated with deep brain stimulation of Parkinson disease: theoretical review, Suma Psicológica 18 (2) (2011) 89–98.

[44] C. Llamoca, Y. Kioko, Diseño de un prototipo de pulsímetro inalámbrico para la monitorización de pacientes pediátricos, in: Proyecto de titulación, Pontificia Universidad Católica del Perú, Lima, 2012.

[45] R. Dobrescu, D. Popescu, M. Nicolae, S. Mocanu, Hybrid wireless sensor network for homecare monitoring of chronic patients, Int. J. Biol. Biomed. Eng. 3 (2) (2009) 1–8.

[46] R. Rivera-Rodríguez, A. Serrano-Santoyo, R. Tamayo-Fernández, A. Armenta-Ramade, Sistema móvil de teleasistencia médica para la atención en tiempo real de casos de urgencia, Ingeniería, investigación y tecnología 13 (1) (2012) 1–8.

[47] F.J. Rincón, L. Gutiérrez, M. Jiménez, V. Díaz, N. Khaled, D. Atienza, M. Sánchez-Elez, J. Recas, G. De Micheli, Implementation of an automated ECG-based diagnosis for a wireless body sensor platform, in: Proceedings of the International Conference on Biomedical Electronics and Devices (BIODEVICES 2009), vol. 1, Springer, 2009, pp. 88–96.

[48] J.B. Wendt, M. Potkonjak, Medical diagnostic-based sensor selection, in: SENSORS, 2011 IEEE, IEEE, 2011, pp. 1507–1510.

[49] H. Alemdar, Y. Durmus, C. Ersoy, Wireless healthcare monitoring with RFID-enhanced video sensor networks, Int. J. Distrib. Sens. Netw. 6 (1) (2010) 473037.

[50] R. Paradiso, A.M. Bianchi, K. Lau, E.P. Scilingo, Psyche: personalised monitoring systems for care in mental health, in: 2010 Annual International Conference of the IEEE Engineering in Medicine and Biology, IEEE, 2010, pp. 3602–3605.

[51] M. Avvenuti, C. Baker, J. Light, D. Tulpan, A. Vecchio, Non-intrusive patient monitoring of Alzheimer's disease subjects using wireless sensor networks, in: 2009 World Congress on Privacy, Security, Trust and the Management of e-Business, IEEE, 2009, pp. 161–165.

[52] S. Pathak, Development and Performance Evaluation of Healthcare Systems and Services for Telemedicine, PhD dissertationMotilal Nehru National Institute of Technology Allahabad, 2017.

[53] W. Ye, J. Heidemann, D. Estrin, Medium access control with coordinated adaptive sleeping for wireless sensor networks, IEEE/ACM Trans. Netw. 12 (3) (2004) 493–506.

[54] P. Lin, C. Qiao, X. Wang, Medium access control with a dynamic duty cycle for sensor networks, in: Proceedings of the IEEE Wireless Communications and Networking Conference (WCNC'04), vol. 3, 2004, pp. 1534–1539.

[55] J. Polastre, J. Hill, D. Culler, Versatile low power media access for wireless sensor networks, in: Proceedings of the Second International Conference on Embedded Networked Sensor Systems (SenSys'04), November, ACM Press, 2004, pp. 95–107.

[56] L. Tang, Y. Sun, O. Gurewitz, D.B. Johnson, PWMAC: an energy-efficient predictive-wakeup MAC protocol for wireless sensor networks, in: Proceedings of the IEEE INFOCOM, 2011, pp. 1305–1313.

[57] W.B. Heinzelman, A.P. Chandrakasan, H. Balakrishnan, An application-specific protocol architecture for wireless microsensor networks, IEEE Trans. Wirel. Commun. 1 (4) (2002) 660–670.

[58] M. Buettner, G.V. Yee, E. Anderson, R. Han, X-MAC: a short preamble MAC protocol for duty-cycled wireless sensor networks, in: Proceedings of the 4th International Conference on Embedded Networked Sensor Systems (SenSys'06), November, 2006, pp. 307–320.

[59] S.C. Ergen, P. Varaiya, PEDAMACS: power efficient and delay aware medium access protocol for sensor networks, IEEE Trans. Mobile Comput. 5 (7) (2006) 920–930.

[60] J. Ben-Othman, L. Mokdad, B. Yahya, An energy efficient priority-based QoS MAC protocol for wireless sensor networks, in: Proceedings of the IEEE International Conference on Communications, 2011, pp. 1–6.

[61] H. C. Foundation, Wireless Devices Specification, HCF SPEC 290 Revision 1.0(2007).

[62] D.-K. Kim, S.K. Yoo, I.-C. Park, M. Choa, K.Y. Bae, Y.-D. Kim, et al., A mobile telemedicine system for remote consultation in cases of acute stroke, J. Telemed. Telecare 15 (2009) 102–107.

[63] A. Adarsh, A. Tiwari, B. Kumar, Performance analysis of data sensitive adaptive MAC protocol for intra-hospital scenario, in: Tenth International Conference on Computing, Communications and Networking Technologies (ICCCNT), IEEE, 2020. (submitted for publication).

[64] P. Pace, G. Aloi, R. Gravina, G. Caliciuri, G. Fortino, A. Liotta, An edge-based architecture to support efficient applications for healthcare industry 4.0, IEEE Trans. Ind. Inform. 15 (1) (2018) 481–489.

[65] R.M. Aileni, G. Suciu, C.M. Balaceanu, C. Beceanu, P.A. Lavinia, C.-V. Nadrag, S. Pasca, C.A. V. Sakuyama, A. Vulpe, Body Area Network (BAN) for Healthcare by Wireless Mesh Network (WMN), in: Body Area Network Challenges and Solutions, Springer, Cham, 2019, pp. 1–17.

[66] L. Kong, J.-S. Pan, V. Snášel, P.-W. Tsai, T.-W. Sung, An energy-aware routing protocol for wireless sensor network based on genetic algorithm, Telecommun. Syst. 67 (3) (2018) 451–463.

[67] Y.K. Ever, Secure-anonymous user Authentication scheme for e-healthcare application using wireless medical sensor networks, IEEE Syst. J. 13 (1) (2018) 456–467.

A secure lightweight mutual authentication and key agreement protocol for healthcare systems

16

Amiya Kumar Sahu[a], Suraj Sharma[a], and Ashish Nanda[b]

Department of Computer Science and Engineering, International Institute of Information Technology Bhubaneswar, Bhubaneswar, India[a] Faculty of Engineering and Information Technology, University of Technology Sydney, Sydney, NSW, Australia[b]

1 Introduction

Many devices in recent decades have become smart and have improved many facets of human life because they are enabled with Internet of Things (IoT) technologies. Let us consider one such sector that is mostly influenced by IoT applications. Devices specifically related to healthcare (e.g., fitness trackers, smartwatches, smart spectacles) collect users' real-time data (such as step count, blood-glucose level, heart rate, pulse rate, etc.); and send them to cloud for analysis and better healthcare services. The data sent through a smartphone gateway and subsequently to the cloud contain sensitive and private user information that is vulnerable to attacks, for example, replay, impersonation, man in the middle (MITM), and many more. The release of private data may also be life-threatening; for instance, if an intruder manages to impersonate a healthcare device that sends data through a gateway, then the adversary may manipulate the data and make the system supply false blood-glucose information to the user. Thereby, the user's life may be endangered with improper insulin intake. The release of sensitive data may also affect the personal life of the user; furthermore, it can also open many pathways for attackers. This implies an essential requirement for a security mechanism to preserve the privacy of the user's sensitive data, and even a mechanism to guarantee mutual authentication between healthcare device and smartphone gateway. However, healthcare wearable devices are resource constrained, that is, they usually possess a limited amount of primary memory and processing power. Therefore devising a security mechanism that would fit into these small devices needs to be lightweight. Moreover, the mechanism must not compromise the privacy and security of the data communicated over the unsecured channel of a network.

In this chapter, we focus on a set of wearable healthcare devices that are vulnerable to many attacks, such as MITM, replay, impersonation, and many more. To counter the aforementioned challenges, we propose a lightweight, secure, anonymous mutual authentication protocol between healthcare device and smartphone (Gateway). It also provides a key establishment mechanism for secure communication using only cryptographic hash function and X-OR functionalities.

Intelligent Data Security Solutions for e-Health Applications. https://doi.org/10.1016/B978-0-12-819511-6.00016-9

The primary contributions to this chapter are

- A lightweight authentication system model for body area network (BAN) healthcare devices is proposed.
- The protocol is devised using a one-way cryptographic hash function and X-OR function for key establishment between the healthcare device and smartphone gateway.
- The protocol is tested using a formal security tool—Automated Validation of Internet Security Protocols and Applications (AVISPA)—to show resistance from various attacks under the influence of Delov-Yao and Cennetti-Krawczyk threat models.
- Session key agreement is supported by formal proofs using BAN logic.
- The computational cost of the proposed protocol is evaluated and compared with other work.

1.1 Organization of the chapter

The organization of the rest of this chapter is as follows.

Section 2 presents the fundamental building blocks required to understand the proposed protocol. Section 3 enumerates the literature related to authentication schemes using hash function and X-OR functionalities. Section 4 explains the proposed network model and the considered threat model. Section 5 describes the proposed security scheme. Section 6 supports the proposed security scheme with security analysis using AVISPA, BAN authentication logic, and communication cost comparisons. Section 7 provides a conclusion followed by references to the chapter.

2 Essential building blocks of the proposed protocol

This section introduces the biometric fuzzy extraction function and bitwise X-OR functionalities, which play the roles of fundamental building blocks to the proposed protocol.

2.1 Biometric fuzzy extractor function

A fuzzy extractor consists of two functions: $Gen()$ and $Rep()$. $Gen()$ is a probabilistic generation function that inputs the personal biometrics BIO_u of user U and outputs a specified length biometric secret key, $\sigma_u \epsilon \{0, 1\}$ and a public reproduction parameter, τ_u. The function can be stated as $Gen(BIO_u) = (\sigma_u, \tau_u)$. However, the function $Rep()$ is a deterministic reproduction function, which takes the biometric impression of the user, say BIO_i, and the reproduction parameter τ_u to generate the secret parameter σ_u. The function can be stated as $Rep(BIO_u, \tau_u) = \sigma_u$.

2.2 Bitwise X-OR function

The bitwise X-OR function inputs two binary arguments of equal length, say l, and outputs an l bit length value. The output bit will be 1 if the input bits are different from one another, otherwise it results in 0. Consider an input $X, Y \epsilon \{0, 1\}^n$, then, it is computationally feasible to evaluate $Z = X \oplus Y$, where $Z \epsilon \{0, 1\}^n$. In contrast, it is computationally hard to find both the inputs X and Y if only Z is known. Nevertheless, if any two of the operands are known from the set $\{X, Y, Z\}$, then the third operand can be computed easily, for example, if X and Z are known, then Y can be evaluated as $Y = Z \oplus X$.

3 Literature review

Wong et al. [1] presented the first lightweight user authentication protocol using a cryptographic hash function and X-OR functionalities; nevertheless, it suffered from various attacks such as stolen verifier and replay attacks. Later, Das [2] recognized these attacks and presented an improved version of the security protocol, which used password-based two-factor authentication and a gateway between user and sensor nodes. Khan and Alghathbar [3] showed that the proposed scheme by Das [2] was unable to achieve key agreement and mutual authentication and also suffered from various attacks such as impersonation and node capture attacks. For improvement, they proposed a hashed password and pre-shared keys for mutual authentication between user and sensor nodes. In the same year, Vaidya et al. [4] also showed the failure of the scheme to deal with stolen smartcard attack and impersonation.

Later, Das et al. [5] presented a password-based mutual authentication scheme using only hash function and X-OR functionalities. However, due to its flawed design, it was infeasible for implementation. The several attacks to the Das et al. [5] scheme are presented by Shuaiwen and Xiaoming [5a] and Turkanović and Holb [6]. Turkanović et al. [7] suggested a protocol for wireless sensor networks (WSNs) based on a smartcard authentication mechanism. The protocol claimed energy efficiency and anonymity of users but contained security issues such as stolen verifier and stolen smartcard attacks. It also failed to support backward secrecy shown by Refs. [8–10]. Furthermore, Chang and Le [9] proposed an improvised scheme with forward secrecy but at the cost of high storage requirement. Farash et al. [8] too presented an advanced key establishment and authentication scheme; however, it failed to deal with the user anonymity problem, stolen smartcard attack, and impersonation. These drawbacks are shown by Amin et al. [11].

Gope and Hwang [12] presented an anonymous authentication protocol for WSN that was later shown by Adavoudi-Jolfaei et al. [13] to be vulnerable to disclosure of session key and unfit to provide secure user authentication. Sahu et al. [14] proposed an authentication protocol for a smarthome-based architecture. It provided authentication between an IoT smart hub and an external but registered user of the system. However, it did not provide the energy requirement and proof of security. Li et al. [15] also suggested another mutual authentication scheme, Koya and Deepthi [16] discovered a key escrow problem in it. They even sensed the scheme was susceptible to both gateway and sensor node impersonation attacks. In the following year, Das et al. [17] proposed a mutual authentication protocol for wearable healthcare devices by using a fuzzy extractor to extract biometric features. However, it suffered from high computational overhead, and their protocol was required to have time synchronization. The time synchronization would require a more powerful backup to maintain synchronous transmission, which demands improvisation for the protocol.

Two-way communications between users and a utility in a smart grid makes the utility smart. However, securing data transmission in an insecure public channel is challenging. Zhang et al. [18] proposed an authentication and key agreement protocol for a smart grid environment. The model was based on a real-or-random oracle model. It also provided a prototype for it. In the same year, Gope [19] proposed a fog computing-based security architecture along with three different authentication protocols for various scenarios. The research paper claimed the provision of anonymity of the devices in the system. However, it did not consider the human identity and its interaction with the proposed system. It also lacked the provision of energy requirements for the protocols. Gupta et al. [20] presented a security protocol for authentication between a wearable device and its user through a fog server. It used only X-OR and cryptographic hash functions to achieve a lightweight protocol. However, its efficiency needed further improvement.

Along with an X-OR and hash function-based lightweight security mechanism, there are other authentication schemes. Zhou et al. [21] proposed an authentication framework that worked on the collected sensor data of human action-related features and identified distinct patterns. It could authenticate and identify users on widely available commercial smartwatches. Researchers have also attempted to explore motion-based IoT-enabled objects that needed lightweight authentication. In this regard, Abdel Hakeem et al. [22] proposed a security protocol for authentication and privacy protection for vehicle to everything. The scheme used two security devices such as a biometric device and a tamperproof device to verify driver and secure the keys, respectively. It decentralizes certificate-authority's functions by generating a pseudoidentity and private keys to obtain authentication in vehicle-to-vehicle communication network. Besides, it also provided an authentication signature protocol using a hash chain key generation mechanism. In a similar fashion, Cui et al. [23] presented a reputation system-based message authentication framework and an elliptic curve cryptosystem-based protocol for 5G-enabled vehicular networks. The reputation system was managed by a trusted authority and provided a reputation score to the vehicle. The reputation score acts as a threshold to participate in the communication system. This score limits the number of untrusted messages in the network.

From the foregoing literature review, we found that the many authentication protocols formulated and implemented were lacking in several aspects. The combination of effective user mutual authentication, anonymity of participating users, energy efficiency, forward and backward secrecy, and resistance to attacks related to authentication is rarely found in the proposed protocols. The need for a secure, lightweight authentication and key agreement protocol motivated us to propose a new security mechanism.

4 System model

4.1 Network model

Fig. 1 depicts a typical communication network model for a healthcare environment. A user uses various wearable healthcare devices to track several medical features such as heart rate, step counts, body motion, pulse count, blood pressure, calories burnt, and many more. These wearable devices collect

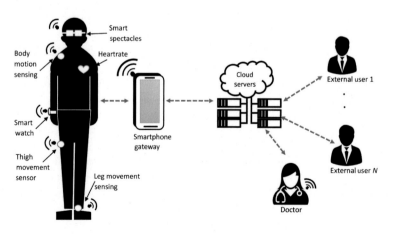

FIG. 1

Network model.

their respective sensed data and forward them to a smartphone, which acts as a gateway to the Internet. Furthermore, the smartphone sends the data to the cloud for storage and analysis. Cloud works as a storehouse of these data where further distribution is done according to the authorization and authentication of external users. The external user could be a doctor or a diet planner of a particular user.

If the user wishes to know their medical health status, they could use the smartphone to communicate and extract the required data from their wearable healthcare devices. The external user can also request the smartphone for desired data, then the smartphone can perform the task for them. This communication model is also suited to military operations where a soldier's health condition could be monitored, and further analysis could be performed to improve it.

4.2 Threat model

This chapter considers the widely adopted [24] threat model and the Canetti and Krawczyk [25] adversary model, where an adversary is able to:

- Eavesdrop on all messages sent on the insecure channel.
- Alter and reroute all messages sent; they can also generate and insert completely new messages.
- Be a legitimate protocol participant (insider) or external party (outsider) or a combination of both.
- Obtain any sufficiently old previously run session keys.
- Start any number of parallel protocol runs for protocol participants.
- Change part of communication system information such as session state, session key, and private key of a compromised user.

5 Proposed security scheme

The proposed security scheme has five stages: (1) set-up phase, (2) registration, (3) log-in phase, (4) authentication and key agreement, and (5) password update steps. Table 1 is a detailed explanation of the steps in the proposed.

5.1 Set-up phase

Fig. 2 depicts the four basic steps needed to set up the system. At the outset, user U_u through mobile M_u generates identity ID_{HD_i} and a corresponding 128-bit random secret r for each healthcare device HD_i. Subsequently, it creates a pseudoidentity PID_{HD_i} by applying a hash function with ID_{HD_i} and r as parameters. This pseudoidentity PID_{HD_i} would help to maintain anonymity of the device in the system. The second step calculates the temporal credential TC_{HD_i} by applying a hash function to ID_{HD_i}, r, and RT_{HD_i}, where RT_{HD_i} is the timestamp of the mobile at that particular instance. This temporal credential would help the mobile user to differentiate between the obsolete and currently active healthcare device. Next, the device HD_i saves its pseudoidentity PID_{HD_i} and temporal credential TC_{HD_i} in its memory. The mobile M_u also stores the credentials for the ith healthcare device HD_i, such as $ID_{HD_i}, RT_{HD_i}, TC_{HD_i}$, and r, in its memory.

Table 1 Notations used in security protocol.

Acronym	Description
U_u	User U
HD_i	ith healthcare device
M_u	Mobile of user U
PID_{HD_i}	Pseudoidentity for ith healthcare device
BIO_u	Biometric impression of user U
ID_{HD_i}	Unique identity for ith healthcare device
RT_{HD_i}	Timestamp for ith healthcare device
SK_{ui}	Session between user U_u and HD_i
r	128-bit random secret number computed by the mobile M_u
$\oplus$	Bitwise X-OR operator
$\parallel$	Concatenation operation
$H()$	One-way hash function
$Gen(.)$	Fuzzy extractor probabilistic generator function
$Rep(.)$	Public deterministic reproduction function
T_{id}	Transaction ID between HD_i and M_u
r_{HD_i}	Random nonce generated by HD_i

User(U_u)/mobile (M_u)   **Healthcare device (HD_i)**

1. U_u generates a unique identity ID_{HD_i} and a 128-bit random secret r. Calculate its pseudoidentity:
$PID_{HD_i} = h(ID_{HD_i} \parallel r)$

2. U_u calculates temporal credential
$TC_{HD_i} = h(ID_{HD_i} \parallel r \parallel RT_{HDi})$

3. U_u stores the PID_{HD_i} and TC_{HD_i} in the HD_i's memory.

4. Simultaneously, U_u stores $\{ID_{HD_i}, RT_{HD_i}, TC_{HD_i}\}$ in its mobile

FIG. 2

Healthcare device deployment.

5.2 Mobile registration

Fig. 3 depicts the association of the user with their mobile. User U_u has to be registered for the mobile smartphone M_u before using it for the service. In this process, user U_u chooses their identity ID_u and password PW_u. They also put their biometric impression on the smartphone's sensor. The smartphone invokes the fuzzy extractor probabilistic function to the biometric impression obtained

User (U_u)   **Mobile (M_u)**

1. U_u chooses ID_u and PW_u and imprints BIO_u in the sensor of mobile M_u.

2. Apply fuzzy extractor function
$Gen(BIO_u) = (\sigma_u, \tau_u)$

3. Evaluates $e_u = h(ID_u \| PW_u \| \sigma_u)$
And $F_u = TC_{HD_i} \oplus h(ID_u \| \sigma_u \| PW_u \| PID_{HD_i})$
And $G_u = PID_{HD_i} \oplus h(ID_u \| \sigma_u \| PW_u)$

4. Store following in M_u's memory:
$\{ Gen(.), Rep(.), \tau_u, h(.), e_u, F_u, G_u \} \quad \forall u \in HD_i$

FIG. 3

Mobile registration.

---

from the user (i.e., BIO_u) and extracts a pair of parameters σ_u and τ_u as biometric secret key and public reproduction parameters, respectively. Next, the smartphone M_u calculates three parameters: first, it evaluates $e_u = h(ID_u \| PW_u \| \sigma_u)$ to identify the user's identity. Second, it finds $F_u = TC_{HD_i} \oplus h(ID_u \| \sigma_u \| PW_u \| PID_{HD_i})$ to incorporate TC_{HD_i} and extract it whenever required. Third, it evaluates $G_u = PID_{HD_i} \oplus h(ID_u \| \sigma_u \| PW_u)$, which can be used to extract pseudoidentity PID_{HD_i} whenever required. At the end of all these computations, smartphone M_u stores $Gen()$, $Rep()$, τ_u, $h()$, e_u, F_u, and G_u in its memory for each healthcare device HD_i.

5.3 Log-in phase

The first three steps of Fig. 4 depict the log-in procedure of the registered user in the system. A user who wishes to read the data from the healthcare service needs to log in to the system by supplying their credentials, that is, identity (ID_u), password (PW_u), and biometric impression (BIO_u). The smartphone retrieves the biometric secret key τ_u of that user and reproduces σ'_u using the deterministic reproduction function $Rep()$ and its supplied two arguments as BIO and τ_u. Furthermore, it computes $e'_u = h(ID_u \| PW_u \| \sigma'_u)$ and checks if it is equal to the stored value of e_u in the smartphone's memory. If the equality holds, then log-in is successful, and the user U_u will be allowed to proceed further; otherwise, the session will be terminated.

5.4 Authentication and key agreement phase

Steps 3–14 of Fig. 4 provide the mutual authentication and session key establishment between smartphone and healthcare device. Once the registered user U_u is authenticated, then the smartphone extracts the PID'_{HD_i} and TC'_{HD_i} from G_u and F_u by using the expressions $PID'_{HD_i} = G_u \oplus h(ID_u \| \sigma'_u \| PW_u)$ and $TC'_{HD_i} = F_u \oplus h(ID_u \| \sigma'_u \| PW_u \| PID'_{HD_i})$. Next, it generates a random nonce r_m and prepares M_1 and M_2 using $M_1 = h(PID'_{HD_i} \| TC'_{HD_i}) \oplus r_m$ and $M_2 = h(M_1 \| r_m)$, respectively. Then, it sends prepared M_1 and M_2 to healthcare device HD_i for the authentication process.

The corresponding healthcare device HD_i receives the sent pair M_1 and M_2. It then calculates $M_3 = h(PID_{HD_i} \| TC_{HD_i})$ and retrieves r_m from M_1 using the expression $r'_m = M_1 \oplus M_3$; further using r_m,

User (U_u) / Mobile (M_u)	**Healthcare Device (HD_i)**

User (U_u) / Mobile (M_u)

1. U_u inputs: ID_u , PW_u, BIO_u
2. Computes $\sigma_u' = Rep(BIO_u' , \tau_u)$
   And $e' = h(ID_u \parallel PW_u \parallel \sigma_u')$
3. Check if $e' == e$? If yes, then calculate
   $PID_{HD_i}' = G_u \oplus h(ID_u \parallel \sigma_u' \parallel PW_u)$, and
   $TC_{HD_i}' = F_u \oplus h(ID_u \parallel \sigma_u' \parallel PW_u \parallel PID_{HD_i}')$
4. Generate a nonce r_m
   Evaluate $M_1 = h(PID_{HDi}' \parallel TC_{HDi}') \oplus r_m$
   and $M_2 = h(M_1 \parallel r_m)$
5. Sends $\{M_1 , M_2\}$ to HD_i as login parameters

Healthcare Device (HD_i)

6. Receive $\{ M_1, M_2 \}$, then
   Calculates $M_3 = h(PID_{HD_i} \parallel TC_{HD_i})$
   and find $r_m' = M_1 \oplus M_3$
   and calculate $M_4 = h(M_1 \parallel r_m')$
7. Check if $M_4 == M_2$? If yes,
   then HD_i authenticates M_u
8. Generate random nonce r_{HD_i} , and
   Calculate $M_5 = h(PID_{HD_i} \parallel TC_{HD_i}) \oplus r_{HD_i}$
   and $SK_{ui} = h(PID_{HD_i} \parallel TC_{HD_i} \parallel r_m' \parallel r_{HD_i})$
   and $M_6 = h(M_1 \parallel M_5 \parallel SK_{ui})$
9. Send $\{M_5 , M_6\}$ to Mobile M_u

User (U_u) / Mobile (M_u)

10. Receive $M_5, M_6\}$, then
    Calculate $r_{HDi}' = M_5 \oplus h(PID_{HDi}' \parallel TC_{HDi}')$
    and $SK_{ui}' = h(PID_{HDi}' \parallel TC_{HDi}' \parallel r_m \parallel r_{HDi}')$
    and $M_7 = h(M_1 \parallel M_5 \parallel SK_{ui}')$
11. Check if $M_7 == M_6$? If Yes,
    then Mobile authenticates HD_i
12. Generate a new Transaction ID T_{id}
    and Calculate $M_8 = T_{id} \oplus SK_{ui}$
13. Sends M_8 to Healthcare Device HD_i

Healthcare Device (HD_i)

14. Calculate $T_{id} = M_8 \oplus SK_{ui}$
    Both shares SK_{ui} as their Session Key
    and T_{id} as their transaction id.

FIG. 4

Login, authentication, and key agreement.

it calculates $M_4 = h(M_1 \parallel r'_m)$. Subsequently, it step checks if M_4 is equal to M_2; if it is, then the device HD_i authenticates the user M_u.

After this one-way authentication, we need to establish a session key along with mutual authentication. To achieve this, the healthcare device HD_i generates a random nonce r_{HD_i} and calculates $M_5 = h(PID_{HD_i} \parallel TC_{HD_i}) \oplus r_{HD_i}$, $M_6 = h(M_1 \parallel M_5 \parallel SK_{ui})$, and a session key $SK_{ui} = h(PID_{HD_i} \parallel TC_{HD_i} \parallel r'_m \parallel r_{HD_i})$. Next, it sends the values M_5 and M_6 to the user M_u.

The smartphone receives the pair M_5 and M_6. Then, it extracts the sent random nonce r_{HD_i} and session key SK_{ui} by calculating $r'_{HD_i} = M_5 \oplus h(PID'_{HD_i} \parallel TC'_{HD_i})$ and $SK'_{ui} = h(PID'_{HD_i} \parallel TC'_H D_i \parallel r'_m \parallel r'_{HD_i})$, respectively. Furthermore, it evaluates $M_7 = h(M_1 \parallel M_5 \parallel SK'_{ui})$ and checks if it is equal to the received value of M_6. If it is, then the smartphone authenticates the device HD_i; hence, mutual authentication; otherwise, it terminates the session immediately. If mutual authentication is successfully achieved, then the mobile user M_u generates the transaction timestamp T_{id} and X-ORs it with the session key, that is, $M_8 = T_{id} \oplus SK_{ui}$. Then, it sends the evaluated M_8 to the healthcare device HD_i.

Healthcare device HD_i receives M_8 from user M_u. Then, it extracts the transaction timestamp T_{id}. Both mutually authenticated parties (M_u and H_{HD_i}) share a secure session key SK_{ui} as their session key. Hence, the communicated T_{id} will be secure, and further communication using the key will also be secure.

5.5 Password update phase

In a practical set-up, if a user wishes to change their credentials, then the step depicted in Fig. 5 would help the user to update their credentials. The following is a detailed explanation of the steps.

User (U_u) **Mobile (M_u)**

1. User U_u input identity ID_u and the current password PW_u^{old} and imprint current BIO_u^{old}.

2. Calculate $\sigma_u^{old} = Rep(BIO_u^{old}, \tau_u)$ and $e'_u = h(ID_u \parallel PW_u^{old} \parallel \sigma_u^{old})$ Check if $e_u == e'_u$? if it is, then ask user to input new password and biometrics.

3. User U_u input new password PW_u^{new} And new biometric BIO_u^{new}

4. Apply fuzzy extractor function $Gen(BIO_u^{new}) = (\sigma_u^{new}, \tau_u^{new})$
5. Compute following in order:
$e_u^{new} = h(ID_u \parallel PW_u^{new} \parallel \sigma_u^{new})$,
$PID'_{HD_i} = G_u \oplus h(ID_u \parallel \sigma_u^{new} \parallel PW_u^{new})$,
$TC'_{HD_i} = F_u \oplus h(ID_u \parallel \sigma_u^{new} \parallel PW_u^{new} \parallel PID'_{HD_i})$,
$F_u^{new} = TC'_{HD_i} \oplus h(ID_u \parallel \sigma_u^{new} \parallel PW_u^{new} \parallel PID'_{HD_i})$,
$G_u^{new} = PID_{HD_i} \oplus h(ID_u \parallel \sigma_u \parallel PW_u)$
6. Replace the values of e_u, τ_u, F_u, and G_u of user U_u with $e_u^{new}, \tau_u^{new}, F_u^{new}$, and G_u^{new}, respectively.

FIG. 5

User password update.

The registered user U_u inputs their identity ID_u, current password PW_u^{old}, and biometric impression BIO_u^{old}. Then, the smartphone reproduces the secret parameter by calculating $\sigma_u^{old} = Rep(BIO_u^{old}, \tau_u)$, and evaluates decision parameter $e'_u = h(ID_u \parallel PW_u^{old} \parallel \sigma_u^{old})$. Next, it checks if stored value e_u is equal to the currently evaluated value e'_u; if it is, then the system prompts the user to input their biometric impression and a new password for the change.

Once the user inputs a new password and biometric, then the smartphone reapplies the fuzzy extractor function to regenerate the pair consisting of a secret key and a public reproduction parameter. Subsequently, it calculates a new value for e_u^{new} using the expression $e_u^{new} = h(ID_u \parallel PW_u^{new} \parallel \sigma_u^{new})$. Then, it finds new values for the pseudoidentity of the healthcare device, PID'_{HD_i}, and temporal credential, TC_{HD_i} using expressions $PID'_{HD_i} = G_u \oplus h(ID_u \parallel \sigma_u^{new} \parallel PW_u^{new})$ and $TC'_{HD_i} = F_u \oplus h(ID_u \parallel \sigma_u^{new} \parallel PW_u^{new} \parallel PID'_{HD_i})$, respectively. Using these newly computed values it also recomputes three protocol parameters such as $F_u^{new} = TC'_{HD_i} \oplus h(ID_u \parallel \sigma_u^{new} \parallel PW_u^{new} \parallel PID'_{HD_i})$, and $G_u = PID'_{HD_i} \oplus h(ID_u \parallel \sigma_u^{new} \parallel PW_u^{new})$. The smartphone stores all these newly computed values, that is, $e_u^{new}, \tau_u^{new}, F_u^{new}$, and G_u^{new}, replacing the old values in its memory.

6 Analysis of proposed work

6.1 Security analysis using AVISPA

Armando et al. [26] devised an AVISPA, which is a widely accepted role-based formal security verification tool. It inputs security protocol specifications using the high-level protocol specification language (HLPSL) format. The tool uses an HLPSL2IF translator to convert the HLPSL specifications into an intermediate format (IF). It can test the IF specifications using four back-end test suites independently. We specified the Delov-Yao adversary model with the multiple session scenarios. It also checks the secrecy of the session key shared between the healthcare device and the smartphone. The proposed protocol is expressed in HLPSL format and tested using two of its back ends. The protocol is simulated using Security Protocol ANimator (SPAN) for AVISPA and two of its back ends. The results for the two back ends, that is, On-the-Fly-Model-Checker (OFMC) and Constraint-Logic-Based Attack Searcher, are shown in Fig. 6. The other two back ends lack support for the bitwise X-OR function. The shown results imply that the protocol is safe against MITM and replay attacks. The CL-AtSe back end checked for 48 states and all the tested states are reachable without any security attacks. A similar result is expressed in the AVISPA tool using the OFMC back end. In OFMC, the visited node is 108, and the depth is 4.

6.2 Security proof using Burrows-Adabi-Needham logic

In this section, security proof for the session key using Burrows-Adabi-Needham is provided. This would establish the shared secret key between wearable healthcare devices and the registered user. The following notations will be used in the proof:

- $A| \equiv X$: A believes that the message X is true.
- $A \lhd B$: A receives/sees a message containing B.
- $A| \sim X$: A has sent the message X, but it is not known whether the message was sent long ago or during the current run.

```
SUMMARY
 SAFE

DETAILS
 BOUNDED_NUMBER_OF_SESSIONS
 TYPED_MODEL

PROTOCOL
 /home/span/span/testsuite/results/MyAuthentication2.if

GOAL
 As Specified

BACKEND
 CL-AtSe

STATISTICS

 Analysed   : 48 states
 Reachable  : 48 states
 Translation: 0.06 seconds
 Computation: 0.12 seconds
```

```
% OFMC
% Version of 2006/02/13
SUMMARY
 SAFE
DETAILS
 BOUNDED_NUMBER_OF_SESSIONS
PROTOCOL
 /home/span/span/testsuite/results/MyAuthentication2.if
GOAL
 as_specified
BACKEND
 OFMC
COMMENTS
STATISTICS
 parseTime: 0.00s
 searchTime: 0.43s
 visitedNodes: 108 nodes
 depth: 4 plies
```

FIG. 6

AVISPA simulation results under CL-AtSe and OFMC back ends.

- $A \Rightarrow X$: A has jurisdiction over X. Principal A has authority over message X; hence, it should be trusted.
- $\#(X)$: X is a freshly generated value.
- $\langle X \rangle_Y$: X is combined with secret Y.
- $\{X\}_Y$: X is encrypted with Y.
- $A \overset{k}{\leftrightarrow} B$: K is a good key for communication between P and Q.
- $\overset{k}{\mapsto} B$: k is the public key of B.
- $A \overset{k}{\rightleftharpoons} B$: A and B have a shared secret key k.

The following are the postulates/rules provided by Burrows et al. [27], which would help in proving the establishment of a key agreement in the proposed protocol.

Rule 1: Message meaning rule (MMR)

   Shared key: If A believes that k is a shared key between A and B, and it receives a message encrypted by the key k, then A believes that B once said X. That is: $\frac{A|\equiv B \overset{k}{\leftrightarrow} A, A \triangleleft \{X\}_k}{A|\equiv B|\sim X}$.

   Public key: If A knows the public key k of B and it receives a message X encrypted by the private key of B, then A believes that B once said X. That is: $\frac{A|\equiv \overset{k}{\mapsto} B, A \triangleleft \{X\}_{k^{-1}}}{A|\equiv B|\sim X}$.

   Shared secret: Similar to the above, if A receives the message accompanied by a shared secret known to A and B only, then A believes that B once said X. That is: $\frac{A|\equiv B \overset{k}{\rightleftharpoons} A, A \triangleleft \{X\}_k}{A|\equiv B|\sim X}$.

Rule 2: Nonce verification rule (NVR): If A believes that X is recently generated and B once said X (either in the past or in the present), then A believes that B believes X. That is: $\dfrac{A| \equiv \#(X), A| \equiv B| \sim X}{A| \equiv B| \equiv X}$.

Rule 3: Jurisdiction rule (JR): A believes that B has jurisdiction over X, then A trusts B on the truth of X. That is: $\dfrac{A| \equiv B \Rightarrow X, A| \equiv B| \equiv X}{A| \equiv X}$.

Rule 4: Freshness rule (FR): If a single component of a message is fresh, then the entire message must also be fresh. That is: $\dfrac{A| \equiv \#(X)}{A| \equiv \#(X,Y)}$.

Rule 5: Principal implication rule (PIR): If A sees a formula and knows its required secret keys, then A also sees its components. That is: $\dfrac{A \lhd X, YA \lhd \langle X \rangle_Y}{A \lhd X} \quad \dfrac{}{A \lhd X} \quad \dfrac{A| \equiv B \overset{k}{\leftrightarrow} A, A \lhd \{X\}_k}{A \lhd X} \quad \dfrac{A| \equiv \overset{k}{\mapsto} B, A \lhd \{X\}_{k^{-1}}}{A \lhd X}$

$\dfrac{A| \equiv B \overset{k}{\leftrightarrow} A, A \lhd \{X\}_k}{A \lhd X}$.

The following are the goals of the proposed key establishment protocol:

G1: $HD_i| \equiv (HD_i \overset{SK}{\leftrightarrow} M_u)$
G2: $M_u| \equiv (HD_i \overset{SK}{\leftrightarrow} M_u)$

The following are the assumptions upon which the security mechanism works:

A1: $M_u| \equiv \#(r_m)$,
A2: $HD_i| \equiv (r_{HD_i})$,
A3: $M_u| \equiv (M_u \overset{PID}{\leftrightarrow} HD_i)$,
A4: $HD_i| \equiv (M_u \overset{PID}{\leftrightarrow} HD_i)$,
A5: $M_u| \equiv (M_u \overset{TC}{\leftrightarrow} HD_i)$,
A6: $HD_i| \equiv (M_u \overset{TC}{\leftrightarrow} HD_i)$,
A7: $HD_i| \equiv M_u \Rightarrow r_m$, and
A8: $M_u| \equiv HD_i \Rightarrow r_{HD_i}$.

The following are the messages exchanged in our proposed key establishment protocol:

M1: $M_u \rightarrow HD_i$: $\{M_1 = h(PID'_{HD_i} \| TC'_{HD_i}) \oplus r_m, M_2 = h(M_1 \| r_m)\}$
M2: $HD_i \rightarrow M_u$: $\{M_5 = h(PID_{HD_i} \| TC_{HD_i}) \oplus r_{HD_i}, M_6 = h(M_1 \| M_5 \| SK_{ui})\}$
M3: $M_u \rightarrow HD_i$: $\{M_8 = T_{id} \oplus SK_{ui}\}$

Furthermore, the rules, assumptions, and messages will be taken into consideration for achieving the proposed goals.

Consider message M1 sent by M_u that arrives at HD_i. By applying the PIR, we obtain

$$HD_i \lhd (r_m)_{HD_i} \overset{TC,PID}{\longleftarrow} M_u \tag{1}$$

Applying the MMR using Assumptions A4 and A6 and Eq. (1), we obtain

$$HD_i| \equiv M_u| \sim (r_m)$$ (2)

Then, applying the FR using Eq. (2) and Assumption A1, we derive

$$HD_i| \equiv \#(r_m)$$ (3)

Furthermore, applying the NVR using Eqs. (2), (3), we obtain

$$HD_i| \equiv M_u| \equiv r_m$$ (4)

Again, applying the JR using Eqs. (3), (4), we derive

$$HD_i| \equiv HD_i \overset{r_m}{\longleftrightarrow} M_u$$ (5)

Now, consider message M2. By applying the PIR, we obtain

$$M_u \triangleleft (r_{HD_i}) \underset{HD_i \longleftarrow}{\overset{TC,PID}{\longrightarrow}} M_u$$ (6)

Applying the MMR using A3, A5, and Eq. (6), we get

$$M_u| \equiv HD_i| \sim (r_{HD_i})$$ (7)

Furthermore, applying the FR using Eq. (7), we extract

$$M_u| \equiv \#(r_{HD_i})$$ (8)

Then, applying the NVR using Eqs. (7), (8), we obtain

$$M_u| \equiv HD_i| \equiv r_{HD_i}$$ (9)

Subsequently, applying the JR using Eqs. (8), (9), we derive

$$M_u| \equiv HD_i \overset{r_{HD_i}}{\longleftrightarrow} M_u$$ (10)

By using Assumption A1 and Eq. (10), we obtain a shared key r_{HD_i} between HD_i and M_u. Similarly, using Assumption A2 and Eq. (5) we get r_m as the shared key between HD_i and M_u. Furthermore, a combined shared key can be generated using these two shared secret keys by X-ORing them, that is, $SK = r_{HD_i} \oplus r_m$. Hence, goals G1 and G2 are achieved.

6.3 Computation cost estimation and comparison with other works

The computation cost estimation and comparison with other works are shown in Table 2. Our work requires only 11 hash functions along with one computation of the fuzzy extractor, which is comparatively very efficient from other research work. The efficiency in computation is attained due to elimination of time synchronization functionality, but without compromising the security requirements.

306 **Chapter 16** A secure lightweight mutual authentication

Table 2 Computation cost comparison.

Scheme	Computation cost
Sun et al. [28]	$3T_h + 4T_enc/T_dec + 4T_exp$
Liu et al. [29]	$6T_h + 6T_enc/T_dec + 2T_qrc$
Liu et al. [30]	$27T_h + 4T_p$
Das et al. [17]	$17T_h + 1T_{fe}$
Our scheme	$11T_h + 1T_{fe}$

Notes: T_p, computation time required for physically unclonable function; T_h, hash function computation time; T_{enc}/T_{dec}, encryption/decryption function computation; T_{qrc}, QR code generation; T_{exp}, time for modular exponentiation; T_{fe}, fuzzy extractor computation time.

7 Conclusion

In this chapter, a lightweight, secure authentication protocol was proposed using a simple cryptographic function, a fuzzy extractor, and X-OR functionalities. It used three factors during authentication: a password, a smartphone, and a biometric feature. The biometric feature is extracted using a fuzzy extractor, which was more reliable and error free than biohashing mechanisms. The proposed protocol was tested using a widely known automated security validation tool, AVISPA, which testified that the protocol was safe from the known attacks related to authentication. In addition to this, its secure key agreement was established using a well-known BAN authentication logic. Furthermore, the chapter also estimated the computation cost and compared it with other related works. It was found that the security protocol was computationally better than the rest of the mechanisms because it used only three message communications with lightweight computational operations such as X-OR and hash functions. Hence, it is best suited for resource-constrained IoT objects like healthcare wearable devices.

References

[1] K.H.M. Wong, Y. Zheng, J. Cao, S. Wang, A dynamic user authentication scheme for wireless sensor networks, in: IEEE International Conference on Sensor Networks, Ubiquitous, and Trustworthy Computing (SUTC'06), vol. 1, 2006, p. 8. https://doi.org/10.1109/SUTC.2006.1636182.
[2] M.L. Das, Two-factor user authentication in wireless sensor networks, IEEE Trans. Wirel. Commun. 8 (3) (2009) 1086–1090, https://doi.org/10.1109/TWC.2008.080128.
[3] M.K.K. Khan, K.A. Alghathbar, Cryptanalysis and security improvements of "two-factor user authentication in wireless sensor networks", Sensors (Basel, Switzerland) 10 (3) (2010) 2450–2459, https://doi.org/10.3390/s100302450.
[4] B. Vaidya, D. Makrakis, H.T. Mouftah, Improved two-factor user authentication in wireless sensor networks, in: 2010 IEEE 6th International Conference on Wireless and Mobile Computing, Networking and Communications, 2010, pp. 600–606. https://doi.org/10.1109/WIMOB.2010.5645004.
[5] A.K. Das, P. Sharma, S. Chatterjee, J.K. Sing, A dynamic password-based user authentication scheme for hierarchical wireless sensor networks, J. Netw. Comput. Appl. 35 (5) (2012) 1646–1656, https://doi.org/10.1016/j.jnca.2012.03.011.

[5a] X. Shuaiwen, W. Xiaoming, Int. Rev. Comput. Softw. 8 (1) (2014). https://www.praiseworthyprize.org/jsm/index.php?journal=irecos&page=article&op=view&path%5B%5D=11211.

[6] M. Turkanović, M. Holb, An improved dynamic password-based user authentication scheme for hierarchical wireless sensor networks, Elektron. Elektrotech. 19 (6) (2013), https://doi.org/10.5755/j01.eee.19.6.2038.

[7] M. Turkanović, B. Brumen, M. Hölbl, A novel user authentication and key agreement scheme for heterogeneous ad hoc wireless sensor networks, based on the internet of things notion. Ad Hoc Netw. 20 (2014) 96–112, https://doi.org/10.1016/j.adhoc.2014.03.009.

[8] M.S. Farash, M. Turkanović, S. Kumari, M. Hölbl, An efficient user authentication and key agreement scheme for heterogeneous wireless sensor network tailored for the internet of things environment, Ad Hoc Netw. 36 (2016) 152–176, https://doi.org/10.1016/j.adhoc.2015.05.014.

[9] C. Chang, H. Le, A provably secure, efficient, and flexible authentication scheme for ad hoc wireless sensor networks, IEEE Trans. Wirel. Commun. 15 (1) (2016) 357–366, https://doi.org/10.1109/TWC.2015.2473165.

[10] R. Amin, G.P. Biswas, A secure light weight scheme for user authentication and key agreement in multi-gateway based wireless sensor networks, Ad Hoc Netw. 36 (2016) 58–80, https://doi.org/10.1016/j.adhoc.2015.05.020.

[11] R. Amin, S.K.H. Islam, G.P. Biswas, M.K. Khan, L. Leng, N. Kumar, Design of an anonymity-preserving three-factor authenticated key exchange protocol for wireless sensor networks, Comput. Netw. 101 (2016) 42–62, https://doi.org/10.1016/j.comnet.2016.01.006.

[12] P. Gope, T. Hwang, A realistic lightweight anonymous authentication protocol for securing real-time application data access in wireless sensor networks, IEEE Trans. Ind. Electron. 63 (11) (2016) 7124–7132, https://doi.org/10.1109/TIE.2016.2585081.

[13] A. Adavoudi-Jolfaei, M. Ashouri-Talouki, S.F. Aghili, Lightweight and anonymous three-factor authentication and access control scheme for real-time applications in wireless sensor networks, Peer-to-Peer Netw. Appl. (2017). https://doi.org/3-017-0627-8.

[14] A.K. Sahu, S. Sharma, D. Puthal, A. Pandey, R. Shit, Secure authentication protocol for IoT architecture, 2017 International Conference on Information Technology (ICIT), 2017, pp. 220–224, https://doi.org/10.1109/ICIT.2017.21.

[15] X. Li, M.H. Ibrahim, S. Kumari, A.K. Sangaiah, V. Gupta, K.-K.R. Choo, Anonymous mutual authentication and key agreement scheme for wearable sensors in wireless body area networks, Comput. Netw. 129 (2017) 429–443, https://doi.org/10.1016/j.comnet.2017.03.013.

[16] A.M. Koya, P.P. Deepthi, Anonymous hybrid mutual authentication and key agreement scheme for wireless body area network, Comput. Netw. 140 (2018) 138–151, https://doi.org/10.1016/j.comnet.2018.05.006.

[17] A.K. Das, M. Wazid, N. Kumar, M.K. Khan, K.R. Choo, Y. Park, Design of secure and lightweight authentication protocol for wearable devices environment, IEEE J. Biomed. Health Inform. 22 (4) (2018) 1310–1322, https://doi.org/10.1109/JBHI.2017.2753464.

[18] L. Zhang, L. Zhao, S. Yin, C.-H. Chi, R. Liu, Y. Zhang, A lightweight authentication scheme with privacy protection for smart grid communications, Futur. Gener. Comput. Syst. 100 (2019) 770–778, https://doi.org/10.1016/j.future.2019.05.069.

[19] P. Gope, LAAP: lightweight anonymous authentication protocol for D2D-aided fog computing paradigm, Comput. Secur. 86 (2019) 223–237, https://doi.org/10.1016/j.cose.2019.06.003.

[20] A. Gupta, M. Tripathi, T.J. Shaikh, A. Sharma, A lightweight anonymous user authentication and key establishment scheme for wearable devices, Comput. Netw. 149 (2019) 29–42, https://doi.org/10.1016/j.comnet.2018.11.021.

[21] J. Zhou, Z. Cao, Z. Qin, X. Dong, K. Ren, LPPA: lightweight privacy-preserving authentication from efficient multi-key secure outsourced computation for location-based services in VANETs, IEEE Trans. Inf. Forensics Secur. 15 (2019) 420–434, https://doi.org/10.1109/TIFS.2019.2923156.

[22] S.A. Abdel Hakeem, M.A. Abd El-Gawad, H. Kim, A decentralized lightweight authentication and privacy protocol for vehicular networks, IEEE Access 7 (2019) 119689–119705, https://doi.org/10.1109/ACCESS.2019.2937182.

[23] J. Cui, X. Zhang, H. Zhong, Z. Ying, L. Liu, RSMA: reputation system-based lightweight message authentication framework and protocol for 5G-enabled vehicular networks, IEEE Internet Things J. 6 (4) (2019) 6417–6428, https://doi.org/10.1109/JIOT.2019.2895136.

[24] D. Dolev, A.C. Yao, On the security of public key protocols, in: Proceedings of the 22nd Annual Symposium on Foundations of Computer Science, SFCS '81, IEEE Computer Society, Washington, DC, USA, 1981, pp. 350–357. https://doi.org/10.1109/SFCS.1981.32.

[25] R. Canetti, H. Krawczyk, Analysis of key-exchange protocols and their use for building secure channels, in: B. Pfitzmann (Ed.), Advances in Cryptology—EUROCRYPT 2001, Springer, Berlin, Heidelberg, 2001, pp. 453–474.

[26] A. Armando, D. Basin, Y. Boichut, Y. Chevalier, L. Compagna, J. Cuellar, P.H. Drielsma, P.C. Heám, O. Kouchnarenko, J. Mantovani, S. Mödersheim, D. von Oheimb, M. Rusinowitch, J. Santiago, M. Turuani, L. Viganò, L. Vigneron, The AVISPA tool for the automated validation of internet security protocols and applications, in: K. Etessami, S.K. Rajamani (Eds.), Computer Aided Verification, Springer, Berlin, Heidelberg, 2005, pp. 281–285.

[27] M. Burrows, M. Abadi, R. Needham, A logic of authentication, ACM Trans. Comput. Syst. 8 (1) (1990) 18–36, https://doi.org/10.1145/77648.77649.

[28] D. Sun, J. Huai, J. Sun, J. Zhang, Z. Feng, A new design of wearable token system for mobile device security, IEEE Trans. Consum. Electron. 54 (4) (2008) 1784–1789, https://doi.org/10.1109/TCE.2008.4711235.

[29] S. Liu, J. Weng, S. Zhu, Z. Chen, A novel asymmetric three-party based authentication scheme in wearable device environment, J. Netw. Comput. Appl. 60 (2016) 144–154.

[30] W. Liu, H. Liu, Y. Wan, H. Kong, H. Ning, The yoking-proof-based authentication protocol for cloud-assisted wearable devices, Pers. Ubiquit. Comput. 20 (3) (2016) 469–479, https://doi.org/10.1007/s00779-016-0926-8.

Index

Note: Page numbers followed by *f* indicate figures and *t* indicate tables.

Printed in the United States
By Bookmasters